Navigating the Complexity Across the Peace–Sustainability–Climate Security Nexus

Bernard Amadei

CRC Press
Taylor & Francis Group
Boca Raton London New York

CRC Press is an imprint of the
Taylor & Francis Group, an **informa** business

Designed cover image: © Shutterstock

First edition published 2024
by CRC Press
2385 NW Executive Center Drive, Suite 320, Boca Raton FL 33431

and by CRC Press
4 Park Square, Milton Park, Abingdon, Oxon, OX14 4RN

CRC Press is an imprint of Taylor & Francis Group, LLC

ISBN: 978-1-032-56338-1 (hbk)
ISBN: 978-1-032-56339-8 (pbk)
ISBN: 978-1-003-43500-6 (ebk)

DOI: 10.1201/9781003435006

Typeset in Times
by codeMantra

Dedication

In memory of Robin Amadei (1955–2019).

Contents

Preface

Voyagers navigating today's planetary ocean of complexity and uncertainty will quickly recognize that deterministic and reductionistic tools have limited use in addressing the "volatile, uncertain, complex, and ambiguous" (VUCA) world they are facing (Tooley, 2021) and its "predictable unpredictability" (The *Economist*, 2021). When maneuvering in that world, our voyagers will soon realize that nexuses (which tie or link things together, from Latin) are the norms rather than the exception. Before embarking on their oceanic voyage, our voyagers must equip themselves with skills, knowledge, resources, and a systems-thinking mindset; adopt new mental models; possess the right attitude; and arm themselves with various multisolving tools to deal with the complexity they are likely to face.

This book acknowledges that the planetary issues affecting human development and security as we enter the third decade of the Twenty-first century are complex and need to be treated as such. They unfold in a fragmented, evolving landscape shaped by multiple factors and technologies. In that landscape, peace, sustainability, and climate security have become topics of growing interest over the past 30 years. Yet, the intersection of these three sectors or their opposites (i.e., conflict, unsustainability, and climate vulnerability) is rarely articulated with a systemic mindset. The traditional approach has been to look at them and their opposites in a categorized and compartmentalized manner. The academic and policy worlds are populated with experts who make a living focusing on disciplinary and compartmentalized silos and who work in isolation. This dominant deterministic and reductionistic approach, referred to as "specialization barbarism" by Ortega y Gasset (1994), is counter to how the three sectors of peace, sustainability, and climate security interact daily (i.e., their nexus). It is also counter to how the world works.

This book addresses the systemic interaction across the peace–sustainability–climate security (PSC) nexus. This approach does not mean, however, that experts are not needed. They are helpful, but the interaction between their expertise is necessary to explore the nexus. This recommendation is not limited to the PSC nexus considered in this book. It also applies to multiple double, triple, and quadruple nexuses that underlie the dynamics of many complex human development problems we face today. They include the water-energy-land-food nexus, the humanitarian aid-development-peacebuilding nexus, the food-nutrition-security nexus, the food-healthcare-nutrition nexus, the environment-fragility-peace nexus, and the climate-fragility-peacebuilding nexus, to name a few. We can add a nexus of all these nexuses to that list (i.e., a metanexus, which better describes the real world).

A nexus approach to any complex problem requires adopting (i) a new mindset on looking at the problem, using more integrated tools in addition to deterministic ones and (ii) a methodology to address issues requiring flexibility and adaptability from decision-makers. Creating change does not start by putting Band-Aids on issues. It requires first looking at the mental models behind the problems, investigating how they translate into structural and behavioral patterns, and how they manifest in the world. This book emphasizes that dynamic. It contradicts the usual way of addressing problems expeditiously and deterministically, often resulting in unintended consequences that do more harm than good.

Changing the mindset and adopting new mental models represent critical leverage to address complex problems such as those at the crossroads between peace, sustainability, and climate security. Change is not easy and is more than blindly adopting new technologies and selecting the latest gadgets to address world issues. It is more than just talking about it. Unfortunately, many who speak of change do not necessarily walk the talk. Schmidheiny remarked in 1992 regarding putting sustainable development into practice:

> The painful truth is that the present is a relatively comfortable place for those who have reached positions of mainstream political or business leadership. This is the crux of the problem of sustainable development and perhaps the main reason why there has been great acceptance of it in principle but less concrete actions to put it into practice: many of those with the power to effect the necessary changes have the least motivation to alter the status quo that gave them the power.

The same could be said about promoting peace and climate security today, as too many private interests are at play for change to gain traction. A corollary of this quote is that, without changing the inner priorities humans operate with on our planet, external interventions will remain shallow and likely result in unintended consequences for life in general (Dhiman, 2018).

This book follows a two-volume book published by Momentum Press in 2019 that explored the value proposition of using a nexus approach in managing and allocating water, energy, land, and food (WELF) resources at the community level. The acronym WELF-X was suggested in that book to capture the interaction between all four sectors of the WELF nexus and other areas where X could be peace, health, climate, transportation, human rights, etc.

The security of WELF resources is one of the many global issues that need to be addressed in human development in the Twenty-first century, along with climate security, national and international security, economic security, rapid urbanization, population growth, migration, environmental protection, natural resources management, risks and emergencies, and peacebuilding. The value proposition of promoting peace and sustainability in human development while accounting for the risks associated with climate change has become more imperative than ever when addressing these issues.

There is ample evidence that peace, sustainability, and climate security are entangled and integral to human development and security. Understanding their inter- and intra-dependencies in different contexts and scales remains an open-ended question. Their intersection or that of their opposites (i.e., conflict, unsustainability, and climate vulnerability) is rarely articulated with a systemic mindset. As a result, there is still much confusion and uncertainty in the literature about the nature of appropriate interventions to address these issues.

There are many ways of approaching the wholeness of human development and security challenges and the coherence between peace, sustainability, and climate security. This book makes a case for using an integrated, coherent, participatory, and practical approach to human development and security issues. It recognizes that peace, sustainability, and climate security do not reside in a specific place in a community. Peace, sustainability, and climate security are considered three interconnected *states* (or cultures) that *emerge* from the interactions of multiple systems in a community landscape (environment or ecosystem) subject to various constraints (political, social, cultural, economic, environmental, etc.) and adverse events. All three states cannot be reduced to their parts and are contained in the emergent and evolutionary community wholeness. They are inherently dynamic (i.e., they change as a community develops over time and vice versa). What happens across the landscape systems depends significantly on many social-psychological factors shaping human thought, preferences, and behaviors.

Addressing the PSC nexus requires decision-makers (practitioners and policy-makers) to be systems thinkers who can use a sound, flexible, and adaptive systems-based methodology that includes (i) participatory assessment and capacity mapping of the environment in which the issues take place; (ii) problem identification in an integrated manner, taking into account context and scale, (iii) development and ranking scenarios of intervention that account for multiple constraints and stressors; (iv) selection and implementation of appropriate intervention scenarios; and (v) adoption of some coherence in governance and policymaking in the short and long term.

Because of its systemic nature, the proposed approach may appear more challenging to decision-makers than traditional approaches, as it requires embracing complexity and change and learning new tools. Awakening to the idea that problems cannot be solved with the same level of thinking that created them, as suggested by Albert Einstein, should not be regarded as a roadblock. Instead, it opens the door to creativity, change, betterment of society, and multiple opportunities. The challenge becomes adapting to a new way of thinking that embraces complexity and not being afraid of change. It must be remembered that change is not always welcome in established fields of science and engineering. The quote, "The only person who likes change is a baby with a wet diaper" (Anonymous), is not far from the truth in today's institutions.

The idea of writing this book came to mind as I witnessed the evolution of the COVID-19 pandemic starting in early 2020. The pandemic was preceded and followed by a series of worldwide crises, many of which have continued to this day. As a super "disease without borders," COVID-19 revealed our world's complexity, fragility, interdependencies, and systemic nature of human and economic development. It also (i) revealed multiple forms of existing injustice and inequality (i.e., ecological, racial, social, economic, and gender), (ii) impacted peace negatively worldwide by pushing more people into poverty, (iii) negatively affected all the systems involved in socio-economic development, and (iv) negatively disrupted public life. Finally, the pandemic demonstrated human life's diversity and fragility, the close linkages between humans and their environment, and the multiple systems upon which they depend.

Conversely, extraordinary times create unique opportunities. The pandemic and the multiple crises during the first two decades of the Twenty-first century represent a wake-up call for humanity to change and learn how to build better resilient societies when exposed to future pandemic events and existential threats. Whether as bad omens or much-needed signs for change, all these crises provide opportunities for humanity to develop "dynamic new normal(s)" (if we want to call it that) and adopt a new and holistic vision toward a more sustainable, stable, and equitable world where all humans can live with dignity and peace. Although developing that new mindset is still a work in progress, some of its characteristics include (i) using an integrated approach to socio-economic development (and humanitarian aid) based on principles of complexity and systems science; (ii) adopting more authentic forms of leadership, compassion, education, and consciousness in the management and operation of our institutions and occupations; (iii) investing in scientific and technical innovation that embody the five aspects of sustainability (people, planet, profit, partnership, and peace); (iv) developing socio-economic partnerships and collaborations that respect participation and empowerment; and (iv) accounting for the inner and outer dimensions of human development.

A post-2020 world mindset needs to consider two goals (Moritz, 2020); (i) immediately prevent further decline in socioeconomic development affecting society's poorest sections the most and (ii) plan for medium- to long-term sustainability, peace, and climate security. To these goals, one can add reconnecting with what it is to be genuinely human in a more consuming, crowded, and connected world than ever, where living systems and cultures are increasingly in jeopardy.

Addressing these priorities and developing an action plan that guarantees a certain level of success is not easy and takes time. But as the TWI2050 (2020) report remarked, "Success is a matter of choice. Choice requires deploying economic, political, and social instruments, technological and cultural innovations, and lifestyle changes to bring about the needed transformational changes at every scale." Unfortunately, the past 30 years have shown policymakers and practitioners' lack of will to change and how geopolitical issues often hinder socioeconomic development progress. Multiple intended and unintended roadblocks that limit progress are inherent to the history of socioeconomic development and have affected the most marginalized groups on our planet.

This book is the first of a series of books that I plan to release in 2024 and 2025. A common thread in these books is the belief that technology alone will not address the development and security issues humanity faces. These issues are the symptoms of the myopic inner work of our institutions and, as a result, of their operating mindsets. Quoting the Thirteenth-century mystic Meister Eckhart, "The outward work can never be small if the inward one is great, and the outward work can never be great or good if the inward is small or of little worth." Hence, external interventions in human development and security must also consider the inner work of the institutions and the mental models of the decision-makers involved in the interventions. Short of examining institutions' inner perspectives and priorities and getting decision-makers to develop better mental models and new mindsets, build internal capacity, and recalibrate their moral compass, humanity will remain a significant roadblock to its progress.

Where do we start on this transformation pathway? My answer to that question resides in you and me and the decision-making of 8 billion of us daily. As suggested by Mahatma Gandhi, "We need to be the change we want to see in the world." A fundamental question remains whether we can mobilize the compassion and leadership of enough "better angels" to create a world where *all* humans have fulfilling lives, meet their basic needs, and live with dignity and peace. The answer is yes if there is a willingness to do so and those who talk about change are walking the talk. It is a matter of human choice (UNDP/HDR, 2022) and embracing a culture of peace, sustainability, and climate security that benefits all. Simply put, a sustainable world will be peaceful, just, equitable, inclusive, and climate secure, or it will not exist.

Bernard Amadei
Boulder, CO
May 2023

REFERENCES

Dhiman, S. (2018). Selfishness, greed, and apathy. In J. Marques (ed.), *Handbook of Engaged Sustainability* (pp. 3–35). https://doi.org/10.1007/978-3-319-71312-0_1

Moritz, R. E. (2020, July 17). To reinvent the future, we must all work together. https://www.weforum.org/agenda/2020/07/to-reinvent-the-future-we-must-all-work-together

Ortega y Gasset, J. (1994). *The revolt of the masses*. W. W. Norton & Company.

Schmidheiny, S. (1992). *Changing course: A global business perspective on development and the environment* (1st ed.). MIT Press.

The Economist. (2021, December 18). The new normal is already here. Get used to it. The era of predictable unpredictability is not going away. https://www.economist.com/leaders/2021/12/18/the-new-normal-is-already-here-get-used-to-it

The World in 2050 (TWI2050). (2020). Innovations for sustainability. Pathways to an efficient and post-pandemic future. Report prepared by The World in 2050 initiative. International Institute for Applied Systems Analysis (IIASA), Laxenburg, Austria. https://www.twi2050.org

Tooley, C. (2021, January 18). What systems thinking actually means – and why it matters for innovation today. The World Economic Forum. https://www.weforum.org/agenda/2021/01/what-systems-thinking-actually-means-and-why-it-matters-today/

UNDP Human Development Report (UNDP/HDR). (2022). *The Human Development Report 2021/2022. Uncertain times, and unsettled lives, shaping our future in a transforming world.* https://www.undp.org/timor-leste/publications/human-development-report-2021/2022

Acknowledgments

I want to thank Taylor & Francis Publ. for giving me the opportunity to publish my work. I also want to thank Tanya Unger and Allison Goldstein for their thorough editorial work. Finally, I especially thank my children, Elizabeth Ann and Alex, for their support, patience, and love.

About the Author

Dr. Bernard Amadei is a Distinguished Professor and Professor of Civil Engineering at the University of Colorado at Boulder. He is the Founding Director of the Mortenson Center in Engineering for Developing Communities (now Global Engineering). He is also the Founding President of Engineers Without Borders - USA and the Engineers Without Borders - International network co-founder. Among other distinctions, Dr. Amadei is an elected member of the US National Academy of Engineering and the National Academy of Construction. He is also a Senior Ashoka Fellow.

About the Author

Dr. Bernard Amadei is a Distinguished Professor and Professor of Civil Engineering at the University of Colorado at Boulder. He is the Founding Director of the Mortenson Center in Engineering for Developing Communities (now Global Engineering). He is also the Founding President of Engineers Without Borders - USA and the Engineers Without Borders - International network co-founder. Among other distinctions, Dr. Amadei is an elected member of the US National Academy of Engineering and the National Academy of Construction. He is also a Senior Ashoka Fellow.

1 Introduction

1.1 BACKGROUND

With the third decade of the Twenty-first century well underway, humanity is navigating in rough waters through what Tooley (2021) referred to as "volatile, uncertain, complex, and ambiguous" (VUCA) times and an era of "predictable unpredictability" (The *Economist*, 2021). As emphasized in the 2021/2022 Human Development Report (UNDP/HDR, 2022),

> A new "uncertainty complex" is emerging, never before seen in human history. Constituting it are three volatile and interacting strands: the destabilizing planetary pressures and inequalities of the Anthropocene, the pursuit of sweeping societal transformations to ease those pressures, and the widespread and intensifying polarization.

In that context and in a changing global environment, the question arises whether it is possible to envision a world anytime soon where *all* humans have fulfilling lives, meet their basic needs, and live with dignity and peace without degrading the ecosystems and services they depend on.

Meeting that overarching goal (vision) of human development will not be easy. There is ample evidence that humanity will continue to face significant development challenges into the rest of the Twenty-first century, short of adopting a new global mindset (i.e., a new attitude toward creation in general). The challenges that started in the twentieth century involve a confluence of complex socioeconomic, environmental, cultural, and geopolitical world issues. Although this list is not exhaustive, such challenges include (i) climate change and security risks; (ii) rapid urbanization; (iii) population growth, migration, and human resettlement; (iv) water, energy, food, and land resources security; (v) access to education, shelter, healthcare, information and communication technology, and employment; (vi) environmental damage and biodiversity loss; (vii) natural and human-induced risks and emergencies; (viii) peacebuilding and violent conflict prevention and recovery; (ix) social equality and inclusive growth; and (x) national and global security. Most of these issues do not stand alone and interact with each other (The Millennium Project, 2017; INCOSE, 2021).

Alone or combined, many of these issues are prone to create risks and instability if not addressed. According to the most recent global risk report of the World Economic Forum (WEF, 2023), the risks can be divided into five categories: economic, environmental, geopolitical, societal, and technological. The top ten risks by order of severity over the long term (i.e., ten years) include: "failure to mitigate climate change; failure to mitigate climate adaptation; natural disasters and extreme weather events; biodiversity loss and ecosystem collapse; large-scale involuntary migration; natural resource crises; erosion of social cohesion & societal polarization; widespread cybercrime and cyber insecurity; geoeconomic confrontation; and large-scale environmental damage incidents." The WEF report also emphasizes how these

DOI: 10.1201/9781003435006-1

risks are interconnected. The question arises regarding how to proactively address these risks now and in the future rather than reactively by emphasizing: (i) environmental protection; (ii) conflict resolution; (iii) economic and political stability; and (iv) climate change awareness, adaptation, and mitigation.

This book looks more specifically at the constraining and combined effects of conflict and climate change on community livelihood and security and, more importantly, at the value proposition of enabling peace, sustainability, and climate security in community development. Understanding that dynamic is critical in understanding what drives the risks listed above.

The abovementioned issues share similar characteristics that make any human development intervention challenging to plan, design, and implement. For instance, they are shaped by multiple factors (socioeconomic, political, environmental, regulatory) and technologies. They are systemic and involve shared interconnected systems and subsystems (social, economic, cultural, ecological, and technical). The issues unfold in landscapes that are context-specific (e.g., urban vs. rural, cultural, geopolitical) and scale-specific (i.e., local, regional, global). Moreover, these systems have elements that are often (i) ill-defined, messy, and adaptive; (ii) constantly changing partly due to feedback mechanisms and complex causal chains; and (iii) characterized by different degrees of uncertainty, ambiguity, and unpredictability. As a result, clear solutions to the issues cannot be established entirely using the traditional deterministic thinking and reductionistic tools applied in science and engineering over the last century. Instead, a systems multisolving perspective derived from the systems and complexity sciences is better suited to (i) map, analyze, and capture complex issue dynamics; (ii) explore different intervention scenarios; and (iii) implement, monitor, and evaluate integrated solutions.

The second characteristic of the world issues mentioned above is that they unfold on a dynamic globalized planet, a rapidly changing geopolitical and socioeconomic landscape, and within a "complex, open system" rather than a closed system of nation-states (Mr. Y, 2011). In that landscape, populations are more consuming, crowded, and connected than ever, with living systems and cultures increasingly in jeopardy. By 2050, global food demand is expected to grow by 60%, energy demand by 80%, and water demand by 55% (Ferroukhi et al., 2015). If these resources are not allocated adequately due to natural hazards or poor policies, trade-offs in their development, management, and distribution could create unintended consequences and uncertainties. These, in turn, could negatively affect large populations and create socio-political instability, geopolitical conflict, and long-lasting environmental damage. As summarized by the World Business Council for Sustainable Development (WBCSD, 2009), the challenge of resource security in the Twenty-first century is "to feed more people with less water, in a context of climate change and growing energy demand, while maintaining healthy ecosystems." A challenging task indeed!

The third common characteristic of world issues is that they affect humanity's most vulnerable sections, many of whom have limited to no voice or representation to deal with the problems. Vulnerable communities worldwide have limited capacity and resilience to adapt and cope with crises and adverse events (some created elsewhere) and even less when facing the burden of multiple issues such as conflict, limited access to resources, marginalization, and climate-related hazards. Their vulnerabilities are further increased due to non-existent and poor-quality infrastructure, the unavailability of services, weak institutions, and limited land rights (Dodman et al., 2022). This dynamic is especially present in informal settlements (UN-Habitat, 2015).

The fourth characteristic of world issues is how they often transcend national boundaries and require regional and international collaboration to be addressed successfully (Frej and Ramalingam, 2011; OECD, 2019). The global impact of climate change, the COVID-19 pandemic, and the war in Ukraine serve as three key examples. They are not contained within the confines of geopolitical borders. Another example deals with water and energy security across borders in the Middle East that calls for transboundary cooperation. The November 2021 water and solar energy agreement between Israel and Jordan brokered by the UAE represents an example of regional collaboration and applied environmental diplomacy between three countries particularly affected by climate change. Under this agreement, Israel would purchase solar power from Jordan, and Jordan would buy water from Israel. As of the end of 2022, energy and water facilities are yet to be constructed in each country (TOI, 2021).

The fifth characteristic of world issues is addressing them amid the spread of disinformation and misinformation, also called an "infodemic" (Zarocostas, 2020; Eysenbach, 2020). As remarked by Himelfarb and Howard (2021), because of bad-faith information, we are "in danger of becoming incapable of dealing with existential threats, such as climate change and pandemics," or even down-to-earth community livelihood. The manipulation of information has many negative socio-economic ramifications and geopolitical consequences, especially for marginalized groups. A recent survey by Pew Research involving 24,525 people from 19 countries with advanced economies has shown that misinformation online and climate change ranked the highest as significant threats, with 70% for misinformation and 75% for climate change (Thompson, 2022). Other identified threats included cyber-attacks from other countries (67%), the condition of the global economy (61%), and the spread of infectious diseases (61%).

The sixth shared characteristic of world issues is that there is more to address them than just (i) proposing scientific, technical, and engineering innovative gadgets and solutions to remedy socioeconomic and technological deficiencies and (ii) developing idealized models of rational human behavior (Karwat et al., 2014). Despite an accelerating pace and advances in science and technology innovation, humanity has not advanced much in how people treat each other and the natural systems on which they depend. Wolfe and Smith (2021) remarked that potential solutions to world issues "are also deeply intertwined with psychological, cultural, economic, and political factors that operate mainly at the level of individuals, communities, and societies." Furthermore, according to these authors, the leverage points to address global issues reside deep in the mental models of society among the "social-psychological factors that shape human thought, preferences, and behaviors." Unfortunately, these leverage points are usually ignored by most people and science in general.

Finally, unless the world issues mentioned above are addressed in a multisolving, intelligent, systemic, equitable, and compassionate manner for the benefit of all rather than in a haphazard, deterministic, and compartmentalized one driven by fear and for the use of a few, it is hard to imagine a just, peaceful, and sustainable world in the foreseeable future as initially envisioned in the Earth Charter (1987). There is indeed a paradox between the strong desire of humans to build a more sustainable and equitable planet and their behavior and funding priorities contrary to that desire. It is time to realize that a sustainable world is peaceful, equitable, and compassionate for *all*—or the planet will not be! As summarized by the National Academy of Engineering (2008), "A world divided by wealth and poverty, health and sickness, food and hunger, cannot long remain a stable [and peaceful] place for civilization to thrive."

Promoting peace and sustainability in human development while accounting for the risks associated with the impact of climate change on society has become more imperative than ever when addressing the global issues mentioned above (Gaston et al., 2023). There is ample evidence that peace, sustainability, and climate security are entangled with multiple complex interactions and cannot be dealt with in isolation (i.e., decoupled) and independently from the environment and the numerous systems with which they interact. A multisolving nexus approach is more appropriate to capture the complexity and uncertainty of how the three sectors of peace, sustainability, and climate security play a role in community development, the nature of their causal chains, and the feedback on how community development affects the three sectors. This book explores the value proposition of using a systems approach, methodology, and tools to comprehend and model that dynamic.

1.2　HUMAN DEVELOPMENT AND SECURITY

Since the publication of the Human Development Report in 1990 (UNDP/HDR, 1990), many initiatives and reports have advocated for a paradigm shift in how humans interact with each other and the environment upon which they all depend. Human development is about "creating an environment in which people can develop their full potential and lead productive, creative lives according to their needs and interests" (UNDP/HDR, 1990). It is also about providing people with the skills and resources to address their basic human needs (e.g., food, health, safe shelter, access to services and resources) as pre-conditions for subsequent economic growth, poverty reduction, aid delivery, debt reduction, individual empowerment, community participation, small-scale technology, and local capacity building. The 2010 UNDP/HDR report further emphasizes that human development expands people's choices, opportunities, and freedoms combined with equity, empowerment, and sustainability. Access to human, economic, cultural, and political development is a human right per the UN Declaration on the Right to Development (UN, 1986).

Multiple back-to-back worldwide crises impacted human development during the first two decades of the Twenty-first century and continue to do so to this day. They include continuous global food and energy crises since 2007 (von Grebmer et al., 2012; Allouche et al., 2015), the economic crisis of 2008 and its subsequent recession, the growing incidence of violent conflicts in fragile states (OECD, 2018), the global COVID pandemic and unrest of 2020–2021, the Ukrainian-Russian war starting in 2022 and its associated destabilizing global effects, and the ongoing security risks related to climate change (National Intelligence Council, 2021; IPCC, 2023). Together, these crises have exposed and exacerbated the fragility and flow in various systems (socioeconomic, political, technical, and environmental) involved in addressing planetary challenges at scales from the local to the global. They also revealed numerous forms of injustice and inequality (i.e., social, ecological, racial, economic, and gender) and negatively impacted peace worldwide (IEP, 2020a). Armed conflicts have added further insecurity with multiple social, political, environmental, and economic ramifications.

Furthermore, the complexity and interdependencies of the crises mentioned above combined with poor decision-making at different levels (political, societal, and managerial), democratic structures under attack, the never-ending pursuit of profit growth, the limited institutional capacity to handle the crises, and the low levels of individual and community resilience (i.e., high vulnerability), especially in disadvantaged areas, have created confusion, uncertainty, and insecurity, and consequently inaction, regarding the future of humanity and how to intervene in these systems (Jacobs, 2016). Even before the COVID outbreak, "more than 6 in 7 people worldwide perceived feeling moderately or very insecure" (UNDP, 2022). That number has increased ever since.

The COVID-19 pandemic, believed to have started at the end of 2019, represents a unique event that derailed a continuous range of efforts to improve human development since the early 1990s. COVID-19 evolved into a democratic "super disease without borders" (Cherkaoui, 2020; Tanabe, 2020). The pandemic revealed the complexity, fragility, and interdependencies in our world and the systemic nature of human and economic development. It also (i) revealed multiple forms of justice, equity, diversity, and inclusion (JEDI) issues; (ii) impacted peace negatively worldwide by pushing more people into poverty; (iii) negatively affected all the systems involved in socioeconomic development; and (iv) negatively disrupted public life. Finally, the pandemic demonstrated the diversity and interdependence of human life, the importance of the close linkages between humans and their environment, and the need to honor and respect the sanctity of all forms of life on our planet.

Conversely, the *early* days of the pandemic brought out "better angels" (Reckford, 2019) and "some of the best human characteristics; self-sacrifice in helping others; empathy and solidarity despite the need for social distancing" (TWI2050, 2020). Another positive outcome has been how rapidly new vaccines were developed through international scientific collaboration (UNDP/HDR, 2022). Finally, the pandemic represents a wake-up call for humanity to collaborate and learn how to deal with future pandemic events, current and future existential threats such as climate change (Palinkas et al., 2021), and possible multiple confluent crises (e.g., climate change and COVID). It is also a wake-up call for humanity to remember its stewardship toward the environment it depends on. Short of that, it is likely that the same dynamics that spread COVID-19 worldwide could happen as global earth systems would collapse due to climate change.

It is appropriate to pause and reflect on (i) what a post-2020 world would look like for a growing and more urbanized world's population (IEP, 2020b), (ii) how to prevent further decline in socioeconomic development that would affect society's poorest sections the most, (iii) how to build back better (rather than return to the old normal) more resilient and equitable inclusive societies that put all people back at the center of human and economic development (UN, 2021), and (iv) how to build capacity and create a culture of resilience at different scales (household, community, national, regional, and global) to adapt to future adverse events and challenging conditions (e.g., climate change and natural disasters). Answering these questions will hopefully create a sustainable and peaceful world for all.

The overarching goal of building a more sustainable, stable, peaceful, and equitable world where all humans live with dignity and peace is not new. It was already in the mind of many constituencies during the twentieth century, starting with the League of Nations (1920–1946) and followed by the United Nations. It was the underlying thrust behind the publication of *Our Common Future* (WCED, 1987) by the Brundtland Commission and *Agenda 21* (UNCED, 1992) following the 1992 Rio Summit. Both documents emphasize integrating sustainability and sustainable development in policies at different scales. They also recognize that (i) technology enables humanity to affect planetary change faster than human's ability to understand and manage the non-technical consequences of such change and (ii) unintended consequences of technology result in division, conflict, and possibly violent disputes.

Following *Agenda 21*, the *1994 UN Development Report* (UNDP/HDR, 1994) extended the development concept with the broader picture of *human security*. This differs from traditional national or territorial security (i.e., protecting the nation or state from external threats using military measures) as it incorporates the protection of individuals everywhere in three main areas: (i) freedom from fear (physical security), (ii) freedom from want (economic and food security, security of livelihoods, access to resources), and (iii) freedom from indignity (political freedoms, equal rights, and justice). Closely related and complementary, but not identical, to human development, human security is people-centered and focuses on human vulnerability, which exists at all levels of development (Dorn, 2003). As Gomez and Gasper (2013) note, human security is about "understanding the particular *threats* experienced by particular groups of people, as well as the participation of those people in the analysis process." Among all possible threats are "proactive crises, violent conflicts, natural disasters, persistent poverty, epidemics, and economic downturns" (UN Trust Fund for Human Security, n.d.).

Since 1994, there has been an international acceptance that human security's basic tenets recognize that people have "the right to live in freedom and dignity, free from poverty and despair... with an equal opportunity to enjoy all their rights and fully develop their human potential." In addition, human security "recognizes the interlinkages between peace, development, and human rights, and equally considers civil, political, economic and cultural rights" (UNDP/HDR, 1994).

The standard definition of human security was accepted in 2012 under UN resolution 66/290, whereby "human security is an approach to assist the Member States in identifying and addressing widespread and cross-cutting challenges to survival, livelihood, and dignity of their people." It calls for "people-centered, comprehensive, context-specific and prevention-oriented responses that strengthen the protection and empowerment of all people."

Seven categories of security were postulated in the 1994 UNDP/HDR report and are listed in Table 1.1. Indicators for each type of security have been proposed by

TABLE 1.1

Seven Categories of Human Security Postulated in the 1994 UNDP/HDR Report and Summarized by the Global Development Research Center (GDRC, n.d.)

Categories of Human Security	Description
Economic	Ensured basic income and employment and access to a social safety net.
Food	Access to essential nutrition and food supply.
Health	Access to safe water, living in a safe environment, access to health services, access to safe and affordable family planning and essential support during pregnancy and delivery, prevention of HIV/AIDS and other diseases, and having the basic knowledge to live a healthy life.
Environmental	Prevention of water pollution and air pollution, prevention of deforestation, irrigated land conservation, and natural hazards such as droughts, floods, cyclones, earthquakes, etc.
Personal	Protection of people from physical violence, whether from the state or external states, from violent individuals and sub-state actors, domestic abuse, or predatory adults.
Community	Conservation of traditional cultures, languages, and commonly held values. It also includes abolishing ethnic discrimination, preventing ethnic conflicts, and protecting indigenous people.
Political	Protection of human rights and well-being of all people. It also includes protection of people from state repression, such as freedom of the press, speech, and voting. Political security also covers abolishing political detention, imprisonment, systematic ill-treatment, and disappearance.

Source: Human Security: Seven Categories (gdrc.org). Used by permission of the GDRC.

the Global Development Research Center (GDRC, n.d.). In late 2010, the Human Security Index was introduced to rank countries based on their level of human security. It combines three economic, environmental, and social fabric indices (Hastings, 2011).

Other types of security can be added to those listed in Table 1.1. Examples include state security (i.e., security in military terms), climate security (i.e., security risks associated with climate change), infrastructural security (e.g., prioritizing critical infrastructure), and resource security (e.g., water, energy, land, food, and shelter).

The *Our Common Future*, *Agenda 21*, and the 1994 UNDP/HDR reports, as well as many other studies and global initiatives, paved the way for the Millennium Development Goals (1990–2015), followed by the Sustainable Development Goals (SDGs, 2015–2030), also known as Agenda 2030. The SDGs framework, consisting of 17 goals and 169 targets, represents a comprehensive worldwide action plan involving five critical sustainability aspects: people, planet, prosperity, peace, and partnerships (UN, 2015). Sustainability can also be seen as having four parts: human, social, economic, and environmental.

The noble vision of a more sustainable, peaceful, equitable, and stable world emphasized by the SDGs since 2015 is worthy of consideration. Its importance has been emphasized multiple times, including recently by 126 Nobel Laureates during the 2021 *One Planet, One Future* (NASEM, 2021) meeting. However, the question arises as to whether the original SDGs' vision and the associated mindset and precepts are still relevant after 2020. As noted by Sachs et al. (2021), "For the first time since the adoption of the SDGs in 2015, the global average SDG Index score for 2020 has decreased from the previous year: a decline driven to a large extent by increased poverty rates and unemployment following the outbreak of the COVID-19 pandemic." The 2023 sustainability development report (Sachs et al., 2023) concluded that "at the midpoint of the 2030 Agenda, all of the SDGs are seriously off track."

An open-ended question is how to recover from the pandemic and attain the SDGs. There seems to be a consensus that there is a need to readjust the timeline of Agenda 2030 to reflect the "new normal" of a post-2020 world (Lu, 2020; Sumner et al., 2020; Sachs et al., 2020; UNDP, 2021) while paying particular attention to equitable progress across different world's economies. This recommendation was echoed by the authors of the 2021/2022 United Nations Development report, who reported a nearly universal decline of the HDI scores back to their 2016 levels (UNDP/HDR, 2022).

1.3 HUMAN DEVELOPMENT AND PEACE

Peace is closely related to human development and security concepts (Dews, 2013). As emphasized in Agenda 2030, "Sustainable development cannot be realized without peace and security; and peace and security will be at risk without sustainable development" (UNESCAP, 2018). The development literature has acknowledged the importance of the so-called sustainability-peace nexus (Sharifi et al., 2021).

Peace brings personal security, environmental security, economic security, and an environment conducive to developing desirable socioeconomic partnerships. The alternative to peace is conflict, which can take different forms, ranging from peaceful manifestations, low-intensity violence, high-intensity violence, and armed conflicts (Lemos, 2018). When violent, conflicts can become destructive and costly. In their book *Breaking the Conflict Trap*, Collier et al. (2003) described the relationship between war, violent conflicts, and development as follows:

> Where development succeeds, countries become progressively safer from violent conflict, making subsequent development easier. Where development fails, countries are at high risk of becoming caught in a conflict trap in which war wrecks the economy and increases the risk of future war.

In 2019, the cost of violent conflict was estimated at $14 trillion or $5 per day per person on the planet (IEP, 2021). As noted by Hayden (2018), "The world bank estimates that loss of productivity, failure of state institutions, capital flight, and increased military spending, reduces average income at the end of civil wars by 15% less than they would have been otherwise, driving people into extreme poverty and deprivation." Intra-state conflicts have dominated inter-state disputes since WWII, especially in developing countries.

The noble goal of promoting lasting and sustainable peace for all people has been a topic of intense discussion by various governmental and non-governmental organizations since the publication of *An Agenda for Peace* by the United Nations (Boutros-Ghali, 1992). This document helped define the concepts of preventive diplomacy, peacemaking, peacekeeping, and peacebuilding. Since 1992, multiple papers and policy statements have been written to clarify the nature of peace and its relation to human development and global security. For example, the United Nations Sustainable Development Goal 16 (Peace, Justice, and Strong Institutions) is to "promote peaceful and inclusive societies for sustainable development, provide access to justice for all and build effective, accountable and inclusive institutions at all levels" (SDSN, 2020). SDG 16 covers a broad spectrum of topics with 12 targets and 24 indicators. As noted in a report by the National Academies of Sciences, Engineering, and Medicine (NASEM, 2022), many of these indicators "were established despite the absence of globally agreed-upon methodology or data."

Meeting SDG 16 is about developing the right relationships, a concept contained in principle 16f of the Earth Charter (1987), where peace is defined as "the wholeness created by right relationships with oneself, other persons, other cultures, other life, earth, and the larger whole of which all are a part." Peace also appears in the SDG cross-cutting issues of gender equality, governance, health, inequalities, security, support of vulnerable states, and sustainable cities (UN, 2015). Although the SDGs community has recognized that not effectively addressing peace may jeopardize all other SDGs (Virji et al., 2019), that relationship is yet to be practically demonstrated in different landscapes.

Although peace is intimately linked to socioeconomic development (Milante and Oxhorn, 2009; Dews, 2013), it is essential to note that not all forms of peace contribute positively to socioeconomic development and vice versa. Whether peace is beneficial depends mostly on how peace resolution and transformation in peacebuilding, peacemaking, and peacekeeping activities are designed, implemented, and evaluated (Ricigliano, 2012). For instance, not addressing the root causes and underlying factors of conflict may result in resuming the conflict and negatively affecting development in the foreseeable future (Ricigliano). A case in point is the fragility of stability, security, and economic development that has been mainstream in Somalia since 1991 due to intermittent armed civil conflict (Hayden, 2018).

Likewise, development can positively or negatively impact peace, depending on the type of development being implemented. It can have consequences or create unintended issues (Bush, 1998). For instance, a combination of inappropriate decision-making and trade-offs in activities such as the supply and demand of water, energy, and food resources; inadequate associated infrastructure planning and design; poor decisions in resource management and allocation; and poor governance may result in divisions, unrest, conflict, violence, and insecurity. In short, not all forms of development lead to long-term peace and vice versa (Brown and Nicolucci-Altman, 2022).

1.4   HUMAN DEVELOPMENT AND CLIMATE SECURITY

Another open-ended question in human development is how to deal with the growing existential threats of climate change. Climate change adds to existing natural (geological) hazards. As summarized by Ban-Ki Moon in his 2012 address to the UN General Assembly (UN, 2012), "Climate change is destroying our path to sustainability." Climate action is addressed as SDG 13 (i.e., urgent action to combat climate change and its impact). Like peace, addressing climate change through awareness, adaptation (addressing its effects), and mitigation (addressing its causes) is instrumental to the success of Agenda 2030.

Starting with the Industrial Revolution, human activities have increasingly affected the climate and caused global warming and climate change. Since the 1960s, worldwide temperatures have increased, hotter each year than before; 2013–2022 has been the period with the warmest years on record (WMO, 2022). According to NASA (n.d.), the evidence of climate change cannot be ignored. It includes global temperature rise, warming oceans, shrinking ice sheets, glacial retreat, decreased snow cover, sea level rise, declining Arctic Sea ice, increased severity and frequency of certain events, erratic precipitation patterns, and ocean acidification. These phenomena directly affect the security of people's livelihoods (water, energy, food, shelter, health), ecosystems and biodiversity, the economy, and infrastructure. One of humanity's challenges in the Twenty-first century is coping and adapting to rapidly changing conditions, developing policies, and building capacity and resilience with awareness, adaptation, and mitigation methods to minimize climate change impact (UN, 2021; IPCC, 2023) and eventually create a net-zero, climate-resilient future (UNFCCC, 2022).

The contribution of anthropogenic effects to climate change was recognized in the late 1980s and led to the Intergovernmental Panel on Climate Change (IPCC) under UN resolution 43/53 on December 6, 1988 (UNGA, 1988). Shortly after, the UN framework convention on climate change (UNFCCC) was signed and represented the first step in creating worldwide awareness of climate change. The framework focused primarily on adaptation measures for agriculture. Since then, there has been a growing realization that climate change associated with anthropogenic greenhouse emissions (CCGs) creates risks that transform the entire security landscape at multiple scales, from the local to the global.

More specifically, climate change has potentially detrimental effects on (i) well-being, the security of livelihood, and the quality of life of individuals and communities (FAO, 2019; UNICEF, 2019); (ii) physical and mental health (McMichael et al., 2006; WHO, 2021; Palinkas et al., 2021); (iii) the enjoyment of all human rights (Human Rights Council Tenth Session, 2009: UNHR, 2021); (iv) ecosystems survival, biodiversity, agriculture, and food security (Hammond and Dube, 2012); (v) infrastructure planning and adaptation (Bergmüller et al., 2018), (vi) social stability and security (Barnett, 2003; NIC, 2021); (vii) human migration and resettlement (Brown, 2008; Null and Herzer, 2016; White House, 2021; Peacedirect, 2022); (viii) the economy (Stern, 2006; World Bank, 2015); (ix) the melting of glaciers and sea level rise (WMO, 2022); and (x) peace, conflict, and unrest (Busby, 2013; Center for Climate & Security, 2021; WCSR, 2021), among others. Table 1.2 lists various effects of climate change on human security identified by the National Intelligence Council

TABLE 1.2
Multiple Effects and Impacts of Climate Change on Human Security as Greenhouse Gas Emissions and Temperatures Increase Outlined by the National Intelligence Council (NIC, 2021)

Climate Change Effects	Impacts on Human Security
Heat	More intense and frequent heat waves will reduce labor productivity, increase the frequency and intensity of wildfires, undermine human health, and lead to loss of life.
Heavy Precipitation and Flooding	Increased flooding will lead to economic losses, increased calls for humanitarian assistance, and loss of life.
Drought	More frequent, intense, and prolonged droughts will undermine food security in developing countries, cause more extreme wildfires, increase political instability, and drive migration.
Sea Level Rise	Rising sea levels will increasingly imperil coastal cities and exacerbate storm surges that damage infrastructure and inundate water systems.
Arctic Ice Melt	The accelerated melting of Arctic ice sheets will affect ocean circulation and salinity, threaten local ecosystems and increase competition over resources and transit route access.
Tropical Cyclones	More frequent, destructive, and shifting tracks of cyclones will lead to trillions of dollars in economic losses in tropical zones, increase calls for humanitarian assistance, drive population displacement and migration, and lead to loss of life.
Coral Reefs	The disappearance of coral reefs will eliminate an ecosystem that serves 500 million people, impacting economic and food security.
Biodiversity	Loss of species will increase human health risks and threaten food security.

(NIC, 2021). Climate change-generated risks affect health, ecosystems, infrastructure, economy, equity, justice, migration, conflict, etc.

There is also a worldwide consensus that climate change is a "threat multiplier" and a "threat catalyst" as it may amplify existing natural and human-made risks. Attention has been directed to *climate injustice*. The stakes are predominant in fragile states and least-developed communities, where climate change and poverty create a double burden for the world's most disadvantaged people (Anguelovski and Martinez-Allier, 2014; Jamieson, 2014; Dehghan, 2022; WMO, 2022; Harvey, 2022; WEF, 2023). As noted by the IPCC (2023), the people most vulnerable to climate change and in need of adaptation and mitigation efforts include those who are "socially, economically, politically, institutionally or otherwise marginalized," and more specifically, indigenous people, women, children, migrants, IDP, and people with disabilities (UNHR, 2021). These also include people living, for instance, in low-lying coastal areas, the Arctic, sub-Saharan Africa, East Africa (Kenya, Ethiopia, Somalia, Uganda, and South Sudan), arid land areas, and sensitive ecosystems. A report by the US National Academies (2022) also emphasized that poor and disadvantaged communities in the US are also subject to the environmental and health burdens associated with events exacerbated by climate change, increasing inequities, and discrimination. All these risks to security change over time and have the potential to reach catastrophic levels during the Twenty-first century (WCSR, 2021).

The climate crisis is a water crisis, an energy crisis, a food crisis, a physical security crisis, an environmental crisis, etc. The statistics about the estimated impact of climate change on humans and the natural environment they depend on are alarming. Some examples:

- Between 2030 and 2050, climate change could cause 250,000 deaths yearly from malaria, malnutrition, diarrhea, and heat stress alone (WHO, 2021).
- The impact of climate change could push another 132 million people into poverty by 2030 (Jafino et al., 2020).
- A billion people will endure unbearable heat for each 1°C rise in temperature (Earth.org, 2020).
- "The cost between 2010 and 2050 of adapting to an approximately 2°C warmer world by 2050 is in the range of $70 billion to $100 billion a year." It will likely increase if nothing is done (World Bank, 2011).
- Climate change may create 200 million climate migrants by 2050 (Forman and Ramathan, 2019).
- "Annual adaptation [to climate change] costs in developing countries alone are estimated at USD 70 billion. This figure is expected to reach USD 140–300 billion in 2030 and USD 280–500 billion in 2050" (UNEP, 2020).
- "More than 20 million people in Kenya, Ethiopia, Somalia, Uganda, and South Sudan have been affected by the drought, with more than 2.2 million displaced in Somalia and Ethiopia and severe maternal risks to hundreds of thousands of expectant or breastfeeding women" (United Nations, in Associated Press, 2023).

Closely related to human security, *climate security* has been proposed to capture the effects of climate change and changes in climate patterns on different aspects of society. It refers to "the security to risks induced, directly or indirectly, by changes in climate patterns" (Wikipedia). The UK Foreign Secretary Margaret Beckett first suggested the concept during a speech at the UK embassy in Berlin on October 23, 2006. Climate security is also about ecological security (WAAS, 2021) and the "maintenance of the local and the planetary biosphere as the essential support system on which all other human enterprises depend." According to McDonald (2013), climate security must also include national and international security, which dominate the discourse on the effect of climate change. Climate security needs to be defined based on whose security is at stake, what threats are implied, and over what scale (physical and time) means of climate security need to be developed. Another question is how to securitize the climate simultaneously as human enterprises and development unfold (Trombetta, 2009).

The 2015 Paris Agreement (COP 21) and more recent 2021 COP 26 and 2022 COP 27 agreements have emphasized the need to curb the effects of climate change during the rest of the Twenty-first century to avoid catastrophic, irreversible consequences to life on Earth. Although plenty of geopolitical obstacles to limiting global warming to 1.5°C or even 2°C above preindustrial levels by 2050 or not reaching a future threshold of 350 ppm of carbon dioxide remain, attention has been paid to developing *climate security practices*. They are defined by von Lossow et al. (2021) as

> Tangible actions implemented by a (local or central) government, organization, community, private actor or individual to help prevent, reduce, mitigate, or adapt to security risks and threats related to the impacts of climate change and related environmental degradation, as well as subsequent policies.

Militaries and security institutions have raised the alarm about the impact of climate change risks on society and have emphasized the urgency of addressing risks through international collaboration (IMCCS, 2020). In the US, climate security has become a hot topic in the relationship between the three pillars of defense, diplomacy, and development in national and global security (Diamond, 2014; Center for Climate Security, 2020; Scott, 2021; WCSR, 2021). The National Intelligence Council (NIC, 2021) sees climate change as a threat multiplier where risks to US national security through 2040 fall into three categories:

- Geopolitical tensions over climate responses (e.g., competitive security, competition on who controls the responses, bears the responsibility to act, and acquires new minerals and technologies)
- Climate exacerbated geopolitical flashpoints (e.g., disputes around transboundary water, energy, land, and food resources in different biomes such as the Arctic or the Middle East and migration issues)
- Impact on country-level instability (especially in developing countries already least ready in capacity and resilience to cope and adapt to changes)

One can add security risks associated with the unintended adverse effects of poorly considered adaptation and mitigation measures on existing geographical areas under socioeconomic, cultural, or political tension. Examples of this concept, called *backdraft* (Risi, 2017; Peters et al., 2020), include (i) the competitive extraction of minerals (e.g., rare earth elements) used in creating new green technologies, (ii) the impact of decisions made by outsiders on local communities to deal with their natural resources (crops, forests), (iii) proposed but untested geoengineering solutions that may negatively affect natural processes, and (iv) adverse impact of solutions on human rights and equalities.

Conversely, there is also a consensus in the literature that climate change, like COVID, offers unique opportunities for (i) integrating scientific collaboration and peacebuilding at different scales (local, regional, global), (ii) encouraging science diplomacy efforts, (iii) promoting innovative research leading to building back better, (iv) creating more geopolitical stability, (v) strengthening local institutions, and (vi) developing a society more resilient to climate change and future threats through awareness, adaptation, and mitigation.

1.5   A NEW MINDSET AND APPROACH

The human development and security literature contain many case studies demonstrating the consequences of the dysfunctional dynamics between conflict, unsustainable development practices, and climate vulnerability regardless of context and scale. All three seem to be the outcomes of a dominating Western world neoliberal and capitalistic mode of operation in the twentieth century and the first two decades of the Twenty-first century. The associated mindset is characterized by determinism, compartmentalization, impatience, fixation on growth, bias, fear, greed, private property, use of resources without limits, and the brutal exploitation of the environment and people as commodities for the benefit of a few (Cherkaoui, 2020; Monbiot, 2021). As noted by Lent (2021), one can only hope that this pathological mindset is dying and will be replaced soon by one "based on life-affirming values."

Paraphrasing Albert Einstein that problems cannot be solved with the same level of thinking that created them, a new mindset in human interactions is necessary to address the human development and security issues in a post-2020 world. The unique perspective must also be operationalized and accompanied by more authentic forms of leadership and decision-making, compassion, education, higher levels of consciousness, and mindful action. Although developing that new mindset is still a work in progress, another critical aspect of the new perspective is that it must depart from the traditional approach that addresses the world's problems in isolation based on a positivistic and reductionistic view of reality seeking optimal solutions to each situation. That mindset, which originated from the Enlightenment of the seventeenth and eighteenth centuries, has been the dominant one in our institutions (social, political, economic, and educational) up to this day. It is time to realize that it is disconnected from reality, as it does not account for the uncertainty and complexity of today's world's problems.

This book makes a case for a new mindset to address the complex development challenges in a post-2020 world and handle potential future crises. It is written for decision-makers to approach community development in complex settings using a system perspective. It acknowledges the multisectoral, multidisciplinary, and participatory nature of community development. Generally, a systems perspective is better suited than a traditional reductionistic one at (i) addressing the complexity, uncertainty, and ambiguity of the systems involved in community development and (ii) accounting for the role of peace, sustainability, and climate security.

As part of the new mindset, this book proposes an integrated, coherent, and multisolving approach when addressing what is referred to as the *peace–sustainability–climate security (PSC) nexus* at the community scale. They are no places where peace, sustainability, and climate security reside in a community. Peace, sustainability, and climate security are considered three interconnected and mutually reinforcing *states* (or cultures) that *emerge* from the interactions of multiple systems in a community landscape (environment or ecosystem) subject to various constraints (political, social, cultural, economic, environmental, etc.) and adverse events. All three states cannot be reduced to their parts. They are inherently dynamic (i.e., they change as a community develops over time). Since the causal chains between the three states are not linear and their drivers are known, decision-making across the PSC nexus requires using a systems-based methodology to assess the current level of community development, develop strategies and scenarios of intervention to close the gap between the present and desired levels of development and select and implement the most appropriate interventions.

The approach used in this book acknowledges that there are no one-size-fits-all unified and optimized static states of peace, sustainability, and climate security as they are context- and scale-specific. As a result, what works in one community landscape may not work elsewhere, and multiple "good enough" states (i.e., satisficing states using the terminology of Simon, 1972) are possible. Paraphrasing Dietrich (2012), peace, sustainability, and climate security and their nexus are states that have "to be read as a plural."

It should be noted that throughout this book, a clear distinction is made between the active *processes* and reform leading to peace, sustainability, and climate security and the states themselves. For instance, sustainable development is viewed as a process that leads to a state of sustainability. Likewise, peacebuilding (i.e., building the conditions for peace before and after conflict), peacemaking (i.e., getting parties to find common ground during conflict), and peacekeeping (i.e., supporting sustainable peace before and during conflict) efforts are three complementary and interrelated processes that lead to lasting and sustainable peace. Finally, communities' climate security practices (awareness, adaptation, and mitigation) to deal with climatic pattern changes contribute to climate security. Another way to consider sustainability, peace, and climate security is to see them as *nouns* (i.e., states seen as outcomes or goals) or *verbs* (i.e., processes and actions). The same distinction could be made for the different categories of human security mentioned above.

1.6   THE SYSTEMS STORYLINE

1.6.1   THE ICEBERG MODEL

As we come to terms with deciding what a world for the rest of the Twenty-first century looks like, the success of any new mindset to address human development and security issues and the coherence between peace, sustainability, and climate security depends significantly on the nature of the *mental models* used in decision-making and how these models convert into action. As defined by Sterman (2000), mental models are cognitive and virtual representations of the real world that modelers and decision-makers use to describe and explain (i) the causes and consequences of an issue or problem, (ii) the structure and relationships believed to be responsible for some observed behavior patterns associated with the issue, and (iii) possible circular feedback mechanisms (circular causation) at play within one issue or across multiple issues.

A metaphor often used in systems thinking to explain how addressing practical issues and events is driven by mental models and structural and behavioral patterns is that of an iceberg floating on seawater (Sweeney and Meadows, 2010), where 90% of it is below the seawater surface and 10% above it. Another metaphor proposed by Griffith University (2022) is biological and that of a living organism (e.g., tree roots, mycelium, or ant nest).

A version of the iceberg is shown in Figure 1.1. In this figure, the top of the iceberg emerging above the waterline represents the outward manifestation of the issues (i.e., the easily observable and identifiable events) that unfold at the level of interest. Such issues include climate change effects, migration, poverty, etc. It is also

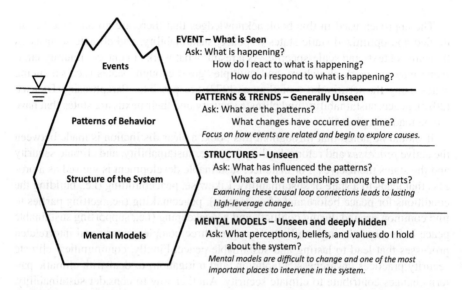

FIGURE 1.1   Iceberg model.

Source: © 2020 Waters Center for Systems Thinking, WatersCenterST.org. Used by permission.

what most decision-makers see first, focus their intention on, and quickly want to correct. However, by providing quick solutions, they ignore what is below the water surface (i.e., the patterns and trends, structures) and, more importantly, the mental (i.e., conceptual) models that explain what is happening above it. The *Titanic* sank because its captain and crew could not detect the lateral extent of the hidden threats below the ocean surface and not because they could not see the ice protruding from the ocean. At that time, there was also the false belief (i.e., mindset) that the ship was indestructible.

The iceberg model concept is often used in the systems literature to recommend approaching complex problems with four levels of thinking. In the context of community development, the first level of thinking considers current community issues represented by the tip of the iceberg in Figure 1.1. Right below the iceberg's surface, the second level of thinking acknowledges the patterns that describe what has happened to the community over time (i.e., the history of the events). These could be patterns of (i) recurring conflict, exclusion, dominance, and competition; (ii) collaboration on joint efforts; (iii) the detrimental effects of climate change (drought, flood); and (iv) economic insecurity. It is likely that some of these patterns and trends are recurring and can be represented by archetypal system behaviors (Kim and Anderson, 2007; Benson and Marlin, 2017; Griffith University, 2022).

Farther below in Figure 1.1, the third level of thinking considers the systemic tangible structures that create the patterns. These structures may include the various community systems and subsystems (i.e., social, economic, cultural, ecological, and infrastructure) at play as issues unfold. In addition, a detailed analysis of the structures may reveal how different systems and embedded subsystems influence each other.

Finally, the fourth level of thinking at the bottom of the iceberg is associated with the mental models, mind maps, and the underlying mindset that drives structural and behavioral performance. Seelos (2020) referred to it as the behavioral architecture consisting of four dimensions (economic, cognitive, normative, and power/politics). That is where intangible factors such as dominant community preferences, values, habits, biases, priorities, culture, religious beliefs, loyalties, policies, and procedures reside. These often unseen aspects represent the inward dimensions of the issues, how the problems are addressed, and how reality is perceived. Even more profound at this level is where "social-psychological factors that shape human thought, preferences, and behaviors" reside (Wolfe and Smith, 2021). It is also where thoughts become words at the individual and community levels, words become actions, actions become habits, habits develop into character, and character becomes destiny (Lao Tzu, n.d.). It is at this level that beliefs control perceptions and vice versa.

When considering the iceberg model in Figure 1.1 from the bottom up, the four levels of thinking inherent in that model form a *systems storyline* relating mental models, structural and behavioral patterns, and events at the scale and context of interest. The storyline contains dynamic hypotheses that are assumed to explain the what, why, who, when, where, and how of the community development issues. The mental model and dynamic hypotheses for each issue can be combined to create a so-called *reference mode* (i.e., "graph(s) showing the[expected] behavior of the [issue] over time") (Rouwette and Vennix, 2015). A graphic representation of the reference mode is sometimes referred to as a "behavior-over-time" graph (Benson and Marlin, 2017) or a "reference behavior pattern" (Ritchie-Dunham and Rabbino, 2001). Mental models must be as comprehensive as possible and require a detailed appraisal.

In community development, it is essential to develop a narrative for the storyline describing the different aspects of the community in its current and desired states. For instance, what are the current and expected conditions of community peace, sustainability, and climate security? Comparison between the current and desired storylines helps to outline possible intervention scenarios. An example of that dynamic can be found in the case study presented by Bosch et al. (2013) and Nguyen and Bosch (2013) about the Cat Ba biosphere in Vietnam. The four levels of thinking in Figure 1.1 were used to decide on interventions addressing the dynamics between conservation and sustainable development. The analysis is summarized in Chapter 12.

1.6.2 Dealing with Mental Filters

The traditional approach to addressing human development and security issues in a specific landscape often ignores what is below the iceberg's surface. It focuses on the external manifestation of the problems by providing quick remedial solutions that ignore the "what, why, who, where, when, and how" of the issues. Unfortunately, shallow and compulsive answers to complex problems often result in short-term solutions and significant unintended consequences. This dynamic is particularly critical when decisions are made with pathological forms of human thought, preferences, behaviors, and values (e.g., selfishness, greed, and apathy). More recently, bad-faith information has permeated the structures of society and affected decision-making.

These mental filters first corrupt the mental models, change the community fabric and structure, create dysfunctional community behavior patterns and trends, and ultimately create harmful unintended consequences for people and their environment.

This dynamic can be attributed to how humans approach complexity and change and, more specifically, how they process information and act upon it. Bounded rationality (i.e., limited rationality in decision-making) limits human's ability to respond to environmental demands and accept change (Simon, 1972; Jones, 1999; Callebaut, 2007; Schön, 1971). When faced with such issues, humans tend to ignore or deny the problems or make them simpler.

Because humans are obsessed with organized simplicity (i.e., simplicity at the group level), individuals or groups often decide on simplified models of reality based on limited understanding, perceptions, perspectives, beliefs, feelings and emotions, experiences, expertise, and habits (Dörner, 1997). These differences often result in disagreements and conflict between distinctive individuals or groups that may impact, for instance, how the different phases of community development are conducted. More specifically, unless they are mediated, the disagreements could control (i) how development interventions are designed, planned, executed, monitored, and evaluated; (ii) how predictable the outcome of those interventions will be; and (iii) how they will yield long-term benefits and sustainability.

1.6.3 FINDING LEVERAGE

The above discussion suggests that the mindset necessary to create systemic changes to complex human development and security issues must include systemic mental models that (i) embrace rather than ignore organized complexity and accept the challenges that this approach brings forth, (ii) break away from equilibrium thinking to dynamic thinking (Scoones et al., 2007), and (iii) see community development as not being static but rather evolving, adapting, and resulting in "learning organizations" as suggested by Senge (1994).

The systemic mental models must also recognize where leverage resides in the different systems involved in human development and security issues. As Meadows (1997) noted, these are deeply rooted places where "a small shift in one thing can produce big changes in everything." Leverage is everywhere but needs to be identified for specific scales and tailored to particular contexts. According to Meadows, the leverage category with the strongest influence resides in the big picture of envisioning systems changes to meet goals, considering new paradigms to change the system, and having the flexibility to change paradigms as needed. All these forms of leverage reside in the lower tier of the iceberg model in Figure 1.1. The following leverage category resides in how systems are structured and how information flows across the structures. They are in the second to last tier of Figure 1.1. Systems structures, in turn, create behavior patterns (third tier in Figure 1.1).

In practice, the challenge of identifying the underlying mental models and structure from observed behavior patterns can be understood as *reverse analysis*. The rationale behind this *inductive* approach is that if the system's mental models and structures could be determined, places to intervene in a complex environment could be identified, and interventions selected and implemented. Following the intervention, the complex environment would show a new behavior pattern more aligned with the desired one. However, the main problem with the reverse analysis of complex systems is that there are no specific existing methodologies, much less a method that would guarantee a definite and successful answer. Furthermore, there are no unique solutions to the reverse analysis of complex non-linear problems, as multiple mental models and structures may generate situations with similar behavior patterns and trends.

It should be noted that leverage is not just about the "where" of any intervention. It is also about the "when" interventions that need to occur when addressing human development and security issues. A crisis may, for instance, be an opportunity for intervention and change, such as not rebuilding vulnerability and increasing community resilience following some natural hazards.

1.7   BOOK CONTENT

This book provides clear guidance on developing systems thinking mindset and using practical systems tools to operationalize that mindset when addressing complex human development and security issues, specifically those at the crossroads between peace, sustainability, and climate security at the community level. All three sectors and their opposites (conflict, unsustainable practices, and climate vulnerability) are interconnected along causal chains and occur in a community landscape (i.e., setting). They are influenced by multiple shared systems and are subject to various socioeconomic, geopolitical, and cultural constraints. In turn, the community landscape depends on how peace, sustainability, and climate security manifest. This book focuses on climate security measures and not explicitly on the physics of climate change itself. Complex earth systems models of climate change are not considered in this book.

Traditional approaches look at complex issues and their underlying structure in a fragmented manner with biased perspectives in favor of linear cause-and-effect thinking and organized simplicity. This compartmentalized approach, driven by a need to reach satisfactory community equilibrium, fails to recognize the interactions and interconnectedness among community systems. If addressed, it could solve multiple issues more effectively. It also does not account for communities' complex, adaptive, and dynamic nature.

A systems perspective offers an alternate process whereby decision-makers can focus, among other things, on the interconnectedness of disparate factors and actors, the nonlinearity of causal relationships, the relevance of feedback structures, patterns, dynamic relationships, and the identification of high leverage points. By embracing organized complexity, this more holistic approach can identify good-enough solutions to existing issues and plan for future events that allow decision-makers to develop meaningful scenarios of intervention, implementation, and assessment at the community level. The value proposition of systems thinking, multisolving related issues, and embracing organized complexity is emphasized throughout this book.

Chapter 2 explores the components of the peace–sustainability–climate security (PSC) nexus, their systemic characteristics, and mutual influence and dependence. It provides the rationale necessary to consider a systems approach to the nexus.

Systems-based definitions of peace, sustainability, and climate security are proposed. All three sectors are defined as states emerging from shared systems (i.e., social, environmental, economic, and infrastructure) interacting in a specific context and scale landscape.

Chapter 3 outlines some desirable characteristics of a new mindset for a post-2020 world and the value proposition for embracing organized complexity and systems science when addressing complex human development and security issues and the PSC nexus at the community level.

Chapter 4 explores the different dimensions of systems thinking and its value proposition when addressing complex human development and security issues and the PSC nexus. Several examples demonstrate how logical reductionistic decision-making combined with well-intended interventions may lead to unintended consequences. Finally, the chapter reviews the habits of systems thinkers that are necessary before systems tools are used in decision-making.

Chapter 5 emphasizes the importance of understanding the context, scale (physical and temporal), and boundaries of the setting/landscape in which community development occurs and the PSC nexus unfolds. Participatory community appraisal through participatory action research provides valuable information about the dynamics of the community landscape and helps identify, outline, and rank critical issues in the community and across the PSC nexus. Integrated capacity, risk, and conflict analyses help convert the information into the knowledge necessary for decision-making across the sectors of the PSC nexus.

Chapter 6 explores how qualitative and semi-quantitative tools can be used to model the systems at play at the crossroads between peace, sustainability, and climate security. The tools include concept maps, cross-impact analysis, and network analysis. These so-called "soft systems modeling tools" provide a basis for understanding the dynamics of the issues and their causes and effects.

Chapter 7 presents the challenges and opportunities in using "hard systems modeling tools" to model community issues. The tools used in this approach include system dynamics (SD) and agent-based modeling (ABM). The challenges and opportunities in using SD to simulate the dynamic across the PSC nexus are discussed. Simple abstract SD models of the dynamic of each sector of the PSC nexus are presented.

Chapter 8 reviews different systems archetypes (i.e., generic structures that tend to be found in multiple human development and security issues). Archetypes may help map various forms of human behavior and identify leverage points of intervention in systems.

Chapter 9 presents the details of a systems-based methodology that can be used by decision-makers involved in addressing complex issues across the PSC nexus. Although the method is generic, it provides a road map and guidelines to address the problems in each sector of the PSC nexus and across the nexus, while considering how each sector of the nexus interacts with the social, economic, environmental, and infrastructure community systems. The methodology is based on the premise that there is a community development story and a narrative describing how the community envisions bridging the gap from its current peace, sustainability, and climate security states to some respective desired states. This approach requires meaningful participation and engagement from different stakeholder groups.

Chapter 10 presents a series of examples illustrating how to use SD to account for community capacity and resilience interactions. SD is also used to model how the three sectors of the PSC nexus interact. The stock and flow models presented in this chapter are generic and can be used to conduct parametric studies on how changes in one sector of the PSC nexus could impact other sectors.

Chapter 11 explores further how to model the interaction between peace, sustainability, and climate security and the multiple systems in the community landscape. Several SD illustrative examples of increasing complexity and generative capacity are presented. One of the examples models the feedback interaction between the PSC nexus and the water-energy-land-food (WELF) nexus.

Chapter 12 presents two case studies to illustrate the value proposition of using SD tools (causal loop diagrams) to capture the complex dynamics in human development and security at two scales: a biosphere reserve in Vietnam and the Syrian crisis.

Chapter 13 describes scenario planning as a *decision support system* to assist decision-makers in exploring several alternative intervention societal scenarios across the community landscape. These scenarios help shape possible intervention pathways to address general PSC nexus-related and community development issues.

Finally, *Chapter 14* draws key conclusions on significant themes addressed in the book and, more specifically, the need for addressing the PSC nexus at the community level in an integrated, dynamic, multidisciplinary, and participatory manner. It emphasizes the need to create a portfolio of case studies to operationalize this new approach and demonstrate its value proposition in human development and security at different scales.

1.8 CONCLUDING REMARKS

Fifty years ago, Borlaug (1970) remarked that a peaceful world cannot be built on "empty stomachs and human misery." One can also add that building a peaceful world requires addressing the economic, environmental, geopolitical, societal, and technological risks outlined at the start of this chapter. Promoting peace and sustainability in human development and security while accounting for the risks associated with climate change has become more imperative than ever when addressing humanity's challenges of the Twenty-first century (Gaston et al., 2023). A new mindset must be embraced by society to address complex human development and security issues with an integrated perspective. The success of that new mindset depends significantly on the nature of the mental models used in decision-making and how these models translate into actual interventions. The new mindset requires embracing change, which according to Schön (1971) can be difficult. As noted by that author, social systems resist with "an energy roughly proportional to the radicalness of the change that is being threatened." Despite such roadblocks, embracing complexity and system sciences is needed to deal with the increasingly complex and challenging problems faced by civilization as it advances in the 21st century.

REFERENCES

Allouche, J., Middleton, C., & Gyawali, D. (2015). Technical veil, hidden politics: Interrogating the power linkages behind the nexus. *Water Alternatives*, *8*(1), 610–626.

Anguelovski, I., & Martinez-Alier, J. (2014). The environmentalism of the poor. Revisited: Territory and place in disconnected glocal struggles. *Ecological Economics*, *102*, 167–176. https://doi.org/10.1016/j.ecolecon.2014.04.005

Associated Press. (2023). Climate change worsened Eastern Africa drought, scientists find. Retrieved April 27, 2023, from https://www.nbcnews.com/news/world/climate-change-africa-drought-worse-world-weather-attribution-rcna81732

Beihoff, B., Oster, C., Friedenthal, S., Paredis, C., Kemp, D., Stoewer, H., Nichols, D., & Wade, J. (2014). A World in motion - systems engineering Vision 2025. https://www.incose.org/about-systems-engineering/se-vision-2025

Benson, T., & Marlin, S. (2017). *The habit-forming guide to becoming a systems thinker*. The Waters Foundation Systems Thinking Group Publ.

Borlaug, N. (1970). The green revolution, peace, and humanity. Nobel peace prize lecture. Retrieved March 1, 2023, from https://www.nobelprize.org/prizes/peace/1970/borlaug/lecture/

Bosch, O. J. H., Nguyen, N. C., Maeno, T., & Yasui, T. (2013). Managing complex issues through evolutionary learning laboratories. *Systems Research*, *30*, 116–135. https://doi.org/10.1002/sres.2171

Boutros-Ghali, B. (1992). An agenda for peace: Preventive diplomacy, peacemaking, and peacekeeping. *International Relations*, *11*(3), 201–218. https://doi.org/10.1177/004711789201100302

Brown, O. (2008, February 15). Migration and climate change. IOM Migration Research series no. 31, Geneva. https://www.iom.int/news/iom-migration-research-series-no-31-migration-and-climate-change

Brown, O., & Nicolucci-Altman, G. (2022). The white paper on the future of environmental peacebuilding. Geneva Peacebuilding Platform, International Union for Conservation of Nature, Peace Nexus Foundation, Environmental Law Institute, Environmental Peacebuilding Association. https://www.ecosystemforpeace.org/

Busby, J. (2013, September 12). Why do climate changes lead to conflict? Provocative new study leaves questions. https://www.newsecuritybeat.org/2013/09/climate-lead-conflict-provocative-study-leaves-questions/

Bush, K. (1998). A measure of peace: Peace and Conflict Impact Assessment (PCIA) of development projects in conflict zones. Ottawa: International Development Research Centre, Working Paper 1.

Center for Climate Security. (2020). A security threat assessment of global climate change. https://climateandsecurity.org/a-security-threat-assessment-of-global-climate-change/

Cherkaoui, M. (2020). *The shifting geopolitics of coronavirus and the demise of neoliberalism (parts 1 and 2)*. Al Jazeera Center for Studies. https://studies.aljazeera.net/sites/default/files/articles/documents/2020-03/The%20Shifting%20Geopolitics%20of%20Coronavirus%20and%20the%20Demise%20of%20Neoliberalism%20%E2%80%93%20%28Part%202%29_1.pdf

Collier, P., Elliott, V. L., Hegre, H., Hoeffler, A., Reynal-Querol, M., & Sambanis, N. (2003). *Breaking the conflict trap: Civil war and development policy*. Oxford University Press. http://hdl.handle.net/10986/13938

Dehghan, S. K. (2022, January 14). https://www.theguardian.com/global-development/2022/jan/14/worlds-poorest-bear-brunt-of-climate-crisis-10-underreported-emergencies?utm_source=newsletter&utm_medium=email&utm_campaign=future_trends_oil_rally_to_continue_berlusconi_s_presidential_bid_us_healthcare_consumerism&utm_term=2022-01-18

Dews, F. (2013, October 17). UN Deputy Secretary-General Jan Eliasson: No peace without development, no development without peace. *Brookings*. http://www.brookings.edu/blog/brookings-now/2013/10/17/un-deputy-secretary-general-jan-eliasson-no-peace-without-development-no-development-without-peace

Diamond, K. (2014, March 7). Climate change and national security in an age of austerity: the 2014 quadrennial defense review. NewSecurityBeat, US Department of Defense. https://www.newsecuritybeat.org/2014/03/climate-change-national-security-age-austerity-2014-quadrennial-defense-review/

Dietrich, W. (2012). *Interpretations of peace in history and culture*. Palgrave Macmillan.

Dodman, D., Hayward, B., Pelling, M., Castan Broto, V., Chow, W., Chu, E., Dawson, R., Khirfan, L., McPhearson, T., Prakash, A., Zheng, Y., & Ziervogel, G. (2022) Cities, Settlements, and Key Infrastructure. In H.-O. Pörtner, D.C. Roberts, M. Tignor, E.S. Poloczanska, K. Mintenbeck, A. Alegría, M. Craig, S. Langsdorf, S. Löschke, V. Möller, A. Okem and B. Rama (eds.), *Climate Change 2022: Impacts, Adaptation, and Vulnerability*. Contribution of working group II to the sixth assessment report of the intergovernmental panel on climate change. Cambridge University Press. https://doi.org/10.1017/9781009325844

Dorn, W. (2003). Human security: An overview. https://walterdorn.net/23-human-security-an-overview

Dörner, D. (1997). *The logic of failure: Recognizing and avoiding error in complex situations*. Perseus Books.

Earth.org. (2020, May 7). For every one °C rise in temperature, a billion people will endure insufferable heat. https://earth.org/for-every-1c-rise-in-temperature-a-billion-people-will-endure-insufferable-heat/

Eysenbach, G. (2020). How to fight an infodemic: The four pillars of infodemic management. *Journal of Medical Internet Research*, 22(6), e21820. https://doi.org/10.2196/21820

Ferroukhi, R., Nagpal, D., Lopez-Peña, A., Hodges, T., Mohtar, R. H., Daher, B., Mohtar, S., & Keulertz, M. (2015). *Renewable energy in the water, energy, and food nexus*. United Arab Emirates: International Renewable Energy Agency (IRENA) Policy Unit. http://www.irena.org/Publications

Forman, F., & Ramanathan, V. (2019). Unchecked climate change, mass migration, and sustainability: A probabilistic case for urgent action. In M. Suarez-Orozco (ed.), *Humanitarianism and Mass Migration: Confronting the World Crisis*, the University of California Press. https://doi.org/10.1525/california/9780520297128.003.0002

Frej, W., & Ramalingam, B. (2011). Foreign policy and complex adaptive systems: Exploring new paradigms for analysis and action. Santa Fe Institute paper 2011-06-022.

Gaston, E., Brown, O., Al-Dawsari, N., Downing, C., Day, A., & Bodewig, R. (2023). *Climate-security and peacebuilding: Thematic review*. UN Univeristy - Center for Policy Research. https://www.un.org/peacebuilding/sites/www.un.org.peacebuilding/files/documents/climate_security_tr_web_final_april10.pdf

Global Development Research Center (GDRC). (n.d.). Human security. https://www.gdrc.org/sustdev/husec/1-def.html

Gómez, O. A., & Gasper, D. (2013). *Human Security: A thematic guidance note for regional and national human development report teams*. UNDP. Human Development Report Office. https://repub.eur.nl/pub/50571/Metis_195152.pdf

Griffith University. (2022). Everyday patterns for shifting systems. https://www.griffith.edu.au/__data/assets/pdf_file/0013/1640002/Everyday-Patterns_YCGU-and-ACL.pdf

Hammond, R. A., & Dube, L. (2012). A systems science perspective and transdisciplinary models for food and nutrition security. *Proceedings of the National Academy of Sciences of the United States of America*, 109(31), 12356–12363. https://doi.org/10.1073/pnas.0913003109

Harvey, F. (2022, November 21). What are the key outcomes of the COP27 climate summit? *The Guardian.* https://www.e-mc2.gr/el/news/what-are-key-outcomes-cop27-climate-summit#:~:text=What%20are%20the%20key%20outcomes%20of%20Cop27%20climate,major%20milestone.%20...%20%202%201.5C%20...%20More%20items

Hastings, D. A. (2011, May 4). The human security index: Potential roles for the environmental and earth observation communities. https://earthzine.org/the-human-security-index-potential-roles-for-the-environmental-and-earth-observation-communities/

Hayden, N. K. (2018). *Balancing belligerents or feeding the beats: Transforming conflict traps.* CISSIM Policy Brief, The University of Maryland Center for International and Security Studies. https://drum.lib.umd.edu/bitstream/handle/1903/20654/Hayden-Balancing%20belligerents%20or%20feeding%20the%20beasts_022618.pdf

Himelfarb, S., & Howard, P. (2021, October 7). What's stunning about the misinformation trend – and how to fix it. https://www.cnn.com/2021/10/07/opinions/facebook-misinformation-and-how-to-fix-it-himelfarb-howard/index.html

Institute for Economics & Peace (IEP). (2020a). *Global peace index 2020: Measuring peace in a complex world.* http://visionofhumanity.org/reports

Institute for Economics & Peace (IEP). (2020b). *COVID-19 and peace.* http://visionofhumanity.org/reports

Institute for Economics & Peace (IEP). (2021). Economic value of peace 2021: Measuring the global economic impact of violence and conflict. http://visionofhumanity.org/resources

Intergovernmental Panel on Climate Change (IPCC). (2023). AR6 synthesis report: Climate change 2023. https://www.ipcc.ch/report/ar6/syr/

International Council on Systems Engineering. (INCOSE). (2021). Systems engineering: Vision 2035. Engineering solutions for a better world. https://www.incose.org/about-systems-engineering/se-vision-2035

International Military Council on Climate and Security (IMCCS). (2020). The world climate and security report 2020. *Product of the Expert Group of the International Military Council on Climate and Security.* Authors: Steve Brock (CCS), Bastien Alex (IRIS), Oliver-Leighton Barrett (CCS), Francesco Femia (CCS), Shiloh Fetzek (CCS), Sherri Goodman (CCS), Deborah Loomis (CCS), Tom Middendorp (Clingendael), Michel Rademaker (HCSS), Louise van Schaik (Clingendael), Julia Tasse (IRIS), Caitlin Werrell (CCS). Edited by Francesco Femia and Caitlin Werrell. Published by the Center for Climate and Security, an institute of the Council on Strategic Risks. https://climate-andsecurity.org/worldclimatesecurityreport2020/

Jacobs, G. (2016, October 26). Integrated approach to peace and human security in the Twenty-first century. https://www.cadmusjournal.org/node/581

Jafino, B. A., Walsh, B., Rozenberg, J., & Hallegatte, S. (2020). Revised estimates of the impact of climate change on extreme poverty by 2030. World Bank Group Policy Research Working Paper 9417. https://openknowledge.worldbank.org/bitstream/handle/10986/34555/Revised-Estimates-of-the-Impact-of-Climate-Change-on-Extreme-Poverty-by-2030.pdf?sequence=1&isAllowed=y

Jamieson, D. (2014). *Reason in a dark time: Why the struggle against climate change failed- and what it means for our future.* Oxford University Press.

Jessen, T. D., Ban, N. C., Claxton, N. X., Darimont, C. T. (2021). Contributions of indigenous knowledge to ecological and evolutionary understanding. *Frontiers in Ecology and the Environment, 20*(2), 93–101. https://doi.org/10.1002/fee.2435

Karwat, D. M. A., Eagle, W. E, Wooldridge, M. S., & Princen, T. E. (2014). Activist engineering: Changing engineering practice by deploying praxis. *Science and Engineering Ethics, 21,* 227–239. https://doi.org/10.1007/s11948-014-9525-0

Kim, D. H., & Anderson, V. (2007). *System archetypes basics: From story to structure.* Pegasus Communications.

Lao Tzu. (n.d.). Retrieved March 10, 2022, from https://www.goodreads.com/quotes/8203490-watch-your-thoughts-they-become-your-words-watch-your-words#:~:text=Quote%20by%20Lao%20Tzu%3A%20%E2%80%9CWatch%20your%20thoughts%2C%20they,character%3B%20watch%20your%20character%2C%20it%20becomes%20your%20destiny.%E2%80%9D

Lemos, C. M. (2018). *Agent-Based Modeling of Social Conflict: From mechanism to complex behavior*. Springer Cham.

Lent, J. (2021, October 9). Solving the climate crisis requires the end of capitalism. Salon, https://www.salon.com/2021/10/09/solving-the-climate-requires-the-end-of-capitalism/

Lu, J. (2020, April 17). What will COVID-19 do to the sustainable development goals? https://www.undispatch.com/what-will-covid-19-do-to-the-sustainable-development-goals/

McDonald, M. (2013). Discourses of climate security. *Political Geography, 33*, 42–51. https://doi.org/10.1016/j.polgeo.2013.01.002

Meadows, D. H. (1997). Places to intervene in a system in increasing order of effectiveness. *Whole Earth, Winter*, 78–84. https://archives-manuscripts.dartmouth.edu/repositories/2/archival_objects/436249

Milante, G., & Oxhorn, P. (2009). *No Development without peace*. World Bank Open Knowledge Repository. https://openknowledge.worldbank.org/handle/10986/4582

Monbiot, G. (2021, October 30). Capitalism is killing the planet – it's time to stop buying into our own destruction. https://www.theguardian.com/environment/2021/oct/30/capitalism-is-killing-the-planet-its-time-to-stop-buying-into-our-own-destruction

Mr. Y. (2011). *A national strategic narrative*. Woodrow Wilson International Center for Scholars, Princeton University.

National Academy of Engineering (NAE). (2018). *NAE grand challenges for engineering*. http://www.engineeringchallenges.org/

National Academies of Sciences, Engineering, and Medicine. (NASEM). (2021). *2021 Nobel Prize summit: Our planet, our future: Proceedings of a summit*. The National Academies Press. https://doi.org/10.17226/26310

National Academies of Sciences, Engineering, and Medicine (NASEM). (2022). Communities, climate change, and health equity state-level implementation. *Proceedings of a Workshop in Brief*. Washington, DC: The National Academies Press. https://doi.org/10.17226/26693

National Academies of Sciences, Engineering, and Medicine. (NASEM). (2022). *Operationalizing sustainable development to benefit people and the planet*. The National Academies Press. https://doi.org/10.17226/26654

National Aeronautics and Space Administration (NASA). (n.d.). Evidence. How do we know that climate change is real? https://climate.nasa.gov/evidence/

National Intelligence Council (NIC). (2021). Climate change and international responses increasing challenges to US national security through 2040. https://www.dni.gov/files/ODNI/documents/assessments/NIE_Climate_Change_and_National_Security.pdf

Nguyen, N. C., & Bosch, O. J. H. (2013). A Systems thinking approach to identify leverage points for sustainability: A case study in the Cat Ba biosphere reserve, Vietnam. *System Research and Behavioral Science, 30*(2), 104–115. https://doi.org/10.1002/sres.2145 Wiley Blackwell.

Null, S., & Herzer, L. (2016). *Navigating complexity: Climate migration and conflict in a changing world*. Office of Conflict Management and Mitigation (CMM). https://www.wilsoncenter.org/sites/default/files/media/documents/publication/ecsp_navigating_complexity_web.pdf

Organization for Economic Co-operation and Development. (OECD). (2018). States of fragility: Highlights. https://www.oecd.org/dac/conflict-fragility-resilience/docs/OECD%20Highlights%20documents_web.pdf

Organization for Economic Co-operation and Development. (OECD). (2019). *Water and violent conflict*. Issues Brief. C:\Users\amade\Downloads\92767-water-violent-conflict_EN.pdf

Palinkas, L. A., Springgate, B., Hancock, J., Sugarman, O. K., Pesson, C. L., Stallard, C. N., Haywood, C., Meyers, D., Johnson, A., Polk, M., Wennerstrom, A., Seay, J. E., & Well, K. B. (2021). Impact of the COVID-19 pandemic on resilience to climate change in underserved communities. *Sustainability and Climate Change, 14*(5). https://doi.org/10.1089/scc.2021.0022

Peacedirect (2022, September 20). Migration and peacebuilding. https://www.peacedirect.org/us/publications/migration-peacebuilding/#:~:text=Migration%20%26%20Peacebuilding%20is%20the%20culmination%20of%20research%2C,academics%2C%20and%20others%20working%20tirelessly%20for%20displaced%20people.

Peters, K., Dupar, M., Opitz-Stapleton, S., Lovell, E., & Cao, Y. (2020). Climate change, conflict, and fragility; An evidence review and recommendations for research and action. https://odi.org/en/publications/climate-change-conflict-and-fragility-an-evidence-review-and-recommendations-for-research-and-action/

Reckford, J. (2019). *Our better angels: Seven simple virtues that will change your life and the world.* St. Martin's Essentials.

Ricigliano, R. (2012). *Making peace last: A toolbox for sustainable peacebuilding.* Paradigm Publishers.

Risi, L. H. (2017, January 12). Backdraft revisited: The conflict potential of climate change adaptation and mitigation. *NewSecurityBeat*, https://www.newsecuritybeat.org/2017/01/backdraft-revisited-conflict-potential-climate-change-adaptation-mitigation/

Ritchie-Dunham, J. L., & Rabbino, H. T. (2001). *Managing with clarity: Identifying, aligning, and leveraging strategic resources.* John Wiley and Sons.

Rouwette, E., & Vennix, J. A. M. (2015). Group model building. In R. Meyers (ed.), *Encyclopedia of complexity and systems science.* Springer, Berlin, Heidelberg. https://doi.org/10.1007/978-3-642-27737-5_264-3

Sachs, J., Kroll, C., Lafortune, G., Fuller, G., & Woelm, F. (2021). *The decade of action for the sustainable development goals: Sustainable development report 2021.* Cambridge University Press.

Sachs, J., Schmidt-Traub, G., Kroll, C., LaFortune, G., Fuller, G., & Woelm, F. (2020). *The sustainable development goals and COVID-19. Sustainable development report 2020.* Cambridge University Press.

Sachs, J.D., Lafortune, G., Fuller, G., & Drumm, E. (2023). *Implementing the SDG Stimulus. Sustainable Development Report 2023.* Dublin University Press.

Schön, D. (1971). *Beyond the stable state: Public and private learning in a changing society.* Maurice Temple Smith Ltd.

Scoones, I., Leach, M., Smith, A., Stagl, S., Stirling, A., & Thompson, J. (2007, January 1.). Dynamic systems and the challenge of sustainability. https://www.ids.ac.uk/publications/dynamic-systems-and-the-challenge-of-sustainability/

Scott, W. (2021, May 26). Climate security: Building a community of practice. https://www.newamerica.org/resource-security/natural-security-blog/climate-security-building-a-community-of-practice/

Seelos, C. (2020). Changing systems? Welcome to the slow movement. *Stanford Social Innovation Review, Winter*, 40–47.

Senge, P. (1994). *The fifth discipline: The art & practice of the learning organization.* Doubleday.

Sharifi, A., Simangan, D., Kaneko, S., & Virji, H. (2021). The sustainability-peace nexus: Why is it important? *Sustainability Science, 16*, 1073–1077. https://doi.org/10.1007/s11625-021-00986-z

Simon, H. A. (1972). Theories of bounded rationality. In C. B. McGuire and R. Radner (eds.), *Decision and Organization* (pp. 161–176). North-Holland Pub.

Sterman, J. (2000). *Business dynamics: Systems thinking and modeling for a complex world.* McGraw Hill.

Sumner, A., Hoy, C., & Ortiz-Juarez, E. (2020). *Estimates of the impact of COVID-19 on global poverty*. United Nations University-WIDER. https://www.wider.unu.edu/publication/estimates-impact-covid-19-global-poverty

Sustainable Development Solutions Network (SDSN). (2020). *Indicators and a monitoring framework: Launching a data revolution for the sustainable development goals*. https://indicators.report/

Sweeney, L. B., & Meadows, D. (2010). *The systems thinking playbook*. Chelsea Green Publishing.

Tanabe, J. (2020). Exploring a post-covid-19 sustainable peace model. *Social Ethics Society Journal of Applied Philosophy*, *Special Issue*, 73–103.

The Earth Charter. (1987). https://earthcharter.org/read-the-earth-charter/

The Economist. (2021, December 18). The new normal is already here. Get used to it. The era of predictable unpredictability is not going away. https://www.economist.com/leaders/2021/12/18/the-new-normal-is-already-here-get-used-to-it

The Millennium Project. (2017). 15 global challenges. https://www.millennium-project.org/projects/challenges/#:~:text=The%2015%20Global%20Challenges%3A%201%20How%20can%20sustainable,democracy%20emerge%20from%20authoritarian%20regimes%3F%20More%20items...%20

The Time of Israel (TOI). (2021, November 22). Israel, Jordan sign huge UAE-brokered deal to swap solar energy and water. https://www.timesofisrael.com/israel-jordan-sign-uae-brokered-deal-to-swap-solar-energy-and-water/

The White House. (2021). Report on the impact of climate change on migration. https://www.whitehouse.gov/wp-content/uploads/2021/10/Report-on-the-Impact-of-Climate-Change-on-Migration.pdf

The World Climate and Security Report (WCSR). (2021). https://imccs.org/wp-content/uploads/2021/06/World-Climate-and-Security-Report-2021.pdf

The World in 2050 (TWI2050). (2020). Innovations for sustainability. Pathways to an efficient and post-pandemic future. Report prepared by The World in 2050 initiative. International Institute for Applied Systems Analysis (IIASA), Laxenburg, Austria. http://www.twi2050.org/

Thompson, S. A. (2022, August 31). Many developed countries view online misinformation as a 'major threat.' *New York Times*. https://www.nytimes.com/2022/08/31/technology/pew-misinformation-major-threat.html?referringSource=articleShare

Tooley, C. (2021, January 18). What systems thinking actually means - and why it matters for innovation today. *The World Economic Forum*. https://www.weforum.org/agenda/2021/01/what-systems-thinking-actually-means-and-why-it-matters-today/

Trombetta, M. J. (2009). Environmental security and climate change: Analyzing the discourse, *Cambridge Review of International Affairs*, *21*(4), 585–602. https://doi.org/10.1080/09557570802452920

UN Development Programme (UNDP). (2021). UNDP annual report. https://www.undp.org/publications/undp-annual-report-2021

UN Development Programme (UNDP). (2022). *New threats to human security in the Anthropocene: Demanding greater solidarity*. https://hdr.undp.org/system/files/documents/srhs2022pdf.pdf

UN Economic and Social Commission for Asia and the Pacific (UNESCAP). (2018). https://www.unescap.org/sites/default/files/PB78_The%20nexus%20between%20peace%20and%20sustainable%20development%20in%20Asia-Pacific%20countries%20with%20special%20needs_final.pdf

UN Environmental Programme. (2020). Adaptation gap report 2020. https://www.unep.org/resources/adaptation-gap-report-2020

UN Framework Convention on Climate Change (UNFCCC). (2022). United Nations climate change annual report 2022. https://unfccc.int/annualreport#:~:text=The%20 UN%20Climate%20Change%20secretariat%E2%80%99s%202021%20annual%20 report,mobilization%20of%20additional%20finance%20and%20private%20sector%20 engagement.

UN General Assembly (UNGA, 43rd session). (1988). *Protection of global climate for present and future generations of mankind: Resolution / adopted by the General Assembly*, 6 December 1988, A/RES/43/53. https://www.refworld.org/docid/3b00eff430.html

UN Human Rights. (2021). Frequently asked questions on human rights and climate change. Fact Sheet 38. https://www.ohchr.org/sites/default/files/Documents/Publications/ FSheet38_FAQ_HR_CC_EN.pdf

UNDP Human Development Report (UNDP/HDR). (1990). *Concepts and measurement of human development*. United Nations Development Progamme, New York.

UNDP Human Development Report (UNDP/HDR). (1994). *New dimensions of human security*. United Nations Development Progamme, New York.

UNDP Human Development Report (UNDP/HDR). (2010). *The real wealth of nations: Pathways to human development*. United Nations Development Progamme, New York.

UNDP Human Development Report (UNDP/HDR). (2011). *Sustainability and equity, a better future for all*. United Nations Development Progamme, New York.

UNDP Human Development Report (UNDP/HDR) (2022). The human development report 2021/2022. Uncertain times and unsettled lives: Shaping our future in a transforming world. https://www.undp.org/timor-leste/publications/human-development-report-2021/2022

UN-Habitat. (2015). Habitat III issue papers 22- Informal settlements. https://habitat3.org/ wp-content/uploads/Habitat-III-Issue-Paper-22_Informal-Settlements-2.0.pdf

United Nations (UN). (1986). The right to development at a glance. https://www.un.org/en/ events/righttodevelopment/pdf/rtd_at_a_glance.pdf#:~:text=%E2%80%9CThe%20 right%20to%20development%20is%20an%20inalienable%20human,%28Article%20 1.1%2C%20Declaration%20on%20the%20Right%20to%20Development%29

United Nations (UN). (2012, January 25). Remarks to the general assembly on his five-year action agenda. "The Future we want." https://www.un.org/sg/en/content/sg/speeches/2012-01-25/ remarks-general-assembly-his-five-year-action-agenda-future-we-want

United Nations (UN). (2015). Transforming our world: The 2030 agenda for sustainable development. https://www.un.org/ga/search/view_doc.asp?symbol=A/RES/70/1&Lang=E

United Nations (UN). (2021). Climate security mechanism. Progress in strengthening the United nations' capacity to address climate-related security risks. https://dppa.un.org/ sites/default/files/csm_progress_report_2021_final.pdf

United Nations Conference on Environment and Development (UNCED). (1992). Agenda 21. http://www.un.org/esa/sustdev/documents/agenda21/english/Agenda21.pdf

United Nations General Assembly (UNGA). (2012). UN resolution 66/290. https://www. un.org/humansecurity/what-is-human-security/

United Nations Trust Fund for Human Security. (n.d.). What is security? https://www.un.org/ humansecurity/what-is-human-security/

Vidal, J. (2016, September 7). Water supplies in Syria deteriorating fast due to conflict, experts warn. *The Guardian*, https://www.theguardian.com/environment/2016/sep/07/ water-supplies-in-syria-deteriorating-fast-due-to-conflict-experts-warn

Virji, H., Sharifi, A., Kaneko, S., & Simangan, D. (2019). The sustainability-peace nexus in the context of global change. *Sustainability Science*, *14*, 1467–1468. https://doi. org/10.1007/s11625-019-00737-1

von Grebmer, K., Ringler, C., Rosegrant, M. W., Olofinbiyi, T., Wiesmann, D., Fritschel, H., Badiane, O., Torero, M., Yohannes, Y., Thompson, J., von Oppeln, C., & Rahall, J. (2012). *Global hunger index, the challenge of hunger: Ensuring sustainable food security under land, water, and energy stresses*. International Food Policy Research Institute. http://doi.org/10.2499/9780896299429

von Lossow, T., Schrijver, A., van der Kroon, M., van Schaik, L., & Meester, J. (2021). Towards a better understanding of climate security practices. https://www.planetarysecurityinitiative.org/sites/default/files/2021-04/PSI-2021_Climate-Security-Practices_final.pdf

Waters Center for Systems Thinking (WCST). https://waterscenterst.org/

Wolfe, S. E., & Smith, L. K. M. (2021). Death becomes US: How our emotions can help avoid climate disaster. https://ernestbecker.org/this-mortal-life/climate-talk/sarah-elizabeth-wolfe-and-lauren-keira-marie-smith/

World Academy of Art and Science (WAAS). (2021). The security and sustainability guide. https://securesustain.org/

World Bank. (2011). Economics of adaptation to climate change. https://www.worldbank.org/en/news/feature/2011/06/06/economics-adaptation-climate-change

World Bank. (2015). Rapid, climate-informed development needed to keep climate change from pushing more than 100 million people into poverty by 2030. https://www.worldbank.org/en/news/feature/2015/11/08/rapid-climate-informed-development-needed-to-keep-climate-change-from-pushing-more-than-100-million-people-into-poverty-by-2030

World Business Council for Sustainable Development (WBCSD). (2009, March 26). *Water, energy and climate change: A contribution from the business community*. Washington, DC. https://www.wbcsd.org/Programs/Food-and-Nature/Water/Resources/A-contribution-from-the-business-community

World Commission on Environment and Development (WCED) (1987). *Our common future*. WCED, Oxford University Press.

World Economic Forum (WEF). (2023). The global risks report 2023. (18th ed.). https://www.weforum.org/reports/global-risks-report-2023/

World Health Organization (WHO). (2021). Climate change and health. https://www.who.int/news-room/fact-sheets/detail/climate-change-and-health

World Meteorological Organization (WMO) (2022, November 6). https://public.wmo.int/en/media/press-release/eight-warmest-years-record-witness-upsurge-climate-change-impacts

Zarocostas, J. (2020). How to fight an infodemic. *Lancet, 395*, 676. https://doi.org/10.1016/S0140-6736(20)30461-X

2 The Peace–Sustainability–Climate Nexus

2.1 INTRODUCTION

The three sectors of peace, sustainability, and climate security are entangled and intimately related to various human development and security issues at different scales, from the local to the global. All three sectors (and their opposites) impact community development and dictate, more specifically, whether a community advances to a higher level of development by building on existing strengths, partnerships, and collaboration among its members. As noted by Barlas (1996), such transformation occurs at four interdependent levels: (i) personal, by ensuring empowerment, freedom, and liberation from oppression and poverty; (ii) household, by improving livelihood at the household level; (iii) community, by respecting diversity, inclusivity, self-reliance, and resilience; and (iv) community of life, by adopting a multigenerational approach that respects people and the environment upon which they depend.

The development literature has recognized how interdependent and mutually reinforcing two or three sectors of the peace, sustainability, and climate security nexus are, a good review of which can be found in Sharifi et al. (2021b, c) and Gaston et al. (2023). It is hard to envision (i) a sustainable community that is not stable and climate-secured, (ii) a peaceful community that has not endorsed practices that sustain livelihoods and the environment and does not support climate security practices, and (iii) a climate-secured community that has not endorsed sustainable practices and is geopolitically unstable. Likewise, it is hard to envision human development and security if one sector of the peace–sustainability–climate (PSC) nexus is weaker or missing. A nexus approach to the linkages between peace, sustainability, and climate security is more appropriate than considering each sector in isolation. There is, however, a range of opinions in the literature about how the three sectors interact and their cause-and-effect pathways. For example, there is disagreement about the direct impact of climate change on undermining peace and how socioeconomic issues may directly or indirectly contribute to conflict (Sharifi et al., 2021a, b; de Coning and Maalim, 2022).

A double- or triple-nexus approach is often recommended in case study publications that report the constraining and threatening dynamic of conflict and the impact of climate change on different aspects of community livelihood and security. For instance, this dynamic has been acknowledged in *environmental peacebuilding*, which relates to the role of natural resource management in conflict prevention (Environmental Peacebuilding Association, n.d.; CDA, 2023). Environmental change combined with the mismanagement of natural resources and climate change increases the risk of conflict, especially "in places already fractured by

DOI: 10.1201/9781003435006-2

socioeconomic inequality, ethnic divisions, or ideological instability" (Brown and Nicolucci-Altman, 2022). At the same time, addressing the mismanagement of natural resources, environmental degradation, and developing climate security measures using a multisolution approach can serve as a "platform for dialogue and a reason for cooperation that can help to resolve differences among communities" (Brown and Nicolucci-Altman, 2022).

Armah et al. (2014) described several case studies of natural resource use conflict in Ghana's mining, land and forestry, fisheries, and oil sectors. All these sectors were found to be interdependent and involved complex dynamics between policy, human rights, the clash between tradition and modernity, and administrative enforcement and regulation. In one of Armah et al.'s case studies, climate change was described as a catalyst feeding existing conflict in Ghana between native farmers and herders around shared common resources, cultural and ethical differences, and land rights. Dysfunctional government policies are also contributing to the conflict. The overall dynamics between climate change, livelihood, drought, conflict, migration, and land use change seem to be recurring in many African countries (Gebre, 2003; Nett and Ruttinger, 2017; Tesfaye, 2022) and Latin America (Rocha et al., 2019). Pakistan is another example of a country in central Asia where those dynamics occur around water management (Mustafa et al., 2013).

Civil unrest and conflict in the Middle East and North Africa (MENA) region following the Arab Spring in 2011 have been attributed to multiple factors such as environmental degradation, significantly reduced water resources due to climate change, unsustainable agricultural practices, low access to services, competition for resources, and other socioeconomic factors (Kelley et al., 2015; Gleick, 2019). The climate security literature is divided into the reasons for the Syrian conflict starting in 2011 (Peters et al., 2020). There is a strong opinion that it began following the worst recorded drought in Syria and the Middle East Fertile Crescent history from 2006 to 2010 (Kelley et al., 2015). That assumption has, however, been disputed by Selby et al. (2017) and others who claimed that the climate change-related drought was not the only single driver of the Syrian conflict. Other factors have been proposed to explain social unrest, violent conflict, and civil war since 2011 (Gleick, 2014, 2019; Vidal, 2016; Suter, 2017). They include weak country governance, poverty, economic liberalization, a lack of environmental and agricultural policymaking, political insecurity, land tenure issues, social inequalities, and corrupt water management.

The Syrian conflict and unrest that started in 2011 led to the migration of rural workers to urban areas that could not absorb the excess population. The migration resulted in a humanitarian crisis, poverty, protests, and an oppressive response from the Syrian government. This dynamic, in turn, brought the country into civil war, forced the migration of refugees fleeing the violence, and fed the refugee crisis in Europe starting in 2015. A possible dynamic between climate change, livelihood, and unrest in Syria is represented by the causal loop diagram shown in Figure 2.1. More detailed causal loop diagrams are presented in Chapter 12. Such graphs depict causality (i.e., how one thing is the cause or effect of something else) and feedback mechanisms.

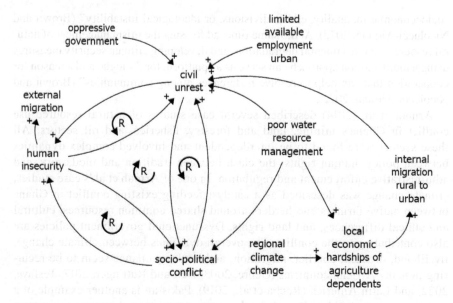

FIGURE 2.1   Causal loop diagram showing the insecurity dynamics in Syria. Legend: R represents reinforcing loops. + signs indicate variables changing in the same direction.

Source: Whitworth (2021). Used by permission of the author.

A similar dynamic happened in Yemen after the unification of the Yemen Arab Republic (North Yemen) with the People's Democratic Republic of Yemen (South Yemen) in 1990. The merger brought together two land rights and water management practices based on Islamic sharia and state law. The resulting confusion, population growth, excessive and uncontrolled water well drilling, groundwater depletion, and increasing water scarcity due to climate change led to water and food insecurity. It fueled a reinforcing cycle of social unrest, protest, violence, and migration in Yemen starting in 1990 (Glass, 2010; Werrell and Femia, 2013; Pulley, 2021).

The uprooting of communities and mass migration fueled by national and trans-boundary conflict, as well as the effects of climate change, has unfortunately become part of our daily news (Peacedirect, 2022: Schwartzstein and Risi, 2023). A combi-nation of land degradation due to climate change and war creates the movement of people to other areas, which may already be environmentally fragile and prone to conflict. Migration to urban areas may create informal and vulnerable settlements. This dynamic triggers a reinforcing loop of social, ethnic, economic, religious, and territorial conflict; environmental damage; and, ultimately, the creation of failed communities and states. Examples abound, such as migration from Bangladesh to India since the 1950s, the Dust Bowl in the 1930s in the United States, the migration out of southern Louisiana after Hurricane Katrina in 2005 (Bendor and Scheffran, 2019), the rural-to-urban migration to five major cities in Fiji starting in the 1990s, due to changing weather patterns and socioeconomic strains (Darwish, 2023), and the MENA region, as mentioned above. Another region where the dynamic men-tioned above is at play is Central America due to the combined effects of changing climate conditions, insecurity, failed democratic governance, corruption, and socio-economic inequalities (Angelo, 2021).

The region above the Arctic Circle is another part of the world where the dynamics between peace, sustainability, and climate security are critical from the local to the regional scale. Global development and pollution have contributed to Arctic warming faster than the worldwide average, with a rise of about 3.1°C between the years 1971 and 2019 (AMAP, 2021). The Arctic has been warming four times faster than the average planetary rate over the last 43 years (PBS, 2022). This warming can create irreversible human, environmental, and infrastructure changes (Hjort et al., 2022). As the Arctic is undergoing unavoidable long-term changes, it is essential to ensure the people, planet, prosperity, and peace components of sustainability in that region, especially when different commercial, indigenous, and security interests are at play and not always in sync. As noted by Hayden et al. (2020), (i) commercial industries are interested in "increased resource extraction and associated shipping activity," (ii) indigenous communities are interested in "food security and participation in sustainable resource development," and (iii) military and security organizations representing the Arctic nations are interested in regional and national security.

All the complex dynamics mentioned above are not new. For instance, one example relates past climate change in the Northern atmosphere due to the eruption of an Icelandic volcano in 1783 that spewed sulfur dioxide for eight months. The explosion resulted in cold winters, with crop failures, famine, disease, and the death of 6 million people worldwide. Claims have even been made that this volcanic event triggered the French Revolution of 1789 (Wikipedia-Laki). A similar but older example is that of the vulnerability of ancient Egypt to changes in climate patterns during the Ptolemaic period (330–30 BC). A volcanic eruption in Alaska in 43 BC led to crop failure and disease in the Mediterranean region and a two-year cold spell in the Northern Hemisphere (McConnell et al., 2020; Birnbaum, 2022).

This chapter further explores the three sectors of the PSC nexus, their systemic characteristics, and their influence and dependence. It provides the background and rationale necessary to consider a system and a multisolution approach to the nexus.

2.2 SUSTAINABILITY

Since the first Human Development Report in 1990 (UNDP/HDR, 1990), sustainability and sustainable development have become mainstream in the development literature. Sustainability has been recognized as the best and most logical way for people to meet their needs while nurturing and restoring the environment. It has been embraced, at least in theory, by all the following sectors of economy: public, private, academia, and government. The value proposition of sustainability is often presented as a radically new platform for research, education, technology, and business opportunities. There is also widespread agreement that quick actions at different scales are needed to accelerate a transition to a more sustainable world.

Despite that agreement, the road map to sustainability has not always been straightforward for multiple reasons. First, opinions about sustainable systems, structures, or communities are divided. Furthermore, humans may have a limited idea of what they want to sustain, such as the natural environment, humanity, and the built environment. We still have questions about the temporal and physical scales of sustainability. More recently, significant issues such as climate change, international conflicts, and the 2020 global pandemic have made it even more challenging to identify what to sustain and for how long. As a result, it has been proposed that resilience—the ability to cope with change, adapt to a new normal, learn, and transform—might be a more appropriate concept to address than sustainability. Finally, it has not been easy to quantify and measure sustainability and understand how sustainability practices express themselves in different economies, contexts, and scales (e.g., project, local, national, regional, and global).

As Rotmans and DeVries (1997) noted, sustainability is "more of a guiding principle to be applied heuristically than a scientific concept waiting for a strict definition." The term is "still ill-defined and somewhat debatable" (Kotob, 2011). Furthermore, the jury is still out about the attributes of sustainable systems, structures, and communities.

Etymologically, the word "sustainability" comes from "sustain," derived from the Latin word "sustenere," which means to uphold and prolong, to keep in existence, to endure and withstand. (Dictionary.com). The term "sustain-ability" can be seen as combining sustaining and the ability (i.e., capacity) to do so. It is generally agreed upon that sustainability, or sustainable development, is characterized by harmonizing three essential elements (i.e., three pillars): people, planet, profit (the 3Ps) or equity, environment, and economics (the 3Es): profit is sometimes replaced by prosperity. This concept, which originally appeared in Common Future (WCED, 1987), is often referred to as the triple bottom line, often represented as three overlapping circles, one for each of the three Es or Ps. The triple bottom line highlights the intimate interaction and balance between society, the environment, and economic/financial systems. Partnership and peace have been added to the triple bottom line, as shown in Figure 2.2. The 3Ps or 5Ps of sustainability must be recognized as dynamic, changing, and adapting over time (Ryan, 2020; UNESCWA, 2021).

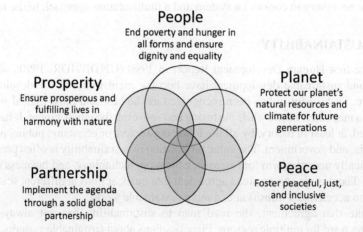

People
End poverty and hunger in all forms and ensure dignity and equality

Prosperity
Ensure prosperous and fulfilling lives in harmony with nature

Planet
Protect our planet's natural resources and climate for future generations

Partnership
Implement the agenda through a solid global partnership

Peace
Foster peaceful, just, and inclusive societies

FIGURE 2.2 The five overlapping components of sustainable development according to Agenda 2030.

Aside from these agreed upon characteristics, there is no such thing as a one-size-fits-all unified definition of sustainability. Instead, various constituencies (e.g., business, education, agriculture, and health) have proposed different definitions to address their needs. Furthermore, the concept of sustainability has changed over time and is still adapting to a dynamic world.

2.2.1 UN SUSTAINABLE DEVELOPMENT GOALS

The 17 sustainable development goals (SDGs) and associated targets and indicators were introduced in 2015 as a new 15-year road map for worldwide sustainable development at the country level. In launching Agenda 2030, the General Assembly of the United Nations "recognize[d] that eradicating poverty in all its forms and dimensions, including extreme poverty, is the greatest global challenge and an indispensable requirement for sustainable development" (UN, 2015). Compared to the preceding Millennium Development Goals (1990–2015), the SDGs apply to all countries regardless of their development level. Table 2.1 summarizes various SDGs that fall into the 3Ps mentioned above. The 5Ps include SDG 17 (Partnerships for the goals) and SDG 16 (peace, justice, and strong institutions). Each goal contains multiple indicators.

Since 2015, the comprehensive SDG agenda has been a work in progress, and the SDG's targets and indicators have been refined further. Significant additions include introducing the SDG index and dashboards to quantify the progress of different countries on the SDGs (LaFortune et al., 2018). The SDG index ranges between 0 and 100 and is calculated as a weighted average of scores of SDGs for which indicator data are available at the country level. It also accounts for the correlation between some indicators.

Another addition to Agenda 2030 was the introduction of six SDG transformations to operationalize SDG implementation at the country level (Sachs et al., 2019; TWI2050, 2020). They include (i) education, gender, and inequality; (ii) health,

---

TABLE 2.1

List of Sustainable Development Goals (SDGs) into the 3Ps of Sustainable Development According to Agenda 2030

People	Planet	Prosperity
SDG 1:	SDG 6:	SDG 7:
No Poverty	Clean Water & Sanitation	Affordable & Clean Energy
SDG 2:	SDG 12:	SDG 8:
Zero Hunger	Responsible Consumption &	Decent Work & Economic Growth
SDG 3:	Production	SDG 9:
Good Health & Well-being	SDG 13:	Industry, Innovation &
SDG 4:	Climate Action	Infrastructure
Quality Education	SDG 14:	SDG 10:
SDG 5:	Life Below Water	Reduce Inequalities
Gender Equality	SDG 15:	SDG 11:
	Life on Land	Sustainable Cities & Communities

well-being, and demography; (iii) energy decarbonization and sustainable industry; (iv) sustainable food, land, water, and oceans; (v) sustainable cities and communities; and (vi) the digital revolution for sustainable development. Each transformation involves multiple SDGs, and a given SDG can be related to various changes. The intensity of how each transformation affects individual SDGs is measured semi-quantitatively using a scale ranging between 0 (neutral) and 3 (directly targets the SDG). The 2021 Sustainable Report (Sachs et al., 2021) proposes short- and long-term guidelines to address these six transformations, considering the COVID pandemic. Despite such efforts, the jury is still out on how the SDGs' targets and indicators need to be updated individually to match the reality of a post-COVID-19 world where the risks associated with climate change are undeniable.

Another question that has always been pertinent to the 2030 agenda is how to meet the goals across different physical scales (country, cities, communities, households, and individuals) and temporal scales (short-, medium-, and long-term). Scharlemann et al. (2020) remarked that progress toward sustainable development might have synergistic benefits at one physical or temporal scale but create negative impacts, requiring trade-offs at other scales. Not including the scale dependence of the SDGs is a severe limitation when relating the SDG ranking at the country scale to community issues. The question remains as to how relevant the SDGs at the local level are when outside experts define them with limited or no input from those who face the actual problems.

Since 2015, there has been an increasing interest in understanding and quantifying how the SDGs interact, because sustainable development is more than meeting a series of independent goals. Addressing the connections among the SDGs in a multisectoral, integrated, and transdisciplinary approach is crucial to ensuring the coherence of Agenda 2030 (Pedercini et al., 2020; Haskins, 2021). From a systems perspective, sustainability can be seen as a state emerging from the interaction of the 17 SDGs, the six SDG transformations, or the five pillars of sustainability: people, planet, profit, partnership, and peace. The SDG index can be used as a measure of that interaction.

Although the SDGs represent an "indivisible whole" (Griggs et al., n.d.), some goals are likely to affect others positively (i.e., creating synergies) or negatively (i.e., requiring trade-offs). In contrast, others may only have indirect interactions or no interaction. Randers et al. (2019) explored, for instance, how the three environmental goals (SDGs 13, 14, and 15) are affected by the other 14 socioeconomic goals for different societal scenarios such as business-as-usual decision-making since 1980.

Furthermore, as noted by Scharlemann et al. (2020), the nature of the linkages across the SDGs being considered depends on (i) the context and groups of actors at the country level and (ii) the perspective (socioeconomic, geopolitical, and geographic) used to explore the interactions (e.g., the environment–human linkage perspective). There is no one-size-fits-all approach to address the linkages between the SDGs systematically. All models are context- and scale-specific and are based on an interpretation of reality but not reality itself. What works on one scale may not work on another scale. Models need to be tailored to specific contexts.

The socioeconomic development literature is rich in contributions that emphasize, mostly *qualitatively*, the value proposition of using an integrated approach to Agenda

2030. Landmark papers, among many others, include those of Griggs et al. (n.d.); Nilsson et al. (2013); Griggs et al. (2013); Waage et al. (2015); Coopman et al. (2016); Vladimirova and Le Blanc (2016); Barbier and Burgess (2017); Morton et al. (2017); Lim et al. (2018); and TWI2050 (2020). Semi-quantitative tools have been used to *quantify* SDG interactions (ICSU, 2015; Schmidt-Traub, 2015; Nilsson et al., 2016; Zhang et al., 2016; Randers et al., 2019).

Two noteworthy contributions to understanding the SDGs' interdependence at the country level include the iSDG framework developed by the Millennium Institute (Pedercini et al., 2020) and the report entitled *A Guide to SDGs Interactions* by the International Council for Science (ICSU, 2017). That report examined the interdependence at the target level between SDGs #2 (zero hunger), 3 (good health and well-being), 7 (energy), and 14 (life below water) with the other goals using a semi-quantitative impact factor ranging over a seven-point scale: neutral impact (0), different levels of positive impact (+1 to +3), and different levels of adverse effect (−1 to −3). More recently, Scharlemann et al. (2020) provided an extensive review of the different formulations proposed in the literature since 2015 that capture the interaction between the SDGs, emphasizing other types of interaction between humans and their environment. Many of these formulations use a double causality analysis. In the case of the 17 SDGs, the analysis would create a 17×17 matrix describing each SDG's direct influence and dependence on the other goals. It becomes even more complicated when analyzing the interaction of SDGs at the target level.

Quantitative tools borrowed from *systems science* have also been proposed to model the SDG interactions. They include, for instance, neural network analysis (Zhou et al., 2018; Gue et al., 2020), cross-impact analysis, and system dynamics (Zelinka and Amadei, 2019a, b). As summarized by Zelinka and Amadei (2019a), using such tools to address the SDGs has a strong value proposition when exploring how complexity and uncertainty in the country's systems affect the decision-making process of policymakers and practitioners.

Of particular interest in this book is how the Agenda 2030 framework accounts for the linkages between SDG 16 (Peace, Justice, and Strong Institution), SDG 13 (Climate Action), and the other SDGs. This interaction can be captured using the SDG interlinkage analysis and visualization tool of Zhou and Moinuddin (2017) from the Institute for Global Environmental Strategies. That tool uses social network analysis to capture the nature and strength of the linkages at the target levels for countries where target interlinkage data are available in the literature. Version 4.0 of the interlinkage web tool involves data from 27 countries (https://sdginterlinkages.iges.jp). Figure 2.3 shows an example of linkages for Bangladesh between the targets of SDG 13, SDG 16, and SDG 1 (no poverty).

2.2.2 SUSTAINABILITY AND INFRASTRUCTURE

Since the 1992 Rio Summit, sustainability has become of interest to various communities of engineers, architects, and contractors involved in infrastructure planning, design, and delivery. The American Society of Civil Engineers (ASCE, 2013) considers sustainability as "a set of economic, environmental, and social conditions [or states] in which all of society has the capacity and opportunity to maintain and

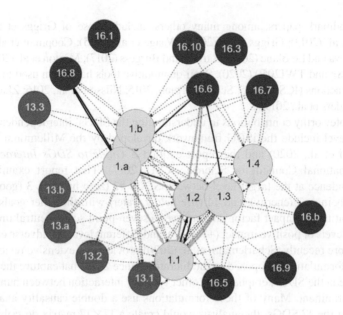

FIGURE 2.3 Causal linkages between targets of SDGs 1, 13, and 16 for the country of Bangladesh created using the interlinkages web tool (Version 4.0) of Zhou and Moinuddin (2017). The line thickness indicates the strength of the causal linkages.[1]

improve its quality of life indefinitely, without degrading the quantity, quality or the availability of natural, economic and social resources."

The ASCE definition of sustainability is at the foundation of Envision®, a framework spearheaded initially in 2012 by the Institute for Sustainable Infrastructure (ISI, 2018) in the United States. Its overall purpose is to evaluate and rate the sustainability of infrastructure projects over their life cycle (i.e., planning, design, construction, operation, and closing) and, more specifically, to improve their "performance" (i.e., how to do technically right projects) with a "social, environmental, and economic perspective" (i.e., how to do the right projects for people and the environment). A third aspect of the framework is to remind all project stakeholders that projects must also be done for the right reasons. It must be noted that the framework only targets specific types of Western infrastructure, such as "roads, pipelines, bridges, railways, airports, dams, levees, landfills, water treatment systems, and other civil infrastructure that make up the built environment." Another sustainability framework, called the *Project Sustainability Management Framework* (FIDIC, 2013), has also been used to measure the sustainability of infrastructure projects.

Table 2.2 summarizes the current version (version 3.0) of the Envision® Sustainable Infrastructure Framework project rating system (ISI, 2018). It consists of five categories of credits (i.e., sustainability indicators) that cut across the people, planet, and profit dimensions of sustainability. They include (i) quality of life (QL) with 13 credits related to well-being, mobility, and community; (ii) leadership (LD) with 11 credits related to collaboration, planning, and the economy; (iii) resource allocation

TABLE 2.2

The Envision® Sustainable Infrastructure Framework Project Rating System for Different Levels of Sustainability

			L1	L2	L3	L4	L5	Points
Quality of Life	Well-being	QL1.1 Improve community quality of life	2	5	10	20	26	200
		QL1.2 Enhance public health and safety	2	7	12	16	20	
		QL1.3 Improve construction safety	2	5	10	14	–	
		QL1.4 Minimize noise and vibration	1	3	6	10	12	
		QL1.5 Minimize light pollution	1	3	6	10	12	
		QL1.6 Minimize construction impacts	1	2	4	8	–	
	Mobility	QL2.1 Improve community mobility	1	3	7	11	14	
		QL2.2 Encourage sustainable transportation	–	5	8	12	16	
		QL2.3 Improve access & wayfinding	1	5	9	14	–	
	Community	QL3.1 Advance equity & social justice	3	6	10	14	18	
		QL3.2 Preserve historic & cultural resources	–	2	7	12	18	
		QL3.3 Enhance views & local character	1	3	7	11	14	
		QL3.4 Enhance public space & amenities	1	3	7	11	14	
Leadership	Collaboration	LD1.1 Provide leadership & commitment	2	5	12	18	–	182
		LD1.2 Foster collaboration & teamwork	2	5	12	18	–	
		LD1.3 Provide for stakeholder involvement	3	6	9	14	18	
		LD1.4 Pursue byproduct synergy	3	6	12	14	18	
	Planning	LD2.1 Establish a sustainable mgt. plan	4	7	12	18	–	
		LD2.2 Plan for sustainable communities	4	6	9	12	16	
		LD2.3 Plan for monitoring & maintenance	2	5	8	12	–	
		LD2.4 Plan for end-of-life	2	5	8	14	–	
	Economy	LD3.1 Simulate economic prosperity & development	3	6	12	20	–	
		LD3.2 Develop local skills & capabilities	2	4	8	12	16	
		LD3.3 Conduct life-cycle economic simulation	5	7	10	12	14	

(Continued)

TABLE 2.2 (Continued)
The Envision® Sustainable Infrastructure Framework Project Rating System for Different Levels of Sustainability

			L1	L2	L3	L4	L5	Points
Resource Allocation	Materials	RA1.1 Support sustainable procurement practice	3	6	9	12	–	196
		RA1.2 Use recycled materials	4	6	9	16	–	
		RA1.3 Reduce operational waste	4	7	10	14	–	
		RA1.4 Reduce construction waste	4	7	10	16	–	
		RA1.5 Balance earthwork on site	2	4	6	8	–	
	Energy	RA2.1 Reduce operational energy consumption	6	12	18	26	–	
		RA2.2 Reduce construction energy consumption	1	4	8	12	–	
		RA2.3 Use renewable energy	5	10	15	20	24	
		RA2.4 Commission & monitor energy systems	3	6	12	14	–	
	Water	RA3.1 Preserve water resources	3	5	7	9	12	
		RA3.2 Reduce operational water consumption	4	9	13	17	22	
		RA3.3 Reduce construction water consumption	1	3	5	8	–	
		RA3.4 Monitor water systems	1	3	6	12	–	
Natural World	Siting	NW1.1 Preserve sites of high ecological value	2	6	12	16	22	232
		NW1.2 Provide wetland & surface water buffers	2	5	10	16	20	
		NW1.3 Preserve prime farmland	–	2	8	12	16	
		NW1.4 Preserve underdeveloped land	3	8	12	18	24	
	Conservation	NW2.1 Reclaim brownfields	11	13	16	19	22	
		NW2.2 Manage stormwater	2	4	9	17	24	
		NW2.3 Reduce pesticide & fertilizer impacts	1	2	5	9	12	
		NW2.4 Protect surface &groundwater quality	2	5	9	14	20	
	Ecology	NW3.1 Enhance functional habitats	2	5	9	15	18	
		NW3.2 Enhance wetland & water functions	3	17	12	18	20	
		NW3.3 Maintain floodplain functions	1	3	7	11	14	
		NW3.4 Control invasive species	1	2	6	9	12	
		NW3.5 Protect soil health	–	3	4	6	8	

(Continued)

TABLE 2.2 (*Continued*)
The Envision® Sustainable Infrastructure Framework Project Rating System for Different Levels of Sustainability

		L1	L2	L3	L4	L5	Points
Climate and Resilience	Emissions						
	CR1.1 Reduce net embodied carbon	5	10	15	20	–	
	CR1.2 Reduce greenhouse gas emissions	8	13	18	22	26	190
	CR1.3 Reduce air pollutant emissions	2	4	9	14	18	
	Resilience						
	CR2.1 Avoid unsuitable development	3	6	8	12	16	
	CR2.2 Assess climate change vulnerability	8	14	18	20	–	
	CR2.3 Evaluate risk and resilience	11	18	24	26	–	
	CR2.4 Establish resilience goals and strategies	–	8	14	20	–	
	CR2.5 Maximize resilience	11	15	20	26	–	
	CR2.6 Improve infrastructure integration	2	5	9	13	18	

Source: Institute for Sustainable Infrastructure (ISI, 2018), used by permission of ISI.
Legend: L1, Improved; L2, Enhanced; L3, superior; L4, conserving; L5, restorative. Maximum total = 1000.

(RA) with 13 credits related to materials, energy, and water; (iv) the natural world (NW) with 13 credits related to siting, conservation, and ecology; and (v) climate and risks (CR) with 9 credits about emissions and resilience. Points (credit values) are assigned to each credit for different project sustainability achievement levels: improved, enhanced, superior, conserving, or restorative.

According to the ISI (2018) report, the five categories can be described as follows:

- *Quality of life* addresses the effects of a project on the host and affected communities, including how well people are doing personally and society as a whole is doing. Quality of life focuses on assessing whether infrastructure projects align with community goals, are incorporated into existing community networks, and benefit the community long-term. Community members affected by the project are considered essential stakeholders in decision-making. The category comprises three subcategories: well-being, mobility, and community. The maximum credit value for the quality of life rating is 200.
- *Leadership* relates to (i) how project teams communicate and collaborate and (ii) how diverse groups contribute ideas and understand the long-term and comprehensive view of the project's life cycle. This category is divided into collaboration, planning, and economy. The maximum credit value for the project leadership rating is 182.
- *Resource allocation* refers to the amount, origin, and properties of project resources and how they affect the project's overall sustainability. Project resources of interest include the physical materials used and discarded in the project, energy, and water. Because they are finite, these resources ought to be used with respect. This category is divided into three subcategories: materials, energy, and water. The maximum credit value for the resource allocation rating is 196.
- *The natural world* is about understanding and minimizing the negative impact of infrastructure on biological systems and increasing synergy. This category is divided into three subcategories: siting, conservation, and ecology. The maximum credit value for the natural world rating is 232.
- *Climate and risks* are about reducing emissions that might contribute to climate change and other immediate and long-term risks and ensuring robust infrastructure investments. To be resilient, the infrastructure needs to be knowledgeable, resourceful, strong, redundant, adaptable, interconnected, and inclusive. This category is divided into two subcategories: emissions and resilience. The maximum credit value for the climate and risk rating is 190.

The sustainability achievement level of a project is that with the highest overall rating, which cannot exceed 1000 credit points. It can be understood as a broad measure of infrastructure sustainability.

Only credits applicable to a given project are considered in all five categories in the current framework version. Furthermore, not all five project achievement levels are possible for each credit. More detailed guidelines about using the framework can be found in the ISI (2018) report about the importance of defining an infrastructure project properly (context, scale, boundary). For each framework category, the report describes the meaning of each level of sustainability achievement in more detail. As an example, Table 2.3 lists the metrics used in determining the level of achievement for CR2.2 (assess climate change vulnerability), ranging between 8 (improved) and 20 (conserving).

The ISI report also describes (i) ways to advance a project to a higher level of achievement, (ii) the explanation of sustainability issues and practices associated with each credit, (iii) how to add credit value for innovation in project delivery, (iv) how some of the credits are interrelated, and (v) how to calculate the overall project sustainability rating. Examples of Envision™ framework applications can be found on the ISI website (https://sustainableinfrastructure.org).

TABLE 2.3

Metrics Used to Determine the Level of Achievement for CR2.2: Assess Climate Change Vulnerability

Improved	Enhanced	Superior	Conserving
A + B	A + B + C	A + B + C + D	A + B + C + D + E
(8) Project Vulnerability	(14) System Vulnerability	(18) Community Vulnerability	(20) Knowledge Sharing

(A) The project team conducts or relies on an existing, comprehensive threat/hazard identification study or assessment because of climate change. Threats/hazards are classified by:

- Duration: acute shocks over hours and days or chronic stressors over years and decades.
- Extent of effects: project site (e.g., localized stormwater overflow), infrastructure system-wide, or community-wide (e.g., climate changes).

The assessment should account for climate change's impact on the frequency, duration, and severity of threats/hazards.

(B) The project team determines vulnerabilities and increased risk to the project, or performance, over its operational life because of climate change-related threats. This should include whether current design variables will continue to meet performance goals over the life of the project under changing operating conditions (i.e., climate, weather patterns, natural hazard frequency, and intensity).

(C) The project team determines vulnerabilities and increased risk to the connected/related infrastructure system or network because of climate change-related threats. This should include how project vulnerabilities may impact system performance and how system vulnerabilities may impact the project. This should consist of direct and indirect impacts such as resource and service availability.

(D) The project team determines vulnerabilities and increased risk to the broader community because of climate change threats. This should include how project vulnerabilities may impact the broader community and how community vulnerabilities may impact the project.

(E) The project team or owner shares climate threat findings to support and facilitate community awareness and their inclusion in future projects.

Source: Institute for Sustainable Infrastructure (ISI, 2018), used with permission from ISI.

The value proposition of the Envision® framework is to encourage decision-makers and practitioners to follow a checklist of criteria that, if met, would lead to infrastructure projects that are better for people and their environment and are profitable. Although comprehensive and forward-thinking, the framework could be improved to explicitly consider possible linkages among the five categories of the infrastructure rating system. These linkages can create synergies or trade-offs at the project level that must be explored.

The Envision® framework provides a unique and rigorous methodology and detailed protocol for assessing semi-quantitative sustainability at the scale of infrastructure community projects in a specific Western context and only in that context. However, with an appropriate selection of indicators, it could be extended to assess semi-quantitatively the sustainability of projects in non-Western world contexts and scales beyond the community project scale.

Furthermore, the Envision® framework could serve as a fundamental and generic framework for policymakers and practitioners to rate community development interventions (e.g., peacebuilding efforts, sustainable development, and climate security practices) and decide whether they are improved, enhanced, superior, conserving, or restorative. A rationale for that suggestion is that the Envision® framework already includes indicators that address, at least in part, four of the 5Ps of sustainability: people and prosperity (quality of life), planet (natural world), and partnerships among decision-makers and practitioners. Peace is not addressed explicitly, however. In addition, the framework accounts for climate change and infrastructure resilience.

2.2.3 SYSTEMS-BASED DEFINITIONS

The two aspects of sustainability considered above (i.e., at the country and infrastructure project scales) deal with people, planet, prosperity, and partnership. They also account for the effects of climate change. Peace is the only component not explicitly included in the ISI framework, even though an argument can be made that it is implicitly related to the quality of life.

The SDG index and the ISI sustainability achievement level represent global sustainability measures at two different scales: country and infrastructure projects. Because sustainability can be seen as emerging from the interaction of multiple systems and subsystems, it is appropriate to consider a systems-based definition of sustainability. A holistic and practical description of sustainability was proposed by USAID (2014), where sustainability refers to

> the ability of a local system to produce desired outcomes over time. Discrete projects contribute to sustainability when they strengthen the system's ability to produce valued results and its ability to be both resilient and adaptive in the face of changing circumstances.

This definition emphasizes the close link between sustainability, resilience, and capacity building. Another pertinent system's definition of sustainability was proposed by Ben-Eli (2012, 2015, 2018), where sustainability is a *desired organizing principle* and a dynamic equilibrium in the processes of interaction between a population and the carrying capacity of an environment such that the population develops to express its full potential without adversely and irreversibly affecting the carrying capacity of the environment upon which it depends.

This definition recognizes the (i) time-changing and balanced (dynamic equilibrium) nature of sustainability, (ii) symbiotic interaction and adaptation between social systems and the environment, and (iii) preservation (i.e., carrying capacity) of the environment on which populations depend. Although that interaction expresses itself differently in different socioeconomic and cultural contexts and scales, it involves standard circular feedback causal loops, as shown in Figure 2.4. As the population of a community grows, its level of activity increases. Growth demands access to natural resources (renewable and non-renewable) and generates byproducts as waste. In turn, the environment's carrying capacity affects the population's well-being and its levels of fertility and mortality.

Ben-Eli's (2018) approach to sustainability emphasized that human (social) and environmental systems continuously hold each other in check through an adaptive and co-creative (or co-evolutionary) process characterized by multiple closed-loop interactions. As a result of this reciprocal causality, these systems maintain a state of equilibrium under normal conditions until enough constraints and stresses, a tipping point, push them to fall into a new balance that is not reversible (Monbiot, 2021).

The feedback dynamic in Figure 2.4 emphasizes that sustainability is closely related to community stewardship. It is about maintaining the natural environment and its eco-services while community activities occur. One lesson humanity will hopefully gain from the 2020 pandemic is that poor stewardship at different scales, from the household to the national or even planetary scale, has many unintended consequences for social well-being, such as putting humans closer to diseases. The same can be said about climate change as it demonstrates the effect of anthropogenic activities on human security. Furthermore, any other dysfunction in the fabric of society can further impact the environment.

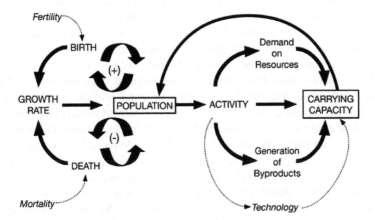

FIGURE 2.4 Feedback loops are involved in the interaction between a population and the environment's carrying capacity on which it depends.

Source: Used by permission of Ben-Eli, the Sustainability Laboratory, 2023.

According to Ben-Eli (2018), sustainability should be seen as a particular system state originating from a particular underlying structure that dictates its behavior. This remark captures the linkage between system structure and behavior patterns and trends, which are inherent to studying systems (Meadows, 2008) and is represented in the iceberg model of Figure 1.1. Ben-Eli introduced five core principles of sustainability associated with five interrelated fundamental domains that play an active structural role in the human–environment feedback mechanism shown in Figure 2.4. The five domains include:

1. The *material domain* (e.g., the flow of resources and materials, infrastructure, and ICT), where the core principle is to limit entropy and ensure that the economy's resource flow is as close to non-declining as is permitted by physical laws.
2. The *economic domain* (e.g., creating and managing wealth, income generation, entrepreneurship, and legal and regulatory frameworks), where the core principle is adopting a suitable accounting system that is entirely in line with ecological processes on the planet and reflects accurate, thorough biospheric pricing to help manage the economy.
3. The *life domain* (e.g., biosphere), where the core principle is to maintain the diversity of life in the biosphere.
4. The *social domain* (e.g., social interactions, education, health services, governance, welfare, and marginal groups), where the core principle is to increase each person's freedom and possibility for self-realization without letting any individual or group have an unfavorable impact on others.
5. The *spiritual domain* (e.g., values, ethics, motivation, aspiration, and well-being), where the core principle is to remember the great mystery and acknowledge the wisdom permeating the web of life.

According to Ben-Eli (2012, 2015), the five core principles of sustainability can be summarized as containing entropy, accounting for externalities, maintaining diversity, gentle self-actualization, and acknowledging the mystery. For each domain and associated core principle, a set of policy and operational implications can be outlined (Table 2.4).

Ben-Eli's sustainability framework lends itself well to a systems approach to sustainability and sustainable community development once temporal and physical scales (individual, household, community, regional, and national) are specified. Despite being comprehensive, the framework would benefit from having a methodology, practical guidelines, and domain metrics. , For instance, many questions remain about (i) what constitutes the components of the five domains for specific scales and contexts, (ii) how to quantify and measure the five-domain interaction, i.e., their influence and dependence, and (iii) how to put the five core principles into practice.

In addition, a more detailed version of Figure 2.4 is necessary to identify specific causal loops between the five domains mentioned above that are more critical to sustainability than others. These loops shown in Figure 2.5, defined as *viability loops* by Hjorth and Bagheri (2006), are "responsible for the viability of all ecosystems, including human-based ecosystems." A stock and flow diagram (see discussion in Chapter 7) represents the loop dynamics.

TABLE 2.4

Policy and Operational Implications for Each Domain and Associated Core Sustainability Principles, According to Ben-Eli (2015)

Domains	Policy and Operational Implications
Material	• Strive for the highest resource productivity. • Amplify performance with each cycle of use. • Employ "income rather than capital" sources and continuously recycle non-regenerative resources. • Affect an unbroken closed-loop flow of matter and energy in a productive planetary infrastructure conceived as a whole. • Control leakages and avoid stagnation, misplaced concentrations, or random diffusion of chemical elements during cycles of use. • Establish a service "performance leasing" orientation for managing durable goods.
Economic	• Employ a comprehensive concept of wealth related to the simultaneous enhancement of five key forms of capital: natural, human, social, manufactured, and financial. • Align the world's economy with nature's regeneration capacity and incorporate critical "externalities" in all cost-and-benefit accounts. • Design regulation and taxation policies to accentuate desirable and eliminate adverse outcomes, optimizing the whole. • Rely on the market mechanism, calibrated to reflect "true" costs, for allocation of capital assets.
Life	• Assume responsible stewardship for our planet's web of biological diversity. • Harvest species only to regeneration capacity. • Conserve the variety of existing gene pools. • Shape land use patterns to reduce human encroachment on other life forms and enhance biological diversity in human habitat areas.
Social	• Foster tolerance as a cornerstone of social interactions. • Enhance universal rights within a framework of planetary citizenship. • Provide for inclusion and effective democracy in governance. • Ensure equitable access to life-nurturing resources. • Establish cooperation as a basis for managing global issues and planetary commons. • Outlaw war and trade in weapon technologies. • Promote sustainability literacy through education at all levels. • Embody sustainability-enhancing concepts in an effective planetary framework of legislation.
Spiritual	• Acknowledge the transcendent mystery that underlies existence. • Seek to understand and fulfill humanity's unique function in the universe. • Honor the Earth with its intricate ecology of which humans are an integral part • Foster compassion and an inclusive, comprehensive perspective in the underlying intention, motivation, and actual implementation of human endeavors. • Link the inner transformation of individuals to the change in the social collective, laying the foundations for the emergence of a new planetary consciousness.

Source: Used by permission of Ben-Eli, the Sustainability Laboratory, 2023.

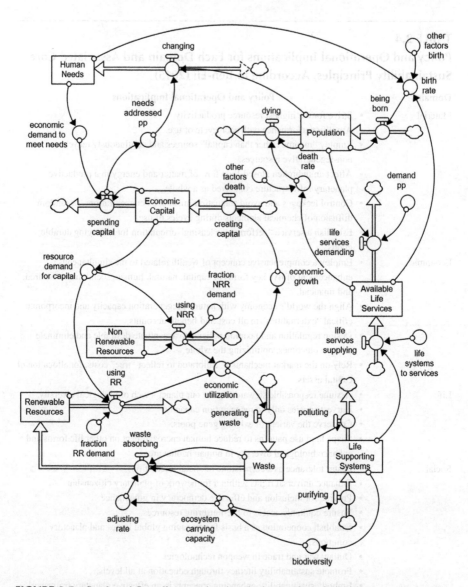

FIGURE 2.5 Stock and flow diagram showing the interaction of viability loops in the real world. Stocks (rectangles) and flows (pipelines) are discussed in Chapter 7.

Source: Hjorth and Bagheri (2006). Used by permission of Elsevier.

Note: The original chart was modified to include additional components and has been redrawn using the STELLA software of Isee systems.

The loops can be regrouped into four categories: human needs, economic capital, the environment, and life support structures. One *loop* involves the interrelationship between human needs and economic capital. An increase in human needs creates an increase in economic demand and the spending of economic capital. This, in turn, creates a circular feedback mechanism leading to a reduction in the needs per person and human needs overall. A *second loop* consists of the dynamic between economic capital and renewable and non-renewable resources. A decrease in economic capital creates a demand for resources contributing to economic growth and capital creation. A *third loop* deals with resource exploitation's environmental consequences (e.g., pollution and reductions in life support systems). As resources are used for economic growth, waste is generated. Some of it, but not all, can be absorbed by natural systems at a specific adjusting rate, which depends on the gap between the waste amount and the ecosystem's carrying capacity to handle the waste. The absorbed waste is returned to the pool of renewable resources. The rest of the waste contributes to pollution and a reduction in the life supporting systems, ecological biodiversity, and ecosystem carrying capacity. A *fourth loop* is about the dynamic between the available services provided by life supporting systems and population growth. Finally, one could add a *fifth loop* relating social systems to environmental and economic systems to these four loops.

If sustainability is achieved, viability loops are critical in maintaining the balance between humans and their environment. According to Hjorth and Bagheri (2006), sustainable development is "the process in which the viability loops are kept functional… and in a healthy state." Although viability loops are different in different socioeconomic and cultural contexts and scales, they represent the "lifelines of natural and human systems" and the necessary components contributing to community sustainability, peace, and resilience. Past a tipping point, their disturbance may lead to significant unintended consequences and irreversible change for all these systems. As a result, viability loops need to be protected in community development, and they are the essential components contributing to system resilience.

2.3 PEACE

2.3.1 POSITIVE, NEGATIVE, AND CULTURAL PEACE

Peace is a concept that has been in the minds of humans since time immemorial. Although countless studies have demonstrated its value proposition in terms of human and economic development, social justice and stability, the promotion of human rights, and well-being in general, peace, like other related community development concepts such as sustainability or resilience, is challenging to conceptualize, let alone quantify for different scales and contexts. An analysis of the various interpretations (philosophical, political, religious, legal, etc.) of peace across different cultures and traditions throughout history can be found in Dietrich (2012) and Stearns (2014). Among all these interpretations, peace can be seen as a state of wholeness, harmony, well-being (physical and spiritual), and *harmonious coexistence*, four emerging properties of human development that are common in the etymological definition of peace in Greek (e.g., *Eirene*) and in Semitic languages (e.g., *shlamah* in Aramaic, *salaam* in Arabic, and *shalom* in Hebrew). The concept of peace as wholeness also appears in the definition proposed by The Earth Charter (1987), where "peace is the wholeness created by right relationships with oneself, other persons, other cultures, other life, Earth, and the larger whole of which all are part."

The literature on conflict management and peace and conflict studies is rich in contributions exploring the different aspects of social conflict and peace. Although peace can be seen as a universal value, it can mean other things to diverse people and cultures (Groff, 2008; Cortright, 2008; Dietrich, 2012; Stearns, 2014). In the same way, as there are different types of social conflict ranging from peaceful demonstrations to armed conflicts (Lemos, 2018), there is no such thing as a one-size-fits-all, unified and optimized static state of peace. It is more realistic to talk about "many [dynamic] peace(s)" (Dietrich and Pearce, 2019). What works in a specific context and scale (physical and temporal) does not necessarily translate elsewhere. Furthermore, conflict and peace are time-dependent.

Peace is not a "measurable commodity" (Diamond and McDonald, 1996) and is more than the absence of hostility and violence. It should be considered "a potential, a possibility, an ever-changing condition [state]... a direction in which to head, one step at a time." Peace can be understood as a state or a process. As a state, peace *emerges* from the interaction of multiple socioeconomic, infrastructure, and environmental systems operating in a constrained landscape of specific context and scale. These systems constitute peace infrastructure in the peace studies and conflict management literature (Lederach, 2012; Davis, 2016).

As a process, peace unfolds over time through peacebuilding (i.e., building conditions for peace), peacemaking (i.e., getting parties to find common ground), and peacekeeping (i.e., supporting sustainable peace) efforts. Another way of looking at peace is to see it as a *noun* (outcome) or a *verb* (process), depending on how it is addressed.

Gittins and Velasquez-Castellanos (2016) noted that "there are about 35 theories of peace, at least at the university level." The conflict and peace studies literature frequently refers to Johan Galtung's work in the early 1960s, which pioneered several approaches to peacebuilding, leading to negative and positive peace (Grewal, 2003; Fischer, 2007; Lawler & Williams, 2008; Galtung, 1964; Galtung, 1990). In short, *negative peace* relates to the *absence* of war and direct or organized violence. Undesirable violence and fear of violence cease to exist due to activities such as nonviolence, disarmament, preventing terrorism and state terrorism, and ceasefires (Fischer, 2007). Negative peacebuilding is about addressing the direct factors that reduce direct violence.

On the other hand, *positive peace* refers to the *presence* and *prevalence* of positive attributes, conditions, and priorities that promote "social and economic justice, environmental integrity, human rights, and development" and contribute to the structural "integration of human society" (Galtung, 1964). As remarked by Fischer (2007), positive peace activities may include establishing good governance, participation, self-determination, and human rights while creating a life-sustaining economy at the local, national, and international levels. Positive peacebuilding is about addressing the indirect factors that may drive violent conflicts. A helpful analogy suggested by Galtung is that negative and positive peace are to peace what *curative* and *preventive* measures are to health.

In addition to positive and negative peace, Galtung (1990) introduced the concept of *cultural peace* as the "aspects of a culture that serve to justify and legitimize direct [negative] peace and structural [positive] peace." Cultural peace activities may include the creation of peaceful deep cultures and deep structures, global communication and conversation, peace journalism, peace education, and the promotion of a culture of peace and mutual learning (Fischer, 2007).

FIGURE 2.6 Peace starts at all corners of the peace triangle. The state of peace resides in the triangle (enabling setting), where the three aspects of peace overlap. PPI (positive peace index), GPI (global peace index), and CPI (cultural peace index).

Source: Amadei (2021), open-access journal.

In a peaceful environment, all three aspects of peace interact with each other and form, according to Galtung (1990), a (virtuous) peace triangle, as shown in Figure 2.6. This contrasts with the so-called (vicious) violence triangle, where direct violence comes from indirect/structural and cultural violence.

Galtung remarked that peace should start at "all three corners [of the peace triangle] at the same time, not assuming that a basic change in one will automatically lead to changes in the other two." In Galtung's peace triangle, one can interpret the area of the triangle as representing the extent of the setting in which peace unfolds over time. Outside the triangle is the external environment (of specific context and scale) that influences the three interacting components of peace over time. A disadvantaged and impoverished environment is unlikely to be a place where peace can thrive. Galtung's representation of peace helps represent peace dynamics at different scales and contexts.

The three forms of peace suggested by Galtung, sometimes referred to as *just peace* (Lederach, 2012), are three forms of *outer peace* usually emphasized in Western cultures. As remarked by Groff (2008), "an essential component and precondition for a peaceful world" requires adding *inner peace* (peace within us) at the individual level, which "draws from the world's rich spiritual-religious traditions" such as Hinduism, Taoism, and Buddhism. Groff (ibid) also considered *Gaia peace* as peace between humans and their environment, particularly emphasized in "earth-based religions and cultures." Regardless of the culture, inner peace is positively correlated with outer peace and is often seen as where peace builds outward at the individual and institutional levels (Cortright, 2008).

2.3.2 THE IEP FRAMEWORK

Because peace is not a direct "measurable commodity" (Diamond and McDonald, 1996) and is difficult to conceptualize at different contexts and scales, questions arise about how to (i) measure it *indirectly* through indicators and proxies and (ii) monitor and evaluate peace over time. The challenge is being able to measure a state that is the outcome of many interacting systems and subsystems (e.g., social, economic, environmental, and infrastructure) with different levels of complexity, uncertainty, and adaptability, and subject to multiple constraints (geopolitical, environmental, cultural, etc.)

Several indices have been suggested in the literature to measure peace (i.e., outer peace) in a qualitative or semi-quantitative manner at the *country* level. Each index consists of multiple indicators. For instance, the Failed State Index (https://fragile-stateindex.org/) uses 12 indicators to measure the risk of countries experiencing internal conflicts. Likewise, the *Peace and Conflict Instability Ledger* (Backer and Huth, 2016) uses five indicator areas to measure states' likelihood of experiencing instability.

A more comprehensive measure of positive peace, called the Positive Peace Index (PPI), was proposed by the Institute for Economics and Peace (IEP) in Sydney, Australia. It considers Galtung's positive peace as "the attitudes, institutions, and structures that create and sustain peaceful societies" (IEP, 2017). According to the IEP, the country level's optimum positive peace environment is founded on eight interdependent pillars or domains, as shown in Figure 2.7.

The PPI is determined at the country level by rating each domain in Figure 2.7. As summarized in Table 2.5, each domain consists of three indicators rated from 1 to 5. The PPI is the weighted average of 24 indicators. It varies on an inverted

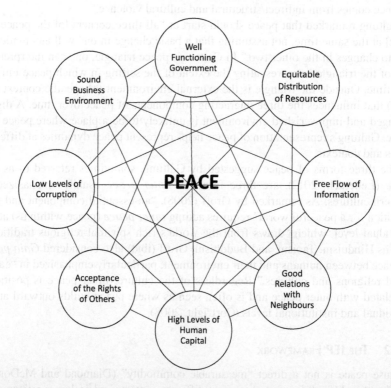

FIGURE 2.7   The eight pillars (domains) create positive peace, according to the IEP (2022).

Source: Used by permission of © Institute for Economics & Peace. Positive Peace Report 2022: Analyzing the factors that sustain peace. Sydney, January 2022. Available from: http://visionofhumanity.org/resources

scale between 1 (most positive peace) and 5 (least positive peace). The indicators and weights in Table 2.5 were selected by the IEP (2018) based on the general characteristics common to peaceful countries. They measure the level of peace and, indirectly, resilience to shocks (endogenous and exogenous) at the country level. The latest report by the Institute for Economics and Peace (IEP, 2022) has shown that globally all eight domains have improved from 2009 to 2020 except for the low levels of corruption.

TABLE 2.5
Positive Peace Index Pillars and Indicators

Positive Peace Pillars	Indicators	Weights, as a % of the total index	Positive Peace Pillars	Indicators	Weights as a % of the Total index
D_1: Well-Functioning Government (WFG)	Democratic political culture	4.49	D_5: Free Flow of Information (FFI)	Freedom of the Press	4.27
	Government effectiveness	5.24		Mobile phone subscription rate	2.13
	The rule of law	5.45		World Press Freedom	3.72
D_2: Sound Business Environment (SBE)	Business environment	4.69	D_6: Good Relations with Neighbors (GRN)	Hostility to foreigners	4.62
	Economic freedom overall score	4.28		Number of visitors	2.34
	GDP per capita	4.07		Regional integration	4.20
D_3: Low Levels of Corruption (LLC)	Factionalized elites	5.03	D_7: Equitable Distribution of Resources (EDR)	Inequality-adjusted life expectancy	3.79
	Perceptions of corruption score	5.38		Social mobility	3.65
	Control of corruption	5.31		Poverty gap	2.27
D_4: High Levels of Human Capital (HLC)	Secondary school enrolment	3.58	D_8: Acceptance of the Rights of Others (ARO)	Empowerment Index	3.31
	Global Innovation Index	4.55		Group grievance rating	4.76
	Youth Development	4.27		Gender inequality	4.48

Source: Amadei (2020). Used by permission of Elsevier. Data Collected from the Institute for Economics & Peace, Positive Peace Report 2018 (IEP, 2018, pp. 68).

The IEP also proposed a Global Peace Index (GPI) to measure negative peace (i.e., the level of country peacefulness) for the same 163 independent states and territories as the PPI (IEP, 2018). It is calculated as the weighted average of 23 indicators divided into three domains: ongoing domestic and international conflict, societal safety and security, and militarization. Like the PPI, the GPI varies between 1 and 5. The values of country GPIs can be found at http://visionofhumanity.org/indexes/global-peace-index/. Analysis of the PPI and GPI overall scores at the *country level* indicates that both indices are highly positively correlated, with a coefficient of correlation $r = 0.75$ for peace data collected from 2008 to 2017 (IEP, 2019). Countries with higher levels of positive peace are less likely to experience violent conflicts and show more coping and adapting resilience to shocks (Killelea, 2021).

The IEP (2019) categorizes countries into four potential peaceful states based on their GPI and PPI values. As shown in Figure 2.8, they include (i) countries with sustainable peace (high positive and negative peace), (ii) countries with a positive peace deficit (low positive peace and high negative peace) that are likely to experience violence in the future, (iii) countries with a positive peace surplus (high positive peace and low negative peace) with the potential to become more peaceful over time, and (iv) countries trapped in violence (low negative and positive peace). Other than sustainable peace, all sectors in Figure 2.8 can represent different aspects of *unsustainable* peace (Amadei 2020). Reychler and Paffenholz (2001) define sustainable peace as

A situation characterized by the absence of physical violence; the elimination of unacceptable political, economic, and cultural forms of discrimination; a high level of internal and external legitimacy or support; self-sustainability; and a propensity to enhance the constructive transformation of conflict.

Although not initially proposed by the IEP, a third index, the Cultural Peace Index (CPI), could be introduced to measure cultural peace (Amadei, 2020). Even though

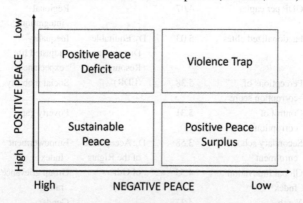

FIGURE 2.8   The four sectors of peace, according to IEP (2019).

Source: Used by permission of the © Institute for Economics & Peace. Global Peace Index 2019: Measuring peace in a complex world. Sydney, June 2019. Available from: http://visionofhumanity.org/resources.

Note: Positive peace and negative peace vary between 1 (high positive and negative peace) and 5 (low positive and negative peace).

its indicators are yet to be determined, the CPI could be designed to range between 1 and 5 for consistency with the PPI and GPI. Amadei (2020) discussed how a 3D peace vector with components PPI, GPI, and CPI could be introduced to represent how the state of peace at the country level evolves.

The framework proposed by the IEP since 2017 acknowledges the multidimensional and multidisciplinary aspects of positive peace at the macro (country) level. It also recognizes that the different components contributing to positive peace are interconnected. In addition, it acknowledges that a systemic approach to positive peace is more appropriate than the assumption that the components act independently of each other in creating peaceful communities. However, the IEP framework is rudimentary in its system formulation for peace. It falls short of exploring how existing systems and complexity science tools could fully capture the systemic nature of positive peace. Amadei (2020) revisited the PPI concept using soft and hard system tools to *explicitly* account for possible interactions (influence and dependence) between the eight domains shown in Figure 2.7.

2.3.3 A System Definition of Peace

Because peace and sustainability *emerge* from the interaction of multiple socioeconomic, infrastructure, and environmental systems operating in a constrained landscape of specific context and scale, it is appropriate to consider a systems-based definition of peace if one is interested in exploring the PSC security nexus with a systemic lens. As suggested by Amadei (2020), peace can be defined as an *organizing principle* and

> an enabling violent-free state of dynamic equilibrium emerging from the right relationships among different populations and their interaction with the various systems in the landscape upon which they depend.

This definition of peace builds on that of sustainability proposed by Ben-Eli (2012, 2015, 2018) and mentioned in the previous section. It also captures the wholeness and relationship aspects of peace suggested by The Earth Charter (1987) and mentioned earlier in this section. The rationale for using this system definition of peace is to recognize that peace and sustainability are states (or cultures) at play emerging from the interaction of shared systems (social, environmental, economic, and infrastructure). Some forms of coherence likely exist, for instance, between the eight domains of peace suggested by the IEP and sustainability. Similarly, it is likely that the five domains of sustainability of Ben-Eli (including the viability loops of Hjorth and Bagheri, 2006) at some specific scale, or the five domains of the Envision® framework at the project scale, are also involved in peacebuilding, peacemaking, and peacekeeping efforts.

Both system definitions of sustainability and peace lend themselves well to using systems modeling tools to capture how the two states of peace and sustainability interact. A challenge in addressing the coherence between sustainability and peace becomes determining all these threads once a specific project has been selected and characterized. Finally, another challenge not addressed here is how inner and outer peace relate to sustainability's inner and outer dimensions.

2.4   CLIMATE SECURITY

2.4.1   A SYSTEM-BASED DEFINITION

Climate change impacts achieving both sustainable development and peace (UN-PPA, n.d.). As mentioned in Chapter 1, climate security captures the effects of climate change and changes in climate patterns on human security and society. Climate security interacts with all types of security mentioned in this book, adds to existing natural (geological) hazards, and is context and scale-specific.

Since its introduction in the 2006 speech of Margaret Beckett, there has been no clear definition of climate security other than dealing with risks and threats related to climate change. According to *Merriam-Webster's Dictionary*, security is the "quality or state of being secure… a state of being protected or safe from harm." Hence, climate security can then be seen as a state of being protected from the risks induced, directly or indirectly, by changes in climate patterns and weather events. It is about creating climate resilience through awareness, adaptation, and mitigation.

As climate security cuts across multiple silos of human development and human security, an attempt can be made to define climate security in an integrated manner using a systems-based definition like those for sustainability and peace. Therefore, the following systems-based definition of climate security is suggested as an organizing principle and as

a secure and resilient state of dynamic equilibrium emerging from the right interactions between populations and the systems they depend on, and where proper practices are used to help prevent, reduce, mitigate, cope, or adapt to the risks and threats related directly and indirectly to the impacts of climate change and related environmental degradation, as well as subsequent policies.

This definition incorporates the concept of climate security practices, which according to the Planetary Security Initiative (Von Lossow et al., 2021), are "tangible actions implemented by a (local or central) government, organization, community, private actor or individual to help prevent, reduce, mitigate or adapt (to) security risks and threats related to impacts of climate change and related environmental degradation, as well as subsequent policies." An issue with climate security practices such as adaptation and mitigation is that they are often "promoted by different communities, and each mostly fails to consider the full [climate] risk spectrum" (Luers and Sklar, 2013).

Although climate security practices have a strong value proposition in terms of socioeconomic return (e.g., "On average every dollar spent on adaptation brings $4 in benefits," according to the World Bank), there are substantial disparities in how such practices are implemented in rich vs. poor communities and countries. Disadvantaged groups have limited initial capacity to implement adaptation and mitigation practices (Schwartzstein and Risi, 2023). A case in point is how countries in Africa with mostly non-irrigated farmland can even start considering such practices.

The Planetary Security Initiative (Von Lossow et al., 2021) cites multiple case studies of climate security practices in different parts of the world to protect natural resources, halt and reverse land degradation, reduce conflict, and enhance peace and stability. Some of these practices are at the macro level and involve government and diplomatic decision-making (e.g., greening the Sahel; phasing out fossil fuel production and consumption). Micro-level practices are at the community level and involve local stakeholders (e.g., community resource security and livelihood, local weather station monitoring) and include, for instance, halting and reversing unsustainable land use changes. Finally, intermediate-level solutions include both local and non-local decision-makers. Examples include WASH strategies at the regional level (e.g., Israel, Palestine, and Gaza) and uni- or bilateral country agreements around trade and management of natural resources. These practices have challenges, such as assessing their direct and indirect impacts. Like all development projects, they also require precise monitoring and evaluation guidelines.

Other examples of climate security practices include introducing "smart" agricultural practices and new and emerging technologies to increase agricultural production (e.g., Agtech, https://www.agtech.com). Other examples related to disaster risk reduction include (i) the development of spatial and non-spatial information monitoring systems that provide early warning of hazards such as floods, droughts, glacier dam bursts, forest fires, etc., and (ii) better management and conservation of ecosystems and biodiversity. For instance, these practices have been developed by the International Center for Integrated Mountain Development (ICIMOD, https://www.icimod.org), a coalition of eight countries in the Hindu Kush and Himalayas mountains.

Other practices include promoting green technical options in the energy field for countries to grow their economies without increasing greenhouse emissions. This change is partly possible because of the declining costs of solar and wind power by 89% and 70%, respectively, from 2009 to 2019 (Lazard, 2019). There is also a strong value proposition to promote changes in consumer behavior, improve the performance of older technologies, promote industry decarbonization, consider carbon sequestration (in soils and oceans), and adopt low-carbon strategies. According to The Nature Conservancy (2018), under a business-as-usual scenario, fossil fuels will still account for 76% of all energy in 2050. By 2050, a more sustainable strategy would bring that share down to 13%. Despite that change, it is important to halt the atmospheric emissions of dangerous greenhouse gases. The Glasgow meeting (COP 26) showed that leadership is still missing in reaching that goal (Galpern, 2021).

Technology for adaptation and mitigation is necessary to secure livelihoods when faced with climate change, but it is insufficient. Another aspect of the systems-based definition of climate security proposed above is the need for proper interactions between people and their environment (natural, social, cultural, etc.) and adopting a culture of resilience. In addition, climate security practices must be rightly done from a practical point of view. Finally, interactions and practices must be carried out for the right reasons. They must also be specific to the risk events climate change creates and their impact or threats (single and multiplying) at different scales (local, regional, global). The Center for Climate and Security (2021) classifies threats into two groups, direct and indirect. The *direct threats* include those affecting critical infrastructure, nations' security, military installations, and the centers (energy, financial, and agricultural) that define economic viability at the national level. The *indirect threats* (i) affect the security of human livelihood resources (e.g., WELF resources), (ii) create migration and population movements, and (iii) generate conflict and unrest, as well as geopolitical tensions at the state level and across states (e.g., the Arctic).

2.4.2 ADAPTATION

Adaptation to climate change and hazards, in general, is critical to human development and security. Climate security requires awareness before adaptation and mitigation practices can be considered. Many worldwide constituencies are conscious of climate change and its consequences on livelihood and the environment they depend on. Despite that awareness, the action part of climate security depends significantly on the engagement of governments and societies whose worldviews may range from denial to full acceptance of climate change and the adoption of national adaptation plans (NAP, n.d.).

A helpful index of climate adaptation supported by indicators is the Notre Dame Global Adaptation Index (ND-GAIN). It was introduced in 2011 by the Global Adaptation Institute to measure how ready and resilient countries are to adapt to climate change (Chen et al., 2015). The index has evolved as a "navigation tool to help prioritize and measure progress in adapting to climate change and other global forces." The index recognizes that climate-related disasters and climate change "will lead to increased risks and costs for business, complicate political decisions, and of most concern, threaten the quality of life for vulnerable populations around the world."

The vulnerability and readiness of each country are plotted on a *Readiness Matrix* as shown in Figure 2.9, which is divided into four quadrants; each quadrant defines the country's challenge level to face climate change or other global forces. The ND-GAIN index has been determined for 182 countries as of 2020.

The latest version of the ND-GAIN framework, released in 2015, consists of 45 indicators of adaptation to climate change at the country level. They are divided into two groups: 36 indicators of vulnerability, divided into six life-supporting sectors listed in Table 2.6, and nine indicators of readiness (capacity) listed in Table 2.7. Each sector of vulnerability and readiness is divided into three components: (i) exposure

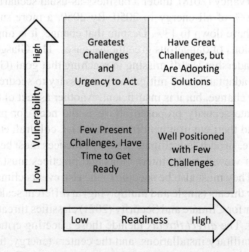

FIGURE 2.9 Country Readiness Matrix: Vulnerability vs. Readiness (or Capacity).

Source: Chen et al. (2015), used by permission of the Global Adaptation Institute, University of Notre Dame.

TABLE 2.6
ND-GAIN Vulnerability Indicators

Sector	Exposure	Sensitivity	Adaptive Capacity
Food	Projected change in cereal yields	Food import dependency	Agriculture capacity (fertilizer, irrigation, pesticide, tractor use)
	Projected population change	Rural population	Child malnutrition
Water	Projected change of annual runoff	Freshwater withdrawal rate	Access to reliable drinking water
	Projected change of annual groundwater recharge	Water dependency ratio	Dam capacity
Health	Projected change of deaths from climate change-induced diseases	Slum population	Medical staffs
	Projected change in length of transmission season of vector-borne diseases	Dependency on external resources for health services	Access to improved sanitation facilities
Ecosystem services	Projected change of biome distribution	Dependency on natural capital	Protected biomes
	Projected change of marine biodiversity	Ecological footprint	Engagement in international environmental conventions
Human habitat	Projected change of warm period	Urban concentration	Quality of trade and transport-related infrastructure
	Projected change in flood hazard	Age dependency ratio	Paved roads
Infrastructure	Projected change in hydropower generation capacity	Dependency on imported energy	Electricity access
	Projection of sea level rise impacts	Population living under 5 m above sea level	Disaster preparedness

Source: Chen et al. (2015), used by permission of the Global Adaptation Institute, University of Notre Dame.

TABLE 2.7
ND-GAIN Readiness Indicators

Components	Indicators			
Economic readiness	Doing business			
Governance readiness	Political stability and nonviolence	Control of corruption	The rule of law	Regulatory quality
Social readiness	Social inequality	ICT infrastructure	Education	Innovation

Source: Chen et al. (2015), used by permission of the Global Adaptation Institute, University of Notre Dame.

to climate change, (ii) sensitivity to how populations react to climate change hazards, and (iii) adaptive capacity (i.e., resilience to hazards). A detailed description of each indicator, including the data each indicator is based on, can be found in Chen et al. (2015).

2.5   THREE INTERCONNECTED STATES

2.5.1   COMMON CHARACTERISTICS

Multiple studies and publications have emphasized the dependencies and relationships between peace, sustainability, and climate security. The emphasis is on whether these sectors create an enabling environment or whether their opposites (i.e., conflict, unsustainable practices, and climate vulnerability) create a constraining (dis-enabling) environment. Several journals have been dedicated to studying the interaction of two-sector nexuses, such as the sustainability–climate change nexus journal (Sustainability and Climate Change | Mary Ann Liebert, Inc., publishers (liebertpub.com) and the sustainability–peace nexus journal (Sharifi et al., 2021a). Still, despite these scholarly publications on the topic, clear and practical frameworks to look at all three sectors of the PSC nexus, especially at the community scale, are missing.

Also missing is an understanding of the causal chains (i.e., pathways) between the three sectors (i.e., how one or two sectors may trigger the others) and how diverse development and security areas may trigger a state of peace vs. conflict, sustainability vs. unsustainability, and climate security vs. vulnerability (Peters et al., 2020). Understanding that dynamic may help in climate- and hazard-related risk management, capacity building, and planning adaptation and mitigation interventions ahead of adverse events. As remarked by Peters et al. (2020), "the relationships between climate factors, natural resource scarcity, and conflict point to a need to integrate stabilization and peacebuilding principles with climate-resilient development interventions at local and sub-regional levels."

The states of peace, sustainability, and climate security defined in the previous sections share several characteristics. First, they are organizing principles and *emerge* from interdependent and interconnected systems (social, environmental, economic, and infrastructure) in complex landscapes. These systems involve different adapting actors and are subject to various enabling and constraining factors and barriers.

The concept of emergence implies that the behavior of the whole (i.e., the emergent wholeness), such as communities, cannot necessarily be determined by adding the behavior of its parts; something happens when the elements interact (Holland, 1999). Although emergence cannot be found anywhere in communities, it is still a system property and creates unique forms of coherent behavior and self-organization. In the complexity science literature, the concepts of emergence, self-organization, connectivity, interdependence, path-dependency, adaptation, and synergy are closely related (Mitleton-Kelly, 2003).

Another shared characteristic of peace, sustainability, and climate security is that their systems-based definitions consider them states of evolutionary dynamic equilibrium (i.e., they change over time and space) involving the interaction of social systems with other systems in a specific landscape. As adaptive systems, social systems undergo irreversible changes (either by keeping their current forms or changing into a different one) with a mixture of stability and instability combined with emerging forms of order, coherence, co-evolution, cooperation, and self-organization. These are all attributes of dissipative structures (Prigogine and Stengers, 1984).

Peace, sustainability, and climate security share the following additional characteristics:

- No single unified and optimized static state of peace, sustainability, and climate security is possible for a given landscape. Multiple coherent states and pathways between states are possible, however. Furthermore, what works at one scale (physical and temporal) may not work at another.
- All three states change with time, hence their dynamic nature. However, they also strive to maintain equilibrium until reaching a tipping point beyond which a new irreversible desirable or undesirable balance is achieved.
- It is easier to define the three states by what they are *not* rather than by what they are. This characteristic allows for exploring many acceptable or satisfactory (i.e., good enough) states. Peace, sustainability, climate security, and the pathways between these states must be read as plural (Dietrich, 2012).
- Because of their entanglement, the three states should not be addressed in isolation but rather integrated once a theory of change has been adopted.
- Addressing the complex dynamics of the three states requires decision-makers to be systems thinkers to handle multiple trade-offs, anticipate synergies, mitigate adverse emergence, and consider different perspective levels from decision-making to field operation.
- The interactions between peace, sustainability, and climate security are complex and hard to disentangle.

All the above characteristics acknowledge that sustainability, peace, and climate security are interconnected, hence the value proposition of considering these three sectors as a nexus. Furthermore, each sector involves intraconnected components. This level of complexity can only be handled using a systems approach. As discussed in the forthcoming chapters, adopting a systems perspective can help to (i) explore the coherence between sustainability, peace, and climate security and (ii) capture the multiple adaptive self-regulating processes and feedback mechanisms (reinforcing and balancing) necessary for the systems to match specific desired goals and objectives.

2.5.2 NEXUS INDICATORS AND PERFORMANCE METRICS

A significant challenge in addressing the PSC nexus is that peace, sustainability, and climate security are not quantitative commodities. Hence, indicators, proxies, and performance metrics are needed to characterize, monitor, and evaluate these three states and their nexus over time. The challenge is measuring conditions that result from many interacting systems and subsystems with different levels of complexity, uncertainty, and adaptability and subject to multiple constraints (e.g., geopolitical, environmental, cultural, etc.) One approach would be to use a scoring framework similar to that used in the ISI sustainability framework described above (Table 2.3), where different levels of achievement of peace, sustainability, and climate security would be considered. These three states could be, for instance, unlikely, possible but restricted, possible but limited, possible and allowed, possible and supported, and likely. Each achievement level would have specific performance metrics. Crossover indicators and performance metrics are also needed across sectors of the PSC nexus. For instance, questions may arise about what crossover indicators in one or two nexus sectors make them essential for the others.

Another challenge, which is relevant to many types of nexus and discussed by the author concerning the WELF nexus (Amadei, 2019), is finding cross-sector indicators that link technical measures that tend to be quantitative with nontechnical (e.g., socioeconomic) measures that tend to be more qualitative. Socioeconomic indicators are often more challenging to measure than technical indicators, despite being equally important in understanding the nexus dynamics. The lack of indicators linking technical and nontechnical issues is a limiting factor in developing comprehensive models to capture the dynamic across the nexuses and their components.

The previous sections discussed several indicators proposed in the literature to assess peace, sustainability, and climate security states. They are summarized in Table 2.8, along with other possible indicators. A few guidelines are necessary when developing an indicator framework, in general.

- The indicators must be appropriate to the context and scale of the landscape in which the PSC nexus unfolds. It is essential to realize that metrics and indicators of importance at one scale and in a given socioeconomic, environmental, and political context may not be relevant at other scales and contexts. Indicators relevant at some regional or national scales may not apply to local sales, and vice-versa. Likewise, the indicators must be tailored to a specific context.
- Interestingly, as the scale increases, indicators become more aggregated and are often replaced by *indexes* in the literature (e.g., the human development index, positive peace, and negative peace indices). A problem with aggregated indicators is that, despite their simplifying aspect, explaining what they mean in practice is often difficult.
- All selected indicators must have at least some specific attributes to be meaningful. In development studies, for instance, Caldwell (2002) suggested that indicators must have many of the following eight characteristics: (i) measurable, (ii) technically feasible, (iii) reliable, (iv) valid, (v) relevant, (vi) sensitive to change, (vii) cost-effective, and (viii) timely. To that list, one could add other characteristics such as indicator specificity and representativeness (Winograd and Farrow, 2011), ease of understanding, and whether the indicators are supported by data that are accessible.
- Regardless of their number, indicators, and performance metrics are necessary but insufficient to understand the nexus, the landscape, and human development and security in general. As mentioned by Raha (2017), "What truly counts is not [always] countable. What is countable does not [always]

TABLE 2.8
Possible Indicators of Peace, Sustainability, and Climate Security and of Influence of One Nexus Sector on the Others

Indicators to Measure…

Peace

- SDG 16 targets and indicators:
  - Target 16.1: Significantly reduce all forms of violence and related death rates everywhere (4 indicators)
  - Target 16.2: End abuse, exploitation, trafficking, and all forms of violence against and torture of children (3 indicators)
  - Target 16.3: Promote the rule of law at the national and international levels and ensure equal access to justice for all (2 indicators)
  - Target 16.4: By 2030, significantly reduce illicit financial and arms flows, strengthen the recovery and return of stolen assets and combat all forms of organized crime (2 indicators)
  - Target 16.5: Substantially reduce corruption and bribery in all their forms (2 indicators).
  - Target 16.6: Develop effective, accountable, and transparent institutions at all levels (2 indicators)
  - Target 16.7: Ensure responsive, inclusive, participatory, and representative decision-making at all levels (2 indicators)
  - Target 16.8: Broaden and strengthen the participation of developing countries in the institutions of global governance (1 indicator)
  - Target 16.9: By 2030, provide legal identity for all, including birth registration (1 indicator)
  - Target 16.10: Ensure public access to information and protect fundamental freedoms, in accordance with national legislation and international agreements (2 indicators)
  - Target 16. A: Strengthen relevant national institutions, including through international cooperation for building capacity at all levels, in particular in developing countries, to prevent violence and combat terrorism and crime (1 indicator)
  - Target 16. B: Promote and enforce non-discriminatory laws and policies for sustainable development (1 indicator)
- Everyday peace indicators (EPI, 2016): indicators in 15 domains at the local level: cohesion and interdependence, leadership, education, social, conflict resolution, discrimination, economic, food and agriculture, infrastructure, health, security (crime), security (daily), security (forces), and transitional justice and human rights
- Positive peace index (PPI): 24 indicators divided into eight domains: well-functioning government, sound business environment, equitable distribution of resources, acceptance of the rights of others, good relations with neighbors, free flow of information, high levels of human capital, and low levels of corruption (IEP, 2017)
- Negative peace index (GPI): 23 indicators divided into three domains: ongoing domestic and international conflict, societal safety and security, and militarization (IEP, 2017)
- Cultural peace index (CPI): indicators to be determined

Influence of Peace on Sustainability and Climate Security

- Equitable access to resources
- Level of climate security practices participation
- Vulnerability of disadvantaged and marginalized people to climate change
- Governance stability and decision-making
- Management and allocation of resources at different scales
- Transboundary exchanges and shared resources management
- Post-conflict rehabilitation and reconciliation
- Adaptation and mitigation efforts to climate change

(Continued)

TABLE 2.8 (*Continued*)
Possible Indicators of Peace, Sustainability, and Climate Security and of Influence of One Nexus Sector on the Others

Indicators to Measure…

Sustainability
- People: SDGs 1–5 targets and indicators
- Planet: SDGs 6, 12–15 targets and indicators
- Prosperity: SDGs 7–11 targets and indicators
- Partnership: SDG 17 targets and indicators
- Envision® framework (five domains and indicators)
- Ben-Eli framework (five domains and no indicators)

Influence of Sustainability on Peace and Climate Security
- Changes in livelihood and health resources
- Changes in societal safety and security
- Changes in conflict and disaster-related risks
- Capacity levels to cope and adapt to shocks and stresses
- Levels of community disagreement, conflict, and violence
- Collaboration levels
- Impact of anthropogenic effects on natural systems

Climate security
- Awareness through social media, education, and communication, citizen involvement, behavior change, and advocacy levels
- Adaptation (GAIN index): 36 indicators to define readiness and nine for vulnerability
- Mitigation indicators may relate to policies and practices for (i) reducing GHG emissions by reducing the burning of fossil fuels for electricity, heat, and transport and (ii) stabilizing emissions to allow for ecosystem adaptation and sustainable development
- Climate change indicators
  - EPA (n.d.): 50 indicators regrouped into six categories: GHG production, weather and climate, oceans, snow and ice, public health and society, and ecosystems
  - CCPI (n.d.): The climate change performance index uses 14 indicators in four categories: GHG, renewable energy, energy use, and climate policy

Influence of Climate Security on Peace and Sustainability
- Changes in conflict dynamics and migration
- Socioeconomic changes
- Recovery time after crises because of increased resilience
- Levels of community stability, strength, and adaptation
- Levels of water, energy, land, and food security
- Changes in disease burden and health-related climate issues
- Changes in biodiversity loss and environmental damage

truly count." In navigating the complexity of the PSC nexus, the challenge is to find a balance between having too many indicators that would give an overly comprehensive understanding of the nexus and the landscape and having fewer. Still, a sufficient number of indicators must provide comprehensible enough insight for decision-makers to develop solutions (using the systems tools discussed in the following chapters) that are meaningful to the community regarding livelihood.

2.5.3 REPRESENTING THE PSC NEXUS

2.5.3.1 Triangular Representation

With the three systems-based definitions of sustainability, peace, and climate security in mind, we can now explore how the three states interact in an integrated manner once the context and scale of their interaction are specified. The interaction can be illustrated in several ways.

Figure 2.10 shows a triangular representation of the interactions between the three sectors of the PSC nexus. Each sector can vary on a qualitative scale from low to high or a semi-quantitative scale from 0 to 100. Depending on the levels of peace, sustainability, and climate security, the cycle between these sectors can range between (i) a full enabling cycle of peace, sustainability, and climate security and (ii) a full constraining (or dis-enabling) cycle of violence, unsustainable livelihoods, and climate vulnerability. The latter is likely to unfold in weak and vulnerable states.

The interactions in Figure 2.10 occur in an environment involving multiple socio-economic, political, and cultural factors. The peace, sustainability, and climate security states (and their opposites) depend on the dynamic of that environment, and the environment depends on how the three sectors interact. Multiple trade-offs or synergies may need to be considered in that feedback interaction.

The development literature is not always clear about what is driving what among the three PSC states in Figure 2.10. There is often weak and contradictory evidence in their causal chains of interaction. That interaction may hinder or not human development and security, depending on capacity. It can follow multiple pathways, take various forms, and change over time. For instance, even though peace may be present, a small level of stability may or may not contribute enough to sustainable development, climate awareness, adaptation, and mitigation. Likewise, a small level of sustainability may be present, but too rapid socioeconomic growth may produce more emissions, challenging climate security measures. Finally, a low level of climate security and sustainability may induce conflict if not properly planned and implemented. The bottom line is that there are multiple ways for human development and security to unfold, and trade-offs and synergies may need to be considered on a case-by-case basis.

2.5.3.2 Cross-Impact Matrix Representation

The interactions in Figure 2.10 are further explored in Table 2.9, which shows possible forms of double *enabling* causality and impact between peace, sustainability,

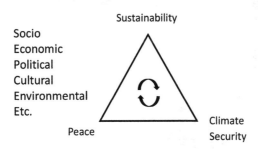

FIGURE 2.10 Interaction between peace, sustainability, and climate security.

TABLE 2.9
Double Entry Table Showing Different Forms of *Enabling Causality* between Peace, Sustainability, and Climate Security

	Peace State (Positive, Negative, Cultural) & SDG 16	Sustainability State (People, Planet, Prosperity, Partnership) & All SDGs	Climate Security State (Awareness, Adaptation, Mitigation) & SDG 13
Peace (Positive, Negative, Cultural) & SDG 16		• Contributes to all SDGs. • Provides stability and security foundation for sustainable development. • Promotes more resilient, prosperous, inclusive, tolerant healthier societies with diversity and integrity. • Creates a safer and more secure socioeconomic environment for stable governance, longer-term productivity and investment, and the management and allocation of resources at different scales. • Provides more reliable planning and design of infrastructure and long-term operation and maintenance. • Promotes more equitable access to resources. • Facilitates transboundary exchanges and shared resource management. • Assists in post-conflict rehabilitation and reconciliation.	• Makes adapting and coping with climate shocks easier. • Provides a platform for dialogue and collaboration at different scales. • Promotes cooperation on climate-related issues. • Reduces vulnerability of disadvantaged and marginalized people to climate change. • Contributes to the presence and prevalence of positive attributes, conditions, and priorities conducive to dialogue and implementation of climate security practices.

(Continued)

TABLE 2.9 (*Continued*)
Double Entry Table Showing Different Forms of *Enabling Causality* between Peace, Sustainability, and Climate Security

	Peace State (Positive, Negative, Cultural) & SDG 16	Sustainability State (People, Planet, Prosperity, Partnership) & All SDGs	Climate Security State (Awareness, Adaptation, Mitigation) & SDG 13
Sustainability (People, Planet, Prosperity, Partnership) & All SDGs	• Creates pathways to more peaceful societies. • Promotes conflict resolution, reconciliation, and peacebuilding. • Contributes to more secure livelihood, reduced poverty, better health and social outcomes, and environmental/ecosystem protection. • Reduces risks of conflict by promoting fairness, equality, and equity. • Increases capacity to cope and adapt to shocks and stresses. • Reduces the likelihood of disagreement, conflict, and violence. • May facilitate bilateral or multilateral agreements. • Practices are conducive to more peaceful communities. • Promotes collaboration. • Provides opportunities for peacebuilding and cooperation. • Promotes peace by addressing causes of environmental degradation.		• Promotes awareness and stewardship. • Reduces the impact of anthropogenic effects on the environment and ecosystems. • Better economic and ecological practices reduce the need for climate-related migration.

(*Continued*)

TABLE 2.9 (Continued)
Double Entry Table Showing Different Forms of *Enabling Causality* between Peace, Sustainability, and Climate Security

	Peace State (Positive, Negative, Cultural) & SDG 16	Sustainability State (People, Planet, Prosperity, Partnership) & All SDGs	Climate Security State (Awareness, Adaptation, Mitigation) & SDG 13
Climate security (Awareness, Adaptation, Mitigation) & SDG 13	• Reduces the likelihood of disagreement, conflict, tension, violence, social friction, and migration. • Enhances social cohesion. • Provides a more stable environment for socioeconomic growth. • Contributes to national and global security. • Creates an enabling geostrategic environment	• Increases community stability, resilience, and adaptation. • Contributes to water, energy, land, and food security. • Contributes to reducing disease burden and health-related climate issues. • Decreases vulnerability to changes in climate patterns and other extreme events. • Reduces biodiversity loss, desertification, and environmental damage. • Reduces migration from rural to urban. • Contributes to all SDGs, the 3Ps/5Ps of sustainability, and the domains of social, economic, material, life, and values.	

and climate security. This representation departs from the dominant literature, which focuses on the *constraining* (dis-enabling) causality and effect between conflict, unsustainability, and climate vulnerability. Table 2.9 has been kept simple for discussion purposes. It represents a high-level cross-impact map of the PSC nexus. A more detailed version of that table could be created if one is interested in looking at the interaction of (i) the positive, negative, and cultural aspects of peace with (ii) the planet, prosperity, and partnership components of sustainability, and (iii) several aspects of climate security such as awareness, adaptation, and mitigation. Other context-specific attributes for each sector of the PSC nexus could also be added to the analysis.

The six off-diagonal boxes in Table 2.9 represent possible enabling feedback mechanisms and interlinkages as two sectors interact interdependently across the nexus. As remarked by Arcade et al. (2014), double causality tables can help identify the influence and dependence of one sector on the others. Hence, each row in Table 2.9 defines how each sector of the PSC nexus *influences* (impacts) the other two sectors. Likewise, each column represents how each sector of the PSC nexus *depends on* (or is sensitive to) the other two sectors.

The intensity of the enabling influence and dependence between the three states in Table 2.9 can be expressed qualitatively as high, medium, and low or semi-quantitatively as scores ranging between 0 (neutral) and 3. Likewise, negative scores between −1 and −3 could also capture constraining effects between the three states. This type of scoring will be used in several examples in the rest of this book.

Each off-diagonal term in Table 2.9 represents the *direct* interaction between two of the three nexus sectors. *Indirect* interactions also exist, involving complex pathways between sectors as one sector influences a second one, affecting another that depends on the second one. For example, one of these pathways could be a state of peace that contributes to reducing the vulnerability of disadvantaged and marginalized people to climate change through adaptation and mitigation efforts. This, in turn, provides (i) increased community stability, security, resilience, and livelihood; (ii) the conservation of natural resources; and (iii) a reduction in greenhouse gas emissions, thus contributing to sustainable development.

2.5.3.3 Pathways Representation

Examples relating climate change to peace/conflict indirectly or directly were proposed by Sharifi et al. (2021b). According to these authors, an indirect pathway corresponds to how "climate change may lead to conflict through diminishing livelihood capacities and/or inducing migration [or internal displacement]," as in the Syrian conflict mentioned in Section 2.1. The direct pathway undermining peace may be "through direct psychological/physiological effects of climate impact or via competition over scarce resources." Figure 2.11 summarizes the results of an extensive literature review of 168 different journals (published since 2015) by Sharifi et al. (2021b), showing the complexity of different pathways between climate stressors, the direct and indirect effects of climate change, and conflict type (e.g., civil conflict, crime, inter-communal violence, interstate conflict, political conflict, and social conflict).

Sharifi et al. (2021b) concluded that (i) indirect effects dominate all types of conflict, and (ii) extreme temperatures are more likely to lead to direct effects. Another

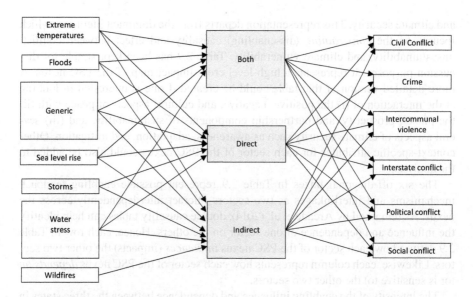

FIGURE 2.11 Different pathways between climate stressors (left), the direct and indirect effects of climate change (center), and conflict type (right). This is a simplified version of the original from Sharifi et al. (2021b) not showing the strength of the pathways.

Source: Sharifi et al. (2021b), open-access journal.

analysis by these authors showed that the "availability and accessibility of resources [especially water] play an important role in the climate-peace nexus" irrespective of climate change's direct or indirect effects.

The bottom line is that whether direct or indirect, the causal links between any of the two sectors of the climate-peace nexus in Figure 2.11 are not straightforward and often involve a third sector. This dynamic also depends on the interplay between pre-existing socioeconomic, political, and institutional factors and different types of capacity (institutional, technical, human resources, financial, environmental, and cultural). The dynamic is also time-dependent, as there may be a delay between the interplay and the time it manifests itself. It is also important to note that the conclusions reached by Sharifi et al. (2021b) highly depend on the data available in different parts of the world. As pointed out by these authors, not much data is available about conflict, climate change, and various other factors in South America compared to Asia and Africa, where more data are available.

2.5.3.4 Tripod Representation

Another representation of the nexus is that of a three-legged tripod, as shown in Figure 2.12. The tripod's overall stability, which represents human development and security, depends on the stability and strength of each leg (i.e., peace, sustainability, and climate security) and all three legs simultaneously (integrated nexus approach).

Figure 2.12 can help illustrate how human development and security would be compromised if at least one of its three nexus sectors were weaker than the others.

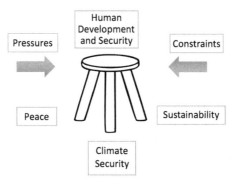

FIGURE 2.12   A tripod representation of the peace–sustainability–climate security nexus.

For example, if one of the tripod's legs were to decrease and the others to increase, this would simulate how not prioritizing one sector of the nexus could affect the others. An example would be where inadequate climate security measures create unsustainable economic growth and conflict.

Furthermore, the tripod's stability depends on how it interacts with its surrounding landscape or environment. That environment creates stressors and constraints (internal or external, soft or hard) on the tripod's existence and stability; too much pressure could even topple the tripod. By analogy, human development and security may be at risk due to socioeconomic, geopolitical, and environmental stressors and constraints (limiters). Stressors and constraints can act synergistically and even exacerbate conflict, poor livelihood, and the impact of climate change. For example, such conditions may be related to urbanization, overexploitation of natural resources, and competition.

Figure 2.12 also shows that interventions selected to address issues across the PSC nexus —whether they are technical or nontechnical and specific to each sector—need to (i) encompass the multiple dimensions of the nexus, (ii) consider the environment in which the nexus unfolds, and (iii) be synchronized across the nexus. Solving one issue associated with one sector of the nexus can affect (positively or negatively) one or several other sectors. This dynamic is because of the dependence and influence properties mentioned in Table 2.9. For instance, inadequate climate adaptation and mitigation practices may influence (intendedly or unintendedly) the management of community resources and resume community conflict.

As discussed further in this book, a challenge in addressing the PSC nexus and any nexus, in general, is how deep one goes into disaggregating the domains and subdomains of each sector and finding the most appropriate attributes. Another challenge is identifying qualitatively or quantitatively how each sector influences the other two sectors. In general, the challenge is to balance capturing the linkages well enough (qualitatively or quantitatively) and being sufficiently comprehensive without falling into paralysis in analysis, which is often the case in systems modeling. Simply put, there are no specific recipes to find that balance short of gaining experience through multiple efforts.

2.5.4 SYSTEMIC QUESTIONS

The study of nexuses, in general, whether it is the PSC nexus discussed herein; the water-energy-food nexus (Hoff, 2011); the water-energy-land-food nexus (Amadei, 2019); the humanitarian-development-peace triple nexus (2019); the agri-food systems, environmental systems, and health disease systems involved in the food-nutrition security nexus (Hammond and Dube, 2012); the food-health-care-nutrition nexus (SPRING, 2015); the climate-fragility-peacebuilding nexus (Wilson Center, 2021); or the Environment-Fragility-Peace nexus (CDA, 2023) brings up a lot of open-ended questions about how to characterize and address the sectors and their causal direct and indirect linkages and pathways. Specifically, practical systemic questions include:

- What is the best way to capture the dynamic of interrelated systems across disciplinary lines?
- How do the nexus sectors interact at various physical (where) and temporal (when) scales?
- What factors support or impede community development, security, and resilience to adverse events and crises?
- What criteria and measures (technical and nontechnical) must be selected to make appropriate decisions when intervening in different sectors?
- What qualitative and quantitative data must be collected about the nexus to best capture the two- or three-way interactions between nexus components and various systems with which the nexus interacts at the community level?
- How should nexus data be collected and analyzed in an integrated manner?
- How should nexus databases be developed, administered, and updated?
- How should context and scale be accounted for in modeling the nexus and making technical, nontechnical, and policy strategic decisions about interventions across the nexus?
- How should objective (rational) and subjective (intuitive) decision-making be balanced when deciding on interventions across the nexus?
- How should interventions be implemented to ensure long-term benefits and resilience at the community level?
- What indicators confirm the integrated nature of solutions across the nexus and the success of these solutions?
- What defines success in integrating the nexus sectors at the community level, and how can synergies be maximized and trade-offs reduced?
- What should the expected quality and comprehensiveness of the solutions to the nexus at the community level be?
- What is the best way to identify the leverage points of intervention across the nexus?

In addition to the questions outlined above, there is also a need to understand the multi-stakeholder dynamic between those who make decisions across the nexus (the outsiders) and those who rely on the community level (the insiders) nexus for their daily well-being. More specifically, there is a need to identify who (i) participates in modeling and making decisions across the nexus, (ii) defines and selects the indicators and performance metrics of success, and (iii) is responsible for the selection, implementation, operation, and assessment (monitoring and evaluation) of the proposed solutions and interventions. These four questions can be framed within the broader discussion of participatory community development, as discussed in Chapter 5.

All the questions above are open-ended and are far from being systemically addressed in the development literature. Systemically answering these questions would help, in general, better understand the dynamics at play across the nexus of interest, develop appropriate solutions, and inform policymaking at the community level. As discussed in Chapter 9, a systems-based methodology is necessary to accomplish these tasks.

2.6   CONCLUDING REMARKS

This chapter focused on defining the three sectors of the PSC nexus and their direct and indirect influence and dependence. There are multiple pathways for human development and security to unfold over time, involving different levels of peace, sustainability, and climate security. There is often weak and contradictory evidence regarding what drives what in nexus situations and the causal chains between peace, sustainability, and climate security, or their opposites. Ultimately, the question is whether decisions made in the landscape of interest support sustainable processes that strengthen peaceful coexistence and decrease the likelihood of vulnerability to climate change and other events.

Many questions remain about what determinants, indicators, and metrics best describe the three states, their direct and indirect interactions, and how they interact with community systems for a specific community context and scale. Another question is how to relate the causal pathways to community development and security.

NOTE

1   More details can be found on the website https://sdginterlinkages.iges.jp/vizualisation-tool.html for Bangladesh.

REFERENCES

Amadei, B. (2019). *A systems approach to modeling the water-energy-land-food nexus*. Vols. *I* and *II*. Momentum Press.

Amadei, B. (2020). Revisiting positive peace using systems tools. *Journal of Technological Forecasting and Social Change*, *57*(11), 1724–1745. https://doi.org/10.1016/j.techfore.2020.120149

American Society of Civil Engineers (ASCE). (2013). The role of the civil engineer in sustainable development. Policy statement 418. Policy Statement 418- The role of the civil engineer in sustainable development | ASCE

Angelo, P. J. (2021, March 22). Why Central American migrants are arriving at the U.S. Border. Council on Foreign Relations. Why Central American Migrants Are Arriving at the U.S. Border | Council on Foreign Relations (cfr.org)

Arcade, J., Godet, M., Meunier, F., & Roubelat, F. (2014). Structural analysis with the MICMAC method and the Actor's strategy with the MACTOR method. In J. C. Glenn and T. J. Gordon (eds.), *Introduction to the futures methods research series*. Futures research methodology, V3.0, The Millennium Project, Washington, DC.

Arctic Monitoring and Assessment Programme (AMAP). (2021). Arctic climate change update 2021: Key trends and impacts. Summary for Policymakers. Arctic Monitoring and Assessment Programme (AMAP), Tromsø, Norway. p. 16. Arctic Climate Change Update 2021: Key Trends and Impacts. Summary for Policy-makers | AMAP

Armah, F. A., Luginaah, I., Tambang, Y. G., Taabazuing, J., & Yawson, D. O. (2014). Management of natural resources in a conflicting environment in Ghana: Unmasking a messy policy problem. *Journal of Environmental Planning and Management*, *57*(11), 1724–1745. https://doi.org/10.1080/09640568.2013.834247

Backer, D. A., & Huth, P. K. (2016). The peace and conflict instability ledger: Ranking states on future risks. In D. Backer, R. Bhavnani and P. Huth (eds.), *Peace and Conflict 2016*. Routledge.

Barbier, E. B., & Burgess, J. C. (2017). The sustainable development goals and the systems approach to sustainability. *Economics E-Journal*, *11*. https://doi.org/10.5018/economics-ejournal.ja.2017-28

Barlas, Y. (1996). Formal aspects of model validity and validation in system dynamics. *System Dynamics Review*, *12*(3), 183–210. https://doi.org/10.1002/(sici)1099-1727(199623)12:3%3c183::aid-sdr103%3e3.0.co;2-4

Beckett, M. (2006). Retrieved May 12, 2021, from Margaret Beckett - 2006 Speech in Berlin - UKPOL.CO.UK

BenDor, T., & Scheffran, J. (2019). *Agent-based modeling of environmental conflict and cooperation*. CRC Press, Taylor & Francis.

Ben-Eli, M. (2012). The cybernetics of sustainability: Definition and underlying principles. Chapter 22. In: J. Murray, G. Cawthorne, A. C. Dey and C. Andrew (eds.), *Enough, For All Forever. A Handbook for Learning about Sustainability (On Sustainability)*. Common Ground Publishing.

Ben-Eli, M. (2015). Sustainability: Definition and five core principles, a new framework. A Sustainability Laboratory publication, New York, NY. SL5CorePrinciples.pdf (sustainabilitylabs.org)

Ben-Eli, M. (2018). Sustainability: Definition and five core principles: A systems perspective. *Sustainability Science*, *13*, 1337–1343. https://doi.org/10.1007/s11625-018-0564-3

Birnbaum, M. (2022, November 17). How climate stress contributed to the collapse of ancient Egypt. *The Washington Post*. Egypt, hosting U.N. climate talks, has a history of climate collapse - The Washington Post

Brown, O., & Nicolucci-Altman, G. (2022). *The white paper on the future of environmental peacebuilding*. Geneva Peacebuilding Platform, International Union for Conservation of Nature, Peace Nexus Foundation, Environmental Law Institute, Environmental Peacebuilding Association. Ecosystem for Peace.

Caldwell, R. (2002). *Project design handbook*. Cooperative for Assistance and Relief Everywhere (CARE).

Center for Climate and Security. (2021). Climate security 101. http://www.climatesecurity101.org/

Chen, C., Noble, I., Hellmann, J., Coffee, J., Murillo, M., & Chawla, N. (2015). Notre dame global adaptation index country index technical report. Environmental change initiative. University of Notre Dame. Microsoft Word - Technical document - Country ND-GAIN Index - Nov 2015.docx

Climate Change Performance Index (CCPI). (n.d.). Climate Change Performance Index (CCPI)

Collaborative for Development Action (CDA). (2023). Environment-fragility-peace nexus. Retrieved April 10, 2023, from Environment-Fragility-Peace Nexus - CDA Collaborative

Coopman, A., Osborn, D., Ullah, F., Auckland, E., & Long, G. (2016). *Seeing the whole: Implementing the SDGs in an integrated and coherent way.* The Stakeholder Forum. Seeing-the-Whole-Implementing-SDGs-in-an-Integrated-and-Coherent-Way.pdf (local2030.org)

Cortright, D. (2008). *Peace: A history of movements and ideas.* Cambridge University Press.

Darwish, S. (2023). *Resilience and social cohesion in Fiji's climate-affected informal settlements: An environment-fragility-peace nexus project case study.* CDA Collaborative Learning Projects, with contributions from Conciliation Resources and the Pacific Center for Peacebuilding. Resilience and Social Cohesion in Fiji's Climate-Affected Informal Settlements - CDA Collaborative

Davis, Q. (2016). Building infrastructure for peace: The role of liaison offices in Myanmar's peace process. A Center for Peace and Conflict Studies learning paper. Australian Government.

De Coning, C., & Maalim, H. M. (2022, November 23). The case for integrating sustaining peace into an expanded climate, peace and security concept. IPI Global Observatory. The Case for Integrating Sustaining Peace into an Expanded Climate, Peace and Security Concept | IPI Global Observatory (theglobalobservatory.org)

Diamond, L. & McDonald, J. (1996). *Multi-track diplomacy: A systems approach to peace.* (3rd ed.). Kumarian Press.

Dietrich, W. (2012). *Interpretations of peace in history and culture.* Palgrave Macmillan.

Dietrich, W., & Pearce, J. (2019). Many violences, many peaces. *Peacebuilding, 7*(3), 1–15. https://doi.org/10.1080/21647259.2019.1632056

Environmental Peacebuilding Association. (n.d.). Environmental Peacebuilding | Welcome to Environmental Peacebuilding Knowledge Platform

Environmental Protection Agency (EPA) (n.d.). Climate change indicators in the United States. View the Indicators | US EPA

Everyday peace indicators (EPI). (2016). Codebook - EPI categories. Microsoft Word - Codebook – EPI Categories copy.docx (everydaypeaceindicators.org)

Federation Internationale des Ingenieurs Conseils (FIDIC). (2013). *Project sustainability management.* International Federation of Consulting Engineers. FIDIC | Project Sustainability Management - Applications Manual - 2nd edition 2013 | International Federation of Consulting Engineers

Fischer, D. (2007). Peace as a self-regulating process. In C. Webel and J. Galtung (eds.), *Handbook of peace and conflict* studies, Chapter 13, Routledge.

Galpern, D. M. (2021). A view from Glasgow. *Sustainability and climate change, 14*(6). https://doi.org/10.1089/scc.2021.0079

Galtung, J. (1964). An editorial. *Journal of Peace Research, 1*(1), 1–4. https://doi.org/10.1177/002234336400100101

Galtung, J. (1990) Cultural violence. *Journal of Peace Research, 27*(3), 291–305. https://www.jstor.org/stable/423472

Gaston, E., Brown, O., Al-Dawsari, N., Downing, C., Day, A., & Bodewig, R. (2023). Climate-security and peacebuilding: Thematic review. UN Univeristy - Center for Policy Research. climate_security_tr_web_final_april10.pdf (un.org)

Gebre, Y. (2003). Resettlement and the unnoticed losers: Impoverishment disasters among the Gumz in Ethiopia. *Human Organization, 62*(1), 50–61. https://doi.org/10.17730/humo.62.1.4ava5ykea9p0vk10

Gittins, P., & Velasquez-Castellanos, I. O. (2016). *Peace and conflict in Bolivia.* Konrad Adenauer Stiftung.

Glass, N (2010). The water crisis in Yemen: Causes, consequences, and solutions. *Global Majority E-Journal, 1*(1), 17–3.

Gleick, P. H. (2014). Water, drought, climate change, and conflict in Syria. *American Meteorological Society, 6*, 331–340. https://doi.org/10.1175/WCAS-D-13-00059.1

Gleick, P. H. (2019). Water as a weapon and casualty of armed conflict: A review of recent water-related violence in Iraq, Syria, and Yemen. WIREs Water. https://doi.org/10.1002/wat2.1351

Grewal, B.J. (2003). *Johan Galtung: Positive and negative peace*. School of Social Science, Auckland University of Technology.

Griggs, D., Reyers, B., & Stafford-Smith, M. (n.d.) *A systems approach: Imperative to achieve the sustainable development goals*. https://futureearth.org/publications/explainers/a-systems-approach/

Griggs, D., Smith, M. S., Gaffney, O., & Noble, I. (2013). Sustainable development goals for people and planet. *Nature*, *495*, 305–307. https://doi.org/10.1038/495305a

Groff, L. (2008). Contributions of different cultural-religious traditions to different aspects of peace - Leading to a holistic, integrative view of peace for the twenty-first century independent world. *FUTUREtakes*, 7(1). v7n1_article8.pdf (futuretakes.org)

Gue, I. H.V., Ubando, A. T., Tseng, M. L., & Tan, R. R. (2020). Artificial neural networks for sustainable development: A critical review. *Clean Technologies and Environmental Policy*, *22*, 1449–1465. https://doi.org/10.1007/s10098-020-01883-2

Hammond, R. A., & Dube, L. (2012). A systems science perspective and transdisciplinary models for food and nutrition security. *Proceedings of the National Academy of Sciences of the United States of America*, *109*(31), 12356–12363. https://doi.org/10.1073/pnas.0913003109

Haskins, C. (2021). Systems engineering for sustainable development goals. *Sustainability*, *13*(18), 10293. https://doi.org/10.3390/su131810293

Hayden, N. K., Hardesty, J. O. E., Bull, D. L., Eicken, H., Bennett, A., Passell, H. D., & Backus, G. A. (2020). Peace Engineering in the Arctic: Accommodating diverse interests in a changing environment. Peace Engineering in the Arctic: Accommodating diverse interests in a changing environment. (osti.gov)

Hjort, J., Streletskiy, D., Doré, G., Wu, Q. Bjella, K., & Luoto, M. (2022). Impacts of permafrost degradation on infrastructure. *Nature Reviews Earth & Environment*, *3*, 24–38. https://doi.org/10.1038/s43017-021-00247-8

Hjorth, P. & Bagheri, A. (2006). Navigating towards sustainable development: A system dynamics approach. *Futures*, *38*, 74–92. https://doi.org/10.1016/j.futures.2005.04.005

Hoff, H. (2011). Understanding the Nexus. Background Paper for the Bonn 2011 Conference: The Water, Energy and Food Security Nexus. Stockholm Environment Institute, Stockholm. SEI-Paper-Hoff-UnderstandingTheNexus-2011.pdf (water-energy-food.org)

Holland, J. H. (1999). *Emergence: From chaos to order*. Basic Books.

Institute for Economics & Peace (IEP). (2017). *Positive peace report 2017: Tracking peace transitions through a systems thinking approach*. http://visionofhumanity.org/reports

Institute for Economics & Peace (IEP). (2018). *Positive peace report 2018: Analyzing the factors that sustain peace. Measuring peace in a complex world*. http://visionofhumanity.org/reports

Institute for Economics & Peace (IEP). (2019). *Global peace index 2019: Measuring peace in a complex world*. http://visionofhumanity.org/reports

Institute for Economics & Peace (IEP). (2022). *Positive peace report 2022: Analyzing the factors that build, predict, and sustain peace*. http://visionofhumanity.org/resources

Institute for Sustainable Infrastructure. (ISI). (2018). *Envision® sustainable infrastructure framework guidance manual*. https://sustainableinfrastructure.org/wp-content/uploads/EnvisionV3.9.7.2018.pdf

International Council for Science (ICSU). (2015). *Review of the sustainable development goals: The science perspective*. International Council for Science.

Kelley, C. P., Mohtadi, S. Cane, M. A., Seager, R., & Kushnir, Y. (2015). Climate change in the Fertile Crescent and implications of the recent Syrian drought. *Proceedings of the U.S. National Academy of Sciences*, *112*(11), 3241–3246. https://doi.org/10.1073/pnas.1421533112

Killelea, S. (2021). *Peace in the age of chaos: The best solution for a sustainable future*. Hardie Grant Books.

Kotob, F. (2011). What is sustainability? https://www.researchgate.net/publication/282184670_What_Is_Sustainability

LaFortune, G., Fuller, G., Moreno, J., Schmidt-Traub, G., & Kroll, C. (2018). *SDG index and dashboards detailed methodological paper*. New York (NY, US): Bertelsmann Stiftung and Sustainable Development Solutions Network (SDSN). 2018 Global Index Methodology.pdf (lmsp.lv)

Lawler, P. & Williams, P. D. (ed.). (2008). Peace studies. In *Security Studies: An Introduction*. Routledge.

Lazard. (2019). *Lazard's levelized cost of energy analysis-Version 13.0*; Lazard: New York, NY, USA.

Lederach, J. P. (2012). The origins and evolutions of infrastructures for peace: A personal reflection. Journal *Peacebuilding & Development*, 7(3), 8–13. https://www.jstor.org/stable/48603417

Lemos, C. M. (2018). *Agent-based modeling of social conflict: From mechanism to complex behavior*. Springer Cham.

Lim, M. M. L., Søgaard Jørgensen, P., & Wyborn, C. A. (2018). Reframing the sustainable development goals to achieve sustainable development in the Anthropocene-a systems approach. *Ecology and Society*, 23(3), 22. https://doi.org/10.5751/ES-10182-230322

Luers, A. L., & Sklar, L. S. (2013). The difficult, the dangerous, and the catastrophic: Managing the spectrum of climate risks. *Earth's Future*, 2, 114–118. https://doi.org/10.1073/pnas.200272211

McConnell, J. R., Sigl, M., Plunkett, G., Burke, A., Kim, W. M., Raible, C. C., Wilson, A. I., Manning, J. G., Ludlow, F., Chellman, N. J., Innes, H. M., Yang, Z., Larsen, J. F., Schaefer, J. R., Kipfstuhl, S., Mojtabavi, S., Wilhelms, F., Opel, T., Meyer, H., & Steffensen, J. P. (2020). Extreme climate after the massive eruption of Alaska's Okmok volcano in 43 BCE and its effects on the late Roman Republic and the Ptolemaic Kingdom. *PNAS*, 17(27), 15443–15449. https://doi.org/10.1073/pnas.200272211

Meadows, D. (2008). *Thinking in systems*. Chelsea Green Publishing.

Mitleton-Kelly, E. (2003). Ten principles of complexity and enabling infrastructures. *Chapter 2 in complex systems and evolutionary perspectives of organizations: The application of complex theory to organizations*. Elsevier.

Monbiot, G. (2021, October 30). Capitalism is killing the planet – it's time to stop buying into our own destruction. Capitalism is killing the planet – it's time to stop buying into our own destruction | Climate crisis | The Guardian

Morton, S., Pencheon, D., & Aquires, N. (2017). Sustainable Development Goals (SDGs) and their implementation: A national global framework for health, development, and equity needs a systems approach at every level. *British Medical Bulletin*, 124(1), 81–90. https://doi.org/10.1093/bmb/ldx031

Mustafa, D.. Akhter, M., & Nasralla, N. (2013). Understanding Pakistan's water-security nexus. Peaceworks No. 88. US Institute of Peace, Washington DC. PW88_cover_final.indd (usip.org)

National Adaptation Plan (NAP). (n.d.). National Adaptation Plans | UNFCCC

Nett, K., & Ruttinger, L. (2017). Insurgency, terrorism, and organized crime in a warming climate. Adelphi. Insurgency, Terrorism and Organised Crime in a Warming Climate (lsu.edu)

Nilsson, M., Lucas, P., & Yoshida, T. (2013). Towards an integrated framework for the SDGs: Ultimate and enabling goals for the case of energy. *Sustainability (Switzerland)*, 5(10), 4124–4151. https://doi.org/10.3390/su5104124

Nilsson, M., Griggs, D., & Visback, M. (2016). Map the interactions between sustainable development goals. *Nature*, 534(15), 320–322. https://doi.org/10.1038/534320a

Public Broadcasting Service (PBS). (2022, August 15). The Arctic is warming nearly four times faster than the rest of the world. The Arctic is warming nearly four times faster than the rest of the world | PBS NewsHour

Peacedirect. (2022, September 20). Migration and peacebuilding. Migration & Peacebuilding - Peace Direct

Pedercini, M., Arquitt, S., & Chan, D. (2020). Integrated simulation for the 2030 agenda. *System Dynamics Review*, *36*, 333–357. https://doi.org/10.1002/sdr.1665

Peters, K., Dupar, M., Opitz-Stapleton, S., Lovell, E., & Cao, Y. (2020). Climate change, conflict, and fragility; An evidence review and recommendations for research and action. Climate change, conflict, and fragility: an evidence review and recommendations for research and action | ODI: Think change

Prigogine, J., & Stengers, I. (1984). *Order out of chaos: Man's new dialogue with nature.* Bantam Books.

Pulley, K. (2021). A systems approach to understanding the Yemen civil war and humanitarian crisis. Term paper, CVEN 5837, University of Colorado, Boulder.

Raha, S. (2017, October 17). What does brushing twice a day have to do with profits and impact? http://www.dailygood.org/story/1737/what-does-brushing-twice-a-day-have-to-do-with-profits-and-impact-somik-raha/

Randers, J., Rockström, J., Stoknes, P., Goluke, U., Collste, D., Cornell, S., & Donges, J. (2019). Achieving the 17 sustainable development goals within 9 planetary boundaries. *Global Sustainability*, *2*, e24. https://doi.org/10.1017/sus.2019.22

Reychler, L., & Paffenholz, T. (eds.). (2001). *Peace-building: A field guide*. Lynne Rienner Publishing.

Rocha, J. C., Baraibar, M. M., Deutsch, L., de Bremond, A., Oestreicher, J. S., Rositano, F., & Gelabert, C. C. (2019). Toward understanding the dynamics of land change in Latin America: Potential utility of a resilience approach for building archetypes of land systems change. *Ecology and Society*, *24*(1). https://www.jstor.org/stable/26796908

Rotmans, J., & deVries, B. (eds.). (1997). *Perspectives on global change: The TARGETS approach*. Cambridge University Press.

Ryan, C. (2020). Introduction to the 5Ps. PowerPoint Presentation (unescap.org)

Sachs, J. D., Schmidt-Traub, G., Mazzucato, M., Messner, D., Nakicenovic, N., & Rockström, J. (2019). Six transformations to achieve the sustainable development goals. *Nature Sustainability*, *2*, 805–814. https://doi.org/10.1038/s41893-019-0352-9

Sachs, J., Kroll, C., Lafortune, G., Fuller, G., & Woelm, F. (2021). *The decade of action for the sustainable development goals: Sustainable development report 2021*. Cambridge University Press.

Scharlemann, J. P. W., Brock, R. C., Balfour, N., & Brown, C. (2020). Towards understanding interactions between sustainable development goals: The role of environment-human linkages. *Sustainability Science*, *15*, 1573–1584. https://doi.org/10.1007/s11625-020-00799-6

Schmidt-Traub, G. (2015). *Indicators and a monitoring framework for the SDGs: Launching a revolution for the SDGs*. Sustainable Development Solutions. Indicators and a Monitoring Framework for Sustainable Development Goals: Launching a data revolution for the SDGs (unsdsn.org).

Schwartzstein, P., & Risi, L (2023, January 26). Climate change and migration: Reporting from Bangladesh, Moldova, and Senegal. Wilson Center environmental change and security program. Climate Change and Migration: Reporting from Bangladesh, Moldova, and Senegal | Wilson Center

Selby, J., Dahi, O.S., Fröhlich, C., & Hulme, M. (2017). Climate change and the Syrian civil war revisited. *Political Geography*, *60*, 232–244. https://doi.org/10.1016/j.polgeo.2017.05.007

Sharifi, A., Simangan, D., Kaneko, S., & Virji, H. (2021a). The sustainability-peace nexus: Why is it important? *Sustainability Science*, *16*, 1073–1077. https://doi.org/10.1007/s11625-021-00986-z

Sharifi, A., Simangan, D., Lee, C. Y., Reyes, S. R., Katramiz, T., Josol, J., dos Muchangos, L., Virji, H., Kaneko, S., Tandog, T., Tandog, L., & Islam, M. (2021b). Climate-induced stressors to peace: A review of recent literature. *Environmental Research Letters*, *16*, 073006. https://doi.org/10.1088/1748-9326/abfc08

Sharifi, A., Simangan, D., & Kaneko, S. (2021c). The literature landscape on peace sustainability nexus: A scientometric analysis. *Ambio*, *50*(3), 661–678. https://doi.org/10.1007/s13280-020-01388-8

Strengthening Partnerships, Results, and Innovations in Nutrition Globally (SPRING). (2015). *A systems thinking and action for nutrition*. USAID/ Project. Systems Thinking and Action for Nutrition | SPRING (spring-nutrition.org)

Stearns, P. N. (2014). *Peace in world history*. Routledge.

Suter, M. (2017, September 12). Running out of water: Conflict and water scarcity in Yemen and Syria. https://www.atlanticcouncil.org/blogs/menasource/running-out-of-water-conflict-and-water-scarcity-in-yemen-and-syria

Tesfaye, B. (2002). Climate change and conflict in the Sahel. Council on Foreign Relations. Center for Preventive action. Climate Change and Conflict in the Sahel (cfr.org)

The Earth Charter. (1987). Read the Earth Charter - Earth Charter

The Humanitarian Development Peace Triple-Nexus Explained. (2019, November 20). The Humanitarian Development Peace Triple-Nexus Explained – Humanitarian Advisors

The Nature Conservancy. (2018, October 13). The science of sustainability. Can a unified path for development and conservation lead to a better future? A Sustainable Future: Two Paths to 2050 (nature.org)

The World in 2050 (TWI2050). (2020). Innovations for sustainability. Pathways to an efficient and post-pandemic future. Report prepared by The World in 2050 initiative. International Institute for Applied Systems Analysis (IIASA), Laxenburg, Austria. www.twi2050.org

United Nations (UN). (2015). Transforming our world: The 2030 agenda for sustainable development. Transforming our world: The 2030 Agenda for Sustainable Development | Department of Economic and Social Affairs (un.org)

UNDP Human Development Report (UNDP/HDR). (1990). *Concepts and measurement of human development*. United Nations Development Progamme.

United Nations Economic and Social Commission for Western Asia (UNESCWA). (2021). the_5ps_of_the_sustainable_development_goals.pdf (unescwa.org)

United Nations Political and Peacebuilding Affairs (UN-PPA). (n.d.). Addressing the impact of climate change on peace and security. Addressing the Impact of Climate Change on Peace and Security | Department of Political and Peacebuilding Affairs (un.org).

U.S. Agency for International Development (USAID). (2014). *Evaluating systems and systemic change for inclusive market development*. USAID.

Vidal, J. (2016, September 7). Water supplies in Syria deteriorating fast due to conflict, experts warn. https://www.theguardian.com/environment/2016/sep/07/water-supplies-in-syria-deteriorating-fast-due-to-conflict-experts-warn

Vladimirova, K., & Le Blanc, D. (2016). Exploring links between education and sustainable development goals Through the lens of UN flagship reports. *Sustainable Development*, *24*(4), 254–271. https://doi.org/10.1002/sd.1626

von Lossow, T., Schrijver, A., van der Kroon, M., van Schaik, L., & Meester, J. (2021). Towards a better understanding of climate security practices. PSI-2021_Climate-Security-Practices_final.pdf (planetarysecurityinitiative.org)

Waage, J., Yap, C., & Bell, S. (2015). Governing the sustainable development goals: Interactions, infrastructures, and institutions. *The Lancet Global Health*, *376*(5), https://doi.org/10.1016/s2214-109x(15)70112-9

Werrell, C. E., & Femia, F. (eds.). (2013, February 28). *The Arab spring and climate change: A climate and security correlations series*. climatechangearabspring-ccs-cap-stimson.pdf (wordpress.com)

Whitworth, H. (2021). Understanding the Syrian Conflict through a system less. *Term paper, CVEN 5837*, University of Colorado, Boulder.

Wikipedia. The Laki volcano. Laki - Wikipedia (Retrieved January 1, 2022).

3 Changing The Narrative

3.1 REDUCTIONISM AND POSITIVISM

Since the seventeenth and eighteenth centuries of the Enlightenment, Western science has been dominated by a default reductionistic view of reality that looks at the universe as a great stable mechanism that consists of fixed parts, is comprised of physical phenomena, and is governed by universal laws (physical determinism). In *Discourse on the Method* (1637), Descartes enunciated four basic rules to evaluate reality:

- "Never accept anything for true which I did not clearly know to be such; that is to say, carefully to avoid precipitancy and prejudice, and to comprise nothing more in my judgment than what was presented to my mind so clearly and distinctly as to exclude all ground of doubt."
- "Divide each of the difficulties under examination into as many parts as possible and as might be necessary for its adequate solution."
- "To conduct my thoughts in such order that, by commencing with objects the simplest and easiest to know, I might ascend by little and little, and, as it were, step by step, to the knowledge of the more complex; assigning in thought a certain order even to those objects which in their own nature do not stand in a relation of antecedence and sequence.
- "In every case to make enumerations so complete, and reviews so general, that I might be assured that nothing was omitted."

The mechanistic worldview envisioned by Descartes was further reinforced by other scientists and Western philosophers of the Enlightenment (e.g., Newton, Bacon, Kant, etc.). Since then, a fragmented and objective approach to understanding reality, where parts are assumed to be independent of each other and addressed in isolation, has dominated Western culture. It was first adopted in the natural and physical sciences and was extended into social and behavioral sciences. This dominant worldview is responsible for how today's institutions (social, educational, economic, etc.) are organized into disciplines, sectors, specializations, parts, etc., and hierarchically run on the power of instructions. It is also responsible for how humanity sees humans as separate from each other and nature as a machine to be controlled. Finally, it relies on the opinion of experts who do not necessarily collaborate and follow a rational decision-making model. As noted by BenDor and Scheffran (2019; based on the remarks of Shmueli et al., 2008), these experts "work in isolation, define problems, collect and select the information they deem to be objective (scientific), build technical models pointing the way toward problem explanations, and thereafter, unilaterally develop optimal solutions for use by formal decision makers." This "barbarism of specialization" approach (Ortega y Gasset, 1994) and "false security

DOI: 10.1201/9781003435006-3

of linear, disciplinary and reductionistic ways of thinking and working" (Woodhill and Milicant, 2023) have been dominant in dealing with human development and security issues.

Combined with positivism, which adds that reality can only be explained rationally and is devoid of choice, values, and consciousness, reductionism has been used to address issues of a world that does not resemble the real one. Because of its tunnel vision, it can only capture a small fraction of the web-like nature of reality.

Another limiting aspect of the reductionistic approach has been its command-and-control approach to how problems, in general, should be addressed. First, to be considered, the issues must be "well-rounded, clearly defined, relatively simple, and generally linear with respect to cause and effect" (Harford, 2012) and quantifiable. Second, problems must have solutions expected to be "direct, appropriate, feasible, and effective over most relevant spatial and temporal scales" (Holling and Meffe, 1995). Third, the solutions must not evolve or adapt over time (Harford, 2012). Finally, the solutions must be predictable and optimal (best). Simply put, such expectations are impossible in the uncertain and unfamiliar settings where development occurs.

As illustrated in Figure 3.1, various Western thinkers have recognized the limitations of the deterministic view of the universe, despite being dominant for the past 400 years (Lent, 2017). There has been a strong realization starting in the 1920s and especially after WWII that Descartes' rules of reality are not universal, and reductionism cannot explain real-world organized complexity, wholeness, and multiple issues that are ill-defined, messy, and sometimes referred to as "wicked" (Rittel and Weber, 1973).

It is not that traditional reductionistic thinking is wrong per se; it is simply not always right. It must be kept in mind that people were sent to the Moon and back

FIGURE 3.1   From reductionism to real-world complexity and wholeness.

Source: Image credit Virpi Oinonen: http://www.businessillustrator.com/ (used with permission).

multiple times with Newton's three fundamental laws and the law of universal gravitation. Reductionist thinking has demonstrated its merits when dealing with simple (predictable and obvious) and complicated systems (we know the unknowns but need experts). Our modern way of life has significantly benefited from using reductionistic thinking in science, engineering, and technology; think of contemporary forms of transportation and telecommunication, medical breakthroughs, etc.

Reductionistic thinking is, however, inadequate to address the complex human development and security issues mentioned in Section 1.1 at the start of this book. These complex issues are often characterized by different degrees of ambiguity, uncertainty, and experience emergence. As explored in this book, they must be handled with more advanced analysis methods borrowed from various branches of systems science and the scientific study of complexity (Waldrop, 1992; Laszlo, 2001; Mitleton-Kelly, 2003). Table 3.1 lists a series of questions for decision-makers to decide whether a "systems practice" is better suited to address challenges they may face or use more traditional reductionistic and deterministic approaches.

The value proposition of using a systems practice and associated tools is especially relevant when addressing nexus problems that cannot be resolved using a compartmentalized approach. By definition, nexus issues involve the interaction of several linked sectors like the peace, sustainability, and climate security sectors considered in this book. Other nexus types that have been addressed using systems thinking include, for instance, the water-energy, water-energy-food, and water-energy-land-food nexus (Amadei, 2019), the humanitarian aid-development-climate change nexus, and the food-healthcare-nutrition nexus (SPRING, 2015). Unlike the traditional reductionist approach to addressing the sectors in isolation (i.e., as decoupled), nexus thinking requires decision-makers to adopt an integrated perspective that considers the characteristics of each nexus component, their connectedness, and the attributes of their linkages. In short, nexus thinking is systems thinking, and decision-makers need to be systems thinkers, as discussed in Chapter 4.

Unfortunately, even though a "systems practice" has been recognized as better suited to address complex problems, the progress in using such a practice has been slow and met with reservations in the literature. There has been a lot of contention, especially in academia, since the 1950s about whether a systems approach could be used in some disciplines (e.g., social, political, and economic sciences) versus more technical ones such as engineering and physics. The jury is still out on that dispute and has many academic opponents, pragmatists, and supporters. Despite that dispute, the first two decades of the Twenty-first century have nevertheless witnessed a new enthusiasm for exploring the value proposition of using a systems perspective in addressing complex world issues. It is likely to gain more momentum in the decades to come.

3.2   A NEW POST-2020 MINDSET

A new mindset is urgently needed for humanity to navigate a post-2020 world, which Tooley (2021) describes as volatile, uncertain, complex, and ambiguous (VUCA). In that unpredictable world:

TABLE 3.1
Choosing Between Traditional and Systems Practices

How Complex is Your Challenge? Use This Chart to Reflect on the Complexity of Your Challenge. A Systems Practice May be a Good Match if You Lean Toward the Right on These Complexity Spectrums

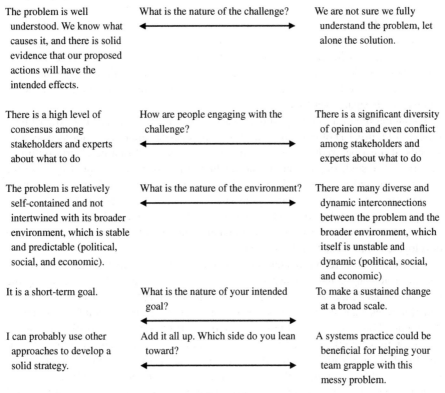

The problem is well understood. We know what causes it, and there is solid evidence that our proposed actions will have the intended effects.	What is the nature of the challenge?	We are not sure we fully understand the problem, let alone the solution.
There is a high level of consensus among stakeholders and experts about what to do	How are people engaging with the challenge?	There is a significant diversity of opinion and even conflict among stakeholders and experts about what to do
The problem is relatively self-contained and not intertwined with its broader environment, which is stable and predictable (political, social, and economic).	What is the nature of the environment?	There are many diverse and dynamic interconnections between the problem and the broader environment, which itself is unstable and dynamic (political, social, and economic)
It is a short-term goal.	What is the nature of your intended goal?	To make a sustained change at a broad scale.
I can probably use other approaches to develop a solid strategy.	Add it all up. Which side do you lean toward?	A systems practice could be beneficial for helping your team grapple with this messy problem.

Source: The Omidyar Group (2017) under Attribution-Share Alike 4.0. International.

- *Volatility* refers to changes becoming more unpredictable and dramatic and happening quicker and more often. Cause and effects are difficult to capture.
- *Uncertainty* deals with the difficulty of anticipating and predicting events, even based on experience.
- *Complexity* deals with nontrivial self-organization, adaptation, feedback mechanisms, emergence, and difficulty relating different events.
- *Ambiguity* is no longer about one-size-fits-all solutions and dualistic deci-sion-making. Paradoxes and contradictions are the norms. Learning lessons from mistakes is critical.

A VUCA world requires individuals and organizations to (i) be flexible and adap-tive to changing conditions, (ii) make decisions when faced with uncertainty, (iii) navigate ambiguous and complex situations, (iv) innovate quickly, and (v) take risks and fail fast to learn and improve. All these require adopting a new mindset, which according to Meadows (1997) and discussed in Section 1.6.3, represents the place (i.e., leverage) to intervene with the highest return on investment. In human development and security, the system can be at the scale of the individual, a community, a country, or the planet.

Changing the mindset can be illustrated as riding two S-shaped curves of change, as shown in Figure 3.2, from the current ways of doing things (i.e., the reductionistic and deterministic approach) with limited interactions to new ways of doing things (i.e., a systemic approach) with more interactions. The new ways of doing things build on innovations and lessons learned from the past. The old ways of doing things decrease with time but still have residual components that may initially create roadblocks to change but dissipate over time.

Changing the mindset deep into the psyche (recall the lower layers of the iceberg model in Figure 1.1) of current institutions and decision-making is not as easy as it sounds. It must be gradual, and its value proposition must first be clearly outlined, understood, tested, implemented, and evaluated before being adopted by multiple stakeholders and decision-makers and becoming mainstream. Moreover, adopting a new mindset is initially challenging since it implies some behavior change and accepting new mental models. This change usually takes time and can be difficult for more conservative stakeholders, policymakers, and practitioners involved in human development and security-related issues.

Interestingly, the recommendation of adopting a new post-2020 mindset is not new and was often suggested in general terms in the 2020 vernacular literature during the COVID-19 pandemic. It was common to read at that time, for instance, that for many constituencies changing the mindset was about "adopting a new normal" and required "pivoting." This naïve concept ignored that there was never a one-size-fits-all normal to start with before the pandemic but rather multiple normal(s), some better than others. In addition, pivoting is okay if a vision is attached to it. Without it, there is the issue of possibly returning to the original direction after rotating by 360 degrees.

With that in mind, creating a more sustainable, stable, and equitable world where all humans live with dignity and peace must be done in an intelligent,

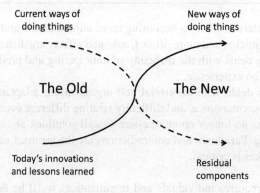

FIGURE 3.2   Riding the old and new S-shaped curves of change.

systemic, fair, and compassionate manner where normal is seen "as a plural." It requires departing from the dominant mindset of the twentieth century and the first two decades of the Twenty-first century characterized by compartmentaliza-tion, fear, greed, and for the benefit of a few. It must be acknowledged that any new normal is dynamic and characterized by "predictable unpredictability" (*The Economist*, 2021).

So, what is that new mindset we are talking about, keeping in mind the human mental filters discussed in Section 1.6.2? I outline below general characteristics (among many others) of a new systemic mindset to address the human development and security issues mentioned in this book and adequately handle potential future crises, whether natural or human-made.

3.2.1   RECONSIDER VALUES AND SOCIOECONOMIC PRIORITIES

The new mindset requires humanity to reconsider first its social, cultural, and eco-nomic values and priorities (i.e., how it sees reality) and put them into practice. A more mature level of consciousness in the day-to-day governance, management, operation, and regulation of our institutions and occupations is needed (Lent, 2021b; Laszlo, 2022). There is a growing realization that unregulated economies built on growth alone measured in terms of GDP are unable to shield society from economic and environmental hazards. As remarked by Churchman (1982) forty years ago, it is a moral outrage that "the human intellect is capable of organizing society to solve the great problems of the world, such as malnutrition, poverty, and war, and yet humanity allows these problems to persist." This statement is still relevant today since human-ity's approach to addressing its complex problems has remained unchanged since the seventeenth century.

As noted by Tanabe (2020), "A critical question is emerging that faces humanity as a whole: what should come in the first place—society or economy, strong public health or profit, citizens' physiological, psychological, intellectual and spiritual well-being or plutocracy." Another question is how to develop the value proposition that each human being can play a crucial and transforming role in fostering long-lasting world peace. The values behind these two recommendations differ from those in tra-ditional human development, where citizens are passive actors subject to policies that maximize the economic benefit [for a solid capitalist elite] while sparingly pursu-ing the social, cultural, and even spiritual development or maturation of humankind (Tanabe). These two recommendations raise the importance of development ethics in practice (Gasper, 2012). As noted by Lent (2021a), "resolving the climate crisis will require a fundamental shift away from our growth-based, corporate-based domi-nated global system" that has been dominant throughout the industrial revolution and the digital revolution up to this day.

The values and socioeconomic priorities need to be formulated and operational-ized by those who want change. As Schmidheiny (1992) noted regarding putting sustainable development into practice, the painful truth is that "many of those with the power to effect the necessary changes have the least motivation to alter the status quo that gave them the power." The same could be said about those promoting peace and climate security.

3.2.2 Promote Collective Activities, Capacity, and Resilience

Cooperation is critical to the new mindset. Collaborative and solidarity activities at different scales, from local to global, that simultaneously respect diversity, equity, and justice are urgently needed to prevent further decline in human development and security in a post-COVID-19 world (UNDP, 2020; Sachs et al., 2020). Despite the "multiple once-in-a-generation crises" faced by humanity today, there is a strong inclination worldwide toward "solidarity and looking for bolder action" to tackle these issues (Open Society Foundations, 2022) outside the spheres of influence of governments.

Collaboration is also required among the disciplines involved in addressing human development and security issues. According to Kania and Kramer (2013), what they call *collective impact* is necessary for "creating effective rules of intervention" that may lead to emerging solutions and opportunities to complex problems. Collective impact has five intentional components: (i) having a common agenda (intentionality), (ii) relying on shared data collection and measurement, (iii) combining reinforcing activities, (iv) providing continuous communication, and (v) having effective management (Kania and Kramer, 2013). Collective impact also recognizes the importance of flexibility in pursuing developmental evaluation across interacting systems. To that list, one can add the necessity of collaborators to share a standard narrative, empathy, be willing to expand the borders of creativity, think in an integrated manner, and be ready to learn from each other.

Collaboration is essential to counteract the traditional reductionistic way of addressing human development and security issues, which is to rely on experts who come up with definite, rational, but isolated well-thought solutions to actual problems in a piecemeal manner. The shortcoming of this compartmentalized and static approach is that there is no interest in understanding whether the issues (i) are interconnected and part of dynamic feedback mechanisms and (ii) share common root causes, which, if addressed together, could solve multiple issues in a more integrated and effective way.

According to Moritz (2020), to avoid further instability worldwide, socioeconomic partnerships and collaboration must simultaneously address short-term improvements to the current situation and long-term sustainability planning along five tracks: (i) *repair* what is currently most damaged; (ii) *rethink* change without going back to how things were (i.e., without rebuilding the vulnerability of business-as-usual); (iii) *reconfigure* change so that it can happen; (iv) *restart* change with the recommendations mentioned above; and (v) *report* how change progresses with the ability for course correction through monitoring and evaluation. Simply put, yesterday's socioeconomic development tools have a limited range of applications in developing the world of tomorrow. The metaphor of not placing new wine into old wineskins but using new wineskins (Mark 2:18–22) comes to mind. Therefore, critical thinking, reflective practice, innovative development tools, and priorities are needed to operate in a new socioeconomic structure. It represents a much-needed development praxis (Karwat et al., 2014; Mahon et al., 2020).

Moritz's five changing tracks emphasize the importance of building capacity and resilience (coping and adapting) at different scales (individual, household,

community, country, region, and global) in the overall discussion on human development and security for the Twenty-first century. These two concepts are not new
and have been part of the development jargon for a long time. However, a traditional
approach to building capacity and resilience has been to identify and address in a
fragmented manner specific issues at play in the systems (institutional, economic,
social, environmental, and infrastructure) in development. This approach could be,
for instance, identifying and addressing roadblocks to peace in specific areas (health,
commerce, education, etc.) by promoting specific peacebuilding practices. In sustainability, the focus might be on addressing particular SDGs. In climate security,
the priority may be to focus on infrastructure resilience to adverse events without
considering societal stability. This compartmentalized approach, driven by a need to
reach satisfactory equilibrium quickly, fails to account for possible dynamics, synergies, and trade-offs across human development and security aspects.

Since the 2020 pandemic is a "wake-up call and a training ground to enhance
our joint and resilient response to future pandemics and other external disturbances"
(TWI2050, 2020), the concepts of capacity and resilience must be reimagined, rede-
fined, and strengthened to handle future crises and not just those related to health. A
systemic approach to capacity and resilience is needed to explore possible synergies
and trade-offs in development interventions in a specific context and scale. Capacity
and resilience cut horizontally across multiple vertical silos of human development and
security. As an example, the continuous provision of services (e.g., water, energy, food,
transportation, communication, health, education, shelter, etc.) to a community requires
considering different interdependent forms of capacity (institutional, economic, human
resources, technical, environmental, cultural) and being able to identify and correct
weak forms of capacity. The vulnerability of these services depends greatly on the community's state of positive peace and its level of resilience to cope and adapt to adverse
events (natural and conflict) through awareness, adaptation, and mitigation.

3.2.3 PROMOTE INNOVATION

In 2009, the World Business Council for Sustainable Development (WBCSD, 2009)
best summarized the challenge of resource security in the Twenty-first century as
"to feed more people with less water, in a context of climate change and growing
energy demand, while maintaining healthy ecosystems." This statement emphasizes
the need for innovation in a world approaching a 10 billion and more affluent population in the Twenty-first century. Berninger (2020) noted that "it will take the brightest
minds and the smartest technologies" to provide resource security for all.

The COVID-19 pandemic has demonstrated "the power of [scientific research]
collaboration to create solutions quickly" (Gil, 2021). The new mindset must build
on such success stories and promote the importance of multisolving innovation in
human and economic development at different scales (individual, household, community, country, regional, and planetary). As suggested by TWI2050, "new thoughts,
frameworks, and methods for the STI (science, technology, and innovation) ecosystem to promote innovation, efficiency, and sufficiency for the achievement of the
SDGs" are needed. One can cite the importance of developing digital technology to
increase connectivity among different groups, especially developing communities.

Bridging the digital divide has the potential to reduce inequalities, increase local capacity, and provide more livelihood opportunities.

Innovation must lead to solutions that preferably embody the five aspects of Agenda 2030. They must be good for the people and the environment, create prosperity, promote human security and social justice, and create meaningful and just partnerships (UNESCWA, 2021). In the context of community development and the PSC nexus, the solutions must contribute to communities with the capacity and resilience to deal with adverse events and risks related to conflict, unstainable community behavior, and climate change.

The question remains regarding how to (i) educate scientists and engineers on the importance of science, technology, and engineering in the service to humanity and (ii) provide them with the necessary attitude, skills, and knowledge to address global challenges at the crossroads between peace, sustainability, and climate security in different contexts and scales. The scientific and engineering professions must embrace a new mission statement for the Twenty-first century: to contribute to building a more sustainable, stable, equitable, and peaceful world where all people have fulfilling lives, meet their basic needs, and live with dignity and peace. This new mission statement requires scientists and engineers to become more global thinkers and doers and be aware of (i) their professional and personal ethical responsibilities; (ii) their role in society as citizens; and (iii) the intended and unintended consequences of their decisions when implementing solutions for different socioeconomic, cultural and political situations. Endorsing the new mission statement represents a challenge for the science and engineering professions since it implies revisiting traditional education and practice. At the same time, it provides a unique opportunity for the scientific and engineering disciplines to demonstrate how beneficial science and engineering are to the world and, as a result, promote both to younger generations.

3.2.4 PROMOTE COMMUNITY EMPOWERMENT

The new mindset requires the interaction and participation of multiple stakeholders at different scales, from the local to the global. The stakeholders include all individuals and groups who can make or influence decisions, even those who may not have a voice in the matter but will be impacted by how the nexus unfolds (Caldwell, 2002; Dearden et al., 2003; Hovland, 2005). Stakeholders can be *critical* stakeholders (who have a strong influence), *primary* stakeholders (who are affected and have a direct stake), or *secondary* or *indirect* stakeholders (who have limited stake and impact). To that list, one can also add specific groups of stakeholders, such as opposition groups and marginalized stakeholders.

Another way to categorize all the stakeholders is to arrange them into three groups: (i) local stakeholders (e.g., community members) who contribute to bottom-up solutions; (ii) governmental institutions stakeholders who provide top-down solutions; and (iii) outsiders (e.g., NGOs, donors, private sector organizations, etc.) who contribute to outside-in solutions. The effectiveness of these three groups of stakeholder dynamics depends on many factors, such as (i) a willingness to participate in dialogue and decision-making, (ii) a capacity to make meaningful contributions, and (iii) having time for dialogue and decision-making.

The dynamic between the stakeholders involved in human development and security projects and programs must be participatory. It must also account for diversity and justice and depart from the neo-colonialist approach of the twentieth century. Until about 30 years ago, the Western world's traditional development approach was mainly top-down informative, contractual, and consultative, with limited input from the bottom-up beneficiaries. More recently, there has been more emphasis on promoting collaborative and collegial practices and transformation through involvement, collaboration, and empowerment (Cornwall and Jewkes, 1995; Checkland and Poulter, 2006). Yet, development shaped by external actors (e.g., multilateral agencies, bilateral in-country agencies, NGOs, and the private sector) is still a dominant way of interacting between the three groups of stakeholders mentioned above. This remark must come with the caveat that many of these external actors are interested in exploring alternative models of participatory interaction using a systems approach but are confused about how to do it.

3.2.5   PROMOTE THE RIGHT RELATIONSHIPS

The new mindset includes a need for humanity to adopt forms of proper relationships (i.e., stewardship) with all forms of life on Earth and not just humans, as described in The Earth Charter and Planetary Health Alliance. It is also the backbone of native and indigenous traditions (Cajete, 2020) that have often been marginalized in Western societies (Jessen et al., 2021). Table 3.2 lists the attributes of two different mindsets (old and new) regarding how humans relate to nature, and as a result, to each other. Greater solidarity is needed at the planetary level to ensure human security in the years to come (UNDP/HDR, 2022).

According to the National Peace Academy (n.d.), right relationships and peace go hand in hand and manifest at five different but synergistic levels: (i) *personal,* with an emphasis on developing proper relationships with ourselves; (ii) *social,* with relationships with others; (iii) *political,* where relationships are established within and between groups of people, communities, and organizations; (iv) *institutional,* with emphasis on relationships within and between all types of organizations, government(s), businesses, systems of organizations and civil society structures; and (v) *ecological,* where relationships are established "with Earth and its ecosystems of which we are a part and on which our survival and quality of life depend."

3.2.6   CONSIDER THE INNER AND OUTER DIMENSIONS
OF HUMAN DEVELOPMENT AND SECURITY

The new mindset must also include the inner dimension of human development and security (i.e., what Maslow (1943) referred to as esteem and self-actualization). Such needs are not explicitly acknowledged in the SDG 2030 agenda, which prioritizes addressing outwardly the bottom tiers of Maslow's pyramid (i.e., meeting physiological and safety needs) even though all needs are interrelated and not just stacked one on top of the other.

Also not included in Agenda 2030 is "the ethical framework to guide decisions, practices, and actions in implementing the SDGs" (Khayesi, 2021). Questions arise

TABLE 3.2

Two Different Mindsets toward Nature

Old Mindset	New Mindset
• Nature is a machine or object with no intrinsic value to be dominated and exploited (e.g., Francis Bacon)	• Nature is sacred, a harmonic web of life; everything needs to be preserved (e.g., native traditions)
• Linear, reductionistic, separate	• Cyclical, systemic, interdependent
• Earth made for humans	• Humans made for Earth
• Violent (brute force)	• Caring and restoring
• Control nature	• Emulate and work with nature
• Short time frames	• Longer time frames
• Earth is a limitless source of resources and sinks for waste	• Earth is a finite source of resources and sinks for waste disposal
• Technology is omnipotent and solves every problem	• Technology as a solution, among many others
• Doing well	• Doing good by doing well
• Extractive processes	• Renewable processes
• Waste as useless stuff	• Waste as resources
• Externalize the externalities	• Internalize the externalities
• Benefits for a few	• Benefits all
• Creates waste	• Creates value
• The Anthropocene: human activities are closely inseparable from Earth's climate and ecosystems	• The Ecocene and Symbiocene: humans work with and in nature

as to (i) whose ethics of development affects whom, (ii) "whose definition and measurement of development [beyond economic indicators] should be considered in programs designed to support the SDGs" (Khayesi, 2021), and (iii) who is accountable at different levels of decision-making. Addressing the ethical dimension of human development and security with proper development ethics practices (Gasper, 2012) and answering these questions is critical if the SDGs need to become mainstream and the world does not revert to past practices.

A quote from Meister Eckhart (Meister Eckhart and Parke, 2010) to support the inner dimension of human development and security is pertinent here: "The outer work can never be minor when the inner work is a major one, and the outer work can never be major or good when the inner work is a minor one and without value." Therefore, any external interventions related to human development and security must also consider revisiting the inner work of the institutions and the dominant values of their decision-makers. With that in mind, one can question the quality of our Western society's inner work, institutions, and decision-makers based on how such groups (including ourselves) have managed planetary challenges over the past 200 years and are likely to handle current and future ones in the so-called Anthropocene, an unofficial epoch of Earth's history where human activities are closely inseparable from Earth's climate and ecosystems. Can we envision a change in mindset from the Anthropocene to the Symbiocene, where humans work with and in nature (Crist, 2019)? Can we expect a better way for humans to treat each other? If not, why not? What is holding humanity back? In recent human history, our "better angels" have always surfaced and dominated when faced with crises (Reckford, 2019). Why is it that we can't be like that all the time?

Lessons can be learned from non-Western mindsets adopted by indigenous cultures (Cajete, 2020) and Eastern traditions (e.g., Taoism, Buddhism, Hinduism, Confucianism) emphasizing interconnectedness and strengthening the whole person's inner dimension concurrently with socioeconomic development and the respect for natural systems. Short of doing that and educating "warrior-sage decision-makers," it is hard to envision adequate and practical solutions to the ongoing planetary issues.

3.3   EMBRACING A SYSTEMS PRACTICE

Another characteristic of the new mindset to address human development and security issues is recognizing that they all involve multiple systems (social, economic, infrastructure, ecological, etc.) that constantly interact and cannot be treated in isolation (Laszlo, 2001). Hence, adopting a systems-aware practice (i.e., understanding systems, becoming a systems thinker, promoting systemic change, and making decisions across systems) is vital to addressing global human development and security issues and a necessary part of the post-2020 mindset. In short, the new perspective must embrace rather than reject the complexity of systems when addressing such issues. By doing so, seeing complexity as an opportunity for change combined with basic systems thinking, tools, and collaboration elements can lead to constructive and innovative outcomes (Leadbeater and Winhall, 2020). A systems practice allows for looking at peace, sustainability, and climate security as states emerging from the interaction of multiple systems.

Figure 3.3 captures the horizontal interaction of each state with traditional vertical systems silos, which are traditionally dealt with using a silo approach. A vertical connection represents the PSC nexus. Other types of nexus can also be added, such as the water-energy-land- food nexus, the food-healthcare-nutrition nexus, the climate-fragility-peacebuilding nexus, and the environment-fragility-peace nexus.

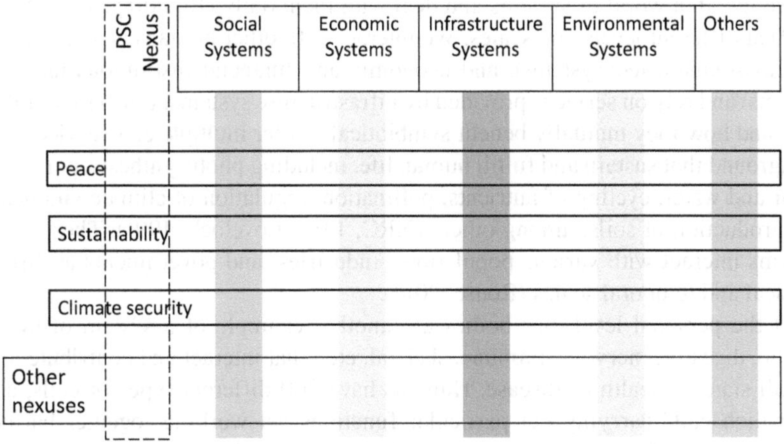

FIGURE 3.3   A silo approach versus systems perspective of the PSC nexus.

3.3.1 What Are Systems?

Etymologically (http://www.etymonline.com), the word 'system' comes from the Greek word 'systema,' which means "an organized whole, a whole compounded of parts." Systems can be broadly defined as groups of interacting (but seemingly independent) parts linked by exchanges of energy, matter, and information (Meadows, 2008). Systems comprise linked components or units that form an integrated whole (Von Bertalanffy, 1973). A common purpose drives the systems to achieve specific goals, even though the systems' parts may have conflicting objectives. This purpose can be seen as unity with differentiation. As noted by Berry (1990), "Nothing is completely itself without everything else in systems."

The behavior of systems is also dictated by various rules that act at the component and system level and by how systems interact with their environment. Finally, people who interact with the systems and the observers who study them become part of them, the observers and the observed. A good example is how exogenous stakeholders in a project (e.g., humanitarian aid, development, and peacekeeping agencies) may become endogenous to the project over time (Hayden, 2018).

Although systems have been recognized since antiquity in ancient Greek culture and Eastern religions (Lent, 2017, 2021b), systems theory is often assumed to have started in Western cultures from at least three different approaches in the first part of the twentieth century (Ramage and Shipp, 2020): *Gestalt* in psychology, the *General Systems Theory* of Ludwig von Bertalanffy (1973), and *Cybernetics* of Wiener (1948) and Ashby (1956). These approaches paved the way for systems science studies and the different mathematical models of systems up to this day. The reader can find a good review of the evolution of systems science and its applications to various practical fields of work in Umpleby and Dent (1999), Myers (2009), and Castellani and Hafferti (2009). Ramage and Shipp (2009) distinguish seven systems approaches: early cybernetics, general systems theory, system dynamics, soft & critical systems, later cybernetics, complexity theory, and learning systems. These authors also review the work of 30 systems thinkers who have contributed to these seven categories.

We live in a world of systems and deal with them daily (Boulding, 1985; Laszlo, 2001) at different levels and scales. We interact with other humans (social systems), the environment (ecosystems), and economic and financial institutions (economic systems) and rely on services provided by infrastructure systems. Earth's natural systems and how they mutually benefit symbiotically offer multiple eco-services in the background that sustain and fulfill human life, including photosynthesis, purification of air and water, cycling of nutrients, pollination, regulation of climate and oceans, and production of soils, among others (NRC, 1988; Lovelock, 1991). These natural systems interact with various populations, industries, and governments at different physical and temporal scales (Rouse, 2014).

At the personal level, our bodies are another example of a system of systems (cardio, digestive, nervous, immune, skeletal, etc.) that interact and contribute to our overall state of health or disease. Humans have 200 different types of cells, about 37 trillion cells carrying out particular functions yet working together harmoniously (Lent, 2021b). In international development and aid, systems (human, natural, infrastructure, economic, and capital) interact at multiple dimensions, from the local scale (individual, households, neighborhood, village, town, and city) to the regional, national, and international levels.

3.3.2 Four System Types

According to the *Cynefin* framework of Snowden and Boone (2007), systems can be divided into four groups: simple, complicated, complex, and chaotic (Table 3.3). As observed by Patton (2011), these systems differ in (i) the "degree of certainty" with which problems can be solved and (ii) "the degree of agreement" on how to solve such problems.

Simple systems have few variables with limited relationships where certainty and predictability are common. In such scenarios, decision-makers "know the knowns" and can find the correct answer to a problem. An agreement can be reached on what to do about addressing the issue. Hence, best practices can be established. At the end of chapters in technical textbooks, problems are formulated in simple systems with a correct answer.

In *complicated* systems, the components are well-defined, but their linkages are more challenging to comprehend and require the input of experts. In such scenarios, decision-makers "know the unknowns," and a solution (but not necessarily the best) is still possible and predictable. There may be multiple reasonable solutions and good practices to a problem that can be analyzed in a cause-and-effect manner. Patton (2011) distinguished between technically complicated and socially complicated systems. A low certainty characterizes technically complicated systems in solving problems but a high agreement that the problem needs to be solved. A high level of confidence describes socially complicated systems in solving the problem but a low level of understanding of how to solve the problem.

As an illustrative example, a technically complicated situation would be, for instance, the implementation by the government of adaptation and mitigation methods against climate change with limited community coordinating services. Still, the population agrees that the methods are necessary and important. A socially complicated situation would be delivering adaptation and mitigation services in a community with coordinating services but with a resisting population that does not believe in climate change. It is generally easier to deal with technical complications where technical and tangible issues must be resolved than social ones where intangible issues are often dominant.

TABLE 3.3

Four Types of Systems with Different Modes of Practice and Response according to The Cynefin Framework of Snowden and Boone (2007)

	Ordered		Unordered	
Types	Simple	Complicated	Complex	Chaotic
Practice	Best	Good	Emergent	Novel
Response	Sense	Sense	**Probe**	**Act**
	Categorize	**Analyze**	Sense	Sense
	Respond	Respond	Respond	Respond

The third group of systems consists of *complex systems* for which we "don't know the unknowns." Complexity can best be described by the meaning of its Latin root, which is "braided together" (Gell-Mann, 1996). Complex systems possess all sorts of unique characteristics that can be hard to comprehend and deal with:

- Nonlinearity, feedback structures, emergence, dynamic behavior, adaptation, uncertainty, coevolution, and self-organization are common (Patton, 2011).
- Unexpected "black swan" or "outlier" events are commonplace (Taleb, 2007).
- They can develop patterns of behavior that may not be predictable from the behavior of each system's part; the whole is greater than the sum of its parts through *synergy* (Fuller, 1975).
- Their behavior depends significantly on the dependencies of its components; removing one element "destroys system behavior to the extent that goes well beyond what is embodied by the particular element that is removed" (Miller and Page, 2007).
- They experience phase transitions leading to the emergence of systems properties and reciprocal causality.
- Best practices cannot be established, but *practical*, *relevant*, and *meaning-ful* ones are still possible (Patton, 2011).
- Only good enough (i.e., satisficing) and not optimal solutions are possible (Simon, 1972).

Examples of complex systems include living systems, Earth's climate, the human body, the stock market, healthcare systems, enterprise network systems, communities and neighborhoods in villages, cities, megacities, etc. The scientific study of complex systems is sometimes called complexity science in the literature (Waldrop, 1992; Mitchell, 2009). It should be noted that there are multiple sciences of complexity with different approaches and lines of research.

When unpredictability is amplified and extreme, complex systems become *chaotic* systems. Such systems are characterized by severe turbulence, small things can have enormous consequences, and bifurcation leading to rapid change is possible (Lorenz, 1972; Briggs and Peat, 1999; Sweeney, 2001). Chaotic systems can sometimes show some temporary emerging synchronicity (cohesion, convergence, or order), leading to additional unintended consequences and unexpected behavior (Waldrop, 1992; Kaufman, 1993). In a vaccination example, a chaotic situation would be one where (i) a contagious disease is quickly spreading among a population that is ill-informed about the importance of vaccination, (ii) no health services are available, and (iii) the population is in a hazardous area. A refugee camp in a conflict area would probably best illustrate such a chaotic situation. Countries experiencing conflict are also chaotic systems. If possible, chaotic systems require immediate action to re-establish a reasonable sense of order so they can be handled as complex systems. Peacebuilding and peacekeeping efforts may provide such activities.

As shown in Table 3.3, different contexts require different approaches to systems and "situation recognition" by decision-makers (Gell-Mann, 1996; Patton, 2011; Britt, 2013; Glouberman and Zimmerman, 2002). As noted by Snowden and

Boone (2007), selecting an appropriate approach when assessing a system and making decisions on how to intervene in that system depends significantly on whether the system is ordered (i.e., simple or complicated) or unordered (i.e., complex or chaotic).

Intervening in any system in a contextually appropriate manner also needs to consider the temporal and physical scales (i.e., the boundaries) in which the system or its parts operate. As an example, different types of intervention are, for instance, needed in the rapid response, recovery, and development phases of a community following an adverse event. Likewise, as noted by Leroux-Martin and O'Connor (2017), different system types could coexist in conflict-affected countries where "the country as a whole may be a complex system, but parts of the country may be in chaos due to localized violent conflict." The challenge becomes prioritizing (e.g., triage) the modes of intervention with existing resources.

3.3.3 COMPLEX ADAPTIVE SYSTEMS

In communities, human systems, economic systems, natural systems, and infrastructure (engineered) systems constantly interact dynamically. Some of these systems are complex and require subjective or intuitive analysis tools. Some others may behave in a simple or complicated manner for which objective analysis tools are more appropriate. Living systems (human and natural) add another dimension, *adaptiveness*, to how systems interact. In general, at the community level, there are instances where systems work well together and others when they are at odds with one another (Leadbeater and Winhall, 2020).

Living systems, such as communities, exchange mass and energy with their surrounding environment to achieve a purpose; they are open systems (Von Bertalanffy, 1950). Communities are unique in that, among all their systems, social systems consist of adaptive agents in dynamic (and not stable) equilibrium. Seelos (2020) noted that within a given community, "People differ in their attitudes, motivations, sense of role or purpose, perceptions, beliefs, expectations, and habits." Yet, despite considerable differences, communities are integrated holarchies (i.e., they retain unity toward a common purpose while experiencing differentiation). Communities seldom preserve their forms and constantly evolve and grow as they develop and reach new states of normality (Miller and Page, 2007; Waldrop, 1992). They can experience emergence, self-organization, self-correction, and adaptation by changing their structure, behavior, and rules of interaction through evolutionary and co-evolutionary change (Mitleton-Kelly, 2003). These forms of behavior depend on the environment in which human systems reside and interact (Simon, 1972). As complex adaptive systems, communities can be perceived as evolving organisms using a biological metaphor with some degree of sentience. These organisms depend on their environment to grow but also affect that environment.

Table 3.4 lists multiple potential characteristics of living systems as complex adaptive systems. All these characteristics do not always manifest themselves simultaneously. Some are likely to be more dominant in specific contexts than others. However, they can be closely related in other situations and potentially interact in compounded disruptive ways.

TABLE 3.4

Characteristics, Behaviors, and Attributes of Complex Adaptive Systems

Characteristics	Description	Examples
Agency	"The capacity of individuals to have the power and resources to fulfill their potential" (Wikipedia, 2023)	Humans are conscious and aware of their behavior and impact
Attractor	"A state or behavior toward which a dynamic system tends to evolve represented as a point or orbit in the system's phase space" (dictionary. com).	A community is trapped in a perpetual struggle, with vulnerability to adverse events and dependency on outside help. Failed states.
Autopoiesis	"The property of a living system . . . that allows it to maintain and renew itself by regulating its composition and conserving its boundaries" (*Merriam-Webster*, m-w.com).	Human and natural systems continuously create their organization and complexity at different scales. Life is self-regenerating.
Chaotic	"Completely confused and disordered" (dictionary.com). Structural instability.	An already vulnerable community faces crises and emergencies following an adverse event. War and refugee situations are chaotic.
Coevolution	Evolution or change in one part of a system puts pressure on another and changes its development.	Anthropogenic effects on the environment and climate. From the Holocene to the Anthropocene. From the Anthropocene to the Symbiocene?
Counterintuitive	The cause behind some effects is not necessarily the most logical one or the one that is the closest in time and space	Resources are available but do not reach community members due to poor management.
Dynamic Behavior	"The behavior over time of a system or any of its components" (Meadows, 2008).	Social and natural systems change, adapt, and evolve all the time.
Feedback Structures	The closed chain of causal influences. A variable can be both the cause and effect of another (Hjorth and Bagheri, 2006).	Climate change affects the economy. Pollution created by the economy affects climate change.
Hierarchy	Systems may consist of different levels and sub-levels of interaction.	Different groups of stakeholders make decisions. Some infrastructure systems are more critical than others.
Interconnectedness	All parts of a system, including its sub-levels, are connected to some other parts, but not necessarily the entire system	Social and natural fabric.
Leverage Points	Places within a complex system . . . where a slight shift in one thing can produce significant changes in everything (Meadows, 1997).	Focus on success stories, positive deviance, strength, and existing capacity at the community level (Pascale et al., 2010).

(*Continued*)

TABLE 3.4 (*Continued*)

Characteristics, Behaviors, and Attributes of Complex Adaptive Systems

Characteristics	Description	Examples
Nonlinearity	"A relationship between two elements in a system where the cause does not produce a proportional [linear] effect" (Meadows, 2008).	Population growth and other types of exponential growth.
Open	Exchange of mass and energy with outside the systems.	Inherent to human and natural systems.
Patterns	The dynamic of a system creates repetitive behavior and the same outcome.	Patterns of daily living at different scales. Habits and biases.
Resilience	An acquired capacity "to prepare and plan for, absorb, recover from, or more successfully adapt to [actual or potential] adverse events" (NRC, 2012).	Resilience to climate change and other adverse effects (e.g., conflict). Ability to cope with challenging conditions and adapt to a new normal.
Self-Organization and Adaptation	"The ability of a system to structure itself, to create a new structure, to learn or diversify" (Meadows, 2008).	Communities adapt to change, dynamic equilibrium.
Sensitivity to Initial Conditions and Path Dependency	The behavior of a system depends on how it evolves from its initial state and associated conditions.	The current state (baseline) dictates what is possible—the importance of initial capacity in absorbing some adverse events and challenges.
Synergy and Emergence	The "behavior of integral, aggregate, whole systems unpredicted by behaviors of any of their components or subassemblies of their components taken separately from the whole" (Fuller, 1975).	The interaction among households and individuals creates the behavior of a community. Peace, sustainability, and climate security are emerging states.
Uncertainty vs. Risk	Uncertainty happens if we don't know the odds and likelihood that something will happen. If the odds are known, it is better to talk about risk (Knight, 1921)	It can derail community development. The challenge is to convert uncertainty and define risk levels.
Integration	Unity with differentiation (Lent, 2021b).	Each system part maintains its unique identity while coordinating with other components through intimate feedback loops.

3.3.4 DEVELOPMENT AS A COMPLEX ADAPTIVE SYSTEM

The interplay between human systems and other systems in communities makes "the process of community development inherently unpredictable and [difficult to program]. It depends critically on constant learning and adaptation to be effective" (Morgan, 1998). This dynamic requires all stakeholders involved in community development to become systems- and complexity-aware and take adaptive actions that incorporate "reflection in and on action," adaptation, monitoring and evaluation, and feedback structures. As a result, decision-makers involved in community development are challenged to reduce uncertainty to an acceptable level to estimate risks without prematurely imposing inadequate solutions.

Assuming communities are not complex and adaptive and consist of closed assemblies of static and independent elements can lead to development and aid interventions with limited success or failed projects altogether. Unfortunately, adopting and operationalizing a systems perspective in development and aid has been slow (Ramalingam, 2014). This trend is despite the recommendations made by several authors that "development is a complex adaptive system" and that, in development and aid settings, complexity and systemic behavior are the norms and not the exception (Chambers, 1983; Rihani, 2002, 2005; Breslin, 2004; Barder, 2012).

It is easy to see why decision-makers hesitate to use a systems perspective in development and aid initiatives and prefer to use predetermined solutions in these projects. First, it is challenging to formulate and address issues in complex systems compared to the more ordered, simple, and complicated systems, whether as an insider or an outsider to development and aid projects. Second, making decisions in uncertain and unfamiliar environments is risky and poses a definite challenge to humans' bounded rationality (i.e., lack of objective reality). Finally, there is still a disconnect between the desire of development organizations to adopt a systems perspective and their pathological behaviors regarding processes, cognition, attitude, and values (Seelos et al., 2021).

The hesitation in embracing a systems perspective can also be attributed to mental limitations. As noted by Simon (1957)

> The capacity of the mind for formulating and solving complex problems is very small compared with the size of the problems whose solution is required for objectively rational behavior in the real world—or even for a reasonable approximation to such objective rationality.

As a result, many attempts have been made in development and aid to force the reductionist approach, discussed earlier in this chapter, into solving complex socio-technical-economic world problems. These risk-averse attempts usually assume that complex systems can be simplified and addressed quickly, expecting successful and lasting changes. Unfortunately, this deliberate way of avoiding complexity and reducing mental effort creates unintended consequences despite good initial intentions (Dörner, 1997). This dynamic can be immediate or far apart in time and space. There is enough evidence in the history of development that repeating the past business-as-usual mindset of ignoring the complexity of the systems at play in development and aid and treating them in isolation can do more harm than good. The same could be said of engineering projects that failed to recognize, for instance, the complexity of the interaction between natural and non-natural systems (Holling and Meffe, 1995; Allenby, 2000; Bugliarello, 2003).

As part of the new mindset in a post-2020 world, a recommendation is for decision-makers to embrace (rather than ignore) complexity and accept what that entails in their decision-making process (i.e., having to combine objective and mostly subjective judgment and critical and creative thinking to handle the complexity at hand). As noted by Westley et al. (2007), this approach requires development and aid decision-makers to make "a fundamental [and intentional] shift in perception—from complexity as an obstacle, to complexity as an opportunity" and being constantly and fully aware of that value proposition. Ramalingam (2014) sees this much-needed new approach to development and aid group decisions as breaking away from an "obsession with organized simplicity" to "embracing organized complexity" while accepting the challenges that this new approach brings forth.

3.4 CONCLUDING REMARKS

A new mindset is needed to address the complex planetary issues of the Twenty-first century. Peace, sustainability, and climate security and their opposites are emerging states that cannot be reduced to their parts. A systems approach is needed to capture these three states' entanglement and interactions with multiple systems upon which they depend. A systems practice for decision-making and implementing solutions in each sector of the nexus and across these sectors should be seen as supplementing the more traditional deterministic approach used in human development and security, not as an alternative. The challenge resides in selecting the appropriate decision-making methods depending on the issues being addressed and their context. As noted by Ortega y Gasset (1994), this is especially important as "Civilization becomes more complex and difficult in proportion as it advances. The problems which it sets before us today are the most intricate. The number of people whose minds are equal to these problems becomes increasingly smaller."

REFERENCES

Allenby, B. R. (2000). Earth systems engineering: The world as a human artifact. *The Bridge*, *30*(1), 5–13.

Amadei, B. (2019). *A systems approach to modeling the water-energy-land-food nexus*. Vols. *I* and *II*. Momentum Press.

Ashby, W. R. (1956). *An introduction to cybernetics*. Chapman & Hall.

Barder, O. (2012, September 7). Complexity, adaptation, and results. http://www.cgdev.org/blog/complexity-adaptation-and-results

BenDor, T., & Scheffran, J. (2019). *Agent-based modeling of environmental conflict and cooperation*. CRC Press, Taylor & Francis.

Berninger, M. (2020, March 10). Food security -You can't build peace on empty stomachs. https://www.3blmedia.com/news/food-security-you-cant-build-peace-empty-stomachs

Berry, T. (1990). *The dream of the earth*. Sierra Club Books.

Boulding, K. (1985). *The world as a total system*. Sage.

Breslin, P. (2004). Thinking outside Newton's box: Metaphors for grassroots development. *Grassroots Development*, *25*(1), 1–9. https://www.iaf.gov/wp-content/uploads/2018/07/IAF_2004_Journal_English.pdf

Briggs, J., & Peat, F. D. (1999). *Seven life lessons of chaos - Spiritual wisdom from the science of change*. Harper Perennial.

Britt, H. (2013). Complexity-aware monitoring. Discussion note: Version 2.0. U.S. Agency for International Development. Washington, DC.

Bugliarello, G. (2003). *The biosoma: Reflections on the synthesis of biology, society, and machines*. Polytechnic University, Brooklyn, NY.

Cajete, G. (2020). *Native science: Natural laws of interdependence*. Clear Light Publ.

Caldwell, R. (2002). *Project design handbook*. Cooperative for Assistance and Relief Everywhere (CARE), Atlanta, GA.

Castellani, B., & Hafferti, F. (2009). Mapping complexity. In *Understanding Complex Systems*. Springer. http://doi.org/10.1007/978-3-540-88462-0_10

Chambers, R. (1983). *Rural development: Putting the last first*. Pearson Prentice Hall.

Checkland, P., & Poulter, J. (2006). *Learning for action: Soft systems methodology and its use for practitioners, teachers, and students*. John Wiley & Sons.

Churchman, C. W (1982). *Thought and wisdom*. InterSystems Publications.

Cornwall, A., & Jewkes, R. (1995). What is participatory research? *Social Science & Medicine*, *41*(12), 1667–1676. https://doi.org/10.1016/0277-9536(95)00127-S

Crist, E. (2019). *Abundant earth: Toward an ecological civilization*. University of Chicago Press.

Dearden, P., Jones, S., & Sartorius, R. (2003). *Tools for development: A handbook for those engaged in development activity*. Version 15.1. Department for International Development, London, UK.

Descartes, R. (2004) [1637]. *A discourse on method: Meditations and principles*. Translated by Veitch, John. Barnes & Noble.

Dörner, D. (1997). *The logic of failure: Recognizing and avoiding error in complex situations*. Perseus Books.

Fuller, R. B. (1975). *Synergetics: Explorations in the geometry of thinking*. MacMillan Publishing.

Gasper, D. (2012). Development ethics - Why? What? How? A formulation of the field. *Journal of Global Ethics*, *8*(1), 117–135. https://doi.org/10.1080/17449626.2012.672450

Gell-Mann, M. (1996). Let's call it pleptics. *Complexity*, *1*(5), 3. https://doi.org/10.1002/cplx.6130010502

Gil, D. (2021, January 12). *COVID-19 a year later: What have we learned?* World Economic Forum COVID Action Platform. https://www.ibm.com/blogs/research/2021/01/covid-19-a-year-later/

Glouberman, S., & Zimmerman, B. (2002). Complicated and complex systems: What would successful reform of Medicare look like? *Discussion paper No. 8*. Commission of the Future of Healthcare in Canada, Ottawa. https://www.degruyter.com/document/doi/10.3138/9781442672833/html

Harford, T. (2012). *Adapt: Why success always starts with failure*. Picador; First Picador Edition.

Hayden, N. K. (2018). *Balancing belligerents or feeding the beats: Transforming conflict traps*. CISSIM Policy Brief, The University of Maryland Center for International and Security Studies. https://drum.lib.umd.edu/bitstream/handle/1903/20654/Hayden-Balancing%20belligerents%20or%20feeding%20the%20beasts_022618.pdf

Hjorth, P., & Bagheri, A. (2006). Navigating towards sustainable development: A system dynamics approach. *Future*, *38*, 74–92. https://doi.org/10.1016/j.futures.2005.04.005

Holling, C. S., & Meffe, G. K. (1995). Command and control and the pathology of natural resource management. *Conservation Biology*, *10*(2), 328–337. https://doi.org/10.1046/J.1523-1739.1996.10020328.X

Hovland, I. (2005). *Successful communication: A toolkit for researchers and civil society organizations*. Research and Policy in Development Programme, London, UK. http://www.odi.org.uk/RAPID//

Jessen, T. D., Ban, N. C., Claxton, N. X., Darimont, C. T. (2021). Contributions of indigenous knowledge to ecological and evolutionary understanding. *Frontiers in Ecology and the Environment*, *20*(2), 93–101. https://doi.org/10.1002/fee.2435

Kania, J., & Kramer, M. (2013). Embracing emergence: How collective impact addresses complexity. Stanford Social Innovation Review, January 2.

Karwat, D. M. A., Eagle, W. E, Wooldridge, M. S., & Princen, T. E. (2014). Activist engineering: Changing engineering practice by deploying praxis. *Science and Engineering Ethics*, *21*, 227–239. https://doi.org/10.1007/s11948-014-9525-0

Kaufman, S. A. (1993). *The origins of order: Self-organization and selection in evolution*. Oxford University Press.

Khayesi, M. (2021). What is the ethical reflection of the sustainable development goals? *Sustainability and Climate Change*, *14*(3). https://doi.org/10.1089/scc.2020.0073

Knight, F. H. (1921). Risk, uncertainty, and profit. University of Illinois at Urbana-Champaign's Academy for entrepreneurial leadership historical research reference in entrepreneurship. https://ssrn.com/abstract=1496192

Laszlo, E. (2001). *The systems view of the world: A holistic vision for our time*. Hampton Press.

Laszlo, E. (2022). *The upshift: Wiser living on planet Earth*. Waterside Productions.

Leadbeater, C, & Winhall, J. (2020). *Building better systems: A green paper on system innovation*. The Rockwool Foundation. https://www.systeminnovation.org/green-paper

Lent, J. (2017). *The patterning instinct*. Prometheus Books.

Lent, J. (2021a, October 9). Solving the climate crisis requires the end of capitalism. https://www.salon.com/2021/10/09/solving-the-climate-requires-the-end-of-capitalism/

Lent, J. (2021b). *The web of meaning: Integrating science and traditional wisdom to find our place in the universe*. New Society Publishers.

Leroux-Martin, P., & O'Connor, V. (2017). *Systems thinking for peacebuilding and the rule of law: Supporting complex reforms in conflict-affected environments*. US Institute of Peace. https://www.usip.org/sites/default/files/2017-11/pw133-systems-thinking-for-peacebuilding-and-rule-of-law-v2.pdf

Lorenz, E. N. (1972). *Predictability: Does the flap of a butterfly's wings in Brazil set off a tornado in Texas?* American Association for the Advancement of Science. http://gymportalen.dk/sites/lru.dk/files/lru/132_kap6_lorenz_artikel_the_butterfly_effect.pdf

Lovelock, J. (1991). *Gaia: The practical science of planetary medicine*. Gaia Book Ltd.

Mahon, K., Heikkinen, H. L., Huttunen, R., Boyle, T., & Sjølie, E. (2020). What is Educational Praxis? In K. Mahon, C. Edwards-Groves, S. Francisco, M. Kaukko, S. Kemmis and K. Petrie, (eds.), *Pedagogy, Education, and Praxis in Critical Times*. Springer, Singapore. https://doi.org/10.1007/978-981-15-6926-5_2

Mark 2:18–22. New wine into old Wineskins. http://www.biblehub.com.

Maslow, A. H. (1943). A theory of human motivation. *Psychological Review, 50*(4), 370–396. https://psycnet.apa.org/doi/10.1037/h0054346

Meadows, D. H. (1997). Places to intervene in a system in increasing order of effectiveness. *Whole Earth, Winter*, 78–84.

Meadows, D. (2008). *Thinking in systems*. Chelsea Green Publishing.

Meister Eckhart, & Parke, S. (2010). *Conversation with Meister Eckhart*. White Crow Books, Publ.

Miller, J. H., & Page, S. E. (2007). *Complex adaptive systems: An introduction to computational models of social life*, Princeton University Press.

Mitchell, M. (2009). *Complexity: A guided tour*. Oxford University Press.

Mitleton-Kelly, E. (2003). Ten principles of complexity and enabling infrastructures. Chapter 2 in *Complex systems and evolutionary perspectives of organizations: The application of complex theory to organizations*. Elsevier.

Morgan, P. (1998). Capacity and capacity development - Some strategies. CIDA Policy Branch, http://nsagm.weebly.com/uploads/1/2/0/3/12030125/strategies_for_capacity_development_cida_1998.pdf

Moritz, R. E. (2020, July 17). To reinvent the future, we must all work together. https://www.weforum.org/agenda/2020/07/to-reinvent-the-future-we-must-all-work-together

Myers, R. A. (ed.). (2009). *Encyclopedia of complexity and systems science. 11* volumes, Springer.

National Peace Academy. (n.d.). *A conceptual framework for peace education and peacebuilding programs*. https://nationalpeaceacademy.us/images/files/ProgramFramework1.pdf

National Research Council. (NRC). (1988). *Earth system science: A closer view*. The National Academies Press. https://doi.org/10.17226/19088

National Research Council (NRC). (2012). *Disaster resilience: A national imperative*. The National Academies Press. https://doi.org/10.17226/13457

Open Society Foundations. (2022). Fault lines: Global perspectives on a world in crisis. https://www.opensocietyfoundations.org/publications/fault-lines-global-perspectives-on-a-world-in-crisis

Ortega y Gasset, J. (1994). *The revolt of the masses.* W. W. Norton & Company; Reissue edition

Pascale, R., Sternin, J, & Sternin, M. (2010). *The power of positive deviance: How unlikely innovators solve the world's toughest problems.* Harvard University Review Press.

Patton, M. Q. (2011). *Developmental evaluation: Applying complexity concepts to enhance innovation and use.* Guilford Press.

Ramage, M., & Shipp, K. (2020). *Systems thinkers.* (2nd ed.) Springer.

Ramalingam, B. (2014). *Aid on the edge of chaos: Rethinking international cooperation in a complex world.* Oxford University Press.

Reckford, J. (2019). *Our better angels: Seven simple virtues that will change your life and the world.* St. Martin's Essentials.

Rihani, S. (2002). *Complex systems theory and development practice: Understanding non-linear realities.* Zen Books.

Rihani, S. (2005). Complexity theory: A new framework for development is in the offing. *Progress in Development Studies, 5*(1), 54–61. https://doi.org/10.1191/1464993405ps101pr

Rittel, H., & Webber, M. (1973). Dilemmas in a general theory of planning. *Policy Science, 4,* 155–169. https://doi.org/10.1007/BF01405730

Rouse, W. (2014). Earth as a system. In *Can Earth's and Society's Systems Meet the Needs of 10 Billion People*, The National Academies Press, Washington, DC.

Sachs, J., Schmidt-Traub, G., Kroll, C., LaFortune, G., Fuller, G., & Woelm, F. (2020). *The sustainable development goals and COVID-19.* Sustainable *development report* 2020. Cambridge University Press.

Schmidheiny, S. (1992). *Changing course: A global business perspective on development and the environment.* MIT Press.

Seelos, C. (2020). Changing systems? Welcome to the slow movement. *Stanford Social Innovation Review, Winter,* 40–47.

Seelos, C., Farley, S., & Rose, L. A. (2021). The "Thou shall nots" of systems change. *Stanford Social Innovation Review,* January 14. https://doi.org/10.48558/0bxx-mp20

Shmueli, D. F., Kaufman, S., & Ozawa, C. (2008). Mining negotiation theory for planning insights. *Journal of Planning Education and Research, 27*(3), 359–364. http://doi.org/10.1177/0739456X07311074

Simon, H. A. (1957). *Models of man: Social and rational.* Wiley.

Simon, H. A. (1972). Theories of bounded rationality. In C. B. McGuire and R. Radner (eds.), *Decision and Organization* (pp. 161–176). North-Holland Pub.

Snowden, D., & Boone, M. (2007). A leader's framework for decision making. *Harvard Business Review, 85*(11), 68–76.

Strengthening Partnerships, Results, and Innovations in Nutrition Globally (SPRING). (2015). A systems thinking and action for nutrition: USAID/ project. https://www.spring-nutrition.org/publications/briefs/systems-thinking-and-action-nutrition

Sweeney, L. B. (2001). *When a butterfly sneezes: A guide for helping kids explore interconnections in our world through favorite stories.* Pegasus Communications.

Taleb, N. N. (2007). *The Black swan: The impact of the highly improbable.* Random House.

Tanabe, J. (2020). Exploring a post-covid-19 sustainable peace model. *Social Ethics Society Journal of Applied Philosophy,* Article *4,* 73–103. ses-journal.com/wp-content/uploads/2020/07/Article-4_Tanabe_SESJuly2020.pdf

The Economist. (2021, December 18). The new normal is already here. Get used to it. The era of predictable unpredictability is not going away. https://www.economist.com/leaders/2021/12/18/the-new-normal-is-already-here-get-used-to-it

The Omidyar Group. (2017). Systems practice workbook. https://oecd-opsi.org/toolkits/systems-practice-workbook/

The World in 2050 (TWI2050). (2020). Innovations for sustainability. Pathways to an efficient and post-pandemic future. Report prepared by The World in 2050 initiative. International Institute for Applied Systems Analysis (IIASA), Laxenburg, Austria. http://www.twi2050.org/

Tooley, C. (2021, January 18). *What systems thinking actually means - and why it matters for innovation today.* The World Economic Forum. https://www.weforum.org/agenda/2021/01/what-systems-thinking-actually-means-and-why-it-matters-today/

Umpleby, S. A., & Dent, E. B. (1999). The origins and purposes of several traditions in systems theory and cybernetics. *Cybernetics and Systems, 30,* 79–103. https://doi.org/10.1080/019697299125299

United Nations Development Programme (UNDP). (2020). *COVID-19 and human development: Assessing the crisis, envisioning the recovery.* UNDP, New York. https://hdr.undp.org/system/files/documents/covid-19andhumandevelopmentpdf_1.pdf

UNDP Human Development Report (UNDP/HDR). (2022). *The human development report 2021/2022. Uncertain times, and unsettled lives, shaping our future in a transforming world.* https://www.undp.org/timor-leste/publications/human-development-report-2021/2022

United Nations Economic and Social Commission for Western Asia (UNESCWA). (2021). https://archive.unescwa.org/sites/www.unescwa.org/files/u593/the_5ps_of_the_sustainable_development_goals.pdf

von Bertalanffy, L. (1950). The theory of open systems in physics and biology. *Science, 111*(2872), 23–29. https://www.jstor.org/stable/1676073

von Bertalanffy, L. (1973). *General systems theory.* (4th printing). George Braziller, Inc. Publ.

Waldrop, M. M. (1992). *Complexity: The emerging science at the edge of order and chaos.* Simon & Schuster.

Westley, F., Zimmerman, B., & Patton, M. Q. (2007). *Getting to maybe: How the world is changed.* Vintage Canada.

Wiener, N. (1948). *Cybernetics or control and communication in the animal and the machine.* The MIT Press. The second edition was published in 1961 with a new printing by Martino Publishing in 2013. https://doi.org/10.7551/mitpress/11810.001.0001

Woodhill, J., & Millican, J. (2023). *Systems thinking and practice: A guide to concepts, principles, and tools for FCDO and partners.* Institute of Development Studies. https://doi.org/10.19088/K4D.2023.002

World Business Council for Sustainable Development (WBCSD). (2009). *Water, energy and climate change: A contribution from the business community.* Washington, DC. http://docs.wbcsd.org/2009/03/WaterEnergyandClimateChange.pdf

4 Systems Thinking

4.1 WHAT WENT WRONG?

The last three chapters emphasized the need for decision-makers to embrace a systems practice when dealing with complex world issues and the PSC nexus. In that practice, systems thinking represents a paradigm that provides a unique vantage point and a set of skills when looking at the world in an integrated manner. It is also a learning method that offers a language to communicate the complexity of that world to others. According to Sterman (2006), systems thinking is "an iterative learning process in which we replace a reductionist, narrow, short-term, static view of the world with a holistic, broad, long-term, dynamic view, reinventing our policies and institutions accordingly." Systems thinking acknowledges that the whole of a system is greater than the sum of its parts and has forms of behavior different from those of each component in isolation. Systems thinking also acknowledges that "for every complex problem, there is an answer that is clear, simple, and wrong" (Mencken, n.d.).

Systems thinking has been used in many fields and disciplines. Benson and Marlin (2017) remarked that systems thinking allows system thinkers to "see how concepts, facts, and ideas link together, which can lead to new learning, discoveries, and innovations." Although systems thinking is necessary to address the systems discussed in the previous chapters, it is insufficient to create desired systemic changes in human development and security across the PSC nexus sectors. Systems thinking is just a way of thinking that recognizes the complexity and inter-related nature of the world. It must also be integrated into a methodology, framework, and practice that guides decision-makers when mapping, identifying, and ranking complex problems; developing strategies; implementing holistic solutions and interventions; and proposing coherent governance and policies in the short and long term (see Chapter 9). Systems thinking must be supplemented with modeling tools (Chapters 6 and 7) and methods of decision-making (Chapter 13) that must be appropriately selected to match their applications.

The best way to demonstrate the value proposition of systems thinking in human development and security is to consider a few illustrative examples for which logical and ordered reductionistic but not integrated decision-making and well-intended interventions led to unintended consequences. As a first example, let's consider the dynamics associated with deforestation and farming in a belt of savannah, known as the Cerrado, in Central Brazil. As reported by Monbiot (2021), in that savannah, dew forms when deep-rooted trees soak up groundwater and release it through their leaves, sustaining its vegetation. Over the past few years, vast tracts of the Cerrado have been cleared to plant crops—mostly soya to feed the world's chickens and pigs. Tree clear-cutting dries the air. Smaller plants die, reducing water circulation. Some scientists warn that this vicious cycle and global warming might quickly turn the system into a desert. In addition, rivers flowing north into the Amazon basin originate in

DOI: 10.1201/9781003435006-4

the Cerrado. Less river water may increase rainforest stress. Clearing, burning, and heating are killing the forests and threatening systemic collapse. This affects how the "rivers in the sky" created by the Cerrado and rainforest form. These streams of moist air are known to distribute rainfall over the world and influence the global circulation of air and ocean currents.

A second example deals with the unintended effects of spraying DDT to fight malaria in a community in Borneo in the 1950s. It ultimately led to the parachuting of cats in Borneo due to a series of unintended consequences. Several versions of "Operation Cat Drop" are available in the literature. As summarized by Loftus (2015), malaria struck Borneo's Dayaks in the 1950s. They called the World Health Organization (WHO) which responded by spraying DDT, which in turn killed malaria-carrying mosquitoes on the island. However, DDT also destroyed a parasite that controlled caterpillar populations. The parasite-free caterpillars flourished and devoured islanders' roofs. Island thatched roofs collapsed. DDT also entered a food web that started with DDT-resistant invertebrates and ended with geckos, which the island's cats ate. Unfortunately, the cats couldn't tolerate the DDT in their bellies and died, eventually dwindling to too few to control the rat population. Rats grew by devouring whatever they could find, including the villager's grain, and spreading the plague. In despair, Borneo again turned to the WHO, which parachuted in a battalion of cats (courtesy of the Royal Air Force) to restore balance. Cats hunted rats and balanced Borneo.

A third example relates to UN High Commission of Refugees (UNHCR)'s humanitarian aid efforts during Bosnia's 1992–1995 war (Cutts, 1999). Multiple warring parties were engaged, including the Bosnian government, the Bosnian Croats, and the Bosnian Serbs. The complex negotiation process and the dynamic between the UNHCR, the UN peacekeeping force, and the Bosnian Serb authorities created challenging and often counterproductive situations in providing humanitarian assistance and emergency relief to those who needed it and preventing ethnic cleansing and expulsions. As noted by Cutts (1999), the warring parties and the international community prioritized political and strategic concerns over humanitarian access. The international community's political plan for dealing with the war entailed a high-profile humanitarian operation, but UNHCR did not make the decisions. Internal limits prevented many humanitarian workers from negotiating with warring parties. Unfortunately, well-intentioned humanitarian diplomacy occasionally supported the regimes that caused civilian misery.

The failed solutions in the abovementioned case studies show the unpredictable and complex nature of human development and security issues regardless of context and scale. Despite good intentions, implemented solutions may work in the short term but fail in the long term due to unpredictable situations. They also demonstrate that immediate rational but narrow-minded decisions that are not well thought out in an integrated manner when dealing with such problems (recall focusing on the tip of the iceberg of Figure 1.1) can endanger the environment, well-being, and livelihood of communities. Furthermore, even though the decisions may be local, their consequences can unfold on a bigger scale.

4.2   DEALING WITH MESSY AND ILL-DEFINED PROBLEMS

The challenge decision-makers and practitioners face when addressing issues such as those at play in the three case studies mentioned above is to develop and implement *good enough* decisions that embrace multiple systems and account for the intra- and inter-connectivity among these systems. Trying to account for all these factors simultaneously belongs to a class of problems that cannot be easily formulated and modeled and is sometimes referred to as "wicked" problems (Rittel and Weber, 1973). As initially defined by Churchman (1967), these problems belong to "a class of social system problems which are ill-formulated, where the information is confusing, where there are many clients and decision-makers with conflicting values, and where the ramifications in the whole system are thoroughly confusing." The term "mess" originated from Ackoff (1981) to describe the management of such problems.

The terms "messy" or "ill-defined" have also been proposed in the literature as synonymous with wicked problems; both are used throughout this book. Such issues can be interpreted as "malignant," "vicious," "tricky," or "aggressive." Paraphrasing Rittel and Weber, unlike "tamed" problems, wicked, messy, or ill-defined ones have unique characteristics:

- They show complex interlocking patterns of dysfunction.
- They are challenging to formulate and can be defined differently depending on context and scale (physical and temporal).
- They are characterized by organized complexity.
- There is no finish line (i.e., they have "no stopping rules").
- There are "no true or false answers."
- They are hard to evaluate since they create unintended consequences that are unique.
- They are irreversible, and attempting to correct some unintended consequences may create more disruptions.
- Multiple solutions to the problems require compromises (trade-offs) between numerous objectives.
- Caution, flexibility, and adaptability are needed when selecting the most appropriate solutions if such solutions can even be found.
- They are unique and cannot be regrouped into classes with similar characteristics and solutions.
- They are meant to be discovered in their unique ways.
- They can be the cause or effect of other wicked problems.

Addressing ill-defined and messy problems in general, whether as an insider or an outsider, requires making decisions in uncertain and unfamiliar environments, a definite challenge to our inherent bounded rationality (i.e., lack of objective reality). As noted by Simon (1957), "...The capacity...of the mind for formulating and solving complex problems is very small compared with the size of the problems whose solution is required for objectively rational behavior in the real world—or even for a reasonable approximation to such objective rationality."

As discussed in Chapter 1 regarding the iceberg model in Figure 1.1, when confronted with complex and uncertain information, human decisions are often made on simplified versions of the problems with conceptual models of reality based on human perceptions, perspectives, beliefs, feelings, emotions, experiences, and habits. This inclination to simplify complex problems is best illustrated in the book, *The Logic of Failure* by Dörner (1997). In that book, the author suggested the failure may originate from four reasons associated with human cognition: (i) slowness of human thinking (i.e., we feel obliged to economize and simplify), (ii) slow speed in absorbing new material (i.e., we don't think about problems we don't have), (iii) self-protection (i.e., we need to have things easier and under control to preserve our expectation of success), and (iv) limited understanding of systems (i.e., making false hypotheses and operating out of ignorance). These cognitive limitations affect how problems are addressed in a fragmented way rather than systematically and the nature of their solutions. More specifically, these limitations control: (i) how solutions are designed, planned, executed, monitored, and evaluated differently; (ii) how predictable the outcome of those solutions will be; and (iii) the long-term benefits, or sustainability, of these solutions.

Of interest in this book, peace, sustainability, and climate security and their opposites (conflict, unsustainability, and climate vulnerability) are states that emerge from the interaction of multiple messy or ill-defined issues. Such issues create challenges for those faced with making management decisions, multisolving, and selecting solutions to human development and security issues from the local to the global.

The selection of peacebuilding interventions, sustainable community practices, and adaptation and mitigation efforts to handle the effects of climate change are not straightforward processes and require decision-makers and practitioners to manage multiple trade-offs and synergies and use different perspectives from policy-decision-making to field operations. Although not a panacea, systems thinking represents a unique way to capture the uncertainty and unpredictability of the systems involved in messy and ill-defined issues. Moreover, it can help (i) capture various dynamics and linkages across the issues, (ii) explore different intervention scenarios, and (iii) develop integrated solutions.

In general, there is no singular way to handle messy and ill-defined issues, although several opinions have been proposed in the literature on how to approach them (Vennix, 1996; Metlay and Sarewitz, 2012; Stahl and Cimorelli, 2012). Chapter 13 will discuss the consequences of dealing with complex and ill-defined problems when deciding on interventions across the PSC nexus and at the community level.

4.3   CONVENTIONAL VS. SYSTEMS PERSPECTIVES

Systems thinking originated with the work on open systems of von Bertalanffy (1950), who "gave the field its basic name, many of its core concepts and a common language" (Ramage and Shipp, 2009). Since then, several definitions of systems thinking have been proposed in the literature. According to Richmond (1994), "systems thinking is the art and science of making reliable inferences about behavior by developing an increasingly deep understanding of underlying structure." Systems thinking has also been presented by Senge (1994) as the fifth discipline necessary for organizations to grow and learn. The other four include acquiring personal mastery, creating mental models, building shared vision, and team learning.

Systems thinking uses a holistic-mindful (aware) approach and complexity mindset to decide on messy and ill-defined issues. The decision process often involves a combination of "intelligent guesses" or "approximate solutions" and using a variety of *objective* tools when the situations are predictable and straightforward and *subjective* or *intuitive* tools in more complex and uncertain cases (Elms and Brown, 2012). Systems thinking also adopts an adaptive and flexible approach to decision-making through *reflection-in-action* (Schön, 1983; Barder, 2012). It also acknowledges that the decision-making process is more about *satisficing* than *optimizing* (i.e., coming up with *good enough* solutions rather than *optimal* (perfect or best) ones) (Simon, 1972). Table 4.1 compares the attributes of two perspectives to address world issues: conventional and systemic.

TABLE 4.1
Conventional and Systems Perspectives

A Conventional Perspective	A Systems Perspective
The world is full of problems. Adopt a problem-solving approach and fix them.	The world is full of systems. Adopt a learning approach. Understanding informs action.
Problems should be broken down into parts. Each part should be addressed individually.	Issues exist within complex contexts. Change requires understanding this interconnectedness.
Following a series of predetermined actions, executed in order, solves problems.	Influencing complex systems requires careful planning and adaptive action: monitor the system for its feedback (response) and adjust actions accordingly. Support positive change developing in the system.
Work is assessed based on its intentions. Unintended consequences are no one's fault, and we cannot anticipate them.	Work is assessed based on its effects. We are responsible for all of our results, including unintended consequences, which we should and can anticipate and mitigate.
Events and issues should be monitored and addressed as they arise.	Underlying social structures and dynamics produce discrete events. Change requires addressing underlying issues that drive events.
Outsiders can affect, but are not part of, the problems being addressed.	If you interact with a system, you become a part of it.
With the proper understanding, outsiders are just as capable of creating change as insiders.	Insiders intuitively understand social systems in ways few outsiders can master.
Work that targets specific constituencies can have an impact beyond those constituencies.	Impacts are important at both individual and socio-political levels of change and with both key and more people in a context.

Source: CDA (2016), used by permission of the CDA Collaborative.

4.4 VALUE PROPOSITION OF SYSTEMS THINKING

Since the publication of General Systems Theory by von Bertalanffy (1973) and the work of multiple systems thinkers (Ramage and Shipp, 2009), the value proposition of systems thinking has been demonstrated in diverse fields, from the global to the local. It has been used to explore and predict global planetary and country-level changes in frameworks and integrated assessment models (IAMs) such as World3, World3–03 (Meadows et al., 2004), Targets (Rotmans and deVries, 1997), and the International Futures platform (Hughes and Hillebrand, 2006).

The value proposition of systems thinking has also been demonstrated to address complex issues at local scales. They include peace and conflict (USIP, 2013; USAID, 2011a,b); healthcare (de Savigny and Adam, 2009; Adam, 2014; Peters, 2014); water cycle and management, water, sanitation, and hygiene (Huston and Moriarty, 2018; Adanke et al., 2019); food and nutrition (Hammond and Dube, 2012; SPRING 2015); critical infrastructure, etc. The INCOSE published several reports emphasizing the value proposition of systems engineering in their 2035 vision to address global societal challenges (INCOSE, 2021). Finally, systems thinking has also been popularized in folktales (Sweeney, 2001) and introduced in K–12 education (Benson and Marlin, 2017).

Systems thinking offers an alternate process to traditional reductionist thinking. It allows policymakers and practitioners to decipher the complexity of systems and explore (i) the interconnectedness of disparate factors and actors involved in complex issues, (ii) the nonlinearity of causal relationships, (iii) the relevance of feedback mechanisms, (iv) patterns, (v) dynamic relationships, and (vi) the identification of high leverage points. This section describes the value proposition of systems thinking when dealing with complex and messy problems in general. The following section discusses how systems thinking can help better understand the dynamic across the peace–sustainability–climate security nexus at the community scale.

4.4.1 GENERAL ATTRIBUTES OF SYSTEMS THINKING

According to various authors in the literature (e.g., Richmond, 1994; Sweeney, 2001; Hjorth and Bagheri, 2006; Sterman, 2006), systems thinking helps the thinker to:

- See the world around us in wholes instead of snapshots.
- Look at the world using different perspectives that may force us to step out of our self-inflicted and deeply engrained boxes.
- Sense how parts of systems work together to create structures and patterns.
- Acknowledge relationships between systems components from multiple levels of perspective and circular causation rather than a cause-effect linear chain of reaction viewpoint.
- Look at events not as separate from each other but as parts of behavior patterns created by some internal structure resulting from patterns and modes of thought.
- Understand the dynamic, adaptable, and changing nature of life, including the effect of time and delays (information and materials).

- Understand how one small event can influence another (positively or negatively) and the associated consequences of such interactions.
- Identify leverage points in a system, i.e., critical components or causal links where specific actions yield the most return.
- Understand that what we see happening around us depends on where we are in the system and our attitude and perception toward that system.
- Challenge our assumptions through mental models.
- Become aware of and accept our bounded rationality—that is, a need to make decisions without knowing all the facts due to complexity.
- Realize that complexity is not an obstacle but an opportunity to step out of the boxes created when describing the world.

According to Richmond (1997), the value proposition of systems thinking can also be expressed in terms of the various skills that the systems thinker provides to address complex problems (Table 4.2).

To that list, Richmond (2004) later added the skills of nonlinear thinking (i.e., no proportional relationship between cause and effect) and empathic thinking (e.g., sharing and understanding). Additional skills have been suggested by researchers other than Richmond and are discussed below.

4.4.2 Systems, Critical, and Creative Thinking

According to Vaughan (2013), systems thinking serves as the pivot of a scale that balances critical and creative thinking. Thinking critically and creatively go hand in hand: The "Why?" and "How?" questions [in a system] are the results of critical thinking. This result encourages creative thinking to generate a variety of

---

TABLE 4.2

A Summary of Systems Thinking and Associated Skills According to Richmond (1997)

Types of System Thinking	Description
Dynamic thinking	Account for how situations change and develop patterns over time
System-as-cause thinking	Find causes for a problem or issue residing within the system instead of being driven by external forces
Forest thinking	Look at trends within a system instead of focusing on specific system parts (which could result in analysis paralysis)
Operational thinking	Explore how behavior is generated through the structure of the system and its components (see Figure 1.1)
Loop thinking	Consider causal loops within a system and sees a circular instead of linear one-way causality between cause and effect
Quantitative and scientific thinking	Develop models of problems consisting of quantifiable components, which can be tested to see whether they match what is being observed in the real world and, if needed, require correction.

possibilities, leading to new queries and the improvement of the available options until the preferred course of action [for a system] is determined. Systems thinking serves as a kind of middle ground in decision-making where decision-makers might go after employing the critical and creative thinking modes, depending on the issue at hand, to obtain the broad picture. Both are constantly in play when deciding how to handle problems with human development and security. To make sure that the difficulties are rightly addressed from a technical point of view, critical thinking is required. At the same time, creative thinking is also necessary to address the uncertainty of the issues and ensure that they are suitable for the beneficiaries and their environment.

4.4.3 FIRST AND SECOND-ORDER CHANGE

According to Watzlawick et al. (1974), there are two types of systems thinking: thinking that results in solutions that create first-order change and thinking that results in solutions that create second-order change. First-order solutions address issues without changing the system as a whole. Second-order solutions, on the other hand, completely alter the system through actual change, whether by adopting a new approach or mentality or redefining what the system is capable of. According to Meadows (1997), second-order change can be considered a "change of change."

In reality, to solve complex problems, a combination of first-order and second-order thinking is required. Let's consider the following three illustrative examples related to the PSC nexus. Starting with peace, let's consider a community forced to choose between the conservation of natural resources (that they have been the steward of for a long time) and economic development. A first-order solution is to regard conservation and development in conflict and push for economic development first, which results in violent conflict and the infringement of human rights. A second-order and more peaceful solution would be to develop a synergistic action plan that helps human communities thrive while serving as stewards of natural resources combined with some acceptable level of outside collaborative economic development. In short, this represents a win-win situation for environmental protection and economic development. The Nature Conservancy (2018) remarked that "achieving a sustainable future will depend on our ability to secure both thriving human communities and abundant and healthy natural ecosystems."

Regarding sustainability, let's consider a community having problems securing essential resources such as water, energy, food, and shelter following some stressful natural event. A first-order solution would address each community's immediate need with the assistance of external voluntary aid groups. A second-order solution would be to work collaboratively and multi-solve with the community in developing a pro-active rather than reactive strategic plan of development where the community is (i) aware of its current development situation, (ii) willing to address in a participatory manner its vulnerability and strengthen its resilience to future adverse events, and (iii) can develop a sustainable plan of capacity building over 5–15 years around resource management.

Regarding climate security, a first-order solution would be, for instance, for a community to adopt a culture of external dependence (e.g., governments) when faced with climate change's direct and indirect consequences. A second-order solution would be to create a culture of resilience at the community level that involves implementing adaptation and mitigation measures that all community members have adopted. An excellent example of such an initiative is the San Francisco Bay Area Planning and Urban Research Association (SPUR, n.d.) resilient city program, a citizen-driven initiative detailing how the San Francisco Bay Area would respond to earthquakes or adverse events.

As a second example, Killelea (2021, p. 97) described the merits of systems thinking to solve conflict around natural resource competition and the environment among nomadic herders and farmers in northern Kenya. Second-order systemic solutions were developed by "farmers, villagers, and the government to create a sustainable ecosystem that balanced the long-term interests of the environment, including endangered wildlife, with those of the herders and the local farming communities."

4.4.4   WHAT IS NOT SYSTEMS THINKING?

It has become popular and progressive to remark that a person or a group has embraced a systems approach to address complex problems in various disputes in science, engineering, politics, and economics (Dent, 2001). Regrettably, this new discourse trend in public life frequently remains at the intellectual level and does not always result in better solutions and political choices.

Given that the concept of systems thinking is frequently misinterpreted or abused, it is essential to clarify what it is not. First, systems thinking is not analysis, which entails dissecting a problem into digestible, bite-sized parts and understanding each component separately. Societies are not only collections of discrete components; they are wholes that are greater than the sum of their parts.

Along such lines, systems thinking does not center on sophisticated complexity typically solved by simulating many variables and intricate arrays of details. This method frequently results in analysis paralysis, generates unmanageable data and information overloads, and obscures the emergence of patterns and correlations. However, this method is commonly applied in business analysis, planning (including engineering), and forecasting.

Finally, systems thinking does not aim to reduce complexity by making things perfect, easy, or simple. It is instead about embracing the distinctive characteristics of the systems mentioned above, not as barriers but as chances for change, as outlined in Section 3.3. The *book Getting to Maybe* by Westley et al. (2007) discusses how treating complex situations as simple or complicated can be ineffective and lead to additional challenges. On the other hand, systems thinking emphasizes "acting deliberately and intentionally in a complex, uncertain world by virtue of being in and of that world" and "welcoming the possibility of change and risk-taking with a mindset of inquiry rather than certainty."

4.4.5   RESERVATIONS TOWARD SYSTEMS THINKING

The value proposition of systems thinking to provide better and more integrated solutions and policy decisions to solve complex social challenges is still not widely accepted, even though it sounds futuristic and is frequently utilized in public discourse and debates. Systems thinking is frequently seen as a challenge to established reductionist thought as if the two were incompatible for some reason. This dualistic argument is absurd because there are occasions when segmented, reductionist decision-making is preferable. In other situations, making decisions necessitates stepping out of silos and seeing the big picture. One of the numerous qualities of system thinkers covered in the following section is their adaptability and sensitivity.

Another reason systems thinking is not always accepted has to do with how frequently public analysis results are presented by systems specialists. When systems concepts are communicated, it can occasionally become so overwhelming that it defies the goal of looking at the larger picture. According to Galloway (2011), there comes a point in systems visualization where "the more information that is represented, the less information is actually conveyed." Based on some workshop talks on systems thinking and health in Baltimore, MD, Knezovich (2014) proposed further difficulties in expressing complexity and systems thinking (Future Health Systems, 2014). The difficulties include (i) employing a language that can be difficult to understand, especially outside of an expert environment, and (ii) presenting models that can be challenging and relate poorly to reality, especially for individuals who haven't contributed to the models. These two difficulties can be overcome by involving stakeholders in a thorough examination of the pertinent issues and involving them in the systems thinking learning process.

4.5   SYSTEMS THINKING AND THE PSC NEXUS

The previous section described the generic attributes of systems thinking when addressing complex human development and security issues. More specifically, systems thinking can capture the influence and dependence among the three sectors of the PSC nexus listed in Table 2.9 and the virtuous cycle of Figure 2.10 and explore different forms of synergy and trade-offs at different scales. More specific to the PSC nexus, systems thinking, combined with systems modeling tools that will be presented in the forthcoming chapters, allows us to:

- Account for complexity, nonlinearities, and emergence in each sector and across the nexus sectors.
- Map, analyze, and model the landscape in which the nexus unfolds more comprehensively and dynamically while integrated with an evidence-based approach.
- Sense from multiple perspectives the dynamics and linkages between systems structure and behavior patterns.
- Gain insight into the different dimensions and attractors of peace vs. conflict, sustainable development vs. unstainable practices, and climate security vs. climate vulnerability practices.
- Identify and address conflicts and barriers to peace, sustainability, and climate security.
- Understand possible emerging issues and leverage points in all three nexus sectors.

- Understand the dynamic, adaptive, and unpredictable nature of different scenarios of interventions across the nexus.
- Analyze how any minor event can affect peace, sustainability, and climate security.
- Explore the importance of trade-offs and synergies in each sector.
- Adopt a flexible, multisolving, and adaptable approach to solving complex issues.

All these attributes help navigate decision-making steps better across the PSC nexus. As discussed further in Chapter 9, these steps include (i) identifying and specifying the issues to be addressed in each sector of and across the nexus, (ii) making assumptions and hypotheses about the issues, (iii) using models (mental, pen-and-paper, numerical) to test the assumptions and hypotheses, and (iv) once the models are deemed acceptable (it may take several iterations to arrive there), communicating the new understanding of the model, and proposing changes and scenarios of intervention to others.

4.6 HABITS OF SYSTEMS THINKERS

Systems thinking requires the "thinker" to embrace a new mindset and adopt habits different from those more familiar with traditional reductionist thinking. As noted by Seelos (2020), "Without changing the mindset and adopting new habits, using the term 'system' is pointless in terms of explanatory power or intervention design."

Based in Pittsburgh, Pennsylvania, the Waters Center for Systems Thinking (WCST, n.d.), formerly the Waters Foundation, proposed a series of habits they deem necessary for decision-makers to adopt when faced with systems. They are listed in Table 4.3 with illustrative examples dealing with one or several sectors of the PSC nexus. Some of the habits also depend on each other.

Even though these habits were developed in the context of integrating systems thinking in K–12 education, they apply to a wide range of situations where the thinker faces messy or ill-structured problems (Benson and Marlin, 2017). These habits represent thinking strategies (visual, listening and speaking, and kinesthetic) that decision-makers might want to follow to address complex problems at the community level and across the peace–sustainability–climate security nexus.

4.7 FINDING GOOD-ENOUGH SOLUTIONS

The systems science and complexity literature acknowledges that when faced with complex, messy, or ill-defined issues, it is impossible to come up with the best and unique solutions. However, "good enough" solutions, sometimes called *satisficing* solutions by Simon (1972), are possible and can account for tangible and intangible factors influencing the issues. Of course, the idea of coming up with just good enough solutions has not always been welcomed by those who see the world using deterministic lenses and expect the "best" and optimized solution to every problem, regardless of its complexity. It is one of the reasons why some individuals have stayed shy of systems thinking and have even been critical of it.

TABLE 4.3

Habits of Systems Thinkers and Linkages and Illustrative Examples of Application

Habits	Description	Human Development and Security Examples
1. Seek to understand the big picture.	A systems thinker focuses on the forest and the details of any single tree.	• Peace, sustainability, and climate security at the local level depend on what's happening globally and vice versa. • Transboundary issues at the regional scale (e.g., the Arctic, Middle East) are common. • Selected interventions create desirable and undesirable patterns of change at different scales (e.g., household, community, and regional).
2. Change perspectives to increase understanding. Related to habit # 5	A systems thinker increases understanding by changing the way they view aspects of the system.	• Stakeholders may have different opinions about peace, capacity building, and climate security practices. • Participatory dialogue is needed to find common ground. • Each intervention's what, why, who, where, when, and how changes from looking at the big picture to examining specific details.
3. Consider how mental models affect current reality and the future. Related to habits # 14 and 5	A systems thinker is aware of how beliefs and attitudes influence how a system behaves.	• Mental models are at the bottom of the iceberg in Figure 1.1. Conflict, unsustainable practices, and climate vulnerability may result from belief systems that are no longer valid. Mental models change. • Different mental models lead to distinctive intervention methods.
4. Observe how elements within systems change over time, generating patterns and trends.	A systems thinker sees change over time as the "dynamics" of a system.	• Identify the story that has led to the current situation and how it has evolved. • How has climate change and its effects affected communities? • How has conflict constrained economic growth over time? • Learning from past events to do better in the future. • The behavior patterns of complex and adaptive systems change over time due to changes in their internal structure and external effects. • A value proposition for monitoring and evaluation of interventions.
5. Surface and test assumptions. Related to habits # 3 and 4	A systems thinker actively tests theories and assumptions, perhaps with others, to improve performance.	• Need to monitor and evaluate implementations, identify and manage risks, and make changes accordingly. • Assumptions behind interventions must be re-evaluated regularly to see if they are still relevant to explain current dynamics. • Avoid making decisions on assumptions and belief systems that are no longer valid and relevant.

(Continued)

TABLE 4.3 (*Continued*)

Habits of Systems Thinkers and Linkages and Illustrative Examples of Application

Habits	Description	Human Development and Security Examples
6. Recognize that a system's structure generates its behavior. Related to habit # 8	A systems thinker focuses on system structure and avoids blaming when things go wrong.	• Peace, sustainability, and climate security are emerging properties from the interaction of multiple systems. • Peace, sustainability, and climate security are entangled. • Decisions to address issues in a system need to be made by first considering the structure and feedback that generate the problems rather than being reactive to these issues. • Avoid applying Band-Aids to immediately address apparent issues and behavior patterns (see Figure 1.1).
7. Identify the circular nature of complex cause-and-effect relationships. Related to habits # 6 and 12	A systems thinker sees the interdependencies in a system and uncovers circular causal connections.	• Multiple feedback loops are at play between the structure and behavior of each sector of the nexus, across the sectors, and the systems with which the sectors interact. • Linear systems where one cause has a specific effect are rare since causes and effects across the nexus are often interchangeable.
8. Recognize the impact of time delays when exploring cause-and-effect relationships. Related to habit # 13	A systems thinker understands that often cause and effect are not closely related in time.	• Effect of time on climate change. • Peacebuilding, peacemaking, and peacekeeping efforts take time. • The delays between implementing an intervention and assessing whether or not it is working. • Addressing nexus-related and community development issues takes time and patience. • It may take several attempts at solving something complex before a permanent solution is in place.
9. Consider short-term, long-term, and unintended consequences of actions.	A systems thinker looks ahead and anticipates the immediate results, actions, and effects down the road.	• Short- and long-term implications on adaptation and mitigation. • Interventions may have short-term consequences that can be evaluated relatively quickly. • Interventions may have long-term consequences that may limit their long-term performance.
10. Consider an issue thoroughly and resist the urge to come to a quick conclusion.	A systems thinker takes the necessary time to understand the dynamics of a system before taking action.	• Problems are never as simple as they seem to be at first glance. • Need to collect and analyze data to identify and rank issues and risks. • Need to understand what drives events.
11. Pay attention to accumulations and their rates of change. Related to habit #4	A systems thinker sees quantities of material or information that have built up or diminished over time.	• If no actions are taken, issues may grow over time at increasing rates, create obstacles or barriers, or spread across the PSC sectors, leading to greater problems with more impactful consequences.

(*Continued*)

TABLE 4.3 (*Continued*)
Habits of Systems Thinkers and Linkages and Illustrative Examples of Application

Habits	Description	Human Development and Security Examples
12. Use an understanding of systems structure to identify possible leverage actions.	A systems thinker uses system understanding to determine what small actions will most likely produce desirable results.	• Identify where to intervene first at the peace, sustainability, or climate security level with a more significant impact on change.
13. Check results and change actions if needed (successive approximations).	A systems thinker establishes benchmarks to help assess gradual improvement.	• Design as you go, adaptive and flexible approach, reflection before, in, and after action. • Learn from failure, change, and experimentation.
14. Make meaningful connections within and between systems. Related to habit # 10	A systems thinker sees how concepts, facts, and ideas link, leading to new learning, discoveries, and innovations.	• The nexus sectors are entangled. • Interventions in one sector of the PSC nexus may have immediate or delayed effects on the other sectors and create cascading intended and unintended consequences. • Multiple cause-and-effect loops are at play in decision-making.

Source: The left and center columns are adapted from Benson and Marlin (2017), used by permission of the © 2020 Waters Center for Systems Thinking, https://waterscenterST.org.

There are no solid road maps and recipes for finding good enough solutions to complex problems. Seelos (2020) noted that solving complex problems is more a journey of discovery than reaching solutions as quickly as possible. In that author's opinion, system work is about "discovering and steering local pathways for change at a pace appropriate for our ability to learn and for what local communities can enact and absorb." Furthermore, the journey is "akin to identifying the essential pieces of a puzzle, understanding how systems are configured to do what they do, and only then devising pathways toward generating a different configuration that everyone sees as an improvement."

The journey of finding solutions to complex problems can best be illustrated using the ancient metaphor of the elephant and the six blind men, each trying to conceptualize precisely the whole when only touching some limited parts of it. Embarking on that journey requires decision-makers to acquire the generic habits listed in Table 4.3. To these general habits, we can add more appropriate practices when making decisions at the local level, such as in community development. They include being able to:

- Adopt an adaptive and reflective practice
- Recognize community behavior patterns and infer their underlying structures

- Operate in qualitative and quantitative ways as needed
- Consider the context, content, and scale of community development
- Identify and make use of feedback structures
- Consider the right development solutions, done right, and for the right reasons
- Consider an integrated approach to planning and design
- Embrace and welcome participation
- Acknowledge one's strengths, weaknesses, humility, patience, and biases
- Learn through experience
- Expect many unintended consequences and adapt to new normal conditions
- Accept not-so-perfect project outcomes (even failure) as a way of learning life-long lessons and gaining insights
- Consider multiple possible scenarios of intervention

Since various decision-making groups are involved in community development, these individual practices must be supplemented by some created at the group level. In community development, groups choose (i) the data to be gathered and analyzed, (ii) the problems that need to be solved, (iii) the best way to represent these problems, and (iv) the intervention scenarios and how they should be carried out.

For a group of decision-makers to effectively collaborate and coordinate their efforts, several practical questions must be addressed, including (i) who the participants are, (ii) how many should be included from different stakeholder groups (community, governments, outsiders), (iii) what skills and knowledge they bring to the group, (iv) what role they will play in the life-cycle of community development, (v) what training they require, and (vi) how diverse the group should be. Creating a "shared reality" that all participants can accept is the main problem in group work (Vennix, 1996). However, it must be remembered that this ideal result is more of an exception than a rule because of the diversity of opinions and levels of bounded rationality that can be expected from group members. Because of this, the group's shared reality is a dynamic idea that needs to be reviewed frequently through reflection-in-action.

Using a systematic approach to deal with complex challenges has fundamental advantages in terms of coming up with "good enough" solutions. It becomes obvious once decision-makers have developed the essential habits and behaviors individually or as a group. However, decision-makers must also be aware of the following when confronted with intricate issues relating to human development and security:

- Predetermined solutions to complex problems do not work. Approaching systems objectively and seeking a deep understanding of these systems does not make sense and is futile. Seelos (2020) referred to the pathologies of "the illusion of understanding" and "the illusion of competence" that decision-makers commonly display when they claim that they have concrete solutions to complex problems.
- Multiple solutions to complex problems are possible. There is no one-size-fits-all approach to mapping, understanding, modeling, and decision-making solutions in complex systems.

- Shallow and quick solutions to complex problems do not last. Patience and humility are necessary when dealing with complex systems, specifically social systems.
- Solutions to complex problems are not just technical. Instead of being pre-determined by some experts, objective and subjective solutions emerge as the environment changes from creative interactions among the stakeholders involved in addressing the problems.

4.8 CONCLUDING REMARKS

The past 30 years have seen a growing interest in systems thinking in multiple disciplines. As noted by Woodhill and Millican (2023), "there are no simple recipes or blueprints for applying systems thinking." As we will see in the forthcoming chapters, numerous tools are available to approach complex issues with a systems mindset and develop intervention scenarios. However, it is essential that before these tools are used, potential users acquire the habits discussed in this chapter. Without developing such practices, systems thinking tools could be misused. Even worse is when the misuse forces decision-makers to revert to a decision process that creates the problems to be solved in the first place.

REFERENCES

Ackoff, R. L. (1981). The art and science of mess management. *Interfaces, 11*(1), 20–26. https://www.jstor.org/stable/25060027

Adam, T. (2014). Advancing the application of systems thinking in health. *Health Research Policy and Systems, 12*, 50. https://doi.org/10.1186/1478-4505-12-50

Adanke, M., Hailegiorgis, B., & Butterworth, J. (2019). A local systems analysis for rural water services delivery in south Ari and Mile, Ethiopia. https://www.ircwash.org/sites/default/files/a_local_systems_analysis_for_rural_water_services_delivery_in_south_ari_and_mile_ethiopia.pdf

Barder, O. (2012, September 7). Complexity, adaptation, and results. http://www.cgdev.org/blog/complexity-adaptation-and-results

Benson, T., & Marlin, S. (2017). *The habit-forming guide to becoming a systems thinker.* The Waters Foundation Systems Thinking Group Publ.

Churchman, C. W. (1967). Wicked problems. *Management Science, 14*(4), B141–142.

Collaborative for Development Action (CDA). (2016). *Designing strategic initiatives to impact conflict systems: Systems approaches to peacebuilding. A resource manual.* CDA Collaborative Learning Projects.

Cutts, M. (1999). The humanitarian operation in Bosnia, 1992–1995: Dilemmas and negotiating humanitarian access. New Issues in Refugee Research, *working paper No. 8.* https://www.unhcr.org/media/humanitarian-operation-bosnia-1992-95-dilemmas-negotiating-humanitarian-access-mark-cutts

Dent, E. B. (2001). System science traditions: Differing philosophical assumptions. *Systems: Journal Transdisciplinary Systems Science, 6*(1–2), 13–30. https://doi.org/10.2139/ssrn.2326323

de Savigny, D., & Adam, T. (eds.). (2009). *Systems thinking for health systems strengthening.* Alliance for Health Policy and Systems Research, World Health Organization.

Dörner, D. (1997). *The logic of failure: Recognizing and avoiding error in complex situations.* Perseus Books.

Elms, D. G., & Brown, C. B. (2012). Decisions in a complex context: A new formalism? *Proceedings of the International Forum on Engineering Decision Making*, 6th IFED, Lake Louise, Canada.

Future Health Systems. (2014). Workshop on complex adaptive systems, Baltimore, June. https://steps-centre.org/blog/complex-adaptive-systems/

Galloway, A. (2011). Are some things unrepresentable? *Theory, Culture & Society*, *28*(7–8), 85–102. https://doi.org/10.1177/0263276411423038

Hammond, R. A., & Dube, L. (2012). A systems science perspective and transdisciplinary models for food and nutrition security. *Proceedings National Academy of Sciences of the United States of America*, *109*(31), 12356–12363. https://doi.org/10.1073/pnas.0913003109

Hjorth, P., & Bagheri, A. (2006). Navigating towards sustainable development: A system dynamics approach. *Future*, *38*, 74–92. https://doi.org/10.1016/j.futures.2005.04.005

Hughes, B. B., & Hillebrand, E. E. (2006). *Exploring and shaping international futures*. Paradigm Publishers.

Huston, A., & Moriarty, P. (2018). Understanding the WASH system and its building blocks: Building strong WASH systems for the SDGs. https://www.ircwash.org/resources/understanding-wash-system-and-its-building-blocks

International Council on Systems Engineering. (INCOSE). (2021). *Systems engineering: Vision 2035. Engineering solutions for a better world*. https://www.incose.org/about-systems-engineering/se-vision-2035

Killelea, S. (2021). *Peace in the age of chaos: The best solution for a sustainable future*. Hardie Grant Books.

Knezovich, J. (2014). Communicating complexity. https://archive.ids.ac.uk/futurehealthsystems/blog/2014/7/30/communicating-complexity.html

Loftus, E. (2015). Operation cat drop. Operation Cat Drop* – heartoftheart. wordpress.com; https://www.heartoftheart.org/?p=1006

Meadows, D. H. (1997). Places to intervene in a system in increasing order of effectiveness. *Whole Earth*, *Winter*, 78–84.

Meadows, D. H., Randers, J., & Meadows, D. (2004). *Limits to growth: The 30-year update*. Chelsea Green Publishing.

Mencken, H. L. (n.d.). https://www.brainyquote.com/quotes/h_l_mencken_129796

Metlay, D., & Sarewitz, D. (2012). Decision strategies for addressing complex, "messy" problems. *The Bridge*, *42*(3), 6–16.

Monbiot, G. (2021, October 30). Capitalism is killing the planet – it's time to stop buying into our own destruction. https://www.theguardian.com/environment/2021/oct/30/capitalism-is-killing-the-planet-its-time-to-stop-buying-into-our-own-destruction

Peters, D. H. (2014). The application of systems thinking in health: Why use systems thinking? *Health Research Policy and Systems*, *12*(51), 166–171. https://doi.org/10.1186/1478-4505-12-51

Ramage, M., & Shipp, K. (2009). *Systems thinkers*. Springer.

Richmond, B. (1994). System dynamics/systems thinking: Let's just get on with it. *System Dynamics Review*, *10*(2–3). https://doi.org/10.1002/sdr.4260100204

Richmond, B. (1997). The 'thinking' in systems thinking: How can we make it easier to master? *The Systems Thinker*, 8(2), 1–15.

Richmond, B. (2004). *An introduction to systems thinking, STELLA software*. isee Systems, Inc.

Rittel, H., & Webber, M. (1973). Dilemmas in a general theory of planning. *Policy Sciences*, *4*, 155–169. https://doi.org/10.1007/BF01405730

Rotmans, J., & deVries, B. (eds.). (1997). *Perspectives on global change: The TARGETS approach*. Cambridge University Press.

San Francisco Bay Area Planning and Urban Research Association (SPUR). (n.d.). The Resilient City. https://www.spur.org/featured-project/resilient-city

Schön, D. A. (1983). *The reflective practitioner: How professionals think in action.* Basic Books,

Seelos, C. (2020). Changing systems? Welcome to the slow movement. Stanford Social Innovation Review, Winter.

Senge, P. (1994). *The fifth discipline: The art & practice of the learning organization.* Doubleday.

Simon, H. A. (1957). *Models of man: Social and rational.* Wiley.

Simon, H. A. (1972). Theories of bounded rationality. In C. B. McGuire and R. Radner (eds.), *Decision and Organization* (pp. 161–176). North-Holland Pub.

Stahl, C., & Cimorelli, A. (2012). A demonstration of the necessity and feasibility of using a clumsy decision analytic approach on wicked environmental problems. *Integrated Environmental Assessment and Management*, *9*(1), 17–30. https://doi.org/10.1002/ieam.1356

Sterman, J. (2006). Learning from evidence in a complex world. *American Journal of Public Health*, *96*(3), 505–514. https://doi.org/10.2105/ajph.2005.066043

Strengthening Partnerships, Results, and Innovations in Nutrition Globally (SPRING). (2015). A systems thinking and action for nutrition: USAID/ Project. https://www.spring-nutrition.org/publications/briefs/systems-thinking-and-action-nutrition

Sweeney, L. B. (2001). *When a butterfly sneezes: A guide for helping kids explore interconnections in our world through favorite stories.* Pegasus Communications.

The Nature Conservancy. (2018, October 13). The science of sustainability. Can a unified path for development and conservation lead to a better future? https://www.nature.org/en-us/what-we-do/our-insights/perspectives/the-science-of-sustainability/

U.S. Agency for International Development (USAID). (2011a). *Systems thinking in conflict assessment: Concepts and application.* USAID, Washington, DC.

U.S. Agency for International Development (USAID). (2011b). *USAID complexity event.* USAID, Washington, DC.

United States Institute of Peace (USIP). (2013). *Harnessing operational systems engineering to support peacebuilding.* The National Academies Press.

Vaughan, M. (2013). *The thinking effect.* Nicholas Brealey Publishing.

Vennix, J. A. M. (1996). *Group model building: Facilitating team learning using system dynamics.* Wiley.

von Bertalanffy, L. (1950). The theory of open systems in physics and biology. *Science*, *111*(2872), 23–29. https://www.jstor.org/stable/1676073

von Bertalanffy, L. (1973). *General systems theory* (4th ed.). George Braziller, Inc. Publ.

Waters Center for Systems Thinking (WCST). (n.d.). https://waterscenterst.org/

Watzlawick, P., Weakland, J. H., & Fisch, R. (1974). *Change: Principles of problem formation and problem resolution.* W. W. Norton & Company; (Reprint ed.). (April 25, 2011).

Westley, F., Zimmerman, B., & Patton, M. Q. (2007). *Getting to maybe: How the world is changed.* Vintage Canada.

Woodhill, J., & Millican, J. (2023). *Systems thinking and practice: A guide to concepts, principles and tools for FCDO and partners.* Institute of Development Studies. https://doi.org/10.19088/K4D.2023.002

5 Defining the PSC Nexus Landscape

5.1 COMMUNITY LANDSCAPE AS A SYSTEM

Understanding the existing setting where conflict and climate change affect community livelihood and security is vital. It represents the frame of reference for developing peace, sustainability, and climate security solutions. The setting usually consists of many interacting systems, each with a hierarchy of embedded subsystems, as shown in Figure 5.1. In that holarchy, issues arise due to multiple observable and unobservable forces as the systems and subsystems share inputs and outputs. The systems are bounded by (i) constraints and barriers, including those resulting from mutual interactions among their components, and (ii) restrictions created by the environment in which the community development unfolds.

Generally, the PSC nexus unfolds in a specific *context* and over a particular geographic area (spatial scale) and time frame (temporal scale) defined by a boundary. Within the border, the community is an emerging and evolutionary whole where various policies, regulations, socioeconomic-cultural factors, etc., influence

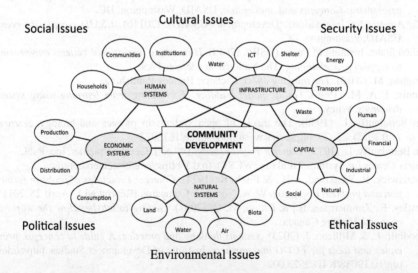

FIGURE 5.1 The holarchy of systems involved in community development and their multiple constraints. Each group consists of various subsystems.

Source: Amadei (2019), used by permission of Momentum Press.

Note: A simpler version of this graph was initially proposed by Jorge Vanegas (personal communication, 2000).

 DOI: 10.1201/9781003435006-5

its dynamic. Once the border has been identified, (i) data and information about the community and the PSC nexus are collected and analyzed, (ii) constraints and issues are identified, and (iii) decisions are made about possible interventions to address these issues. The selected boundary and permeability are critical since they determine the community development's internal (endogenous) or external (exogenous) constraints. The external environment outside the border cannot be ignored, as it may affect the landscape's dynamic. Human-made crises and natural disasters can potentially affect the landscape dynamic. Internal and external factors require community development decision-makers to make decisions in a complex and uncertain environment.

As discussed by the author for the FEW/WELF nexus (Amadei, 2019), it is appropriate to use the term "landscape" to describe the setting or "area of activity" (*Merriam-Webster*) in which community development takes place and the PSC nexus unfolds. The community landscape is the space that encompasses all the systems and subsystems shown in Figure 5.1. A time boundary can also be introduced to define the time window in which the landscape dynamic of Figure 5.1 evolves.

In the literature, the term "landscape" has been used in various integrated landscape management approaches/frameworks, particularly when resolving issues relating to natural resource management, conservation, development, and climate (Sayer et al., 2013; Denier et al., 2015). All of these strategies acknowledge that (i) the landscape is a complex and ill-defined system of systems that necessitates adopting flexibility and adaptability in its management, (ii) there are adequate but not ideal solutions to address landscape issues, (iii) multi-stakeholder participation is essential for resolving these issues, and (iv) any interventions across the landscape need to include numerous system components while attempting to increase synergies and reduce trade-offs.

As a result, the community landscape is a dynamic, complex system comprising various system types that interact to create a larger structure. In this book, the systems are reorganized into four categories for clarity, as indicated in Figure 5.1: human (social), infrastructure, natural, and economic systems and their subsystems. For instance, houses, tribes, communities, and institutions are all examples of human systems. Infrastructure systems, sometimes called engineered systems, are composed of several parts that deliver services, including water, telecom, housing, electricity, food, transportation, health care, waste disposal, etc.

Likewise, the natural systems consist of the hydrosphere (water), the geosphere (land), the atmosphere (air), and the biosphere (plant and animal life). Finally, economic systems consist of various production, distribution, and consumption processes associated with different sectors of the economy. These four systems groups involve other forms of capital (natural, intellectual and human, social, financial, and physical). The systems in Figure 5.1 could also be replaced by the five domains of sustainability suggested by Ben-Eli (2018) discussed in Section 2.2.3.

The community landscape is a system because the various systems and their subsystems mentioned above are interrelated and synergistic. The PSC nexus is embedded in their interactions and cannot be extracted from the landscape.

The fact that the PSC nexus's components interact with the systems and subsystems of the community landscape to create an evolving "space of possibilities" (Mitleton-Kelly, 2003) is another reason to think of the community landscape as a system. The enabling environment is subject to numerous environmental, political, social, cultural, ethical, and security stressors and limiting factors, as indicated in Figure 5.1. They create rules and constraints dictating the behavior of the systems, their subsystems, and the behavior patterns of the landscape. While some of these stressors originate from the external environment, others are contained within the internal environment of the landscape. The space of possibilities or the enabling environment at the community level dictates potential community states or the levels of development that are constantly changing. The space of possibilities at the PSC nexus level describes how each sector of the nexus manifests itself and can be managed.

Finally, a reason to consider the community landscape as a system is that its embedded systems and subsystems have several functions and purposes that support the PSC nexus. For instance, social systems may include institutions that provide governance, the rule of law, and conflict resolution. Infrastructure systems provide services needed for sustainable development (e.g., water, wastewater, energy, telecommunications, transportation, shelter, and so on), adaptation to, and mitigation of adverse events. Natural systems provide multiple eco-services such as air and water purification, the cycling of nutrients, pollination of crops and vegetation, and production of soils, among others. Climate change may affect these eco-services. The type of economic system dictates the production, distribution, and consumption of services. Furthermore, all these forms of service interact with each other.

In general, using the system's classification discussed in Section 3.3.2, the community landscape is a *complex* system in the sense that (i) uncertainty and ambiguity are the norms, (ii) complex interactions with circular and nonlinear causality take place among its components, (iii) unpredictability in one, or several of its components is commonplace, (iv) unintended consequences unfold, and (v) it is not easy to reach an agreement on how to address problems in the landscape since they are interconnected. In complex systems such as the landscape, the unknowns must be handled as they are discovered. Furthermore, the complexity of the landscape can be defined as "organized" and characterized by "a sizable number of factors which are interrelated into an organic whole" and for which no probable system's behavior can be defined (Weaver, 1948). Organized complexity is in direct contrast to disorganized complexity, where the number of factors is vast, and statistical methods can predict the system's behavior.

Although the landscape in Figure 5.1 is complex overall, some of its systems and subsystems may display varying degrees of complexity. Infrastructure systems are one example of something that may not be complex but rather *complicated*, and even though the unknowns are recognized, experts are still required to solve them. In rare instances, some systems can be *simple* and demonstrate predictability and certainty. Complicated and simple systems are easier to control and less likely to have unintended repercussions than complex ones. Decision-makers must utilize various modes of intervention, depending on the complexity of the landscape, as stated in Section 3.3.2: categorizing for simple systems, analyzing for complicated systems, probing for complex systems, and responding rapidly to chaotic systems.

The community development landscape is not only intricate but also has *adaptive* characteristics and components that adjust to internal and external changes. These elements are primarily present in social and ecological systems that (i) are in a state of dynamic equilibrium, (ii) are defined by organization and structure, and (iii) are changing through time through various processes at various speeds. By altering their structures, behaviors, and interactional rules through evolutionary and coevolutionary feedback mechanisms, these systems are capable of different levels of organization, reorganization, self-organization, self-correction, and adaptation (Mitleton-Kelly, 2003). The last unique characteristic of social systems is "intent."

Other unique properties of complex systems that might be important to consider in understanding the community landscape include the following:

- Repetitive behavior patterns, feedback processes, and the role of attractors
- Interdependency and synergy between components leading to a global landscape emerging behavior that cannot be predicted from that of its parts taken separately
- Nonlinear relationships between components linking causes and effects often counterintuitively (Meadows, 2008)
- Uncertainty in how the landscape and its components behave and for which odds and likelihood cannot be estimated with confidence due to the organized complexity (Knight, 1921; Luce and Raiffa, 1957; Duncan, 1975)
- Places of leverage where a slight change in the landscape has the potential to have a more significant impact across multiple systems and subsystems (Meadows, 2008)
- Irreversible hysteresis behavior once tipping points have been reached; and
- Dependence on and sensitivity to initial conditions.

The community landscape of Figure 5.1 more closely resembles a *biological organism* with a changing metabolism than an assemblage of static pieces as a result of all the above characteristics. This physical metaphor often describes complex and adaptive systems, such as communities (Batty, 2010). The organism's systems, subsystems, and interdependent interactions produce its overall behavior pattern (or performance). Based on that pattern, the PSC nexus will develop in a certain way.

In community development practice, the challenge becomes identifying the overall landscape structure responsible for its behavior pattern, systems, and subsystems and how the PSC nexus unfolds. As discussed for the iceberg model of Figure 1.1, the main challenge with this type of *reverse analysis* is that there are no specific existing methodologies for doing so, much less a method that would guarantee a definite and successful answer since complex systems are nonlinear. Even if possible, the solution at one scale could not be extrapolated to another and would likely be time-dependent. Another limitation of the reverse analysis is that it is impossible to account for all the dynamics processes, components, and causal links responsible for the observed behavior. Finally, a third limitation is that the reverse analysis can only go so far regarding the level of disaggregation.

In short, reverse analysis and modeling of behavior patterns of interacting human, ecological, economic, and engineered systems in the landscape can only be done iteratively, incrementally, and by trial and error, and requires multidisciplinary backgrounds. Finding models that explain common behavioral patterns in a way experts and laypeople can comprehend requires striking a balance between complexity and simplicity.

Despite the abovementioned limitations, a reverse analysis might be easier for engineered and economic systems that are more predictable and show more consistent behavior than human and natural systems. However, this does not mean that reverse analysis of human systems such as households, communities, and institutions is random. Human behavior often follows patterns explained by archetypes (see Chapter 8). The dynamics and structure behind these archetypes are relatively well understood, although they cannot be generalized to represent all forms of behavior. The same could be said of the structure of natural systems in the landscape, whether natural or human-modified (i.e., engineered), based on what is known of their dynamics, evolution, and how they provide ecosystem services. Nevertheless, their uncertainty and complexity remain in their response to global phenomena such as climate change (Schneider, 2004; Burkett et al., 2005).

5.2   CONTEXT, SCALE, AND BOUNDARIES

Context, scale, and boundaries are three critical landscape characteristics defining how community development occurs and the PSC nexus unfolds. Mapping of these characteristics is needed before any community landscape appraisal is carried out, community issues identified and modeled, and solutions proposed. They control what data and information need to be collected and what community interventions are more appropriate than others.

5.2.1   CONTEXT

Context is defined in the *Merriam-Webster* dictionary as "the situation in which something happens... the group of conditions that exist where and when something happens." Community development and the dynamic between peace, sustainability, and climate security are likely to be different for different (i) rural and urban settings, (ii) climatic regions, (iii) elevations, (iv) cultures, and (v) adverse events settings. They are also different in the context of pre-conflict, ongoing conflict, and post-conflict. Finally, context may not be static and change over time, thus requiring monitoring and evaluation of the important social, technical, economic, environmental, political, legal, and ethical aspects of the community landscape.

As discussed by the author for the WELF nexus, geography provides practical tools for decision-makers to understand the role that context plays in decision-making. It contributes valuable spatial and temporal insights into Earth's physical (physical geography) and how populations interact with the Earth and its natural processes (human geography). Geography impacts all the systems in Figure 5.1. It also shapes the effect of conflict and climate change on social and natural systems (Bendor and Scheffran, 2019). As noted by Marshall (2021)

Geography is a key factor shaping what humanity can and cannot do... The choices people make, now and in the future, are never separate from their physical contact. The starting point of any country's story is its location in relation to neighbors, sea routes, and natural resources.

Ignoring geographic information in community development will likely lead to inappropriate technical and socioeconomic solutions to community issues and possible conflicts (Marshall, 2021). Based on De Blij's (2012) work, geography affects the systems of Figure 5.1 in multiple ways.

For the socioeconomic systems, geography

- Explains why populations convene in specific locations and prioritize certain activities, how they trade with each other, and why some have more advantages than others
- Offers insights into how populations make decisions for a specific ecological and climatic setting based on their belief systems, cultural preferences, value systems, and so on
- Provides insights into the management and allocation of nature's resources while considering possible geopolitical and socioeconomic risk drivers, constraints, and limitations

For the environmental systems, geography

- Provides a methodology to assess the nature (quality and quantity) and distribution of natural resources
- Combined with geology, it yields valuable information about the availability of local geological materials for construction, land stability or road construction, and land use in general
- Provides information about the depth and recharge of groundwater and the location of springs

For the infrastructure systems, geography

- Contributes to making appropriate decisions about what types of infrastructure would work best at certain locations to provide specific services such as water, energy, roads, telecom, and transportation to populations
- Is critical to land use and community planning. It may help to decide, for instance, how land is used and whether communities may need to be relocated due to changes in natural conditions following some adverse events

Among all disciplines of geography, climate (i.e., the average weather) impacts all the systems in Figure 5.1. According to the Köppen classification system (Means,

2016), Earth climates are divided into five groups: tropical humid (equatorial or low latitude), dry (sub-tropical to mid-latitude), mild (temperate) mid-latitude, severe (continental) mid-latitude, and polar.

Climates and their intra-variability (over one year) or inter-variability (from one year to the next) affect all three sectors of the PSC nexus. Climates can jeopardize stability and peace. Climate-related risks and uncertainties can create socioeconomic, geopolitical, and environmental problems that could lead to crises or unrest at different scales and over long periods, especially in disadvantaged communities. As discussed in Section 2.1, this was the case with the sustained drought in Syria and the Middle East Fertile Crescent starting in 2011, combined with weak country governance and a lack of environmental and agricultural policymaking. This dynamic led to political unrest and human migration from rural to urban areas (Kelley et al., 2015) and fueled a worldwide refugee crisis starting in 2015.

Climate change affects the people, planet, prosperity, partnership, and peace aspects of sustainable development by:

- Controlling (i) where and how populations live, (ii) the quality and quantity of the natural resources, (iii) the planning, design, operation, and maintenance of infrastructure systems; and (iv) what is possible for socioeconomic development
- Defining the extent and intensity of dry and wet seasons and the land's hydrology, which in turn (i) controls how much freshwater is available for domestic, industrial, and agricultural use and (ii) affects food and energy security
- Creating socioeconomic challenges in countries with "difficult hydrology" (i.e., insufficient or too much water). In arid and semiarid climates, there may be (depending on the location) enough water for domestic and industrial use but not enough to grow food—a situation that is likely to deteriorate over time due to rapid population growth and urbanization in that region
- Affecting how land is used—for instance, if it is subjected to desertification, land can no longer be used for agriculture

Finally, the rate and intensity of climate change and the development of erratic climate patterns control how populations should prepare to cope and adapt to one or several adverse events. They include floods, tropical storms, landslides, heat waves, droughts, wildfires, sea-level rise, and temperature rise. Recognizing climate change helps develop guidelines regarding the nature of the climate security adaptation and mitigation practices to be implemented at the community level.

Figure 5.2 shows the result of an extensive literature review (papers published in 168 journals) by Sharifi et al. (2021) on the linkages between climate change stressors and different types of conflict. The authors also considered 16 geographic regions. As noted by the authors, conflicts in the Middle East are mostly related to water stress. Southeast Asia is linked to climate stressors such as "water stress, extreme temperatures and floods, and civil, interstate, and political conflicts."

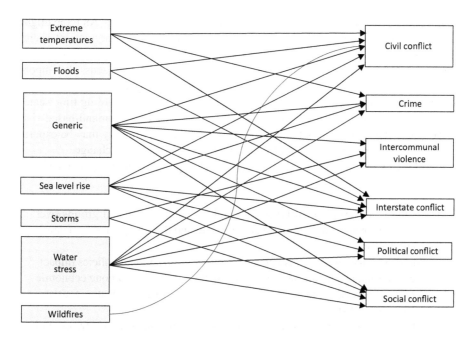

FIGURE 5.2 Interlinkages between climate stressors and conflict types. This is a simplified version of the original from Sharifi et al. (2021) not showing the strength of the pathways and geographic regions.

Source: Sharifi et al. (2021), open-access journal.

5.2.2 Spatial and Time Scales

Systems exist at different scales, from the individual/household level to the community, national, and global scales. Even if all community development issues appear to unfold in the community only, the problems may also manifest at a larger scale and have a considerable impact. In that case, more encompassing systems and their subsystems must be considered.

The dynamic across the PSC nexus is not the same at different scales, from the global (country or state) to the regional and local or functional scale, such as villages or households. All three sectors may be balanced states at one scale and unbalanced at another, where one or several sectors are weaker. A case in point is what happened in Rwanda before 1994, where plots of family land were divided from one generation to the next. This unsustainable situation resulted in plots of land that became too small to provide proper household economic support—a dynamic that scholars have suggested was correlated with political unrest, ethnic divisions, and the violent 1994 country-wide genocide (Diamond, 2005; Boudreaux, 2009).

Across the PSC nexus, the *spatial* scale plays a critical role in making decisions and who makes them. Decisions are made by community members at the local (bottom-up) level and by various forms of government in the country, state, or region (top-down). It is essential to explore whether development issues at one scale are related to problems at another and whether solutions to these issues scale up. An issue might be how tensions at one scale may impact conflict at another. Decisions to intervene in one or multiple sectors of the nexus at the national level may not be relevant at the regional and local levels, and vice versa. Reynolds et al. (2003) discuss the importance of scale when distinguishing between local land degradation and regional desertification due to climate change. The same could be said regarding time scale, as a community may be resilient to specific supply-based and demand-based risk drivers over the short term but not in the long term. The community may be experiencing long periods of stasis disturbed by sudden events requiring change.

The OECD (2005) considered water-related tensions at four interdependent physical scales:

- At the local level: for instance, in conflicts between societal groups over access to a water source or between the state and those impacted by a dam's construction.
- At the national level: for instance, in discussions on national policies impacting water management, such as the redistribution of water among economic sectors, between various interest groups (e.g., farmers, industry, tourism, environmentalists).
- At the international level: for instance, in disputes between upstream and downstream states over using shared rivers.
- At the global level, for instance, in the global food market, between importers and exporters.

Furthermore, physical and time scales, both dynamic, also affect each other. Zurek and Henrichs (2007) noted that more aggregated processes at the regional or global scale take longer to unfold than less aggregated processes at the local scale. A good example is how the dynamic of global climate change that has taken place over decades affects livelihood and security at the community level on a yearly or seasonal basis. The reverse is true since problems may start locally and evolve to become critical at larger scales (Winograd and Farrow, 2011). An example would be the drought in Syria and the Middle East Fertile Crescent that led to the European refugee crisis starting in 2015.

Pakistan is another example where water issues unfold at two different scales: interstate with India and Afghanistan and intrastate across provinces. Both are threatening the political and environmental security of the region and at the local level in a country that is experiencing rapid urbanization and population growth. A complex dynamic in Pakistan involves (i) the unequal and inequitable availability and accessibility of land and resources such as water, energy, and food; (ii) the overexploitation of surface water and excessive underground water withdrawal; (iii) the effect of climate change on weather patterns; (iv) increased rural-urban migration; and (v) local and regional conflict and protest in urban and rural areas. This complex dynamic is best summarized by Mustafa et al. (2013): "Water scarcity, floods, droughts, and domestic mismanagement can embitter interethnic relations and prompt political tension, which can, in turn, lead to violence."

Interventions in the PSC nexus at one scale may impact interventions at other scales (Zurek and Henrichs, 2007). For example, large-scale water, energy, and agricultural infrastructure projects necessary to fulfill the needs of large urban areas may impact smaller community projects, particularly in terms of socioeconomic effects (Flammini et al., 2014; FAO, 2014). They can also create conflict. A case in point is what has been happening to the ecology and economics of the Colorado River delta estuary region that used to rely on upstream water and sediments. Due to significant water withdrawal in the southwestern part of the U.S., the river has not reached the ocean since the 1990s (Wiles, 2014). In Pakistan, farmers located at the tail end of canals have less access to water and are less productive (Mustafa et al., 2013).

Another example is the social and environmental impact of constructing and operating dams, such as the Three Gorges Dam in China, affecting many upstream and downstream places (Xu et al., 2013). Dams in Iran and Turkey along the Tigris-Euphrates River systems, combined with climate change, have created severe land and environmental degradation in Iraq starting in the 1960s up to today (Bruneau and Rasheed, 2021; Shemakov, 2022).

In general, the effect of scale (spatial and temporal) on decision-making and intervention scenarios in community development is challenging to understand and manage since too many factors are at play. One challenge is dealing with the non-linearity inherent in all the systems and subsystems in Figure 5.1. This property implies that solutions cannot be extrapolated from one scale to another. Despite that limitation, synchronizing solutions and interventions across the PSC nexus at different physical scales (local, regional, global) and temporal scales (short-, medium-, or long-term) is essential to avoid united consequences. According to Zurek and Henrichs (2007), interventions scenarios across scales can be of five types: (i) *equivalent*, where scenarios are transferrable between scales (e.g., climate change), (ii) *consistent* (e.g., shortage of resources related to unreasonable national policies), (iii) *coherent* if decision-making is based on the same logic, (iv) *comparable* but different in their outcomes (e.g., climate security practices at different scales), or (v) *complementary* (e.g., human and economic policies). Furthermore, the intervention scenarios can be coupled differently and involve different processes. They can be run jointly, in parallel, in an iterative manner, consecutively, or independently of each other.

5.2.3 Boundaries

Whether natural or artificial, physical and temporal boundaries are needed to define the spatial and temporal scales at which the PSC nexus is studied. What are the boundaries of the conflict or areas where climate change has had an impact? Do these boundaries change over time? Once boundaries are selected, questions arise about: what data need to be collected and analyzed, their aggregation level, where data should be collected and over what time frame, what issues need to be addressed, and the characteristics of proposed solutions.

It is difficult to define the boundaries of a complex problem since "everything is somehow connected" (Seelos, 2020). Social systems have no proper boundaries that can be established. Once arbitrarily selected, a boundary sends a clear message that some components and their attributes and relationships (endogenous) are included within the boundary, whereas others (exogenous) are purposely excluded. Boundaries may have different levels of permeability with the exchange of tangible resources (e.g., food, energy, water, shelter) and intangible resources (e.g., information). According to Friedman and Allen (2014), the more porous the border, the more interaction the system has with its surroundings and the more open it is. This openness, in turn, makes the analysis more challenging.

A challenge in selecting boundaries is that some systems' boundaries may not coincide. An example would be a boundary that defines the resources a population depends on and the administrative/political boundary with jurisdiction over a region. A temporal boundary would be to look at what's happening to a community during the dry or wet seasons only. The challenge is to select, somewhat subjectively, an overall boundary that is good enough and "aligns best" with the boundaries of each component of the nexus.

Boundary selection is a more subjective than objective process, but it is also not random, and general guidelines can be followed. For instance, it is essential to select boundaries that are not too narrow or too wide, too shallow or too deep, or too short or too long. Narrow boundaries may limit what causes and effects are considered. Broad boundaries may include too much information that cannot possibly be analyzed. Boundary selection can be accomplished, as mentioned by Ricigliano and Chigas (USAID, 2011), by selecting *reasonably* defined boundaries that balance inclusiveness (breadth or extension) with clarity (depth or intensity). Striking this balance is not always easy when multiple variables are at play. In the PSC nexus, breadth concerns the cross-disciplinary interaction between the nexus's sectors and the landscape's various components. The depth component entails how deeply to go (in a reductionist manner) into each sector of the nexus and the landscape and to what level of detail. The challenge of boundary selection can also be understood by choosing boundaries that offer some trade-offs "among [model] realism, precision, and generality" (Costanza et al., 1993). The nature of the trade-offs depends on what attributes are essential in the context of interest.

Another guideline is to explore whether some phenomena at play in the PSC nexus are confined to well-defined geographic/natural boundaries. For instance, if water is an issue that could lead to conflict, the limit of a watershed (catchment, drainage basin) may be appropriate for identifying the dynamic of a community and how its members use natural resources if the community operates in an isolated manner and within the confines of the watershed. However, if community members interact with other communities and social units outside the boundary regarding culture, politics, administration, and economics (trade), which occurs more frequently than not, the boundary loses significance. For instance, Day (2009) discusses the challenges of establishing watershed boundaries in sub-Saharan Africa for community-based water resource management. Due to the remoteness of the villages, Day concluded that micro-watersheds were better suited than major watersheds to comprehend how local inhabitants used the aquifer systems.

Another illustrative watershed with geopolitical constraints deals with the Hebron-Besor-Wadi Gaza basin, shown in Figure 5.3. Starting from Hebron, the river flows westward, crosses different political boundaries, and involves several ethnic and cultural groups: Palestinians (West Bank), Israelis, Bedouins, and Palestinians (Gaza). Many communities in the basin are remote and are off the water, sanitation,

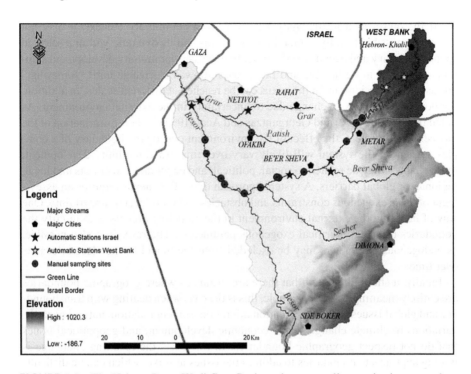

FIGURE 5.3 The Hebron-Besor-Wadi Gaza Basin and water quality monitoring network.

Source: Tal et al. (2010), used by permission of Taylor and Francis.

and electricity grid, thus making their resilience to climate change more challenging (EcoPeace Middle East, 2018).

In this case, proper watershed management necessitates (i) finding common ground among the four groups; (ii) identifying the needs of the four groups; (iii) collecting and analyzing information; (iv) planning, designing, and implementing interventions; and (v) monitoring and evaluating their continuous performance. All these tasks must be done collaboratively and participatory to be accepted by all groups, representing a challenge in the geopolitical context where the river flows (Lipchin and Albrecht, 2019).

A similar watershed project is the Kidron Valley project, which considers treating municipal raw sewage (50,000 m^3 per year) generated from Jewish and Arab neighborhoods in East Jerusalem combined with waste from several Palestinian communities (Rinat, 2017). The wastewater flows eastward untreated along the Kidron Valley in the Judean Desert and reaches the Dead Sea. Transboundary stream restoration and wastewater treatment options are being explored and implemented for the Kidron Valley (Novick/Maariv, 2022). Asaf et al. (2007) reviewed several polluted rivers considered for transboundary stream restoration in the Holy Land. These projects require complex diplomatic and engineering efforts and defining appropriate geopolitical boundaries. Increasing water scarcity due to climate change in the regional Israel-Palestine-Jordan landscape can potentially affect national and regional security (EcoPeace Middle East, 2019).

At the outset of a nexus study within a given community context, it may not always be possible to fully comprehend the nexus and its dynamic within a selected spatial boundary and over a specific time. In that case, community development solutions may need to be flexible and boundaries allowed to change until "somewhat" consistent conclusions about the nexus can be reached at different scales. In addition, the boundary is likely to change due to uncertainty in the external environment. As noted by Duncan (1972) and Georgantzas and Acar (1995) in their examination of the business environment, the effect of the environment outside the boundary of a complex system on the system will likely vary over time. In community development, these changes may be related to social, political, and economic constraints and local, regional, or global barriers. A system approach to the PSC nexus requires an assessment of these exogenous constraints and obstacles and their level of uncertainty. One way of handling the external environment in the modeling process is to modify the boundaries to bring in critical exogenous parameters. The reverse is also possible, as endogenous parameters may be excluded from the model as they lose relevance over time.

Finally, it should be noted that there are instances where geographic boundaries are entirely meaningless. For example, this is the case when dealing with transboundary and global issues such as population migration, soil degradation, natural hazards, variations in climate change, rogue economic development, and geopolitical issues that do not respect geographic boundaries. In this case, the resulting challenge is finding appropriate boundaries to address the issues at stake, which can be difficult.

5.3 COMMUNITY LANDSCAPE APPRAISAL

The complexity of the landscape in which community development occurs and the PSC nexus unfolds can never be understood entirely, as it is impossible to know all the unknowns in complex and ill-defined systems. Nevertheless, whether one is interested in understanding and modeling the structure behind the patterns of one or several systems shown in Figure 5.1 or the whole landscape, several analyses must be carried out. Although site-specific, they require collecting data and information from a detailed appraisal of the systems and their interaction. Because of the systemic nature of the community landscape, a *systems-aware appraisal* must be carried out where data are collected and analyzed systemically and not just categorized. Key questions in the appraisal are: What do we need to know about the community landscape, and How much information do we need? How does the PSC nexus unfold in the landscape?

An answer to these questions is getting enough information about the landscape to develop a community *baseline profile* that can be used to identify the overall state of the community, its behavior patterns, and its structural components. It is also about reviewing any existing (secondary) information, identifying thematic areas of concern, and mapping existing enabling and constraining factors, including key factors, key stakeholders, what works well, what does not work well, and what could be improved. The appraisal, in turn, helps formulate possible *dynamic hypotheses* and mental models around issues in the landscape (i.e., possible explanations about the causes and consequences of each issue and its underlying structure). As discussed in the methodology presented in Chapter 9, once formulated, the issues can be modeled using systems modeling tools which will be reviewed in Chapters 6 and 7. This step is followed by (i) identifying places to intervene in the landscape (i.e., possible leverage points); (ii) designing, planning, and implementing possible intervention scenarios; (iii) monitoring and evaluating these interventions; and (iv) considering the scalability and sustainability of these interventions. It should be noted that a better picture of the landscape emerges over time as appraisal data are collected and analyzed in a participatory and systemic manner.

This section provides a summary of the critical steps of community appraisal. A more detailed description of the steps can be found in Amadei (2015) and the *Handbook on Tools for Effective Project Planning in Community Development* by the Grassroots Collective (n.d.)

Appraisal of the community landscape is not a neutral activity as those involved in the appraisal (i.e., insiders and outsiders to the community) bring challenges and biases (Cornwall and Jewkes, 1995). Chambers (1983) identifies six groups of biases: (i) spatial (data are collected only in easily accessible places), (ii) project (data from failed projects are ignored, and data from successful projects are emphasized), (iii) person (preference is given to collecting data from more educated people), (iv) season (preference is given to collecting data during traveling seasons), (v) diplomacy (specific issues are not raised because they are not deemed essential or as a matter of courtesy), and (vi) professional (communication is preferred—and perhaps therefore limited to—occurring between expert team members and more educated individuals).

5.3.1 PARTICIPATORY COMMUNITY APPRAISAL

The primary purpose of any appraisal is to learn as much as possible about a particular situation, in our case, the level of development of the community, including its states of peace, sustainability, and climate security. Information is acquired in a participatory manner to develop a community baseline profile with meaningful and appropriate indicators that best describe the current dynamics and structure of the landscape shown in Figure 5.1. Table 5.1 provides a non-exhaustive list of possible sources of information in community mapping.

In most cases, a pre-appraisal phase precedes the actual appraisal to (i) provide a preliminary idea of what is at stake, (ii) decide what type of appraisal needs to be conducted, (iii) frame questions; and (iv) select who needs to be on the appraisal team. As a *reflection-before-action* activity, pre-appraisal can help decide whether the current situation in which the PSC nexus and community development unfold is worth addressing further and if a reasonable intervention success can be expected. It also identifies whether the community is in a pre-conflict, ongoing conflict, or post-conflict setting. That decision process can use criteria such as safety, relevance, complexity level, required efforts, and community stakeholders' engagement. Under certain conditions, proceeding beyond the pre-appraisal phase may not be possible.

Community appraisals often use participatory methods that can be regrouped under the broader concept of *participatory action research* (PAR). PAR is a recognized form of practical action research (Lewin, 1946) that emphasizes the

TABLE 5.1
Possible Sources of Information in Community Mapping

Aspects	Examples of Information Needed
People	Who lives in the area? What are their structure and composition? What divisions exist? What is the basic profile regarding health, education, employment, income, and so forth? What are the patterns of leadership? What aspects of people's beliefs, values, and practices seem essential? Do some groups have more power or influence than others? How do people with different identities (tradition, gender, patriarchy/matriarchy, ethnicity, race, caste, childhood, aging, disability) experience poverty, conflict, violence, oppression, and climate issues? Who are existing community changemakers who do things differently and successfully (positive deviance)? How do people make a living and earn money?
Environment	Where are the physical and social boundaries of the community? What aspects of climate, topography, natural resources, or seasonal variations seem essential? What outstanding natural features mark the area? How is the environment connected with a household's livelihood?
Infrastructure	What institutions, organizations, facilities, or services exist? What is their relationship to local populations, now and in the past? What is likely to change in the future? What types of technology are present, and what is their performance?
Resources	What important assets does the community possess or have access to? These might include financial, intellectual, human, and informational resources. How are these assets held and managed? What rules govern their use? What are the community resources, skills, strengths, and capacity (institutional, human resources, technical, economic/financial, energy, environmental, social, and cultural), and the quality, quantity, and state of those resources and skills?
Modes of livelihood	What are the principal bases of the economy? How are people organized for work and community activities? How are they connected or differentiated? Are there extremes of wealth and poverty? What are current economic trends? How are resources and benefits distributed? How is time patterned? What is the livelihood dynamic across seasons (e.g., dry and wet seasons)?
Issues and concerns	What has engaged the time, thinking, and energy of people here? What are people's main concerns, priorities, risks, community concerns, sense of vulnerability, and risks (real and perceived) that could harm people, property, services, livelihoods, and the environment people depend on? How do they see these issues? Are there differences of opinion regarding these? What sorts of options are acceptable or workable for dealing with them?
Principal constraints	What factors or conditions (e.g., geopolitical and adverse events) lying mainly outside the control or prediction of the community are essential for understanding what is happening in the community? How do people see these things? Have they changed over time? What are the in-country governance, policy, and socio-political-economic issues at the regional and national levels that the community needs to consider in its development; examples include regional and national policies in public health and sanitation, education, job creation, shelter, transportation, energy, poverty reduction, natural hazards, and climate adaptation and mitigation, and others?

Source: Adapted from Nolan (2002), used by permission of Taylor and Francis.

collaborative nature of the work of researchers and stakeholders to identify areas of concern and develop joint solutions. PAR can also be interpreted as a bottom-up approach to community development because it (i) begins with people's problems, concerns, and local knowledge; (ii) is motivated by collective action; and (iii) ends in action. Researchers and stakeholders actively participate in data collection and analysis in PAR appraisal. The work is done through progressive critical inquiry and adaptive learning with *reflection-in-action* by all parties involved. This approach differs from starting the appraisal with hypotheses in mind and looking for data that support or repudiate them, as is customarily done in traditional appraisal methods (Checkland and Holwell, 1998).

Different PAR appraisal methods are available in the literature, a review of which can be found in Chapter 5 of *Engineering for Sustainable Human Development* (Amadei, 2014). They differ primarily based on the field methods and tools (e.g., group and team dynamics, sampling, interviewing, visualizing, mapping) they use to collect and analyze data and whether the appraisal is rapid or in-depth. A common characteristic of all these appraisal methods is that as thorough as they may be, there are incomplete, as there are always gaps when collecting data.

Figures 5.4.a and 5.4.b summarize customary steps in conducting an appraisal and associated feedback loops. Its overarching goal is to acquire enough knowledge and understanding to identify and rank the most significant issues and problems at stake in the landscape, the PSC nexus, and the community. Once collected, the information is analyzed and commonly regrouped into several categories, as shown in Figure 5.4b and summarized in Table 5.2. More details of these analyses can be found in Amadei (2014).

Regardless of the PAR tools used to carry out the community landscape appraisal, a key priority in data collection is to make sure that information comes from data that are authentic, valid, appropriate, meaningful, inclusive, truthful, and accurate; in other words, that conclusions about the community can be drawn with enough confidence. According to Barton (1997), good quality data and information must show the following attributes: accuracy, relevance, timeliness, credibility, attribution, significance, and representativeness. In general, quantitative and qualitative data collection methods differ in the data collected, the methods used, the skills required of those collecting the data, and the scope and scale of data collection. A review of the different forms of data collection can be found in Barton (1997), Caldwell and Sprechmann (1997a,b), and Chambers (1983, 2002, 2005).

5.3.2 SYSTEMS-AWARE COMMUNITY APPRAISAL

It is essential to recognize that pre-appraisal and participatory appraisal of complex adaptive systems requires a different approach from a traditional participatory assessment. *Systemic action research* is sometimes used to describe action research carried out systematically (Burns, 2007).

Decision-makers must adopt and encourage an open, flexible, and systemic mindset in the pre-appraisal phase and when acquiring and analyzing data and information

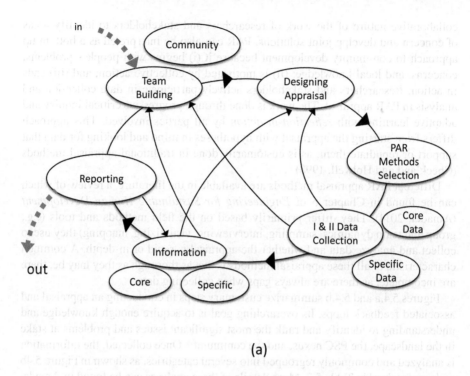

(a)

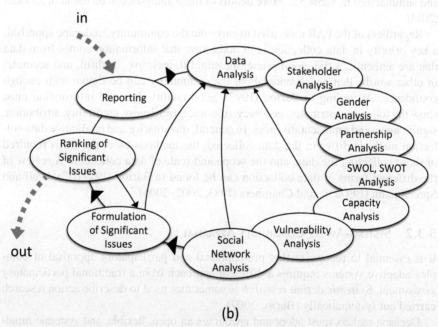

(b)

FIGURE 5.4   (a) Key steps involved in the appraisal; (b) Analyzing the appraisal results.

Source: Amadei (2019), used by permission of Momentum Press.

TABLE 5.2
Different Categories of Analysis of Community Appraisal

Types of Analysis	Description/Purpose
Stakeholders (including power and institutions)	• Identify all individuals and groups who make or influence decisions directly or indirectly, including those who may not have a voice in the matter but will be impacted. They can be generally grouped into three categories: community members, governments, and outsiders. • More specific stakeholders: political, economic, social and cultural, legal, environmental, technical, etc. • Map actors' and stakeholders' positions, interests, needs, and willingness to contribute to change, peace, sustainability, and climate security. • Rank stakeholders in terms of influence and importance. • Identify relationships (collaboration and conflict issues) between various stakeholders and their respective levels of participation: *key* stakeholders (strong influence), *primary* stakeholders (affected), and *secondary* or indirect stakeholders (with little stake and impact), and their respective levels of participation. Other stakeholders are opposition stakeholders and marginalized stakeholders. • Identify (i) Who depends on community development projects, (ii) Who is interested in the outcome of the projects, (iii) Who could influence the projects, (iv) Who will be affected by the projects, (v) Who could be against the projects (threat), and (vi) Who may be left behind in the projects?
Partnership	• Who are the partners, and their values? • What level and type of experience and expertise can be expected from each partner: strengths, weaknesses, opportunities, challenges, participation level? • How is a working partnership likely to take shape? Including (i) the roles and responsibilities of different partners in proposed projects, (ii) any information sharing, (iii) any joint project planning, (iv) resource sharing, (v) dealing with conflict, and (vi) defining phase-in and phase-out strategy for all partners.
Social	• Identify how different stakeholders/actors are related, their power dynamics, and their relation to peace, sustainability, and climate security. • Gender analysis: how men and women currently conduct their socioeconomic activities; their specific needs, roles, and areas of interest; their relationships; their areas of empowerment and participation; their project impact and contributions; and any gender risks. • Identify what divides and connects people. • Governance mechanisms and political analysis. • Human-right (inequalities and discriminatory practices). • Map relationships among actors, stakeholders, and institutions (social network analysis).

(Continued)

TABLE 5.2 (*Continued*)
Different Categories of Analysis of Community Appraisal

Types of Analysis	Description/Purpose
Capacity	• Identify "the abilities, skills, understandings, attitudes, values, relationships, behaviors, motivations, resources and conditions that enable individuals, organizations, networks/sectors, and broader social systems to carry out functions and achieve their development objectives over time" (Bolger, 2000). • Identify what works, how well it works, and the constraints preventing how things could work better.
Risk	• Identify and rank potential risk events (natural and human-made, climate change), probability, consequences, impact, and how risks are handled and managed. How have past threats been dealt with? What risk management strategies (avoidance transfer, redundancy, or mitigation) were used in the past?
Livelihoods/Vulnerability/ Fragility	• Community weaknesses in livelihood: food and nutrition, health, habitat and shelter, water and sanitation, education, economy, environment, and civil society. • Current and past exposure to adverse events.
SWOT(C/L)	• Identify community strengths, weaknesses/vulnerabilities, opportunities for change, and threats/challenges/limitations.
Conflict	• Map the "causes, actors, and dynamics of conflict" (GPPAC, 2017). Develop and implement solutions that best match the phase of conflict (prevention, ongoing, and post-conflict).
Climate security	• Identify risks induced, directly or indirectly, by changes in climate patterns (past and present). • Map existing methods of mitigation and adaptation to climate change and environmental degradation.

about the different systems at play at the community level. A traditional reductionistic tendency is for decision-makers to focus too quickly on the pre-appraisal with preconceived ideas on a particular issue that resonates with them or has been emphasized by a specific interest group in the community. This narrow mindset can derail decision-making and undermine community participation in addressing issues that matter to most.

Another constraining aspect of traditional participatory appraisal is its pigeonholed approach to data collection and analysis, whether the data are about people's needs, infrastructure, or specific issues related to conflict and climate change. No attempt is made to examine how data from different PSC nexus systems or sectors interact. For instance, data related to conflict are connected to climate security and livelihood. This myopic approach often leads to narrowly focused decision-making and possibly unintended consequences, which could have been avoided if data had been cross-examined for dependency.

In comparison, a *systems-aware appraisal* is better suited to capture the complexity of the community landscape in Figure 5.1. It starts with the different categories of information listed in Table 5.1. Compared to traditional appraisal, the data and information are collected, analyzed, presented, and interpreted in an integrated or systemic way. As discussed in Amadei (2014), this means: (i) seeing and seeking connections in the data, including using triangulation methods; (ii) engaging multiple stakeholders in the different stages of the appraisal; (iii) being able to manage different conflicting opinions among different groups of stakeholders; (iv) using reflection-in-action and adaptive practices to assess (monitor and evaluate) the appraisal and the results of the appraisal; (v) formulating issues and problems in the landscape and its components in a non-compartmentalized (i.e., integrated) manner; and (vi) and selecting appropriate dynamic hypotheses and models about the what, who, where, when and how of the issues structures and dynamics.

Conducting a systems-aware appraisal of a community landscape requires decision-makers to have acquired unique systems practice skills to recognize and address the complexity of community development. In addition to having the habits of systems thinkers discussed in the previous chapter, decision-makers also need to adopt a complexity-mindful (or aware) step-by-step approach to community development that combines objective tools when dealing with complicated systems and subjective or intuitive tools in more complex and uncertain situations. In conducting such analyses, decision-makers are expected to be more than just traditional value-neutral individuals capable of producing linear blueprints and predictable solutions delivered on time and within budget for well-defined problems. As systems thinkers, decision-makers need to be creative, innovative, and interactive to account for uncertainty, complexity, ill-defined issues, and constraints in a cultural context with which they are likely unfamiliar.

Another challenge in conducting community landscape analyses with a systems perspective is extracting from the collected data the information necessary to comprehend the different systems of Figure 5.1 and how the PSC nexus unfolds in that landscape. It is about selecting systems characteristics, appropriate variables, and processes essential to understanding community development issues under normal and adverse conditions without falling into paralysis in analysis. Unfortunately, there are no objective ways to decide when enough data and information have been collected to provide a "good enough" understanding of the landscape. Using triangulation methods and analyzing consistency between different data sources may help.

Finally, a systems-aware participatory community landscape appraisal also implies that the appraisal team is aware of and willing to accept and deal with the feedback mechanisms between the different components of the appraisal shown in Figures 5.4a and b. For example, as the appraisal proceeds, the reflective and adaptive practice may require the appraisal team to supplement its expertise with the opinion of other individuals in specific areas of study and critical stakeholders. Likewise, more information may be needed, and data collected as a gap is noticed in a particular domain during data analysis. Finally, another possible feedback mechanism could occur if there is a need to change the way the team operates due to cultural or other issues that emerge as the appraisal unfolds.

5.3.3 CORE INFORMATION

Many ways of regrouping the information collected during the community landscape appraisal could impact community development and the PSC nexus. Before going into the details of the data necessary to assess the different systems of Figure 5.1 and their interactions and the data to understand how the nexus unfolds on the landscape, core information is needed to acquire an overall picture of the community landscape itself. At a minimum, the following core information must be sought in the pre-appraisal and appraisal:

- Physical geographic information about climate (variability and trend) and weather; landforms and topography; soil and rock types and their distribution (also related to geology); natural resources; forests; vegetation; fauna and flora; and surface and underground water (also related to hydrology and hydrogeology) including watersheds, rivers, streams, and aquifers. Current and past geographic information is essential.
- Adverse events (small, medium, large) the community has experienced or is likely to experience. They might be related to natural (geologic) hazards and processes (e.g., earthquakes, floods, drought, landslides, subsidence, wildfire, coastal storms, tornadoes/hurricanes, and tsunamis) and non-natural activities (e.g., conflict and war). The history of these hazards must be analyzed, including type, significance, location or extent, intensity, severity, duration, surprise effect, signs (warnings), probability of occurrence, trends, risk drivers, and corresponding impact drivers.
- Human geographic information about the structure, distribution, concentrations, growth, and movements of populations and their overall state of development; demography; human activities; land use and ownership; transportation (roads, railways, waterways); human economy; culture; human health; belief systems; education and literacy; existing labor vs. available jobs; evolution of these various characteristics (historical geography); and so on.
- Infrastructure information about the major types of engineered (non-natural) systems that provide services (e.g., water, energy, food, land, transportation, health, shelter, communications) to populations at the landscape and community levels.
- Economic and financial information about the type of economy at play (traditional, command, market, mixed); its dominant production, consumption, and distribution processes; its dominant sectors (agricultural, industrial, domestic); the private vs. public sector; financial systems; levels of subsidies; pricing; forms of capital; etc.
- Institutional information about existing institutions, governance, law rules, decision-making processes, regulations, policies, etc.
- Social and cultural information such as languages spoken, gender, stability, equity, support systems, social networks, vulnerable groups, citizen participation, etc.
- Healthcare information about diseases, health practices, child mortality, health services provided, and sanitation practices.
- Human security information, especially regarding past and present conflicts and peacebuilding efforts.

From a practical point of view and in the best-case scenario, the information mentioned above should be available from various in-country government agencies (local, regional, national), nongovernmental agencies, or commercial entities in the form of reports, maps, sketches, Geographic Information Systems (GIS) databases, and so on. In the worst-case scenario, data may not be available or are incomplete about one or several specific issues that matter to the appraisal team, especially at the community landscape scale of interest. Another situation may arise when some data are available but have not been updated for a while. In all of these circumstances, there is a need for the appraisal team to collect more data or make guesses based on experience. Once organized, collated, and analyzed, new data sets should provide up-to-date information and help better understand the current landscape.

5.3.4 SYSTEMIC INFORMATION

The core information mentioned above is necessary but insufficient to understand the dynamic and structure of the community landscape in Figure 5.1. It needs to be supplemented with more specific details about each of the four major systems groups in Figure 5.1; how they interact; and how peace, sustainability, and climate security unfold across these systems.

5.3.4.1 Social Systems

The social (human) systems of interest include populations, communities, and institutions created for specific purposes. These systems can be further subdivided into subsystems such as households, different ethnic groups, marginalized groups, special interest groups (e.g., farmers, men, women, teachers), and different types of institutions (e.g., public or private, economic, financial, educational, and health). These subsystems and groups interact with each other in multiple ways. For instance, populations form households and groups and interact with institutions. The sense of community influences how people interact. Finally, institutions provide services to populations in normal and adverse conditions and encourage (or discourage) a sense of community.

Determining how populations, communities, and institutions influence and depend on each other requires selecting metrics and measures that best describe how these subsystems interact. A non-exhaustive list of structural variables (indicators) that can further define human systems' behavior can be found in Appendix A. The variables have been regrouped in different arbitrary categories around (i) demography, education, health, and employment for populations; (ii) households/families and groups in the communities; and (iii) social, economic, financial, governance, and public services institutions. Some of these variables are *quantitative* (tangible), such as the demographic breakdown of population by age, gender, and education; the number of households; or the number of schools or clinics. Other variables are *qualitative* (intangible) and expressed by a certain level of impact or effectiveness ranging from low to medium to high (e.g., levels of water, energy, food, and transportation security; levels of educational, health, and governance services; levels of positive or negative impacts of various groups or individuals; or the level of effectiveness of governance, banking, cooperative groups, and institutions). Only variables deemed necessary to describe the human systems in the landscape in their present state must be selected and supported by data. Historical data might also be helpful to determine possible chronological trends to capture how human systems in the community landscape have changed over time and foresee how they could evolve in the future.

One way of representing how human systems and their subsystems interact is to conduct a social network analysis (SNA). As discussed in Section 6.4, SNA is a systems tool to show the connections between different social agents (e.g., people, households, communities, institutions) facing a common issue. The issue may be how information flows across a group of individuals, how community decisions are made, how decisions about resource allocation are made in a community, or how different sources of conflict affect various groups or individuals. SNA maps clearly show whether decisions or information flows between agents, who control what and critical actors, existing clusters of decision-makers, where roadblocks occur, and who is marginalized. In general, SNA maps show how the structure of a network controls its overall behavior and the behavior of each agent.

5.3.4.2 Environmental Systems

Environmental (natural) systems provide eco-services and resources through their symbiotic nature. They include the hydrosphere (water), the atmosphere (air), the geosphere (land), and the biosphere (animal and plant life). Their carrying capacity is limited, especially when subjected to stress associated with natural hazards like floods, soil erosion, landslides, desertification, and fauna and flora extinction. Biological systems influence and depend on each other. For instance, water controls surface and groundwater and replenishes and supports life. Land and soil affect water percolation, desertification, and vegetation growth or decay. Air influences precipitation and evaporation affects the weather. Forests reduce soil erosion, control ground temperature, sequester carbon, and contribute to biodiversity.

Appraisal of natural systems implies determining the characteristics of each system and assessing their interactions, which is not simple. A *non-exhaustive* list of structural variables that may need to be considered to describe the behavior of natural systems can be found in Appendix A. Qualitative and quantitative data at the landscape level are required to obtain information about both the current state of the various environmental systems and their past variability, whether over one year, several seasons, or several years during which some of the systems may have been stressed due to changes in weather patterns and natural or non-natural hazards.

5.3.4.3 Engineered Systems

Various infrastructure (i.e., engineered) systems interact with social, natural, and economic systems. Among many possible indicators, the availability, level of functioning, continuous downtime, reliability, operating and maintenance, and sustainability of these systems are critical to adequately managing resources at the community level. Engineered systems provide many services related to water, energy, agriculture, food production and processing, wastewater treatment, sanitation, telecommunications, transportation, health, shelter, etc. The services can be complex (sometimes complicated) and depend on each other. A breakdown of various systems related to water, energy, agriculture/food, education, transportation, and healthcare can be found in Appendix A.

The various infrastructure systems and their subsystems in the landscape could interact in multiple ways. The types and levels of interaction depend on the context and scale of interest, such as urban vs. rural, centralized vs. decentralized infrastructure, and emergency vs. non-emergency situations. Critical infrastructure systems require special attention among all the infrastructure systems essential for the functioning of a society and economy. They are the lifeline parts of the infrastructure whose destruction or incapacitation would significantly impact society's security, health, wealth, etc. Community resilience to adverse events depends greatly on the critical infrastructure's role in community development.

One challenge in assessing infrastructure vulnerability is mapping and modeling the intra- and interdependencies operating in the networked infrastructure systems and their connections (Chai et al., 2008). These dependencies contribute to possible infrastructure vulnerability and dictate possible cascading effects and unintended consequences associated with natural and non-natural events (Pederson et al., 2006; Walsh et al., 2009).

5.3.4.4 Economic Systems

Economic systems consist of production, distribution and trade processes, and consumption of goods and services in a society. These processes involve countless interactions with the social, natural, and engineered systems mentioned above. The dynamic of these interactions depends on whether the economy is traditional, command, market, or mixed (Krugman and Wells, 2015).

Appraisal of economic systems requires that metrics and indicators be selected to measure the processes mentioned above in response to supply and demand. The appraisal needs to be done for different sectors of the economy, such as agriculture, industry, and services. It must also consider interactions within the landscape and outside of it.

More specifically, a practical way to carry out the appraisal of economic systems is to identify for each sector of the economy: (i) what goods and services are being produced (quantity and quality); (ii) how they are produced and with what resources and forms of capital or assets (e.g., social, natural, financial, institutional, technical); (iii) how they are distributed; (iv) who in society benefits from and receives the production output; and (v) what institutions, groups, and individuals decide, coordinate, regulate, and control the processes of production, distribution, trade, and consumption. Other issues that must be addressed include the quality and quantity of productions, existing and potential markets, wages and earnings, GDP per capita, GDP annual growth, and employment versus existing labor.

5.3.5 Systems Interactions

The four systems groups described above interact in the community landscape. There are several ways of showing that interaction. For example, Figure 5.5 shows possible connections between environmental, social, and economic systems as modeled in the iSDG system dynamics framework (Pedercini et al., 2020). The states of peace, sustainability, and climate security are emerging properties of such interactions.

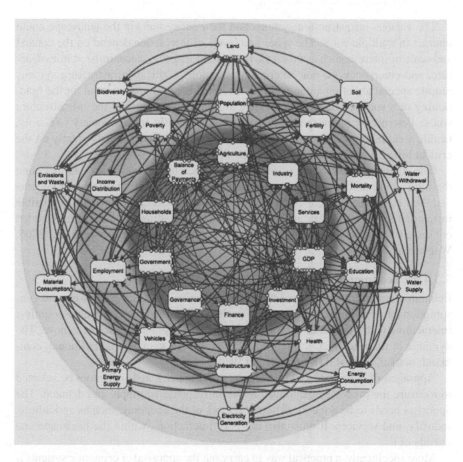

FIGURE 5.5   Interactions among environmental (outer ring), social (medium ring), and economic (inner ring) systems variables as used in the iSDG framework.

Source: Pedercini et al. (2020). Used by permission of Wiley and Sons.

Another way of illustrating the interaction between the systems in Figure 5.1 is to use a cross-impact interaction matrix, as shown in Table 5.3. It is a high-abstraction representation of the interdependencies among the four systems groups of Figure 5.1 and natural hazards. Each row describes the direct impact of each system group on the others, and each column describes how each system group depends on (is sensitive to) the others. As in Table 2.7, the interactions between the systems can be direct or indirect, as one type of system influences a second one, which affects the third one. For example, engineered systems may impact natural systems, affecting human health.

In practice, the challenge consists of breaking down the content of each off-diagonal cell in Table 5.3 using landscape-specific and context- and scale-dependent indicators. However, handling that level of disaggregation in the landscape appraisal is challenging. First, all the systems' intra- and inter-connectivity (mostly nonlinear)

TABLE 5.3

Cross-Impact Representation of The Four Systems Groups of Figure 5.1 and Natural Hazards

	Human Systems	Natural Systems	Engineered Systems	Economic Systems	Natural Hazards
Human Systems		Drive agri. practices and urbanization. Degradation of natural systems if not properly managed	Design, build, operate, maintain, and use engineered systems	Drive supply and demand. Production, distribution, and consumption	May amplify or reduce the impact of natural hazards
Natural Systems	Provide resources and values. Land use and productivity	Degradation of natural systems if not properly managed	Provide resources (e.g., water, energy, wood, etc.)	Affect production, distribution, consumption	May amplify or reduce the impact of natural hazards
Engineered Systems	Have a positive or negative impact on human systems	Degradation of natural systems if not properly managed		Interact with production, distribution, and consumption	May amplify or reduce the impact of natural hazards
Economic Systems	Have a positive or negative impact on human systems	Degradation of natural systems if not properly managed	Necessary for loan and investment		May amplify or reduce the impact of natural hazards
Natural Hazards	Increase vulnerability	Potential to change natural systems	Could create damage	Could create additional costs	

Source: Amadei (2019), used by permission of Momentum Press.

cannot *all* be mapped and analyzed. Another challenge is tracking how the systems and their interactions change over time and express themselves at different physical scales. Climate change impacts many of the exchanges. Conflict may also arise due to the constraining aspects of one system's group on the others.

With these limitations in mind, a special effort needs to be made to (i) identify the critical components of each systems group in Figure 5.1; (ii) create metrics and measures for several of their components as comprehensively as possible, either qualitatively, semi-quantitatively, or quantitatively; and (iii) consider their most dominant interactions and feedback dynamics at the system and subsystem levels. Analysis of that information may help identify the states of peace, sustainability, and climate security at the community level.

5.4 COMPREHENSIVE COMMUNITY LANDSCAPE ANALYSES

Among the different types of analysis shown in Figure 5.4b and listed in Table 5.2, capacity analysis, conflict analysis, and the analysis of risks associated with conflict, unsustainability, and climate change require special attention. These analyses integrate the core information and characteristics of the four systems described above. They focus on the ability of a community to reach some goals, provide services, and manage the risks associated with various adverse events, climate change, and conflict situations. All these analyses are not an end in themselves but contribute to creating a more integrated view of the landscape and provide a better understanding of how issues across the PSC nexus unfold.

5.4.1 Capacity Analysis

In community development, it is essential to understand whether community stakeholders (e.g., individuals, households, institutions, governments, etc.) currently have the capacity (i.e., the ability) to achieve specific goals (e.g., the different types of security listed in Table 1.1) and access services (e.g., water, energy, sanitation, health, education, etc.) to satisfy their needs and secure their livelihood. Sustainability can be seen as the ability (capacity) to sustain.

Among the multiple definitions of capacity available in the literature, the Canadian International Development Agency (Bolger, 2000) captured the concept of capacity well in its various expressions and scales. It is defined as:

> The abilities, skills, understandings, attitudes, values, relationships, behaviors, motivations, resources and conditions that enable individuals, organizations, networks/sectors, and broader social systems to carry out functions and achieve their development objectives over time.

Community capacity defines the enabling environment of the community, where community members can cope with various situations and adapt to new needs, challenges, changes, and opportunities. Capacity is a vital attribute of resilient communities to events of diverse adversity (e.g., conflicts, natural hazards, climate change). In that context, capacity can be (i) *inherent* to capture how community stakeholders cope with these events and (ii) a*daptive* to describe how they adapt to them over time.

Regardless of how capacity is defined, it is generally agreed that capacity as an emerging community state (i) is critical to the success of human development and security; (ii) is a vital attribute of resilient, peaceful, and sustainable communities; (iii) takes time to acquire with multiple twists and turns and sometimes some set-backs, and (iv) is scale- and context-specific.

A capacity analysis provides a way to assess the state of a community in its current state of development, identify areas for improvement, and develop an action plan to increase capacity through *capacity building*. Sometimes referred to as *capacity development* or *asset-based community development* in the development literature, capacity building can be seen as

> a process through which individuals, organizations, and societies obtain, strengthen, and maintain the capabilities to set and achieve their own development objectives over time (UNDP, 2015).

Even though there is no one-size-fits-all approach to capacity building that would work for all community landscapes, building capacity represents a strategic means to an end, which is to create sustainable, peaceful, and resilient communities. This process has unique characteristics:

- It creates an enabling environment with context-specific development (individual, institutional, organizational) strategies.
- It is scale-dependent (physical and temporal) and cannot be easily extrapolated from one scale to another.
- It does not happen by itself and builds on local ownership and self-reliance.
- It promotes partnership and long-lasting broad-based community participation.
- It takes time and depends on the capacity baseline and the enabling aspect of the environment in which it unfolds. The higher the baseline, the faster capacity building can be expected. It is mainly a challenge for poor communities with low initial capacity.

The process of community capacity building is not random. It starts with assessing the current level of community development based on its existing capacity to provide specific services and security and respond to the needs of its constituents. It is about mapping what the community can do, what it cannot do, and what it could do if it were to reach a higher level of development through strengthening.

Capacity building is also about investigating the level of community development the community aspires to reach, over what time frame, and addressing existing gaps between current and desired capacities. The goal might be to get to a certain level of sustainability, recover from conflict and peacebuilding, or be able to cope and adapt to climate change. The gap between current and desired capacity drives the need for change. Comparing present and desired capacity helps identify, rank, plan, prioritize, and implement the most appropriate community development interventions to build capacity over time.

5.4.2 CAPACITY MAPPING

Capacity mapping and analysis start after answering two fundamental questions. The first is what "capacity to do what, in what context, and over what time and physical scale" needs to be mapped; the "what" may be some goals or specific services to the community or how to adapt and cope with adverse events. A second question is what significant capacity domains need to be considered to address the "what." A capacity mapping method developed by researchers at the University of Virginia in Charlottesville (UVC) is presented below. It emphasizes that whether a community is interested in meeting some goals or service provision, multiple sectors and their interaction need to be considered to reach some level of success.

The framework referred to as UVC below was initially developed to assess the capacity of small-scale developing communities to manage the delivery of local community municipal sanitation services related to drinking water supply, wastewater, and sewage treatment and the management of solid waste (Bouabid, 2004; Bouabid and Louis, 2015; Ahmad, 2004). The framework is comprehensive enough to be generalized for the delivery of other types of community services as well, such as coping and adapting to climate change, health, energy, food, shelter, transportation, education, telecommunication, the management of critical infrastructure, and the prevention of violence and injury. The steps of the methodology are the same and are discussed below.

Step 1: Once a desired community goal or service has been identified, up to seven categories of capacity deemed to be important are considered. They are shown in Figure 5.6. The UVC framework assumes that these seven capacity categories are independent. The linkages between the seven categories shown in Figure 5.6 are considered further in Chapter 10.

Step 2: Each capacity category has several requirements (or constituents). Since many requirements are possible, the challenge is to select those more likely to play a critical role in community development for the context (sociocultural, economic, geopolitical), scale, and boundary in which the capacity analysis is carried out. Table 5.4 gives a non-exhaustive list of such requirements.

If necessary, other forms of capacity could be added to that list, such as the ability to (i) handle crises and emergencies related to specific adverse events and hazards, (ii) absorb displaced populations, or (iii) recover from conflict. Likewise, other capacity requirements (and sub-requirements) could be considered.

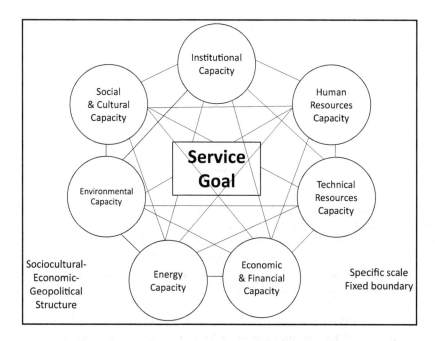

FIGURE 5.6   Seven related capacity categories deliver a specific community goal or service in an environment with a particular structure, context, and scale.

Source: Amadei (2020), open-access journal.

TABLE 5.4

A Non-Exhaustive List of Capacity Types and Requirements

Capacity Type	Possible Requirements
Institutional	Policies (laws, regulations), Programs (administration, jurisdiction), Processes (permits, performance)
Human Resources	Professional, Skilled Labor, Unskilled Labor – Literate and Illiterate
Technical	Operations, Maintenance, Adaptation, Supply Chain: Spare parts, Supplies, Services
Economic/Financial	Private sector %, Bonds Rating, User Fees, Budget, Asset Values
Energy	Grid electricity access, Other electricity access, % of budget, reliability factor (annual hours/8766)
Environmental/Natural Resources	Annual withdrawal % of (stock + recharge), Background quality
Social/Cultural	Community, Stability, Castes/Clan/Ethnicity/Women Participation

Source: Bouabid and Louis (2015). Used by permission of Academic Press.

Note: The authors considered an eighth type of capacity (service) which is not included here.

Step 3: A total of N_i requirements $C_{ij}(j = 1-N_i)$ are selected for each capacity category ($i = 1-7$). Each requirement is assumed to be rated based on an agreed-upon metric. It can be qualitative (high, medium, low) or quantitative, between 0 and 100, and broken down into several rating groups. For instance, Bouabid (2004) uses five rating groups of 20 units each.

Step 4: Each capacity category is assigned a capacity factor $CF_i(i = 1-7)$ equal to

$$CF_i = \sum_{j=1}^{N_i} C_{ij}\, w_{ij} \tag{5.1}$$

In this equation, C_{ij} and w_{ij} ($j = 1-N_i$) represent the requirements scores and weights associated with the i-th capacity factor CF_i ($i = 1-7$). Compared to the original UVC framework, each capacity factor CF_i is assumed to depend somehow on the other six CF_k ($k \neq i$). Likewise, each requirement score C_{ij} depends on all other possible scores (C_{kl}, $k \neq i$, $l \neq j$). This formulation accounts for the various feedback mechanisms among the different capacity categories.

Step 5: The UVC framework uses the weakest link or pessimistic rule decision criterion to determine the capacity factor with the lowest score among all the capacity factors. It is defined as the *Community Capacity Assessment C_A.*

$$C_A = Min(CF_i;\ i = 1 - 7) \tag{5.2}$$

According to Bouabid (2004), C_A can be understood as the place in the community that is most vulnerable and where intervention to improve a specific service or reach a goal is first needed. It can also be interpreted as a measure of the stage of development of a community and its readiness to provide the service.

Bouabid (2004) introduced a community capacity level (*CCL*) over a five-point scale. Table 5.5 shows how the *CCL* relates to C_A for delivering local community municipal sanitation services. Once the *CCL* has been identified for a given goal or type of service, decisions can be made about the supply chain service options and technologies most appropriate to reach the goal or provide the service to the community in its current level of development (Ahmad, 2004).

Remarks:

1. The UVC approach is quite conservative by using a pessimistic rule criterion to calculate the Community Capacity Assessment C_A value. Bouabid (2004) noted that other measures could be used, such as calculating C_A as the weighted average of all capacity factors with weights reflecting the importance of different capacity types. Another observation made by Bouabid (2004) was that the C_{ij} scores in eq. (5.1) are best guesses only. A sensitivity analysis might also be needed to analyze the impact of their variation on deciding what solutions are appropriate.

TABLE 5.5

Community Capacity Levels to Provide Sanitation Services

Score C_A	CCL	Stage/ Interpretation	Community Profile Description
1 – 20	1	High entropy	Initial stage where there is no formal public service provided.
21 – 40	2	Pre-community	Limited local service is provided with no regulatory or administrative control.
41 – 60	3	Community-Based	A mix of public and informal private services is provided with minimal controls.
61 – 80	4	Centralized	Regional public service is provided with adequate controls.
81 – 100	5	Diversified	Regional public and selective private service is provided with improved control.

Source: Bouabid and Louis (2015), used by permission of Academic Press.

2. As an illustrative example, Appendix B presents an analysis carried out by Bouabid (2004) and Bouabid and Louis (2015) to assess the capacity of a rural village consisting of 230 households and a population of 1250 in Southern Morocco to adopt a new strategy for wastewater and sewage treatment management.
3. The UVC methodology described above considers one goal or type of service at a time. The situation becomes challenging when several goals or forms of services need to be addressed simultaneously. For example, one might be interested in determining the capacity of a community to ensure sustainable peace, develop specific sustainable practices, and guarantee climate security, all at the same time. The lowest capacity factor, C_A, and *CCL* need to be determined first for each goal or type of service. However, there is no guarantee that all goals and types of service would have the same kind of limited capacity. In other words, the security of the entire nexus and *CCL* may be limited by one form of capacity for peace, another for sustainability, etc. In this case, interventions at the nexus and community level may require addressing the limiting factors for each goal or type of service while ensuring that the interventions do not create unintended consequences for the other goals or services.
4. As discussed in Chapter 10, the UVC framework can be integrated into systems models of community capacity that capture the evolution of community development from an initial level to the desired level.

The UVC framework is general enough to address the capacity of a community to meet some goals or provide multiple services. Another capacity framework worth mentioning is that of Huston and Moriarty (2018). It was proposed to account for the different factors involved in the service delivery of WASH-related (water, sanitation, and hygiene) systems at the community level. The framework recognizes that WASH-related services involve nine types of capacity called building blocks:

- Institutions: Coordination, roles, responsibilities, capacity, sector mechanisms
- Policy and legislation: Sector policy and strategy, legal framework, norms and standards, by-laws
- Finance: Flows and responsibilities, clear frameworks including life-cycle costs and source identification
- Planning: Planning and budgeting, capacity, and frameworks for planning
- Infrastructure management and development: Development and mainte-nance, project cycles, asset management, roles
- Monitoring: Frameworks and routine implementation, service levels, use of data
- Regulation and accountability: Accountability mechanisms, regulatory framework, and capacity
- Learning and adaptation: Capacity and frameworks to capture and feedback lessons learned, update and adapt various building blocks
- Water resources management: Allocation and management of resources abstraction, water quality, coordinated efforts

An illustrative example of applying the framework to two districts (South Ari and Mile) in Ethiopia was proposed by Adanke et al. (2019). The focus was determin-ing their capacity to provide operation and maintenance services to water systems through proper coordination, collaboration, and learning. An attractive character-istic of this framework is how it *qualitatively* recognizes the interaction between the nine building blocks. Like the UVC framework, the WASH-related framework relies on developing semi-quantitative indicators ranging between 1 and 5 for the components of each building block. It can also be extended to analyze the capacity to provide services other than WASH.

5.4.3 Risk Analysis

Communities must identify and increase their capacity and identify and reduce their vulnerabilities. The dynamic between capacity and vulnerability defines the risk environment and community resilience. In general, the risk is the possibility that an undesired outcome (or the absence of the desired result) associated with an event has "adverse effects on lives, livelihoods, health, economic, social and cultural assets, services (including environmental), and infrastructure" (NRC, 2012). When faced with an event, risk can be related to community capacity and vulnerability as follows

$$\text{Risk} = \text{Exposure} \times \text{Event} \times \left(\frac{\text{Vulnerability}}{\text{Capacity}} \right) \qquad (5.3)$$

In this equation, "exposure" varies between 0 (no exposure) and 100% (total expo-sure). The variable "event" varies over a specific scale based on the event's adversity and impact. It should be noted that all variables in this equation depend on time.

The risk environment at the community level is twofold. These are risks associ-ated with various issues and adverse and uncontrollable events or hazards the com-munity could face. They exist before any development intervention is conducted and can be internal or external to the community, small or large. The events range from everyday events (e.g., lack of water and sanitation, poor shelter, living condi-tions, livelihood, illness, economy, etc.) to extreme events (e.g., floods, volcanoes, earthquakes, landslides, wildfires, hurricanes, etc.) Several small-scale or periodic medium-scale events may arise, such as drought (periodic, chronic), soil degradation, deforestation, epidemics, health risks, hazards, etc. Another class of adverse events deals with those associated with war, conflict, and the breakdown of governments that may have disastrous consequences at the local and global levels.

The second risk environment is associated with development interventions and capacity-building issues. For example, there may be a risk that some community stakeholders will create roadblocks to the interventions. The risks may result from poor planning, design, management, or execution of the interventions. They can also be created by poor decisions made by policymakers and institutions not fully involved in the interventions or those that prioritize access to resources such as water to special groups such as in Pakistan (Mustafa et al., 2013).

There may also be the risk that the collected data are inaccurate, incomplete, poorly analyzed, or strongly biased during the systems-aware appraisal. There is a risk that the data analysis leads to vague dynamic hypotheses. There is a risk that the intervention may fail because of unintended consequences resulting in conflict and loss of life or resources, whether right after the interventions are completed or dur-ing their implementation. These situations may lead to negative results, intervention delays, or cost overruns. Finally, there is a risk that the interventions are no longer what the community needs or, in some cases, were never needed in the first place.

It should be noted that the risk environments mentioned above are not necessar-ily independent. They may be situations where one feeds onto the other and even accentuates the severity of some issues in a cascading manner; new risks may even be created.

Since risks are integral to community development and resilience, they must be managed. Risk management contributes to protecting and preserving human secu-rity, well-being, and quality of life at the community level through coping, adapting, and mitigating measures. An added value of risk management is that it helps com-munities become more resilient over time and creates better interventions overall.

According to Smith and Merritt (2002), the first step in risk management is identifying each risk, its impact, and its probability of occurrence. As an illus-trative example, let's consider the conceptual framework of climate security proposed by the WCSR (2021) to capture the dynamic between climate change, climate-related events, risk factors, and adverse impacts. Figure 5.7 shows a framework representation using the cascading risk model proposed by Smith and Merritt (2002). A risk event defined as "erratic changes in climate patterns" has multiple consequences and impacts, which take time to manifest. All three have their respective drivers. Suppose the magnitude of the total loss associated when the risk event occurs, L_t, could be determined and the probabilities of occurrence of the risk event, consequences, and impact estimated. In that case, the expected

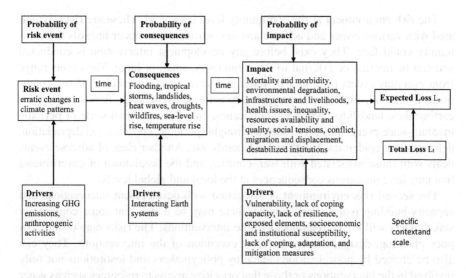

FIGURE 5.7   Cascading risk representation of the conceptual framework for climate security (WCSR, 2021) showing the consequences and impact of erratic changes in climate patterns.

loss, L_e, could be calculated as the product of L_t and these three probability values. The dynamic of Figure 5.7 is context- and scale-specific.

A challenge in Figure 5.7 is mapping all the consequences and their respective impact for a specific context and scale. Another challenge is how to estimate the value of the total loss quantitatively, which could be expressed in financial/economic terms, time, loss of lives or infrastructure, etc. Another option is to qualitatively describe the total loss, such as high, medium, low, or semi-quantitative, using a scale ranging between 1 and 10.

Once the risks are identified and analyzed, a *risk heat map* can also be created to show the likelihood and impact of each risk. This map helps to prioritize the risks and develop appropriate action plans and risk-coping strategies. According to Smith and Merritt (2002), these can be (i) avoiding the risks, (ii) transferring the risks, and (iii) reducing the effect of the risk events by providing parallel solutions paths and backup options. Another strategy is to tolerate the risks but at the same time mitigate their impact and impact drivers (to make them less severe), either by developing a prevention plan (to reduce risk and risk drivers), a contingency plan (works on impact and impact drivers), or a reserve plan (risk occurs and losses are covered). Once the risks are resolved, a risk monitoring and evaluation plan must be developed and implemented to identify whether the risk management strategies are working and if new risks are created.

Regarding climate risk management, Luers and Sklar (2013) proposed that the effectiveness of climate security measures such as adaptation and mitigation depends on the impact severity of the risk event and time. As shown in Figure 5.8, beyond a "limit of mitigation" time, mitigation and adaptation (low-impact severity) or mitigation only (high-impact severity) have an impact. Below that time, adaptation is the

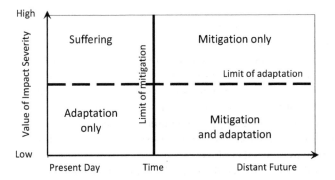

FIGURE 5.8 Risk management quadrants. Conceptual map of options for managing climate risks. The limits of adaptation and mitigation are uncertain.

Source: Luers and Sklar (2013). Used by permission of John Wiley and Sons.

only climate security option when the severity is low. The other option is suffering when the impact severity of the risk event is high. It should be noted that the "limit of mitigation" line and the "limit of adaptation" line do not have to be vertical and horizontal and can change over time.

The risk model of Figure 5.7 is generic enough to be applied to issues the community faces related to resources, conflict, or climate change. In all cases, the risk model requires deep introspection into the impact and consequences of each issue and its respective drivers. A systems-aware approach to risk also requires looking at (i) how different issues may contribute to some collective impact and loss and (ii) how cumulative risk events may lead to complicated situations (e.g., the 2010 Haiti earthquake, combined with political absenteeism and subsequent hurricanes) that are hard to recover from. However, it must be kept in mind that different constituencies perceive, map, and manage risks and consider the impact of risk events over time differently.

5.4.4 CONFLICT ANALYSIS

Conflict analysis is another context-specific analysis involving the different systems of the community landscape. It aims to study the "causes, actors, and dynamics of conflict" (GPPAC, 2017) and come up with solutions that best match the phases of conflict (i.e., preventive, ongoing, or post-conflict). Among the many definitions of conflict available in the literature, the following one is selected:

> Conflict is an escalated competition at any system level between groups whose aim is to gain an advantage in the area of power, resources, interests, and needs, and at least one of the groups believes that this dimension of the relationship is mutually incompatible. (Rasmussen, 1997 in GPPAC, 2017)

Social conflict, which is of interest here, is defined as a "confrontation of social powers" (Lemos, 2018). It can involve multiple actors, from individuals to institutions, groups, associations, etc. There are various reasons for conflict to be triggered. For instance, environmental conflicts, which can be seen as a type of social conflict, manifest themselves as disputes following ecological degradation and the overuse of natural resources, leading to resource scarcity and unequal resource distribution (BenDor and Scheffran, 2019). As noted by OECD (2005), water availability and allocation can be a source of tension (or even low-scale violence) but not necessarily a significant reason for violent conflicts. Environmental and water-related conflicts "frequently overlap with other types of conflicts on gender, class, territory, or identity" (Scheidel et al., 2020). Adverse events such as war and climate change also contribute to environmental conflict.

Lemos (2018) noted that conflicts could manifest in multiple ways and across a spectrum ranging between peaceful manifestations, low-intensity violence, high-intensity violence, and armed conflicts. Lemos (2018) cited the work of Collins (1975) about the general characteristics of social conflict in historical and geopolitical contexts: (i) potential conflicts are caused by inequities in the distribution of scarce socioeconomic, cultural, and power resources; (ii) potential conflicts become actual conflicts when opposing groups are mobilized; (iii) conflicts create subsequent conflicts; and (iv) the intensity of the conflicts decreases when mobilization resources are used. Lemos (2018) also referred to the work of Gurr (1968), who examined the influence of psychological factors that may affect civil violence. Among these factors is the relative deprivation of some members of society, which translates into frustration and aggression.

It is apparent in the literature that conflict, as such, is not always destructive as it may contribute positively to change in the creative tension that drives community development, as mentioned above. Of more significant concern is the impact of violent conflicts on development. As noted by Collier et al. (2003)

> Where development succeeds, countries become progressively safer from violent conflicts, making subsequent development easier. Where development fails, countries are at high risk of becoming caught in a conflict trap in which war wrecks the economy and increases the risk of future war.

As discussed in Chapter 2, violence, according to Galtung (1964, 1990), can take multiple forms and be direct (i.e., physical and psychological and exercised by an actor), indirect/structural (i.e., formed by structures that prevent meeting some desired needs and create scarcity), and cultural (i.e., legitimized by some social culture in the form of prejudices and attitudes). It can start in one of these three poles and affect the others. Identifying the causes of violent conflicts is essential in the different phases of conflict management.

A model like that of Figure 5.7 can be introduced to relate the consequences and impact of conflict, seen as a risk event, and account for their respective drivers. The losses associated with conflict can be estimated once the total losses (financial/economic, time, loss of lives and infrastructure, environmental damage, etc.) are evaluated. The probabilities of the conflict and its consequences and impact need to be estimated to do so.

Conflict analysis aims at mapping conflict, its stages, timeline, driving forces, dynamics, and the factors and the key actors/stakeholders (connectors and dividers) of conflict. Guidelines and tools for participatory conflict analysis can be found in CDA (2016), GPPAC (2017), and the GSDRC (Herbert, 2017). The why, what, who, where and when, and how of conflict must be identified. What is the nature of the conflict? Why is there a conflict in the first place? Who is involved in the conflict and could resolve the conflict? What are the physical and temporal boundaries of the conflict? And how does the conflict express itself and its impact on livelihood and the different aspects of human security? Answering these questions requires collecting data that supplement those mentioned in the previous sections. Table 5.6 gives a non-exhaustive list of input data necessary for conflict analysis according to the *Global Partnership for the Prevention of Armed Conflict* (GPPAC, 2017).

In addition to the list of data mentioned in Table 5.7, there is also a need to collect data that are more specific to the phase of conflict the community is experiencing and the intensity of the conflict. For instance, the *Global Partnership for the Prevention of Armed Conflict* (GPPAC, 2017) considers different data for the following phases of conflict prevention: early intervention, urgent intervention, intervention in periods of open violence or cyclical violence, and intervention in post-violence/post-war/post-peace agreement situations.

TABLE 5.6

A Non-Exhaustive List of Input Data for Conflict Analysis Suggested by The *Global Partnership for The Prevention of Armed Conflict* (GPPAC, 2017)

Categories of Data	Description
Positive factors for peace/resolution/ transformation (political, economic, social, technical, legal, environmental)	• Factors that bring people together • Elements that can be strengthened or built upon in peace work. Prominent individuals or groups, traditional institutions, mechanisms for conflict resolution?
Negative factors producing conflict/tension/ barriers to peace (political, economic, social, technical, legal, environmental)	• Key factors of conflict • Factors that push people apart • Factors that contribute to migration • Patterns of violence and dehumanization
Key actors/stakeholder analysis	• Roles, means of power/influence, interests, needs, values, positions, willingness to negotiate, etc.? • Actors for peace and actors that contribute to conflict
Long-term structural issues and short-term operational issues/triggers	• Latent conflicts, emergent, already manifest but not yet violent, violent conflicts.
Effects of conflict on different people/groups.	• Differences across groups, genders, ages, and geographic areas? • Cohesion and coherence between migrants and host communities.
Elements that contribute to conflict	• Historical factors, economic factors, social/ relational factors, political factors, security factors, justice/human rights factors, environmental factors.

(Continued)

TABLE 5.6 (*Continued*)

A Non-Exhaustive List of Input Data for Conflict Analysis Suggested by The *Global Partnership for The Prevention of Armed Conflict* (GPPAC, 2017)

Categories of Data	Description
Specific questions	• What changes are needed? • Immediate and long-term threat analysis (current, past, forthcoming, potentially violent). • Orientation to specific groups, such as women, youth, minority groups, religious leaders, businesspeople, etc. • Examining various layers/levels of conflict (local to province/state to national to regional, etc.) • Issues of particular interest (land issues, environmental, ethnicity, religious tensions, youth, gender, etc.) • Existing peace efforts: who is doing what? What have been the results (positive and negative)? Are there significant gaps, issues not addressed, groups not involved, etc.?

5.5　ENABLING OR CONSTRAINING LANDSCAPE

One of the outcomes of a systems-aware community appraisal is identifying whether the landscape's internal environment is enabling or constraining change. Core attributes of enabling environments could consist of having:

- A community with existing and prospective *capacity* (institutional, financial, technical, human, and so on) to provide multiple aspects of human development and security
- A *resilient* community with strategies for dealing with risks over different physical and time scales, including those associated with adverse natural and non-natural events
- A community with a level of *participation* where community members: (i) are aware of the economic and social values of peace, sustainability, and climate security; (ii) can articulate security issues; (iii) can mobilize, organize, and suggest solutions (including trade-offs) to the issues in collaboration with other stakeholders; (iv) can assess (monitor an evaluate) progress and make adaptive changes as deemed necessary; (v) can handle sources of conflict; and (vi) can make decisions with different global, local, and integrative perspectives
- A community where *collaboration* between different groups of stakeholders exists

- A community with sound economic and social *policies and legislations* that promote security and human rights equitably and transparently when dealing with PSC issues.

These attributes are likely to vary from one community to the other. They dictate possible and appropriate interventions across one or several nexus sectors. In general, as the enabling environment of a community increases, more sophisticated interventions across the peace, sustainability, and climate security sectors can be implemented with a higher level of success expected in the short and long term.

The above core attributes must be supplemented with context- and community-specific features around social, economic, infrastructure, and political issues. These attributes are context-specific and are determined during the community appraisal phase discussed above. For instance, the enabling environment is likely to be different for a community in an urban or peri-urban setting compared to a community in a rural setting. The same could be said about communities in different climatic conditions.

The enabling or constraining nature of the community landscape also depends on external factors. A community is not an island; its dynamic also depends on interactions with other communities and institutions at the regional and even global scale. Various socioeconomic-political constraints and policies may originate outside the landscape boundary and limit or promote the range of interventions at the local level. Exogenous issues are often hard to define, show different levels of uncertainty, and are likely to change with time—a characteristic of complex and dynamic environments (Duncan, 1972).

5.6   FROM APPRAISAL TO DYNAMIC HYPOTHESES

5.6.1   FORMULATING THE ISSUES

At the end of the systems-aware community appraisal, there should be enough information to start formulating preliminary conceptual (or structural) models to explain the current state of community development, its deep structure (Omidyar group, 2017), and how the PSC nexus unfolds in the community landscape. More specifically, the systems-aware appraisal is expected to identify and formulate as comprehensively and integrated as possible:

- The most significant (key) issues, concerns, and needs the community faces and their prioritization and opportunities for leverage
- The perceived cause-effect relationship for each issue, including possible feedback mechanisms
- Each issue's consequences, impacts, drivers, probabilities, and expected losses.
- The current and desired community's capacity and available resources and assets (natural, human, social, economic, and infrastructure capital)

- The issues important to different groups: what works (or has worked) well, does not work, what could be improved, what changes are envisioned by whom and for whom, and current roadblocks to improvement
- The ranking and importance of issues based on gender, age, employment/unemployment, caste, belief systems, married/single individuals, etc.
- Possible linkages between the issues and how they may have common causes and effects.
- The role played by conflict, unsustainable behavior, and climate change in the issues
- How peace, sustainability, and climate security can contribute to addressing the issues

An issue is understood here as a *dynamic gap* between the current state and desired state of (i) one or several sectors of the PSC nexus (e.g., conflict vs. peace, climate vulnerability vs. security, unstainable vs. sustainable behavior); (ii) one or several service components or security indicators within a sector; and (iii) one or several aspects of the social, natural, infrastructure, and economic systems interacting with the nexus. When considered together, these different types of gaps contribute to an overall gap between the current levels of community development, peace, sustainability, and climate security and the more desirable ones. The challenge is to develop interventions to bridge the overall gap over time with new mental models that create structure and promote better behavior patterns for the community. It should be noted that the rate of reducing the gap depends on the current community development level and capacity. The higher that level is compared to the desired one, the faster change will likely occur. In all cases, bridging the development gap takes time and often requires accepting incremental steps of adaptation and transformation and considering multiple feedback processes. This dynamic is captured in the system dynamics models in Chapters 10 and 11.

A systems approach to community development requires formulating dynamic hypotheses to explain how the issues unfold and interact (i.e., possible explanations that relate structures to behaviors). This approach requires addressing each issue's what, why, who, where, when, and how. If the *what* of a single issue is the starting point, the issue must be described in a quantitative, qualitative, or semi-quantitative manner. What internal and external factors in the landscape contribute to and affect the issue? The *why* comes next since there must be one or multiple reasons for an issue. For instance, there may be insufficient resources available compared to some minimum standards, or the government or community members expect a desired level (but not met). Another example is that there is not enough capacity to address the issue.

Following the why of an issue comes the *who* deals with who is being, has been, or could be affected by the issue, or who could contribute to its solutions. Then comes the *where* and *when,* which define the physical and time scales over which the issue is at play or has manifested itself before: is there a recurring pattern? Finally comes *how* the issue currently plays or has played before across the community landscape and the PSC nexus, including its causes and effects. It is also about how the issue could manifest itself in the future if not addressed and how it could interact with other issues.

For example, let's consider the case of a specific geographical area where resource security is a source of conflict between settled farmers and pastoral nomad groups (what, who, where). The available resources, especially water and food, are scarce during the dry season (when) and create conflict. The settled farmers object to the passage of nomadic groups who demand the movement of people and herds as a guaranteed right. The area's preliminary capacity analysis shows that the conflict results from a lack of agreement between the two groups, unreasonable expectations, the clash between tradition and modernity, and the absence of government enforcement and regulation policies (why). In summary, poor resource management, inequity, and marginalization have created tension and resentment between farmers and herders, violence, lack of economic development, and insecure livelihood (how). Some of that dynamics can be found in the Sahel region of Africa (Tesfaye, 2002), where conflict has arisen due to the combined constraining effect of climate change on climate-sensitive rain-fed agriculture-based livelihood, political instability, insurgency, ethnic tension, and state fragility. Rapid population growth creates a demand for cultivated land, restricting the movement of nomadic herding. Land tenure is also controlled by customary land practices that affect that movement.

If multiple issues are at play and show connectivity, the *what* requires describing what the issues are and what makes them interconnected and dependent on each other? Then comes *why* these issues are essential and related and why some may be more critical than others and cannot be addressed. Then, the *who* defines the multiple groups of stakeholders who may be affected by one or several issues and could influence each other. The *where* and *when* define the physical and temporal extent of the issues, some being more active and critical at one physical and time scale than others. Finally, the *how* of the multiple issues must demonstrate how they are presently interconnected and have been interconnected in the past and whether they may have mutual causes and consequences.

A more complex version of the above example includes the combined dynamic of climate change, livelihood, drought, conflict, migration, and land-use change. The area's water and food security issues are compounded by the encroachment of migrating herders on farmers' land, destroying crops. The farmers and herders also get political support from two opposite government factions. Multiple drought episodes due to climate change have forced farmers to abandon their lands and move to big cities to find living wages. This migration has put pressure on city living. The lack of work has created unrest and repression from the government. Growing city insecurity has forced people to leave and become refugees, affecting other communities. In summary, multiple consequences arise from the overall dynamics between climate change, livelihood, drought, conflict, migration, and land-use change.

5.6.2 Ranking the Issues

In the complex community development landscape of Figure 5.1, multiple issues are likely to exist, and the question arises of how to choose among them. Some issues might be specific to community needs (water, energy, food, health, etc.). In contrast, others might involve several community needs, such as those across peace, sustainability, and climate security. Once these issues are formulated and their dynamic hypotheses adequately outlined, the next step is to list and rank/prioritize them to be addressed in order of importance. Key questions that should help in the ranking are as follows (Seelos, 2020):

- Are the issues legitimate?
- Are the issues identified the most critical ones?
- Are the issues identified capturing the concerns of multiple stakeholders?
- Are the issues identified addressing the *current needs* in the community (i.e., inadequate services, key grievances, and resiliencies)?

Another way of ranking issues is to use *multi-criteria or multi-attribute analysis* tools from the field of decision science (Keeney and Raiffa, 1976; Decision Sciences Institute, 2017). One such tool is *Multi-Criteria Decision Analysis* (MCDA). It is formulated to rank decisions based on several critical criteria or objectives deemed necessary in the decision process (Delp et al., 1977; Mendoza and Macoun, 1999; Figueira, 2005; Nathan and Reddy, 2011; Huang et al., 2011). The Department for Communities and Local Government (DCLG, 2009) in the United Kingdom published an excellent review of different multi-criteria analysis techniques. The range of applications of the MCDA method in community development can be found in Amadei (2014, 2019).

5.7 CONCLUDING REMARKS

As summarized by Zoellick (2010), "People don't live their lives in health sectors or education sectors or infrastructure sectors, arranged in tidy compartments. People live in families and villages and communities and countries where all the issues of everyday life merge." Hence, the community landscape must be addressed in an integrated manner.

There are multiple ways of assessing the landscape in which peace, sustainability, and climate security unfold. Not all development and security projects require all the analyses discussed in this chapter. Assessment tools such as capacity and risk analysis are site-specific. As the GPPAC (2017) noted, the question remains about what represents a good enough conflict analysis. The same question applies to capacity analysis. A possible answer to that question depends on the purpose and depth of the analyses. More in-depth analyses will likely be used to meet specific community goals and objectives.

The issues outlined and ranked at the end of the appraisal phase need to be formulated systematically rather than as a list of things to address. Furthermore, special attention must be placed on whether solving one issue may help address another or create new ones due to non-linearities, synergy, and emergence. An example would be how poorly executed development projects could trigger or re-energize conflict among different groups in a community and weaken the community's coherence and resilience when subject to adverse events. The following two chapters present a series of systems tools that can capture each issue's dynamics, interactions, and contribution to the overall community landscape.

REFERENCES

Adanke, M., Hailegiorgis, B., & Butterworth, J. (2019). A local systems analysis for rural water services delivery in south Ari and Mile, Ethiopia. https://www.ircwash.org/sites/default/files/a_local_systems_analysis_for_rural_water_services_delivery_in_south_ari_and_mile_ethiopia.pdf

Ahmad, T. T. (2004). A classification tool for selecting sanitation service options in lower-income communities. MS dissertation, University of Virginia, Charlottesville, VA, USA.

Amadei, B. (2014). *Engineering for sustainable human development: A guide to successful small-scale development projects.* ASCE Press.

Amadei, B. (2015). *A systems approach to modeling community development projects.* Momentum Press.

Amadei, B. (2019). *A systems approach to modeling the water-energy-land-food nexus* (Vols. *I* and *II*). Momentum Press.

Amadei, B. (2020). A systems approach to community capacity and resilience. *Challenges, 11*(2), 28. https://doi.org/10.3390/challe11020028

Asaf, L., Negaoker, N., Tal, A., Laronne, J., & Khateeb, N.A. (2007). Transboundary stream restoration in Israel and the Palestinian authority. In C. Lipchin, E. Pallant, D. Saranga and A. Amster (eds.), *Integrated water resources management and security in the middle East.* NATO Science for Peace and Security Series. Springer. https://doi.org/10.1007/978-1-4020-5986-5_13

Barton, T. (1997). *Guidelines for monitoring and evaluation: How are we doing?* CARE International in Uganda, monitoring and evaluation task force, Kampala, Uganda.

Batty, M. (2010). Complexity in city systems: Understanding, evolution, and design. Paper 117. UCL Center for Advanced Spatial Analysis, University College, London, UK.

BenDor, T., & Scheffran, J. (2019). *Agent-based modeling of environmental conflict and cooperation.* CRC Press, Taylor & Francis.

Ben-Eli, M. (2018). Sustainability: Definition and five core principles: A systems perspective. *Sustainability Science, 13,* 1337–1343, https://doi.org/10.1007/s11625-018-0564-3

Bouabid, A. (2004). Requirements analysis for sustainable sanitation systems in low income-communities. MS dissertation, University of Virginia, Charlottesville, VA, USA.

Bouabid, M., & Louis, G. (2015). Capacity factors for evaluating water and sanitation infrastructure choices for developing communities. *Journal Environmental Management, 161,* 335–343. https://doi.org/10.1016/j.jenvman.2015.07.012

Boudreaux, K. (2009). Land conflict and genocide in Rwanda. *Electronic Journal of Sustainable Development, 1*(3), 86–95.

Bolger, J. (2000). Capacity development: Why, what, and how. https://www.researchgate.net/publication/268354675_Capacity_development_Why_what_and_how

Bruneau, C., & Rasheed, A. (2021, September 7). As its rivers shrink, Iraq thirsts for regional cooperation. https://www.reuters.com/business/environment/its-rivers-shrink-iraq-thirsts-regional-cooperation-2021-09-06/

Burkett, V. R., Wilcox, D. A., Stottlemyer, R., Barrow, W., Fagre, D., Baron, J., Price, J., Nielsen, J. L., Allen, C. D., Peterson, D. L., Ruggerone, G., & Doyle, T. (2005). Nonlinear dynamic in ecosystem response to climate change: Case studies and policy implications. *Ecological Complexity, 2,* 357–394. https://doi.org/10.1016/j.ecocom.2005.04.010

Burns, D. (2007). *Systemic action research: A strategy for whole system change.* Policy Press.

Caldwell, R., & Sprechmann, S. (1997a). DM&E workshop series: Vol. *1 Handout manual.* M&E Workshop Series, CARE International, Atlanta, GA.

Caldwell, R., & Sprechmann, S. (1997b). DM&E workshop series: Vol. *2,* Facilitators' *manual.* M&E Workshop Series, CARE International, Atlanta, GA.

Chai, C. L., Zhang, W. J., Liu, X., Deters, R., Liu, D., Dyachuk, D., Tu, Y. L., & Baber, Z. (2008). Social network analysis of the vulnerabilities of interdependent critical infrastructures. *International Journal of Critical Infrastructures*, *4*(3), 256–273. http://doi.org/10.1504/IJCIS.2008.017440

Chambers, R. (1983). *Rural development: Putting the last first*. Pearson Prentice Hall.

Chambers, R. (2002). Participatory workshops: A sourcebook of 21 sets of ideas and activities. Earthscan Publications Ltd.

Chambers, R. (2005). *Ideas for development*. Institute for Development Studies. Earthscan Publications Ltd.

Checkland, P., & Holwell, S. (1998). Action research: Its nature and validity. *Systemic Practice and Action Research*, *11*(1), 9–21. https://doi.org/10.1023/A:1022908820784

Collaborative for Development Action (CDA). (2016). *Designing strategic initiatives to impact conflict systems: Systems approaches to peacebuilding. A resource manual*. CDA Collaborative Learning Projects.

Collier, P., Elliott, V. L., Hegre, H., Hoeffler, A., Reynal-Querol, M., & Sambanis, N. (2003). *Breaking the conflict trap: civil war and development policy*. Oxford University Press. http://hdl.handle.net/10986/13938

Collins, R. (1975). *Conflict sociology: Toward an explanatory science*. Academy Press.

Cornwall, A., & Jewkes, R. (1995). What is participatory research? *Social Science & Medicine*, *41*(12), 1667–1676. https://doi.org/10.1016/0277-9536(95)00127-S

Costanza, R., Wainger, L., Folke, C., & Mäler, K.-G. (1993). Modeling complex ecological economic systems: Toward an evolutionary, dynamic understanding of people and nature, *BioScience*, *43*(8), 545–555, https://doi.org/10.2307/1311949

De Blij, H. (2012). *Why geography matters more than ever*. Oxford University Press.

Decision Sciences Institute. (2017). http://www.decisionsciences.org/.

Delp, P., Thesen, A., Motiwalla, J., & Seshadri, N. (1977). *Systems tools for project planning*. International Development Institute.

Denier, L., Scherr, S., Shames, S., Chatterton, P., Hovani, L., & Stam, N. (2015). *The little sustainable landscapes book: Achieving development through integrated landscape management*. Global Canopy Programme,

Department for Communities and Local Government (DCLG) (2009). *Multi-criteria analysis: A manual*. Communities and Local Government Publications, Wetherby, UK.

Diamond, J. (2005). *Collapse: How societies choose to fail or succeed*. Penguin Group.

Duncan, R. B. (1972). Characteristics of organizational environments and perceived environmental uncertainty. *Administrative Science Quarterly*, *17*(3), 313–327. https://psycnet.apa.org/doi/10.2307/2392145

EcoPeace Middle East. (2018). Report on the status of the Hebron- Besor-Wadi Gaza basin. De Bruyne, Charlotte. http://ecopeaceme.org/wp-content/uploads/2017/01/nahal-hevron-for-web.pdf

EcoPeace Middle East. (2019). *Climate change, water security, and national security for Jordan*, Palestine, and Israel. *Amman, Jordan; Tel Aviv, Israel; Ramallah, Palestine*. I. Carry (ed.). C:\Users\amade\Downloads\climate-change-web.pdf

Figueira, J. (2005). Multi criteria decision analysis: state of the art surveys. In J. Figueira, S. Greco, and M. Ehrgott (eds.) Springer International, vol. 78.

Flammini, A., Puri, M., Pluschke, L., & Dubois, O. (2014). *Walking the nexus talk: Assessing the water-energy-food nexus in the context of sustainable energy for all initiatives*. Environment and Natural Resources Working Paper No. 58, FAO, Rome. https://agris.fao.org/agris-search/search.do?recordID=XF2015001455

Food and Agriculture Organization of the United Nations (FAO). (2014). *The water-energy-food nexus: A new approach in support of food security and sustainable agriculture*. FAO, Rome. https://www.fao.org/3/bl496e/bl496e.pdf

Friedman, B. D., & Allen, K. N. (2014). Systems theory. Chapter 1. In J. R. Brandell (ed.), *Essential of clinical social work*. Sage Publ. https://doi.org/10.4135/9781483398266

Galtung, J. (1964). An editorial. *Journal of Peace Research, 1*(1), 1–4. https://doi.org/10.1177/002234336400100101

Galtung, J. (1990). Cultural violence. *Journal of Peace Research, 27*(3), 291–305. https://www.jstor.org/stable/423472

Georgantzas, N. C., & Acar, W. (1995). *Scenario-driven planning: Learning to manage strategic uncertainty*. Quorum Books.

Global Partnership for the Prevention of Armed Conflicts (GPPAC). (2017). Conflict analysis framework: Field guidelines and procedures. https://www.gppac.net/resources/conflict-analysis-framework-field-guidelines-and-procedures

Grassroots Collective. (n.d.). https://www.thegrassrootscollective.org/grassroots-hub

Gurr, T. (1968). Psychological factors in civil violence. *World Politics, 20*(2), 245–278. https://doi.org/10.2307/2009798

Herbert, S. (2017). *Conflict analysis: Topic guide*. GSDRC, University of Birmingham, International Development Department. https://gsdrc.org/wp-content/uploads/2017/05/ConflictAnalysis.pdf

Huang, I. B., Keisler, J., & Linkov, I. (2011). Multi-criteria decision analysis in environmental sciences: ten years of applications and trends. *Science of the Total Environment, 409*(19), pp. 3578–94.

Huston, A., & Moriarty, P. (2018). Understanding the WASH system and its building blocks: Building strong WASH systems for the SDGs. https://www.ircwash.org/resources/understanding-wash-system-and-its-building-blocks

Keeney, R., & Raiffa, H. (1976). *Decisions with multiple objectives: Preferences and value tradeoffs*. Wiley.

Kelley, C. P., Mohtadi, S., Cane, M. A., Seager, R., & Kushnir, Y. (2015). Climate change in the Fertile Crescent and implications of the recent Syrian drought. *Proceedings of the U.S. National Academy of Sciences, 112*(11), 3241–3246. https://doi.org/10.1073/pnas.1421533112

Knight, F. H. (1921). Risk, uncertainty, and profit. University of Illinois at Urbana-Champaign's academy for entrepreneurial leadership historical research reference in Entrepreneurship. https://ssrn.com/abstract=1496192

Krugman, P., & Wells, R. (2015). *Economics* (4th ed.). Worth Publishing.

Lemos, C. M. (2018). *Agent-based modeling of social conflict: From mechanism to complex behavior*. Springer.

Lewin, K. (1946). Action research and minority problems. In G. W. Lewin (ed.), *Resolving social conflicts*. Harper & Row.

Lipchin, C., & Albrecht, T. (2019). A watershed-based approach to mitigating transboundary wastewater conflicts between Israel and the Palestinian Authority: The Besor-Hebron-Be'er Sheva watershed. In J. A. Cahan (ed.), *Water Security in the Middle East* (pp. 93–124). http://www.jstor.org/stable/j.ctt1jktqmk.10

Luce, R. D., & Raiffa, H. (1957). *Games and decisions*. John Wiley & Sons.

Luers, A. L., & Sklar, L. S. (2013). The difficult, the dangerous, and the catastrophic: Managing the spectrum of climate risks. *Earth's Future, 2*, 114–118. https://doi.org/10.1002/2013EF000192

Marshall, T. (2021). *The power of geography: Ten maps that reveal the future of the world*. Elliott and Thompson.

Meadows, D. (2008). *Thinking in systems*. Chelsea Green Publishing.

Means, T. (2016, February 15). The Köppen system of climate classification. http://weather.about.com/od/climatechange/fl/the-koumlppen-system-of-climate-classification.htm

Mendoza, G. A., & Macoun, P. (1999). *Guidelines for applying multi-criteria analysis to the assessment of criteria and indicators.* Center for International Forestry Research (CIFOR) http://www.cifor.org/acm/methods/toolbox9.html (Dec. 13, 2014).

Mitleton-Kelly, E. (2003). Ten principles of complexity and enabling infrastructures. Chapter 2 in *Complex systems and evolutionary perspectives of organizations: The application of complex theory to organizations.* Elsevier.

Mustafa, D., Akhter, M., & Nasralla, N. (2013). *Understanding Pakistan's water-security nexus. Peaceworks No. 88. US Institute of Peace,* Washington, DC. The National Academies Press. https://www.usip.org/publications/2013/05/understanding-pakistans-water-security-nexus

Nathan, H. S. K. & Reddy, B. S. (2011). Criteria selection framework for sustainable development indicators. *Journal of Multi-Criteria Decision Making,* 1(3), pp. 257–279.

National Research Council (NRC). (2012). *Disaster resilience: A national imperative.* The National Academies Press. https://doi.org/10.17226/13457

Nolan, R. (2002). *Development Anthropology: Encounters in the real world.* Westview Press.

Novick/Maariv, L. (2022, July 18). How is Jerusalem's sewage regulated? -new report. *Jerusalem Post,* Business Innovation. https://www.jpost.com/business-and-innovation/all-news/article-712429

Organization for Economic Co-operation and Development (OECD). (2005). Water and violent conflict. Issues Brief. C:\Users\amade\Downloads\92767-water-violent-conflict_EN.pdf

Pedercini, M., Arquitt, S., & Chan, D. (2020). Integrated simulation for the 2030 agenda. *System Dynamics Review, 36,* 333–357. https://doi.org/10.1002/sdr.1665

Pederson, P., Dudenhoeffer, D., Hartley, S., & Permann, M. (2006). *Critical infrastructure interdependency modeling: A survey of U.S.* and international research. Report No. INL/EXT-06-11464, Idaho National Laboratory, Idaho Falls, Idaho.

Rasmussen, J. L. (1997). Peacemaking in the Twenty-First Century: New Rules, New Roles, New Actors. In W. Zartman (ed.), *Peacemaking in International Conflict: Methods and Techniques* (pp. 23–50). United States Institute of Peace Press.

Reynolds, J. F., Stafford-Smith, D. M., & Lambin, E. (2003). Do humans cause deserts? A land problem through the lens of a new framework: The Dahlem desertification paradigm. In N. Allsopp (ed.), *Proceedings of the VIIth International Rangelands Congress,* 26 July–1 August 2003, Durban, South Africa.

Rinat, Z. (2017, July 18). Untreated sewage flowing from West Bank and East Jerusalem is polluting Israeli streams. *Haaretz.* https://www.haaretz.com/life/2017-07-18/ty-article/.premium/untreated-sewage-flowing-from-west-bank-polluting-israeli-streams/0000017f-e2c3-d7b2-a77f-e3c7a6370000

Sayer, J., Sunderland, T., Ghazoul, J., Pfund, J. L., Sheil, D., Meijaard, E., Venter, M., Boedhihartono, A. K., Day, M., Garcia, C., & Van Oosten, C. (2013). Ten principles for a landscape approach to reconciling agriculture, conservation, and other competing land uses. *PNAS, 110*(21), 8349–8356. https://doi.org/10.1073/pnas.1210595110

Scheidel, A., Del Bene, D., Liu, J., Navas, G., Mingorría, S., Demaria, F., Avila, S., Roy, B., Ertör, I., Temper, L., & Martínez-Alier, J. (2020). Environmental conflicts and defenders: A global overview. *Global Environmental Change, 63,* 102104. https://doi.org/10.1016/j.gloenvcha.2020.102104.

Schneider. S. H. (2004). Abrupt non-linear climate change, irreversibility, and surprise. *Global Environmental Change, 14*(3), 245–258. https://doi.org/10.1016/j.gloenvcha.2004.04.008

Seelos, C. (2020). Changing systems? Welcome to the slow movement. *Stanford Social Innovation Review, Winter,* 40–47.

Sharifi, A., Simangan, D., Lee, C. Y., Reyes, S. R., Katramiz, T., Josol, J., dos Muchangos, L., Virji, H., Kaneko, S., Tandog, T., Tandog, L., & Islam, M. (2021). Climate-induced stressors to peace: A review of recent literature. *Environment Research Letters, 16,* 073006. https://doi.org/10.1088/1748-9326/abfc08

Shemakov, R. (2022, July 19). Iraq, Iran, and local residents continue to oppose Turkey's hydroelectric projects along the Tigris. Ihttps://globalvoices.org/2022/07/19/iraq-iran-and-local-residents-continue-to-oppose-turkeys-hydroelectric-projects-along-the-tigris/

Smith, P. G., & Merritt, G. M. (2002). *Proactive risk management.* Productivity Press.

Tal, A., Khateeb, N., Nagouker, N., Akerman, H., Diabat, M., Nassar, A., Angel, R., Sadah, M. A., Hershkovitz, Y., Gasith, A., Aliewi, A., Halawani, D., Abramson, A., Assi, A., Laronne, J. B., & Asaf, L. (2010). Chemical and biological monitoring in ephemeral and intermittent streams: A study of two transboundary Palestinian-Israeli watersheds. *Intternational Journal River Basin Management, 8*(2), 185–205. https://doi.org/10.1080/15715124.2010.491796

Tesfaye, B. (2002). *Climate change and conflict in the Sahel.* Council on Foreign Relations. Center for Preventive Action. https://www.cfr.org/report/climate-change-and-conflict-sahel

The Omidyar Group. (2017). *Systems practice workbook.* https://oecd-opsi.org/toolkits/systems-practice-workbook/

The World Climate and Security Report (WCSR). (2021). https://imccs.org/wp-content/uploads/2021/06/World-Climate-and-Security-Report-2021.pdf

United Nations Development Progamme (UNDP). (2015). Capacity development: A UNDP primer. https://www.undp.org/publications/capacity-development-undp-primer

U.S. Agency for International Development (USAID). (2011). *Systems thinking in conflict assessment: Concepts and application.* USAID.

Vanegas, J. (2000). *Personal communication,* Boulder, CO.

Walsh, S., Cherry, S., & Roybal, L. (2009). *Critical infrastructure modeling: An approach to characterizing interdependencies of complex networks & control systems.* Report No. INL/CON-09-15271, Idaho National Laboratory, Idaho Falls, Idaho.

Weaver, W. (1948). Science and complexity. *American Scientist, 36*(4), 536–544. https://www.jstor.org/stable/27826254

Wiles, T. (2014, December 17). A progress report on the Colorado River pulse. *High Country News.* http://www.hcn.org/articles/progress-report-for-colorado-river-experimental-pulse/print_view

Winograd, M., & Farrow, A. (2011). Sustainable development indicators for decision making: Concepts, methods, decisions, and uses. In *Dimensions of sustainable development, UNESCO-encyclopedia of life support systems,* Paris France.

Xu, X., Tan, Y., & Yang, G. (2013). Environmental impact assessments of the Three Gorges project in China: Issues and interventions. *Earth-Science Reviews, 124,* 115–125. https://doi.org/10.1016/j.earscirev.2013.05.007

Zoellick, R. (2010, September 20). *Remarks for opening plenary of the high-level UN meetings on the MDGs.* United Nations General Assembly.

Zurek, M. B., & Henrichs, T. (2007). Linking scenarios across geographical scales in international environmental assessments. *Technology Forecasting & Social Change, 74,* 1282–1295. https://doi.org/10.1016/j.techfore.2006.11.005

6 Soft Systems Modeling Tools

6.1 INTRODUCTION

6.1.1 MODELING

Once human development and security issues and the PSC nexus's role in these issues have been clearly articulated, an attempt can be made to model their dynamics. Because of their ill-structured aspects, these issues cannot be modeled with simple analytical tools. Instead, as discussed in this chapter and the next one, systems tools are more appropriate for modeling the workings of systems involved in these issues and deciding where to intervene while accounting for their evolution over time.

Approaching the dynamic of the artificial construct of Figure 5.1 with a scientific perspective involves qualitative and quantitative simulation modeling. At the community scale, this may consist of modeling its past and current states of development and characteristics (e.g., capacity, vulnerability, conflict, resilience) and how the PSC nexus unfolds. There is also a need to model the desired state of the community and predict (forecasting and back-casting) its reaction to future specific events and scenarios of intervention. Other than being used for prediction, models can also be used for multiple reasons, as in Table 6.1.

Although the systems modeling tools presented in this chapter and Chapter 7 may appear more realistic and holistic than the traditional reductionist ones (e.g., analytical models, regression analysis) to address community development issues, we must be conscious of their limitations. It must be kept in mind that all models are not an end in themselves and represent virtual representations (mental constructs) needed to

---

TABLE 6.1

Reasons Other Than Prediction to Build Models According to Epstein (2008)
http://creativecommons.org/licenses/by/4.0/

- Explain (very distinct from prediction)
- Guide data collection
- Illuminate core dynamics
- Suggest dynamical analogies
- Discover new questions
- Promote a scientific habit of mind
- Bound (bracket) outcomes to plausible ranges
- Illuminate core uncertainties.
- Offer crisis options in near-real time

- Demonstrate trade-offs/suggest efficiencies
- Challenge the robustness of prevailing theory through perturbations
- Expose prevailing wisdom as incompatible with available data
- Train practitioners
- Discipline the policy dialogue
- Educate the public
- Reveal how what appears to be simple can be complex, and vice versa

---

DOI: 10.1201/9781003435006-6

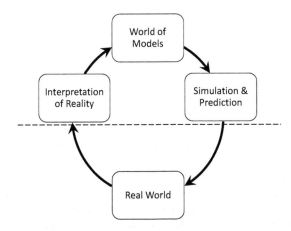

FIGURE 6.1   From the real world to the world of models.

simplify the complexity of the real world so that "more intelligent" or "less stupid" decisions can be made. As shown in Figure 6.1, models are based on an interpretation of reality, not reality itself. They are simplified simulations, interpretations, and explanations of reality (Franck, 2002; Sterman, 2002).

Once the purpose of models has been selected, their usefulness and soundness are dictated by how well they simulate reality and the observed behavior patterns (Forrester, 1969, 1971; Sterman, 2000). The simulations have the advantage of "providing a deep level of insight and understanding and allowing the consideration of many different scenarios which would be impossible to test in reality" (Lemos, 2018).

However, models can never wholly match reality, especially when trying to understand the interaction of multiple systems, such as those involved in the PSC nexus and community development. As such (and as reiterated in this book), the reality in which development and the nexus unfold can indeed be complex, uncertain, and unpredictable. So models are never complete or exact and are "very often systematically flawed" (Senge, 2006). Costanza et al. (2013) compared models to road maps with "many possible purposes and uses, [but] no one map, or model is right for the entire range of uses." Thus, one cannot expect structural models of the PSC nexus and the various community systems of Figure 5.1 with which the nexus interacts to be optimal or elegant interpretations of reality; they can only be interpreted as satisfactory (i.e., satisficing; Simon, 1972) but clumsy (Rittel and Webber, 1973) interpretations of reality. Models are created by individuals who make assumptions based on their mental filters; they interpret their world in a certain way, as discussed in the iceberg analogy in Figure 1.1. In short, models are tools to understand reality and "can be no better than the modelers" (Hannon and Ruth, 2001). Consequently, decision-makers need sound judgment and reflection to account for the models' uncertainty when selecting specific interventions.

Another characteristic of models is that they cannot be validated and are never value-free (Sterman, 2000; Ford, 2010). As noted by Barlas (1996), the validity of a model can be described in its usefulness for some purpose, keeping in mind that "the usefulness of the purpose itself" needs to be formulated, as well. Since system behavior patterns are dictated by structural patterns (Figure 1.1), validating a model is also about its usefulness to some structure and its environment (i.e., the context and scale discussed in Chapter 5). In community development, the purpose would be to address any actual situation that the community is facing or expects to face when dealing with (i) the management of resources and services, (ii) the consistent functioning of infrastructure over one or several years, (iii) conflict, and (iv) the effect of climate change and other adverse events. The usefulness of that purpose is evident regarding the community's survival, resilience, well-being, and economic development at a specific scale and over time. In general, confidence in the usefulness of models increases with time and following good modeling practices.

All these characteristics of models led Box and Draper (1987) to conclude that "essentially all models are wrong, but some are useful" and that "the approximate nature of the model must always be borne in mind." Page (2018) noted that models must ultimately be helpful, comprehensive, and sound enough to "reason, explain, design, communicate, act, predict, and explore" to be valuable in interpreting reality.

Although, as noted by Sterman (2000), "There is no cookbook recipe for successful modeling, [and] no procedure you can follow to guarantee a useful model," systems modeling is not random and requires following a road map. For example, Sterman (2000) considers five interactive activities in developing a dynamic model:

1. *Problem articulation* describes (i) existing observed patterns of behavior over time; (ii) the nature, scale, and boundaries of the problem being addressed and its key variables; (iii) how the problem has manifested itself and was addressed in the past; and (iv) if left unresolved, how the problem would manifest itself in the future.
2. *Dynamic hypothesis formulation* involves mapping the current causes and consequences of the observed behavior and identifying the endogenous issues and feedback mechanisms deemed responsible for that behavior.
3. *Simulation model formulation* comprises building the model, selecting the parameters that enter its structure, deciding on initial conditions, and testing the model for consistency and other attributes.
4. *Model testing* is done by: (i) comparing its predictive behavior with actual behavior, (ii) subjecting the model to unusual and extreme conditions (i.e., testing its robustness), and (iii) seeing how the predictive behavior changes by varying the system variables (sensitivity analysis).
5. *Policy design and evaluation* are conducted by exploring different scenarios or strategies and their consequences, proposing concrete recommendations to address the problem, and foreseeing possible side effects associated with these recommendations.

Activities 1 and 2 were addressed in Chapter 5. This modeling roadmap involves a fair amount of feedback mechanisms between the five activities. One of the many value propositions of following that road map is the learning experience gained by all participants involved, whether as individual modelers or members of a group through group model-building (GMB). According to Hovmand (2014), they go through a discovery journey from recognizing first that they are dealing with systems to ultimately understanding, at least in part, why things happen in the systems. As modelers go through the steps mentioned above, confidence in the model's usefulness grows, starting with clearly understanding what is expected in the five activities of the model building. Confidence also increases over time as the model performance is compared to the real world it is supposed to represent and is corrected accordingly (Sterman, 2000). This feedback can be seen as an ongoing "reality check" to prevent the model from going astray.

As we will see in Chapter 9, the five activities mentioned above can be integrated into a broader systems-based methodology that decision-makers can follow to address community development and the PSC nexus.

6.1.2 MODELING GUIDELINES

Navigating the road map when modeling human development and security issues and the PSC nexus requires following some guidelines. Table 6.2 lists a series of critical thinking questions that individuals and GMB teams must answer before any dynamic community development model is developed.

Among all the modeling guidelines, the first and foremost is the need to identify the model's context and clear physical and temporal boundaries. The boundaries must be *reasonably* defined in breadth or extension (horizontal) and in-depth or intensity (vertical). In the case of community development and security projects, the horizontal characteristic deals with the cross-disciplinary nature of the problems faced by the community (health, water, sanitation, energy, shelter, jobs, conflict, climate change, etc.). The vertical component is associated with how deep and detailed it is necessary to go (in a reductionist manner) into each development discipline to address each problem. Finally, the model's time frame (days, months, years) simulated by the model must be selected, and the system's initial conditions identified by the community baseline are identified through community appraisal.

A second guideline is ensuring the model's goals are clear and well-articulated. Models are developed once there is a clear understanding of how the community landscape has been established, how the nexus unfolds in the landscape, and what behavior patterns (including archetypical ones) are at play as the PSC nexus interacts with the various components of the landscape. This understanding, in turn, dictates the model structure and the selection of critical variables for each sector of the PSC nexus and other systems being considered. The goals of the models might be, for instance, to (i) explore the different types of dual causality among peace, sustainability, and climate security listed in Table 2.6 at the community level; (ii) predict how a community might react to future adverse events (e.g., flood, drought, conflict, climate change); (iii) explore the functioning of some critical community infrastructure or institutions; or (iv) identify the interventions to reduce the gap between the desired level of community development (e.g., desired peace, sustainability, and climate security outcomes) and the current status (i.e., baseline) of community development. It must be kept in mind that not all issues of interest can be addressed, and some aggregation is necessary.

A third guideline is the proper selection of the model boundaries. They determine how systems are framed and differentiate between "what is in and what is out, what is deemed relevant and irrelevant, what is important and unimportant, what is worthwhile and what is not, who benefits and who is disadvantaged" (Williams, 2008).

TABLE 6.2
Questions May Arise When Formulating Dynamic Models

Why	• Why is a dynamic model constructed?
What	• What problems, behavior, and structural patterns are being modeled over what time frame and spatial scale?
	• What boundaries should be selected?
	• What relationships exist between the systems and subsystems and the environment outside the systems?
	• What methods can other than (or complementary to) dynamic modeling be used to model the problem?
	• What changes in the system are desirable or not?
	• What would happen if the problem were or were not addressed?
	• What solutions have been attempted to address the problem in the past, and what were their outcomes?
	• What are the components of the problem being addressed and their connections?
	• What range of responses can be expected from the model?
	• What types of uncertainty and trends need to be included in the model?
How	• How will the model be complementary to the traditional steps of community development?
	• How have the components of the model interacted in the past?
	• How will community members be trained and involved in building, reviewing, and updating the model?
	• How will the model recommendations be presented to the community members?
	• How will decisions in model building, evaluation, and change be reached and disagreement/conflict mediated?
Who	• Who is participating in developing the model (stakeholders)?
	• Who is involved in group model building?
	• Who will coordinate group model building?
	• Who will be involved in deciding on desirable system changes and their implementation?
When	• When should the model be integrated into the management of development interventions?
	• When should the model be started, evaluated, modified, and updated?
Where	• Where should model development and community interaction occur (office, community)?

The boundaries of system dynamics models may sometimes coincide with those in the real world. In community development, the spatial boundaries are likely to be geographical (community, village, household, watershed), and the temporal boundaries may include seasonal, monthly, or yearly activities. If the boundaries cannot easily be identified, artificial boundaries may need to be selected to simplify the complexity at stake. Once the boundaries have been established, a decision needs to be made about the endogenous components (i.e., originating from within) that need to be included in the model and those exogenous (i.e., arising from without) that can be set aside in the modeling process. The latter components can be included later if deemed necessary or as needed.

A fourth guideline deals with deciding whether modeling is qualitative or quantitative. Qualitative modeling will likely remain dominant when modeling social systems for which only soft (subjective) data are available. Proxies or constructs relating a qualitative variable to other variables for which quantitative data can be used. Another option is to use semi-quantitative data. Quantitative information may also be available. Dealing with qualitative and quantitative information requires alternating between critical and creative thinking, as described in Section 4.4.2; together, they produce the systems thinking necessary to develop these models (see Table 4.2).

The modeling literature argues that qualitative modeling has limitations since it cannot give a comprehensive understanding of the issue being addressed; only quantitative modeling can. However, an argument can be made concerning what constitutes such "full understanding," mainly when applied to open and complex adaptive systems like communities, as described by Vennix (1996). Since, as discussed in the previous chapters, there is more interest in the process of "satisficing" than "optimizing" when dealing with complex systems such as communities, it can be argued that qualitative modeling also provides value in (i) the form of a learning environment, (ii) the process of understanding communities better, and (iii) making more intelligent project management decisions. Of course, the fact that there are positive aspects to qualitative modeling should not preclude the use of quantitative modeling when data is available for some parts of the system. Doing so should lead to a fuller understanding of the problem. In community development, the quantitative data collected during community appraisal described in Chapter 5 can be included in the quantitative modeling of specific real issues the community faces related to population (health, demography, workforce, and employment), the management of infrastructure, water, energy, land, and food resources, and the community capacity to provide services.

6.1.3 SOFT AND HARD SYSTEMS MODELING TOOLS

There are many ways of modeling the dynamics of messy and ill-defined complex problems, such as those involved in community development. Checkland and Poulter (2006) noted that there are two different approaches to modeling such situations, a soft systems approach and a hard systems approach. The essence of each approach is illustrated in Figure 6.2.

In the early 1980s, Checkland promoted a soft systems methodology (SSM) to address complex problems in management. It focuses primarily on the systemic process of inquiry and problem situations (Observer 2 in Figure 6.2) and, to a lesser extent, on the problem structure. The methodology emphasizes the importance of systems appreciation of perceiving and understanding reality over time. It also recognizes the value proposition that through group learning, different people with different worldviews perceive and judge the problems and purposefully tackle them differently. Seelos (2020) noted that a soft systems approach focuses on identifying drivers and potential paths forward. It is generally appropriate for complex social settings where subjective decision-making is dominant. However, it stops short of modeling how systems interact.

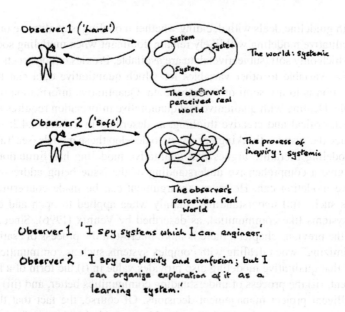

FIGURE 6.2   The "hard" and "soft" systems modeling stances.

Source: Checkland and Poulter (2006). Used by permission of John Wiley and Sons.

The hard systems approach considers the world as systemic (Observer 1 in Figure 6.2). The systems are treated as entities with clearly defined boundaries that can be objectively assessed and improved using available knowledge and tools (Seelos, 2020). The models capture the systemic and structural aspects of the analyzed problems and explore how system structure could explain the observed behavior. According to Seelos (2020), a limitation of the hard systems approach is that "initiatives based on hard system premises are sensitive to even minimal deviations from their assumptions... and robust change might require a more fundamental transformation of the system's architecture to alter its tendency to recreate the same problems." A hard systems approach generally works well for technical systems for which tangible factors can be included.

Of course, both hard and soft modeling perspectives are imperfect, and each has limitations. The approach used in this book includes both views as it is believed that when combined, they provide a better understanding of the systems involved in human development and security and the sectors of the PSC nexus. This approach is integrated into the methodology proposed to address complex community development challenges and discussed further in Chapter 9.

A wide variety of systems thinking theories, methods, and tools available in the literature can be used for different applications, a good summary of which can be found in Peters (2014) about applying systems thinking to health. The rest of this chapter presents primarily qualitative or semi-quantitative causal analysis tools.

They include systems mapping (concept maps, and rich pictures), cross-impact analysis, and network analysis tools. These tools provide a way to display the structure and interaction of systems and show the dynamics of identified issues. As emphasized in the overall methodology in Chapter 9, these tools are prerequisites to the more advanced qualitative and quantitative tools discussed in Chapter 7, including those of system dynamics, agent-based modeling, and discrete modeling.

6.2 CONCEPT MAPS

Concept maps (also called systems maps) represent how different parts of a system relate to each other as cause or effect around a unique idea or concept. Concept maps can be used for various purposes. For instance, they may help illustrate any system's organizational or hierarchical structure. Figure 6.3 is a multilayered mind map showing possible interdependency between the five categories of systems in the community landscape of Figure 5.1.

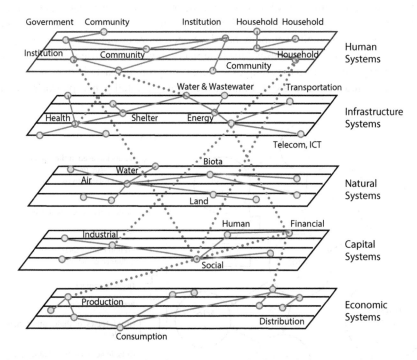

FIGURE 6.3   Intra- and interdependencies between the five major systems of Figure 5.1.

Source: Amadei (2019), used by permission of Momentum Press.

Note: Intraconnections are represented by solid lines connecting the nodes in each layer. Interconnections are represented by dotted lines across layers. Only a limited number of possible linkages are shown.

The components of each system category (i.e., the subsystems) are horizontally integrated; they are intra-dependent. Such a model was proposed, for instance, to show how the linkages that existed between critical water, energy, transportation, information and telecom, and emergency services played a role in the response of the city of New Orleans following Hurricane Katrina in 2005 (Pederson et al., 2006).

Figure 6.4 is another example of a concept map created to show relationships among parties in conflict. In this map, different symbols show different connections among stakeholders involved in the conflict ranging between alliances and discord. Concept maps such as Figure 6.4 can also be complemented with stakeholder maps that illustrate the influence and interests of different stakeholders. A good example of application of this mapping method to represent the conflict dynamics between different groups of actors in the South Kordofan state, Sudan can be found in CDA (2012) and the GPPAC (2017).

Different mind map platforms are available to communicate systems intra- and interconnections. They can be generated using software packages for mind mapping, a review of which can be found in Buzan (2018) and Wikipedia (2021). Pletica (www. pletica.com) and Kumu (www.kumu.io) are other powerful modern data visualization platforms that can organize complex information into interactive systems maps and rich pictures. The Cynefin company has developed more advanced system mapping tools, such as SenseMaker (https://thecynefin.co/how-to-use-sensemaker/) to iden- tify emerging data patterns in complex systems and promote participatory reflection/ engagement and action (praxis). Finally, the strategic intelligence platform of the

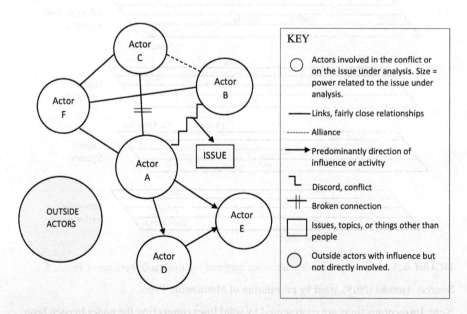

FIGURE 6.4 Example of a concept map showing different types of relationships among parties involved in a conflict.

Source: © Fisher et al. (2000), Zed Books, used by permission of Bloomsbury Publishing Plc. Note: "Actor" is used instead of "party" and the KEY has been simplified.

World Economic Forum enables users to develop mind maps around specific issues. An example of a mind map showing the different domains and subdomains that contribute to peace and resilience can be found at (Strategic Intelligence (weforum.org)).

In general, systems maps help show how things are related once an issue has been identified. However, they do not indicate whether the connections are reinforcing or balancing and do not include feedback mechanisms. The causal loop diagrams discussed in Chapter 7 build on system maps.

6.2.1 GRAPHICAL TREES

Graphical trees (Delp et al., 1977) are unique concept maps that visualize the consequences (or effects) and causes of a problem identified using the systems-aware appraisal presented in Chapter 5. A problem tree has a trunk representing a problem/issue identified at the end of the systems-aware appraisal. A network of tree branches, the visible part of the tree, defines the problem's consequences (or effects). The branches may have smaller units to simulate the impacts and associated sub-effects. The tree roots, the hidden part of the tree, represent the causes, sub-causes, and other linkages. Multiple tree root layers can be introduced until the most profound root causes of the problem are identified. These deep root causes represent places to intervene with the highest leverage.

Several core problems can be represented by several trees sharing roots and branches. The Omidyar Group (2017) considered three types of causes and effects: (i) structural associated with the physical and social environment, the built environment, and social and economic institutions and infrastructure; (ii) attitudinal associated with "beliefs, values, norms, and intergroup relations"; and (iii) transactional associated with "the processes used by and interactions among key people as they deal with important social, political, and economic issues."

Figure 6.5 shows an example of a conflict tree describing the causes and effects of ethnic tension in Burundi. Eight major root causes of the conflict were identified. Individually or combined, they influence ethnic tension and must be addressed accordingly.

The problem tree leads to its counterpart, a *solution tree*, sometimes called a *result tree* or an *objective tree* (Delp et al., 1977). A solution tree has positive roots and optimistic outcomes that overcome the negative causes and effects of the problem tree. The solution to the problem is now at the center of the tree and can be understood as a community development goal. The solution tree gives a comprehensive picture of the desired solution in a hierarchical format. The positive roots represent objectives to reach the goal. Starting from the bottom of the tree and working the way up, they can be regrouped around strategic development themes. For the conflict in Burundi example shown in Figure 6.5, the positive roots would include equal distribution of resources, economic equality, eliminating the side effects of colonialism, ensuring inclusivity, addressing corruption, and stopping the manipulation of history. The strategy to reach the goal of removing ethnic tension is primarily socio-economic and political.

Figure 6.6 shows an example of a problem tree for the Chico Mendes Extractive Reserve (CMER), located in the Acre district near the town of Rio Branco in western Brazil (Sabogal et al., 2015; Kroger, 2019). Illegal encroachment by farmers and cattle ranchers in the bio-reserve has created more deforestation and difficulty for the local forest people to survive economically and sell NTFPs (non-timber forest

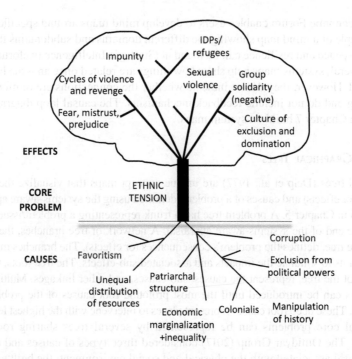

FIGURE 6.5 A problem tree mapping conflict dynamics in Burundi around the issue of ethnic tension.

Source: CDA (2012), used by permission of the CDA collaborative.

products), creating conflict. The main problem is that CMER residents are forced to shift to less sustainable, more profitable, secure livelihoods as cattle ranchers. As shown in Figure 6.6, the consequences of the problem include deforestation, environmental and climatic impact, and a lost sense of community, among others. The CMER residents identified several root causes of the problem, represented by the lower boxes of Figure 6.6.

This problem tree illustrates how the conflict between cattle ranchers and forest people and unsustainable practices contribute to the main problem. In this example, climate change is a consequence of the problem. It could also be a cause if it directly affects the main problem.

Figure 6.7 shows the counterpart of the tree of Figure 6.6 and potential solutions. The strategy to reach the goal of keeping the CMER residents from switching to cattle ranching is of three types. First, an education strategy is needed to educate the community on the benefits of NTFPs, adopting better economic models, new technologies, stewardship, and the pros and cons of converting to cattle ranching. A second strategy is to seek private and public support to improve the infrastructure necessary to bring the NTFPs to market. Finally, a third strategy is socio-economic-political, which fights corruption, creates supportive government regulations, and seeks economic opportunities and subsidies.

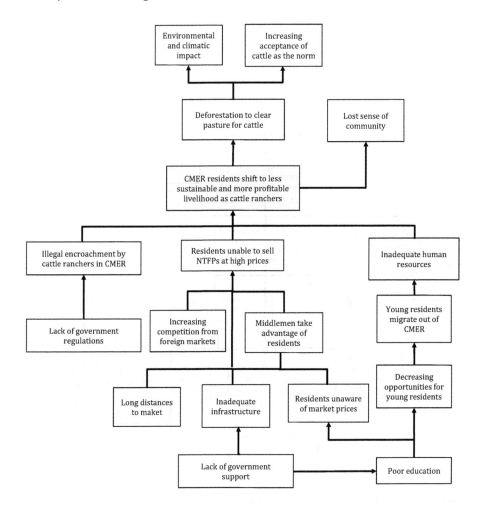

FIGURE 6.6   CMER livelihoods problem tree. NTFPs are non-timber forest products.

Source: Morin et al. (2021), used by permission of the authors.

From a systems point of view, the problem and solution trees are great causality tools that help visualize the hierarchical cause-and-effect dynamics that drive complex systems in community development. Furthermore, most focus group participants can construct and understand problem and solution trees. The tree representation can help people visualize and comprehend linkages between the causes and consequences of issues they may not even be initially aware of.

In Figures 6.6 and 6.7, the problem involves the three sectors of the PSC nexus. In some other instances, problem and solution trees can be created for issues that are specifically critical to each sector of the PSC nexus: (i) conflict and peace, (ii) unsustainable and sustainable practices, and (iii) climate vulnerability and security. These three trees will likely share roots and branches to capture the triple-nexus

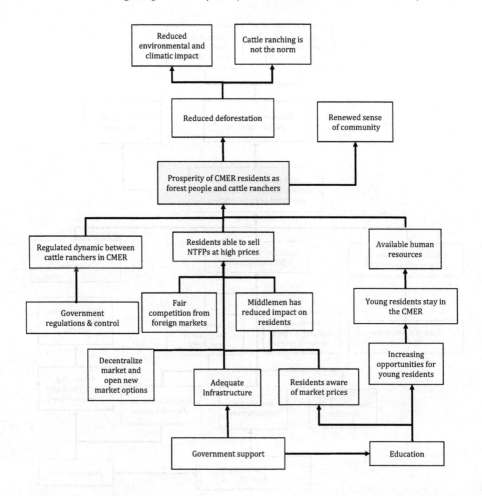

FIGURE 6.7   CMER livelihoods solution tree.

dynamic. Furthermore, the roots of one tree (causes) may connect to branches (effects) of another tree, or vice versa.

The main limitation of problem and solution trees is their static nature. They only show links in one direction and in a hierarchical manner. As a result, they do not capture the closed-loop interactions among different causes or effects or between causes and effects. These can be visualized better with the system dynamics causal loop diagrams graphical tool presented in Chapter 7. Another challenge in using a tree representation is prioritizing which causes and effects to tackle once identified. According to Caldwell (2002), priority should be given to causes that: (i) show good potential to make a significant impact and contribution if eliminated; (ii) are relatable to community members; (iii) provide substantial impact through synergy, collaboration, and partnering; (iv) match the capacity of the community; (v) are recurring in the community; and (vi) can be measured and verified.

6.3   CROSS-IMPACT ANALYSIS

Cross-impact analysis, also called double-causality analysis, is a mathematical approach used in Futures Research studies. It originated in the mid to late 1960s (Gordon & Hayward, 1968; Glenn, 2003; Glenn & Gordon, 2003; Gordon, 2014) and was initially developed to analyze weakly structured systems for which theory-based computational models do not work due to the system's complexity, uncertainty, and disciplinary heterogeneity. Since its inception, cross-impact analysis has been a general approach for assessing the "interrelations [among] the most important influential factors in a system by experts who evaluate [subjectively] pairs of these factors" (Weimer-Jehle, 2010). The different methods of cross-impact analysis differ in how the interrelations are formulated (probabilistically or deterministically) and whether a qualitative, quantitative, or mixed approach is used to describe the causalities (Asan & Asan, 2007).

The first step in any cross-impact analysis is to identify the n interacting variables that play a role in a specific issue. The variables may come from different areas of community development and security. In our present case, some may be related to conflict/peace, unsustainable/sustainable practices, and climate vulnerability/security. All these variables impact and are sensitive to others across the PSC nexus. Cross-impact analysis can also map the relationship between different stakeholders (individuals or organizations) involved in decision-making.

Cross-impact analysis of the n variables is represented by an $(n \times n)$ cross-impact matrix with zeros along its diagonal and $n^2 - n$ off-diagonal terms. The off-diagonal terms define how each variable (row) *directly* influences or impacts the other variables and how each variable (column) depends on or is sensitive to the other variables. It should be noted that the cross-impact matrix, referred to as the *matrix of direct influence* (MDI) by Godet (2000), is not necessarily symmetric. The strengths of the binary influence between two variables can be described qualitatively using qualifiers such as high, medium, or low or scored semi-quantitatively over an appropriate scale (say 0 for no influence, up to three for strong influence). The selected scale is specific to the system being analyzed. The scores can be positive to represent enabling influence and dependence or negative to represent constraining influence and dependence. When using the cross-impact analysis to explore the relationships between stakeholders, the off-diagonal terms in the cross-impact matrix describe the nature of each stakeholder's links with the others, which complements the social network analysis mentioned in the next section.

Table 2.9 is an example of cross-impact analysis showing the influence and dependence of the three sectors of the PSC nexus. Table 5.3 shows different forms of cross-impact between the systems of Figure 5.1. In both cases, influence and dependence are described in qualitative terms. More detailed versions of the tables would require breaking down each sector in Table 2.9 or each system in Table 5.3 into components. For instance, in Table 2.9, three variables could define positive, negative, and cultural peace. Likewise, four variables could represent the people, planet, prosperity, and partnership components of sustainability. Finally, climate security could be broken down into coping, adapting, and mitigating measures. In that case, Table 2.9 would represent a 10×10 cross-impact matrix with 90 off-diagonal terms whose binary interactions would have to be determined. The analysis becomes more complex if one considers further the different attributes of each of the ten variables.

Table 6.3 shows another example of the cross-impact analysis proposed by Amadei (2020) to model the interaction between the $n = 8$ domains of positive peace shown in Figure 2.7. Semi-quantitative scores were assigned to describe the strength of the *direct enabling influence* between interacting domains, two at a time. The scores ranged between 0 for no influence, 1 for low influence, two for medium influence, and three for strong influence. In this example, possible constraining influences (with negative scores ranging between -1 and -3) were not considered.

Scores were assigned to the 56 off-diagonal terms of the double-causality matrix of Table 6.3 based on reading the comprehensive statistical analysis conducted by the IEP and summarized in Appendix A of their 2017 report (IEP, 2017). The challenge in populating Table 6.3 was translating the purely *qualitative* statements made in that appendix into *semi-quantitative* measures. The scores in Table 6.3 were subjectively selected (best guess) to illustrate the methodology and are not associated with any actual case study. Ideally, actual values at the country level would have to be jointly selected by decision-makers with different expertise. The selection process requires time, brainstorming, and consensus-building between all parties involved

TABLE 6.3

Cross-Impact Matrix Showing the Different Levels of Direct Influence and Dependence among the Eight Domains of the Positive Peace Index (0 No Influence; 1 Low Influence; 2 Medium Influence; and 3 Strong Influence)

	WFG	SBE	LLC	HLC	FFI	GRN	EDR	ARO	Net influence
Well-functioning government (WFG)	0	3	3	2	2	2	2	2	16
Sound business environment (SBE)	2	0	2	2	1	1	3	1	12
Low levels of corruption (LLC)	3	3	0	3	2	2	3	1	17
High levels of human capital (HLC)	1	3	1	0	1	2	3	1	12
Free flow of information (FFI)	3	2	3	2	0	2	2	3	17
Good relations with neighbors (GRN)	1	3	1	2	2	0	2	1	12
Equitable distribution of resources (EDR)	2	3	2	3	1	1	0	1	13
Acceptance of rights of others (ARO)	3	3	2	3	1	2	2	0	16
Net dependence	15	20	14	17	10	12	17	10	115

Source: Amadei (2020). Used by permission of Elsevier.

(Arcade et al., 2014). The net dependence and influence values of Table 6.3 are plotted on a single influence (*x*) vs. dependence (*y*) graph (Figure 6.8).

The average direct influence and dependence value for all domains is 14.4. The graph can then help to separate the variables (i.e., domains) into several groups. According to Arcade et al. (2014), they include:

- *Influential variables* (domains) with high influence and low dependence (e.g., acceptance of rights of others [ARO] and free flow of information [FFI])
- *Excluded variables* (domains) with low influence and dependence (e.g., good relations with neighbors [GRN])
- *Relay variables* (domains) with high influence and dependence (e.g., well-functioning government [WFG])
- *Dependent variables* (domains) with low influence and high dependence (e.g., sound business environment [SBE], high levels of human capital [HLC], and equitable distribution of resources [EDR])

Table 6.3 involves a high level of aggregation since each positive peace index (PPI) domain contains multiple indicators, as indicated in Table 2.5. A more comprehensive cross-impact analysis could be carried out by involving the 24 PPI indicators listed in that table. In that case, the 8×8 matrix in Table 6.3, with its 56 off-diagonal terms, would be replaced by a 24×24 matrix containing 552 off-diagonal components. Although more comprehensive, the analysis would become more challenging

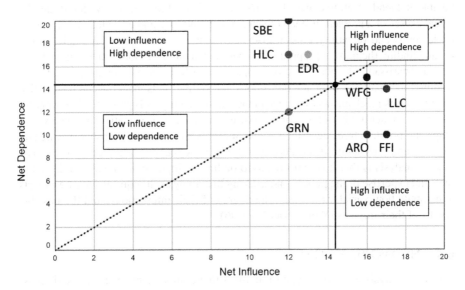

FIGURE 6.8 Graph showing the values of the degrees of direct net influence and dependence for all eight domains of the positive peace index (PPI). The four main sectors are defined by the average values (14.4) of the net influence and dependence in Table 6.2.

Source: Amadei (2020). Used by permission of Elsevier.

as the influence of each indicator on the other 23 would need to be determined semi-quantitatively, two at a time. For this reason, the present analysis is restricted to the eight domains of positive peace.

The value proposition of cross-impact analysis in understanding the dynamics of the eight domains involved in the PPI is defined by its simplicity and ability to determine among all the eight domains (or all 24 indicators) which ones have more influence (dominance, impact) on the others and those that are subordinate to the others. Special attention needs to be placed on the most influential domains (i.e., the high influence and low dependence quadrant in Figure 6.8) as they are crucial and have the highest leverage in the system responsible for positive peace at the country level and may help decision-makers prioritize their decision process.

Finally, the cross-impact methodology presented above considers the *direct* influence and dependence between the eight domains that define the PPI. Any *indirect* dynamic interaction between the eight domains requires a different approach and the introduction of a *matrix of indirect influence* (MII). As suggested by Arcade et al. (2014) and Godet (1986, 2001), a domain may have a limited direct influence on another but have a sizable indirect influence through multiple indirect "feedback effects through paths and loops" across all domains. A total of 8! (40,320) pathways linking the eight domains in Table 6.3 would have to be considered to determine the indirect influence. Another alternative suggested by Arcade et al. (2014) and Godet (1986) is to raise the cross-impact matrix to successive powers (up to 4 or 5) and plot the indirect influence and dependence values using the same format as in Figure 6.8.

The cross-impact analysis is particularly appropriate to tackle societal issues. It is flexible and lends itself to expert discourse, which is vital for effectively identifying the actual causes of a problem instead of using a mere intuitive and educated guess. Due to its flexibility and versatility, cross-impact analysis is apt for comparing multiple scenarios and finding the most appropriate ones based on analytical tools rather than guesses, bias, and partisan influence. The cross-impact matrix helps map the nature and extent of feedback mechanisms and interconnections in a system. This mapping can help decide what feedback mechanisms to include in the hard modeling tools presented in Chapter 7.

Cross-impact analysis has limitations, however. First, it is static, like the system maps and problem trees described above. It represents a system snapshot in time and cannot handle dynamic (time-dependent) issues. A second limitation of the cross-impact analysis is that it is entirely based on human input and depends on the accuracy and expertise of the people undertaking that analysis. It requires judging experts to estimate how variables interact, the degree of their interactions, and the possible results of their impacts (Weimer-Jehle, 2006).

6.4 NETWORK ANALYSIS

Network analysis is another type of analysis that complements causality and cross-impact analysis. It provides another means of mapping the interconnectivity between the systems in Figure 5.1 or the intra-connectivity of the nested subsystems comprising each system, as shown in Figure 6.3 above. The connections can be between individuals, groups, organizations, objects, and processes. Before any analysis, the challenge or opportunity to be investigated must be defined (IRC, 2016). PSC nexus-related examples include who is involved in the conflict between different parties, how community resources management is decided among institutions, how climate changes at geographic locations interact, and how various organizations coordinate climate awareness, adaptation, and mitigation policies and processes to increase resilience to climate change.

Network analysis is more than just a graphical representation of connectivity, as described in the book *Networks: An Introduction* by Newman (2010). When used for mapping social systems, network analysis is referred to as social network analysis (SNA). It can be used to show, for instance, how members of a group or members of several organizations interact and connect in a network (NRC, 2009; Borgatti et al., 2009) and how the components of a social network communicate, express their creativity, and reach consensus (Perkin and Court, 2005).

In general, SNA network diagrams are *graphs* that consist of multiple nodes (vertices) connected by links (edges or ties) that define the social fabric. The nodes represent social agents or actors (individuals, groups, organizations, or partners), and their shapes, sizes, or colors can represent an agent's importance or unique attribute in the network. The links represent how the agents or actors are interconnected when addressing a specific issue at a given time. Different graphical tools have been proposed to show the influence of actors/agents on others. For instance, graphs that show edges pointing inward toward or outward from each node are called *directed* graphs. Symbols of different sizes can indicate each node's strength (attribute). Likewise, the same can be done with the links by changing their thickness or color. These networks with additional information are called *valued networks* (Borgatti et al., 2013) or *weighted networks* (Newman, 2010).

It should be noted that network analysis can also help map the connectivity between nonsocial agents. Figure 2.3 is an example of network analysis showing how the targets of SDG 1 (poverty), SDG 13 (climate action), and SDG 16 (peace, justice, and strong institutions) interact, including their trade-offs and synergies. Other examples include mapping the different components of infrastructure systems that provide a specific type of service under a particular context and at a specific scale. In this case, the network maps may help identify where to intervene in the infrastructure to make a particular service more efficient or accessible to a broader range of customers. Network analysis can also help assess the critical infrastructure necessary for a community to face adverse events and natural hazards, thus increasing its overall resilience (Toole and McCown, 2008; NRC, 2009). It is also helpful in developing awareness, adaptation, and mitigation strategies in response to climate change. Finally, network analysis can map how the economic processes of production, distribution, and consumption of goods and services depend on each other at different scales.

As the IRC (2016) suggested, network analysis can help visualize how network connections change over time, thus affecting the behavior of a system and the components of that system. For example, Figure 6.9 shows the evolution of the relationship between different health-related groups of workers in Sierra Leone. Starting with a functional network between donors, IRC, local NGOs, healthcare providers, and community authorities (scenario A), some division occurs over time in the network for some reasons (scenario B). The divisions, in turn, require investing in new relationships to bring the network to a new level of functionality (scenario C).

Social network analysis maps can also be analyzed using mathematical tools. They can (i) identify the strengths, weaknesses, and patterns of interaction among system components; (ii) identify potential system attractors; (iii) make predictions and assess the

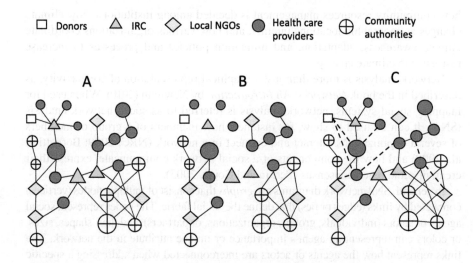

FIGURE 6.9 Scenarios showing three types of relationships between health-related workers in Sierra Leone

Source: IRC (2016), used according to license agreement (http://www.rescue.org/page/term-use).

network's resilience; (iv) map assets and vulnerabilities; (v) conduct simulations; and (vi) plan interventions that leverage or strengthen existing network connections. Borgatti et al. (2009) reviewed some of the measures and properties that can be inferred from SNA maps at the network level (cohesion, shape), the node level (different forms of centrality, betweenness), and the link level (cohesion and equivalence). In turn, these measures and properties can help identify the "underlying processes that account for observed relationships among variables," which, according to Borgatti et al., can be transmission, adaptation, binding, or exclusion processes. Although network analysis focuses on the components of networks and their patterns of interactions (i.e., the network structure), it pays less attention to the *nature* and *dynamic* of those interactions, which can be handled better qualitatively and quantitatively by the hard system tools discussed in Chapter 7.

Cross-impact analysis and network analysis are closely related. For instance, the double-causality matrix of cross-impact analysis becomes the so-called *adjacency matrix* in network analysis. For example, Table 6.3 yields the following adjacency matrix E_{ij} $(i, j = 1–8)$:

$$E_{ij} = \begin{pmatrix} 0 & 3 & 3 & 2 & 2 & 2 & 2 & 2 \\ 2 & 0 & 2 & 2 & 1 & 1 & 3 & 1 \\ 3 & 3 & 0 & 3 & 2 & 2 & 3 & 1 \\ 1 & 3 & 1 & 0 & 1 & 2 & 3 & 1 \\ 3 & 2 & 3 & 2 & 0 & 2 & 2 & 3 \\ 1 & 3 & 1 & 2 & 2 & 0 & 2 & 1 \\ 2 & 3 & 2 & 3 & 1 & 1 & 0 & 1 \\ 3 & 3 & 2 & 2 & 1 & 2 & 2 & 0 \end{pmatrix} \qquad (6.1)$$

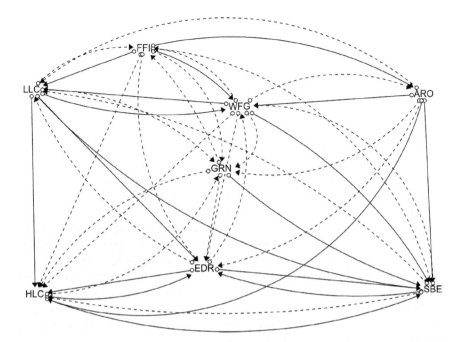

FIGURE 6.10 Value-directed network showing how all eight positive peace domains in Table 6.3 interact. The strong influences (value of 3 in eq. 6.1) and medium influences (values of 2 in eq. 6.1) are represented by solid and dashed lines, respectively. Well-functioning government (WFG), Sound business environment (SBE), Low levels of corruption (LLC), High levels of human capital (HLC), Free flow of information (FFI), Good relations with neighbors (GRN), Equitable distribution of resources (EDR), Acceptance of rights of others (ARO).

This matrix translates into a valued-directed graph (i.e., a network analysis graph showing how the eight PPI domains are connected). As an example, Figure 6.10 shows some of the interactions among the eight domains of the positive peace index defined in Table 6.3. The MICMAC software (www.en.laprospective.fr) developed by Godet (1986) can also be used to construct more complex graphs with multiple degrees of domain interdependence.

The centrality of each node in Figure 6.10, that is, "the contribution the node makes to the structure of the network," can be determined using different measures (Newman, 2010). For instance, using the *degree of centrality* as a measure, the eight domains have *out-degree* centralities (sum of values of outgoing links) of 16, 12, 17, 12, 17, 12, 13, and 16, respectively. The eight domains also have *in-degree* centralities (sum of values of ingoing links) of 15, 20, 14, 17, 10, 12, 17, and 10, respectively. The out-degree centrality indicates the influence of one domain on the others, and the in-degree centrality represents the dependence of each domain on the others.

SNA is a powerful method that can help to make decisions across the PSC nexus where there may be issues about (i) how information flows between populations, households, and institutions at the community level and (ii) how decisions about development and security are made in the community. SNA maps can help show whether information flows, who controls what, the critical actors and clusters of decision-makers, where roadblocks occur, and who is marginalized. As an example, Bodin et al. (2006) showed how these properties and measures of SNA maps could help users to understand better the role that components of social networks play in the adaptive management of natural resources around critical social features such as social memory, heterogeneity, redundancy, learning, adaptive capacity, and trust.

As reviewed by Freeman (2000) and Borgatti et al. (2013), the visualization of networks has evolved from early hand-drawn images in the 1930s to today's computer-generated diagrams. Various tools and software are available today that map the interaction between different network components and help identify the strength of networks (NRC, 2009). Borgatti et al. (2013) showed several examples of how SNA can be applied using the software UCINET (www.analytictech.com), which is available through *Analytic Technologies* based in Lexington, KY (Borgatti et al., 2002). Net-Map (www.netmap.wordpress.com) is another SNA tool.

Examples of application of network analysis in development and aid studies abound in the literature, especially for policy decision-making (Davies, 2003). Among many case studies of the application of network analysis, some well-documented ones can be found in the papers by Moore et al. (2003) for floods in Mozambique; Schiffer and Waale (2008) for the management of water basin resources in Ghana; Dale (2011) for network identification in Timor-Leste; Blanchet and James (2012) for policy and health intervention in Ghana; and Zimmerman et al. (2016) to model the interaction between the water, energy, and food sectors.

The application of network analysis to peace and conflict studies has been demonstrated by Wolfe (2004), Joshi and Henn (2021), and Shaikh et al. (2015), among others. In the area of resilience to climate change and disasters, the study done by the Harvard Humanitarian Initiative (HHI, 2020) provided a detailed analysis of how network analysis can be used to map the engagement and collaboration patterns between multiple actors involved in national climate awareness, adaptation, and mitigation and disaster resilience issues in a district in Bangladesh.

Pramova et al. (2020) used network analysis to carry out *policy network studies* to analyze how different actors focus on developing policies that favor adaptation to mitigation at the national level. Policy network analysis "can reveal some of the barriers to, and provide insights on possible opportunities for, better actor communication and coordination. It can reveal which policy actors are in a better position to connect the adaptation and mitigation policy domains (both usual and unusual suspects)."

The analysis carried out by Pramova et al. (2020) involved 76 agencies engaged in national climate policy in Peru. It was found that some agencies prefer focusing on mitigation, whereas others prefer adaptation; very few linkages were found to exist between the two groups of agencies. The analysis also showed that national governmental organizations control the climate change agenda in Peru and that mitigation involved more agency connections than adaptation. A similar study was done by Di Gregorio et al. (2019) for Brazil and Indonesia. It accounted for the decision process at three levels of country governance: national, provincial, and district. Another interesting social network analysis study was carried out by Farrell (2016) to examine the countermovement toward climate change and the role played by the private and public sectors in controlling the dialogue about climate change. The network consisted of 4,556 individuals tied to 164 contrarian organizations.

Although network analysis focuses on the components of networks and their patterns of interactions (i.e., the network structure), it represents a snapshot of systems interactions at a specific time. The dynamics of those interactions can be handled more effectively (qualitatively and quantitatively) by the modeling tools discussed in Chapter 7. Schoenenberger and Schenker-Wicki (2014) suggested that an ideal time to perform (social) network analysis in community development is during data collection and analysis (i.e., stakeholder and partner analysis). It can also prove helpful, for instance, when deciding who needs to be involved in decision-making.

6.5 CONCLUDING REMARKS

The soft modeling tools presented in this chapter help analyze the critical issues outlined and ranked at the end of the community landscape appraisal discussed in Chapter 5. More specifically, they help identify the root causes and consequences of the issues, possible causality, how different issues influence and depend on each other, and potential relationships. However, they share similar limitations (i.e., being static and unable to capture the inter- and intra- system dynamics). Another restriction of soft modeling tools is that they are qualitative or semi-quantitative. Despite these limitations, they provide a strong foundation for the hard modeling tools discussed in the following chapters. It is highly recommended to use soft modeling tools before using those described in Chapter 7.

REFERENCES

Amadei, B. (2019). *A systems approach to modeling the water-energy-land-food nexus* (Vols. *I* and *II*). Momentum Press.

Amadei, B. (2020). Revisiting positive peace using systems tools. *Technology Forecasting and Social Change, 158.* https://doi.org/10.1016/j.techfore.2020.120149

Arcade, J., Godet, M., Meunier, F., & Roubelat, F. (2014). Structural analysis with the MICMAC method and the Actor's strategy with the MACTOR method. In J. C. Glenn and T. J. Gordon (eds.), *Introduction to the futures methods research series.* Futures research methodology, V3.0, The Millennium Project, Washington, DC.

Asan, S. S., & Asan, U. (2007). Qualitative cross-impact analysis with time consideration. *Technological Forecasting & Social Change, 74,* 627–644. https://doi.org/10.1016/j.techfore.2006.05.011

Barlas, Y. (1996). Formal aspects of model validity and validation in system dynamics. *System Dynamics Review, 12*(3), 183–210. https://doi.org/10.1002/(sici)1099-1727(199623)12:3%3c183::aid-sdr103%3e3.0.co;2-4

Blanchet, K., & James, P. (2012). The role of social networks in the governance of health systems: the case of eye care systems in Ghana. *Health Policy and Planning,* 1–14. https://doi.org/10.1093/heapol/czs031

Bodin, O., Crona, B., & Ernstson, H. (2006). Social networks in natural resource management: What is there to learn from a structural perspective? *Ecology and Society, 11*(2). https://www.jstor.org/stable/26266035

Borgatti, S. P., Everett, M. G., & Freeman, L. C. (2002). *UCINET for windows: Software for social network analysis.* Analytic Technologies.

Borgatti, S. P., Everett, M. G., & Johnson, J. C. (2013). *Analyzing social networks.* Sage Publications.

Borgatti, S. P., Mehra, A., Brass, D. J., & Labianca, G. (2009). Network analysis in the social sciences. *Science, 323*(5916), 892–895. https://doi.org/10.1126/science.1165821

Box, G. E. P., & Draper, N. R. (1987). *Empirical model-building and response surfaces*. Wiley.

Buzan, T. (2018). *Mind map mastery: The complete guide to learning and using the most powerful thinking tool in the universe*. Watkins Publ.

Caldwell, R. (2002). *Project design handbook*. Cooperative for Assistance and Relief Everywhere (CARE). https://www.fsnnetwork.org/resource/cares-project-design-handbook

Checkland, P., & Poulter, J. (2006). *Learning for action: Soft systems methodology and its use for practitioners, teachers, and students*. John Wiley & Sons.

Collaborative for Development Action (CDA). (2012, June 13). *Conflict analysis framework. Field guidelines and procedures*. https://www.cdacollaborative.org/wp-content/uploads/2016/02/Conflict-Analysis-Framework-Field-Guidelines.pdf

Costanza, R., Wainger, L., Folke, C., & Mäler, K.-G. (2013). Complex ecological economic systems. *BioScience, 43*(8), 545–555. https://doi.org/10.2307/1311949

Dale, P. (2011, June 29). Ties that bind: Studying social networks in Timor-Leste. People, spaces, deliberation. https://jano-buti.blogspot.com/2011/06/ties-that-bind-studying-social-networks.html

Davies, R. (2003). Network perspectives in the evaluation of development interventions: More than a metaphor. EDAIS Conference on New Directions in Impact Assessment for Development: Methods and Practice. November 24–25, 2003, https://web.worldbank.org/archive/website01031/WEB/IMAGES/NAPE.PDF

Delp, P., Thesen, A., Motiwalla, J., & Seshadri, N. (1977). *Systems tools for project planning*. International Development Institute.

Di Gregorio, M., Fatorelli, L., Paavola, J., Locatelli, B., Pramova, E., Nurrochmat, D. R., May, P. H., Brockhaus, M., Sari, I. M., & Kusumadewi, S. D. (2019). Multi-level governance and power in climate change policy networks. *Global Environmental Change, 54*, 64–77. https://doi.org/10.1016/j.gloenvcha.2018.10.003

Epstein, J. M. (2008). Why model? *Journal of Artificial Societies and Social Simulation*, 11(4), 12. https://www.jasss.org/11/4/12.html

Farrell, J. (2016). Network structure and influence of the climate change counter-movement. *Nature Climate Change, 6*, 370–374. https://doi.org/10.1038/nclimate2875

Fisher, S., Ibrahim Abdi, D., Ludin, J., Smith, R., Williams, S., & Williams, S. (2000). *Working with conflict: Skills and strategies for action*. Zed books.

Ford, A. (2010). *Modeling the environment*. Island, Press.

Forrester, J. W. (1969). *Urban dynamics*. Productivity Press.

Forrester, J. W. (1971). *World dynamics* (2nd ed. 1973). Productivity Press.

Franck, R. (ed.). (2002). *The explanatory power of models: Bridging the gap between empirical and theoretical research in the social sciences* (pp. 1–8). Springer Verlag.

Freeman, L. C. (2000). Visualizing social networks. *Journal of Social Structure, 1*.

Glenn, J.C. (2003). Introduction to the futures research methods series. In J. C. Glenn and T. J. Gordon (eds.), *Futures research methodology* (2nd ed.). United Nations University, Millennium-Project.

Glenn, J. C., & Gordon, T. J. (2003). The AC/UNU millennium project. In J. C. Glenn, and T. J. Gordon (eds.), *Futures research methodology* (2nd ed.) United Nations University, Millennium-Project.

Global Partnership for the Prevention of Armed Conflicts (GPPAC). (2017). *Conflict analysis framework: Field guidelines and procedures*. https://www.gppac.net/resources/conflict-analysis-framework-field-guidelines-and-procedures

Godet, M. (1986). Introduction to La Prospective: Seven key ideas and one scenario method. *Futures, 18*(2), 134–157. https://doi.org/10.1016/0016-3287(86)90094-7

Godet, M. (2000). The art of scenarios and strategic planning: Tools and pitfalls. *Technological Forecasting and Social Change, 65*(1), 3–22. https://doi.org/10.1016/S0040-1625(99)00120-1

Godet, M. (2001). *Creating futures: Scenario planning and a strategic management tool.* Brookings Institution Press.

Gordon, T. J. (2014). Cross-impact analysis. In *Introduction to the futures methods research series*. Futures research methodology, V3.0, The Millennium Project, Washington, DC.

Gordon, T. J., & Hayward, H. (1968). Initial experiments with the cross-impact matrix method of forecasting. *Futures, 1*(2), 110–116. https://doi.org/10.1016/S0016-3287(68)80003-5

Hannon, B., & Ruth, M. (2001). *Dynamic modeling.* Springer.

Harvard Humanitarian Initiative (HHI). (2020). Network analysis of climate change & disaster resilience actors working in Bagerhat District, Bangladesh. C:\Users\amade\OneDrive\Documents\My Files\BOOKS\Managing Change\Documents\bangladesh_network_analysis_report_final_anonymized.pdf

Hovmand, P. S. (2014). *Community-based system dynamics.* Springer.

Institute for Economics & Peace (IEP). (2017). *Positive peace report 2017: Tracking peace transitions through a systems thinking approach.* Report number 54, IEP: Sydney, Australia.

International Rescue Committee (IRC). (2016). Social network analysis handbook: Connecting the dots on humanitarian programs. https://www.rescue.org/resource/social-network-analysis-handbook-connecting-dots-humanitarian-programs

Joshi, M., & Henn, S. (2021). *Building a network for successful peace negotiations in afghanistan: Social network analysis of the Afghan peace process.* Peace Accords Matrix, Kroc Institute for International Peace Studies, Keough School of Global Affairs. https://doi.org/10.7274/r0-ax7h-g962

Kroger, M. (2019). Deforestation, cattle capitalism and neo-developmentalism in the Chico mendes extractive reserve, Brazil, *The Journal of Peasant Studies, 47*(3), 464–482, https://doi.org/10.1080/03066150.2019.1604510

Lemos, C. M. (2018). *Agent-based modeling of social conflict: From mechanism to complex behavior.* Springer Cham.

Moore, S., Eng, E., & Daniel, M. (2003). International NGOs and the role of network centrality in humanitarian aid operations: A case study of coordination during the 2000 Mozambique floods. *Disaster, 27*(4), 305–318. http://doi.org/10.1111/j.0361-3666.2003.00235.x

Morin, J., Sagaser, M., & Tisdale, J. (2021). Rising deforestation in the Chico Mendes extractive reserve: Causes and effects. Term paper, CVEN 5746, Spring 2021, University of Colorado.

National Research Council (NRC). (2009). *Applications of social network analysis for building community disaster resilience.* The National Academies Press.

Newman, M. E. J. (2010). *Networks: An introduction.* Oxford University Press.

Page, S. E. (2018). *The model thinker: What you need to know to make data work for you.* Basic Books.

Pederson, P., Dudenhoeffer, D., Hartley, S., & Permann, M. (2006). *Critical infrastructure interdependency modeling: A survey of U.S. and international research.* Report No. INL/EXT-06-11464, Idaho National Laboratory, Idaho Falls, Idaho.

Perkin, E., & Court, J. (2005). Networks and policy processes in international development: A literature review. Overseas Development Institute, Working Paper 252, Research and Policy in Development Programme (RAPID), London, UK.

Peters, D. H. (2014). The application of systems thinking in health: Why use systems thinking? *Health Research Policy and Systems, 12*(51), 166–171. https://doi.org/10.1186/1478-4505-12-51

Pramova, E., Locatelli, B., Di Gregorio, M., & Brockhaus, M. (2020). *Usual and unusual suspects: What network analysis can tell us about climate policy integration.* Center for International Forestry Research. https://doi.org/10.17528/cifor/007592

Rittel, H., & Webber, M. (1973). Dilemmas in a general theory of planning. *Policy Science, 4,* 155–169. https://doi.org/10.1007/BF01405730

Sabogal, D., Nascimento, S., & Meneses, L. (2015). *Community-based forest monitoring: Experiences from the Chico mendes extractive reserve.* Global Canopy Programme.

Schiffer, E., & Waale, D. (2008). Tracing power and influence in networks: Net-Map as a tool for research and strategic network planning. Discussion paper 00772, International Food Policy Research Institute, Washington, DC.

Schoenenberger, K., & Schenker-Wicki, A. (2014). Can system dynamics learn from social network analysis? *Proceedings of the International Conference of the System Dynamics Society,* July 20–24, 2014, Delft, Netherlands.

Seelos, C. (2020, December). Changing systems? Welcome to the slow movement. *Stanford Social Innovation Review, Winter,* 40–47.

Senge, P. (2006). *The fifth discipline: The art & practice of the learning organization.* Doubleday.

Shaikh, M., Salleh, N., & Marziana, L. (2015). Social networks content analysis for peace-building application. In A. Abraham, A. Muda and Y. H. Choo (eds.), *Pattern analysis, intelligent security and the internet of things, advances in intelligent systems and computing* (Vol. 355). https://doi.org/10.1007/978-3-319-17398-6_1

Simon, H. A. (1972). Theories of bounded rationality. In C. B. McGuire and R. Radner (eds.), *Decision and Organization* (pp. 161–176). North-Holland Pub.

Sterman, J. (2000). *Business dynamics: Systems thinking and modeling for a complex world.* McGraw Hill.

Sterman, J. (2002). All models are wrong: Reflections on becoming a systems scientist. *Systems Dynamics Review, 18*(4), 501–531. http://doi.org/10.1002/sdr.261

The Omidyar Group. (2017). *Systems practice workbook.* https://oecd-opsi.org/toolkits/systems-practice-workbook/

Toole, C. L., & McCown, A. W. (2008). Interdependent energy infrastructure simulation system. In J. G. Voeller (ed.), *Handbook of science and technology for homeland security.* John Wiley and Sons.

Vennix, J. A. M. (1996). *Group model building: Facilitating team learning using system dynamics.* Wiley.

Weimer-Jehle, W. (2006). Cross-impact balances: A system-theoretical approach to cross-impact analysis. *Technological Forecasting and Social Change, 73*(4), 334–361. https://doi.org/10.1016/j.techfore.2005.06.005

Weimer-Jehle, W. (2010). *Introduction to qualitative systems and scenario analysis using cross-impact analysis.* The University of Stuttgart. http://www.cross-impact.de/Ressourcen/Guideline%20No%201.pdf

Wikipedia. (2021). List of concept- and mind-mapping software. Retrieved May 1, 2022, from https://en.wikipedia.org/wiki/List_of_concept-_and_mind-mapping_software

Williams, R. (2008, December 2). Bucking the system. *The Broker.* http://www.thebrokeronline.eu/Articles/Bucking-the-system

Wolfe, A. W. (2004). Network thinking in peace and conflict studies. *Peace and Conflict Studies, 11*(1). http://doi.org/10.46743/1082-7307/2004.1045

Zimmerman, R., Zhu, Q., & Dimitri, C. (2016). Promoting resilience for food, energy, and water interdependencies. *Journal of Environmental Studies and Sciences, 6,* 50–61. https://doi.org/10.1007/s13412-016-0362-0

7 Hard Systems Modeling Tools

7.1 INTRODUCTION

The previous chapter emphasized the value proposition of soft systems tools in modeling issues identified at the end of the appraisal of the community landscape in Figure 5.1. Despite their qualitative or semi-quantitative limitations and being static, these tools help comprehend and map the relationships (i.e., influence and dependence) and causality among the systems and subsystems in Figure 5.1. Understanding that dynamic is necessary and valuable before developing the more complex qualitative and quantitative models described in this chapter.

Over the past 50 years, advanced systems theories and methods have been proposed to address complex systems (Peters, 2014). Among them, the tools of system dynamics (SD) modeling, agent-based modeling (ABM), and discrete event (DE) modeling have been used in various fields of science, engineering, and economy to model the dynamics of complex systems both qualitatively and quantitatively (Borshchev and Grigoryev, 2020). As shown in Figure 7.1, these three categories address different levels of abstraction and details and can be used at different levels of decision-making (i.e., strategic, tactical, and operational).

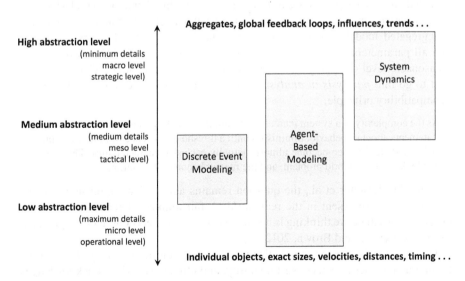

FIGURE 7.1 Systems modeling tools and abstraction levels.

Source: Borshchev and Grigoryev (2004), used by permission of the AnyLogic Company.

DOI: 10.1201/9781003435006-7

In a nutshell, the SD method is *top-down*. It can be applied to systems with high levels of abstraction (i.e., high aggregation) and is, therefore, appropriate at the strategic level of decision-making (Borshchev and Filippov, 2004). The method assumes that all processes are continuous and considers multiple feedback mechanisms, delays, and complex nonlinear processes described by differential equations. A significant limitation of the SD method is that it cannot capture, for instance, the details of the individual agents that comprise the systems under consideration.

If, on the other hand, low and middle levels of abstraction (i.e., low aggregation) are desirable and specified rules of agent behavior are set, the ABM and DE modeling methods become more appropriate than the SD method at the decision-making operation level (Borshchev and Filippov, 2004). Both methods use a *bottom-up* perspective and deal with discrete processes. The difference between these methods is that the ABM method deals with active and interactive evolving agents. In contrast, DE modeling deals with passive and non-interactive processes, such as those involved in value chain processes; it will not be addressed herein. Finally, one can add hybrid modeling tools to the three specific modeling methods that combine the best of each method (Borshchev, 2013; Shieritz and Milling, 2003).

As Rahmandad and Sterman (2008) noted regarding the SD and ABM methods (and it applies to DE), one modeling approach is not better than the others; they are just different. Selecting the most appropriate way to model the dynamics of a given problem depends on "the purpose of the model and the level of aggregation appropriate for that purpose." In short, the selected level of aggregation must match the level of details in the available data sources and provide a balance between "simplicity and realistic depiction of the underlying mechanisms" expected to be at play in the problem of interest. As modeling evolves, different levels of aggregation may need to be considered.

A challenge in using the systems tools discussed in this chapter is to find a balance between less accurate modeling with a higher level of aggregation and more accurate disaggregated modeling that is less precise due to accumulated errors associated with all parameters involved in the analysis (Rastetter et al., 1992). Nevertheless, a reasonable level of aggregation is always necessary for modeling if one does not want to go into *paralysis in analysis* and face the consequences of Zadeh (1973)'s incompatibility principle,

> As the complexity of a system increases, our ability to make precise and yet significant statements about its behavior diminishes until a threshold is reached beyond which precision and significance become almost mutually exclusive characteristics. The closer one looks at a real-world problem, and the fuzzier becomes its solution.

As noted by Rastetter et al., the question remains about what aggregated systems and subsystems represent in the real world. A fair amount of reflection involving objective and subjective thinking is needed when making decisions about aggregated system parts (Elms and Brown, 2012).

This chapter focuses on the challenges and opportunities of using SD to model the interactions across peace, sustainability, and climate security. It acknowledges and builds on the value proposition of using SD in sustainable community development and modeling the water-energy-land-food nexus explored in the books by Amadei (2019).

7.2   SYSTEM DYNAMICS

The system dynamics method is a relatively recent branch of systems science that originated with the work of Dr. Jay Forrester at the Massachusetts Institute of Technology in the 1950s and 1960s. The books *Urban Dynamics* (Forrester, 1969) and *World Dynamics* (Forrester, 1971) helped develop what came to be known as the system dynamics approach to complex problems. The method was subsequently used by various researchers, including Donella H. Meadows and coworkers, in several studies showing the impact of population growth, industrial growth, pollution, and degradation of the environment on world systems (Meadows et al., 1972, 1974, 1992, 2004); a review of these studies can be found in Meadows (2008). The SD method has been used to address complex issues in various disciplines such as engineering, business, economics, health, planning, management, etc.

A simple way to portray system dynamics is to state that it "deals with how things change through time, which includes most of what most people find important" (Forrester, 1997). System dynamics considers systems that are away from equilibrium. Landmark books that have promoted the applications of system dynamics in solving complex problems include those by Senge (1994), Sterman (2000), and Richmond (2004). Other interesting texts on various applications of systems thinking and system dynamics include those by Ford (2010) on modeling environmental processes; Hargrove (1998) on health sciences; Vennix (1996), and Richardson and Andersen (2010) on group model building (GMB) and decision-making; Robinson (2001) on climate sciences; Hannon and Ruth (2001a) on modeling biological systems; Pidd (2004, Part III) on management science; and Stroh (2015) on social change. Other books with multidisciplinary applications of system dynamics include those of Wolstenholme (1990), Hannon and Ruth (2001b), Bossel (2007a, b, c), Richmond et al. (2010), Pruyt (2013), and Ghosh (2017).

The unique characteristics of the SD method that warrant its use in modeling the dynamics of complex systems can be found in the references mentioned above. In a nutshell, they include being able to (i) handle cross-sectoral impacts; (ii) capture both qualitatively and quantitatively how systems continuously change over time due to possible changes in and relationships among components and changes in the overall direction of systems; (iii) account for system non-linearities, feedback mechanisms, and delays; and (iv) demonstrate that as the structure of a system changes, so does its behavior and vice versa. However, a limiting aspect of SD is that it cannot capture the details of the individual components that form the system. More emphasis is placed on the structure, or aggregated nature, of a system than on trying to figure out the details of all its components. Another characteristic of SD modeling is that once a model boundary has been selected, the models are designed to contain the components needed to explain the system's dynamic behavior, including endogenous rules (Sterman, 2000); external influences are not considered explicitly. Finally, another limitation of system dynamics emphasized by Ahmad and Simonovic (2004) is that it can only handle systems and processes that vary in time. Working with processes that vary in time and space requires combining system dynamics with other methods emphasizing spatial variations, such as Geographic Information Systems (Ahmad and Simonovic 2004).

7.2.1 Basic SD Components

One of the unique characteristics of SD modeling is that it captures the feedback mechanisms inherent to complex systems using two types of cause-and-effect circular causations: reinforcing and balancing feedback loops (Richardson, 1999). *Reinforcing* (R) feedback loops model self-reinforcing feedback processes and virtuous and vicious cycles leading to amplification. *Balancing* (B) loops prevent them from growing or declining forever. They create self-correcting processes that lead to stability and equilibrium and reach a goal or objective. In addition to these two essential components, a delay may be added to model the effect of time in linking causes and effects or any adjustment processes. In the decision process across the PSC nexus, delays can be associated with the time it takes different groups of stakeholders to (i) make decisions (information delays), (ii) implement processes (material delays), or (iii) unfold various processes (e.g., supply chains, services, peacebuilding).

Various combinations of reinforcing and balancing loops and delays can be created to model the behavior patterns of complex systems and unique repetitive and generic patterns called archetypes (see Chapter 8). The models (sometimes called conceptual models) can be represented in an object-oriented form of *causal loop diagrams* or *stock and flow diagrams*. Such diagrams illustrate valuable tools in (i) depicting how parts of a system interact and create patterns of behavior, (ii) communicating the dynamics of systems, and (iii) designing and planning interventions to address issues faced by the system.

The two diagrams below are used to model the peace, sustainability, and climate security nexus dynamics. For illustration purposes, each sector of the nexus is assumed to follow a *goal-seeking* dynamic or transition toward some desired goal. In practice, the desired goals of peace, sustainability, and climate security may not be the same for different groups of stakeholders, such as the community, governments, and outsiders. All SD models presented below were developed using the STELLA (Systems Thinking Experiential Learning Laboratory with Animation) Architect software (Version 3.0) by *isee systems, Inc* (www.iseesystems.com). The software is also used to model more complex dynamics of interaction between the three sectors of the PSC nexus, as explored in Chapters 10 and 11.

7.2.2 Causal Loop Diagrams

Causal loop diagrams (CLDs) show how elements of a feedback mechanism are causally related. They are influence diagrams consisting of two basic causal links:

$$A \text{ ----}^+> B$$

and

$$A \text{ ----}^-> B.$$

Both indicate that variable A influences variable B. The first link with a (+) polarity sign suggests that A and B move in the same directions ($\partial B/\partial A > 0$) (i.e., both A and B increase or decrease simultaneously). The second link with a (−) polarity sign indicates that A and B move in opposite directions ($\partial B/\partial A < 0$) (i.e., B decreases as A increases or B increases as A decreases). In some CLDs in the literature, the (+) and (−) signs attached to the arrows can be replaced by the letters "s" (for the same) and "o" (for the opposite), respectively. Figure 2.1 is an example of a causal loop diagram showing the dynamics between climate change, poor livelihood, and civil unrest in Syria since 2010.

The following link represents a possible delay (due to information or material) between A's action and its effect on B.

$$A \text{ --} \| \text{--> } B.$$

In general, causal loops are created by combining the abovementioned links. All loops with links with only positive signs or a combination of positive signs and an *even* number of negative signs are reinforcing loops (R). In contrast, loops with links with an *odd* number of negative signs are balancing loops (B). Guidelines for drawing CLDs can be found in Ghosh (2017).

Figure 7.2 shows a CLD that captures a possible *goal-seeking dynamic* for each sector of the PSC nexus. The current state of each sector, defined generically as X, is compared to the desired goal, *DX*. Corrective action is taken to reduce the gap (*DX − X*) between the goal and the current state. It is assumed to improve the state of the sector. The dynamic of Figure 7.2 creates a balancing loop, B, with two + polarities and one − polarity.

The state of each sector is also assumed to depend on another factor, *Y*, which can be enabling or constraining to X. Delays are also possible anywhere in the balancing loop. For instance, they may represent the time it takes to realize that corrective action is needed once the gap reaches a certain level and is brought to the attention of the decision-makers. Another example would be the time it takes to implement the corrective action.

CLDs such as Figure 7.2 are helpful for mapping, inferring, and visualizing what contributes to growth, decline, delay, or stability and are mainly used at the *strategy* level. Once the mental model of a problem has been outlined, the CLDs show, in a condensed manner, different relationships, trends, connections, and causal feedback mechanisms in a system. However, CLDs are not used to conduct numerical systems

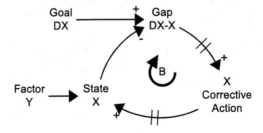

FIGURE 7.2 A CLD showing the goal-seeking dynamic assumed for each sector of the PSC nexus.

simulations. Instead, they help lay out the different structural components of a system in a conceptual manner and show how they interact dynamically in a *qualitative* way. In short, they are helpful "for communication, not for simulation" (Ford, 2010). Despite that limitation, CLDs provide a strong value proposition in the decision process across the PLC nexus. They help decision-makers develop a shared understanding of issues they might be facing. The two case studies described in Chapter 12 emphasize that value proposition.

7.2.3 STOCK AND FLOW DIAGRAMS

Another way to describe systems dynamics is to use stock and flow diagrams consisting of combinations of several building blocks shown in Figure 7.3. They help visualize qualitatively and quantitatively accumulation, flows, delays, and dissipation and incorporate feedback mechanisms and nonlinear dynamics. When combined, they represent the primary language of SD modeling.

Using the terminology used in the *STELLA Architect* software by *isee systems*, these building blocks are defined as follows:

Stocks, represented by rectangles in Figure 7.3, correspond to accumulations of something that can be measured at one point in time. They are *state variables* that define the current state of a system. Examples include the states of conflict/peace, unsustainability/sustainability, and climate vulnerability/security.

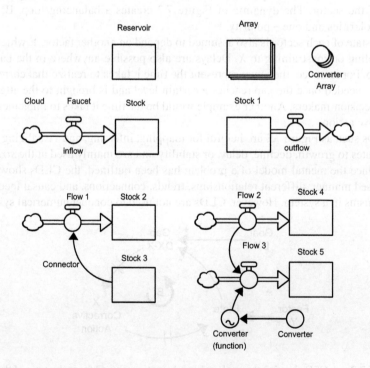

FIGURE 7.3 Basic building blocks of stock and flow diagrams.

Flow (inflow, outflow), is represented in the form of pipelines (with a faucet controlling the flow) in Figure 7.3. Flow (i.e., flux or rate) results in changes (dynamic behavior) in the stock accumulations and the entire system. Flows are *control variables* that create change in a system's state. Examples include (i) sustainable development processes leading to a state of sustainability; (ii) peacebuilding (i.e., building the conditions for peace), peacemaking (i.e., getting parties to find common ground), and peacekeeping (i.e., supporting sustainable peace) processes leading to lasting (sustainable) peace; and (iii) communities' awareness, mitigation, and adaptation practices leading to climate security.

Clouds, in Figure 7.3 indicate infinite sources or sinks outside the system boundaries.

Converters, represented by circles in Figure 7.3, convert or transform information from one stock and flow path to another or feed information into an existing flow. A converter can also mean a stock without inflow or outflow. They are *converting variables.* Converters can change over time and be described in a functional form (~ symbol).

Connectors, represented by arrows in Figure 7.3, indicate transmission or links of actions and information (i.e., causal connections) between variables such as stock-to-flow, flow-to-flow, or converters. One or several variables can provide input to and influence another variable through connectors.

As shown in Figure 7.3, the stocks, flows, and converters can also be represented as layered building blocks to represent arrays. They can be used, for instance, to describe how the different components of each stock change over time. Examples would include (i) the positive, negative, and cultural components of peace; (ii) the people, planet, prosperity, and partnership components of sustainability; or (iii) possible awareness, adaptation, and mitigation components of climate security.

SD models generally combine all the building blocks of Figure 7.3. The models can be made as mathematically complex as necessary to capture complex dynamics. However, it must be remembered that no one-size-fits-all SD model could capture all the possible dynamics of complex systems, such as those in each sector of the PSC nexus and the interaction between peace, sustainability, and climate security in multiple contexts and scales.

The two stock and flow models presented in Figures 7.4 and 7.5 below capture the same nonlinear *goal-seeking* dynamics of Figure 7.2, which is about reducing the gap between the state of each sector, X, of the PSC nexus, and some desired goal, DX. More advanced SD models are presented in Chapters 10 and 11.

7.2.3.1 Model 1

Starting with an initial value X_o, the stock X is assumed to vary with time toward a desirable value DX with an adjustment rate ARX (per year). The actual ARX rate is the product of an estimated basic adjustment rate (i.e., possible intervention), a multiplying corrective factor FX whose value decreases as the ratio $RX = X/DX$ increases (i.e., as the gap $DX - X$ decreases), and a factor that depends on another variable, Y (~ influence factor $ARX(Y)$).

In Figure 7.4, the change of the stock X over time ("adjusting X") is equal to:

$$\frac{dX}{dt} = ARX \times (DX - X) \tag{7.1}$$

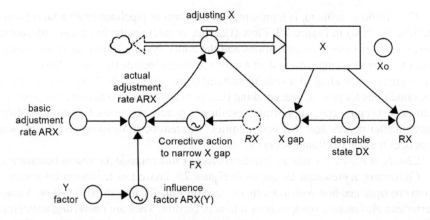

FIGURE 7.4 Goal-seeking stock and flow model.

This first-order differential equation can be solved for X and the ratio $RX = X/DX$ with X_o as the initial condition if we know the functional forms of $ARX(Y)$ and FX. The biflow in Figure 7.4 accounts for a possible increase or decrease in stock X. For instance, the current state X may decrease if the "adjusting X" flow rate becomes negative, which could result, for example, from the effect of a negative (constraining) influence factor $ARX(Y)$.

This model can be used, for instance, to show the variation of each sector of the PSC nexus. It accounts for possible external parameters' enabling or constraining effect on the rate of change in peace, sustainability, and climate security.

7.2.3.2 Model 2

As shown in Figure 7.5, the stock and converters are now arrays of dimension N. Equation (7.1) is now replaced by N-independent equations:

$$\frac{dX_i}{dt} = ARX_i \times (DX_i - X_i) \tag{7.2}$$

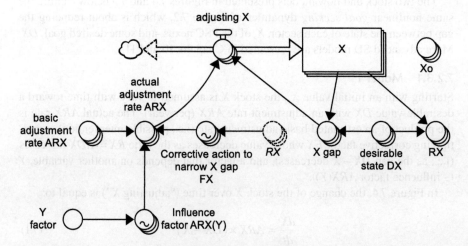

FIGURE 7.5 Arrayed goal-seeking stock and flow model.

For example, $N=3$ if Figure 7.5 models the variation of peace, sustainability, and climate security over time. In this model, these three sectors, X_i ($i=1$–3), are assumed to be independent and change over time toward three desired goals, DX_i, and at different adjustment rates, ARX_i. The Y factor may affect the three adjustment rates differently (enabling or constraining).

As an illustrated numerical example, we will assume that the three sectors of the nexus can be expressed respectively in generic peace units (pu), sustainability units (su), and climate security units (cu) ranging over three [0–100] scales. These arbitrary units are introduced here as semi-quantitative peace, sustainability, and climate security measures. An interactive user interface of the SD model shown in Figure 7.5 can be found on the web.[1]

The peace, sustainability, and climate security scales can be broken down into several achievement-level groups from very low to very likely using a semi-quantitative rating scale, as shown in Table 7.1. Each group is specific to the context in which the PSC nexus analysis is carried out. Metrics can be introduced to describe each level of achievement as done, for instance, with the ISI project sustainability framework discussed in Section 2.2.2 (see Table 2.3).

An illustrative SD analysis was carried out assuming that initially (i) peace is very low with an initial value of 20 pu; (ii) sustainability is low with an initial value of 30 su, and (iii) climate security is low with an initial value of 40 cu. The desired peace, sustainability, and climate security values are equal to 100 pu, 100 su, and 100 cu, respectively, and the corresponding adjustment rates are 0.01/year, 0.02/year, and 0.03/year. Furthermore, the three correcting factors FX_i for peace, sustainability, and climate security are assumed to decrease linearly from 2 to 1 as the $RX_i = X_i/DX_i$ ($i=1$–3) ratios increase from 0 to 1. In other words, less correction is needed as each $DX_i - X_i$ gap decreases. Finally, the influence factor $ARX(Y)$ is constant and equal to 1, 1, and -0.1 for peace, sustainability, and climate security, respectively. Figure 7.6 shows the variations of the RX_i ratios for the three nexus sectors over 50 years. In this example, peace and sustainability increase toward their desired values, but climate security decreases with time.

The SD model shown in Figure 7.5 can also be used to model how the components of each sector of the nexus change with time. For instance, eq. (7.2) with $N=3$ could be used to model how positive peace, negative peace, and cultural peace independently change with time. Similarly, eq. (7.2) with $N=5$ could help analyze how the 5Ps of sustainability (people, planet, prosperity, partnership, and peace) change with time. Finally, eq. (7.2) with $N=3$ could be used to model how climate awareness, adaptation, and mitigation change with time. In all three cases, the influence of an external factor, Y, on each component of peace, sustainability, and climate security can be considered.

TABLE 7.1

Possible Sustainability, Peace, and Climate Security Achievement Levels

	1–20	21–40	41–60	61–80	81–100
Sustainability	Very low	Low	Somewhat possible	Very possible	Very likely
Peace	Very low	Low	Somewhat possible	Very possible	Very likely
Climate security	Very low	Low	Somewhat possible	Very possible	Very likely

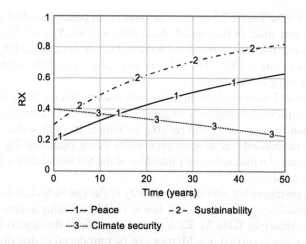

FIGURE 7.6 Variation of $RX_i = X_i/DX_i$ ($i = 1$–3) over time.

7.2.4 Discussion

The models in Figures 7.4 and 7.5 are two of many possible SD models that could be developed to explore the goal-seeking dynamic of each sector of the PSC nexus. In these models, the X_i ($i = 1$–N) variables are independent. The interaction of peace, sustainability, and climate security will be analyzed further in the models of Chapters 10 and 11.

The arbitrary peace units (pu), sustainability units (su), and climate security units (cu) used in the two models need to be tangible and quantifiable. For instance, in the model of Figure 7.4, the overall state of peace could be SDG 16, the positive peace index (PPI), the global peace index (GPI), or a combination of PPI and GPI, as discussed in Chapter 2. Likewise, the sustainability variable could be some measure of sustainability, such as the SDG index (Sachs et al., 2019) or one of the 17 SDGs. Climate security could be SDG 13 or any measure of adaptation and mitigation climate security practice.

In the model of Figure 7.5, the peace and sustainability stocks now have multiple dimensions. Besides the 5Ps of sustainability, the arrayed stock could be represented by some of the 17 SDGs or the six SDG transformations (TWI2050, 2020; Sachs et al., 2019). The dimensions of peace could be the three types of peace used above.

Finally, in Figures 7.4 and 7.5, the basic adjustment rates of peace, sustainability, and climate security could be time-dependent if necessary. Whether positive or negative, they dictate how one or several of the three sectors and their components continuously increase or decrease in value over time.

7.2.5 SD Applications

Multiple models in the literature use the principles of systems thinking to address various aspects of sustainable community development (see review in Amadei, 2015 and

2019). Some of these models use system dynamics commercial software packages such as *STELLA* (www.iseesystems.com), *Powersim* (https://powersim.com), and *Vensim* (https://vensim.com). The models can be divided into those that address global changes and specific issues. Global change models include those of Rotmans and deVries (1997), Meadows et al. (1972, 1974, 1992, 2004), Bazilian et al. (2011), Davies and Simonovic (2011), Hermann (2012), Howells et al. (2013), Welsch et al. (2014), Dale et al. (2015), Pasqualino et al. (2015, 2020), Hughes (2016), and Moyer and Hedden (2020), among others. The iSDG model of the Millennium Institute (www.isdgs.org) is another global change integrated system simulation tool that explores scenarios linking strategies and policy as a country progresses toward reaching the 17 SDGs (Pedercini et al., 2020).

As remarked by Amadei (2019), all these global change frameworks can handle high levels of complexity, involve high levels of aggregation, and allow for high levels of decision-making around development issues. However, all of them possess two general shortcomings. First, they have been mainly used to model the complex dynamics of change and development at the global, regional, or country scale. Second, they all reveal how difficult it is to obtain data to quantify the causal links considered in the frameworks. With some modifications, however, they could be applied to model the dynamics at play in the complex smaller-scale landscape shown in Figure 5.1 and account for the complex interactions between the PSC nexus and social, natural, infrastructure, and economic systems.

On the other end of the spectrum of system models addressing sustainable community development from the global change ones described above are those that focus on sector-specific issues such as water resources management, energy resources management, agro-food, land resources management, health, conflict, etc. Like the global models mentioned above, these frameworks address issues at the country, regional, or global scales. Sohofi et al. (2016) gave an excellent review of many of these different topical models. It should be noted that many of the sector-specific formulations also incorporate, in a comprehensive manner, topics such as climate change. Still, few include both conflict/instability and climate vulnerability/security.

Choucri et al. (2005) used SD to model state instability, resilience, and capacity (institutional, technical, social, financial, and so on). The rationale is that the stability of the state is driven by a multitude of interacting social, economic, and geopolitical pressures, which, when combined, may reach a tipping point beyond which state resilience is exceeded, and conflict arises. It is not difficult to envision, for instance, how water, energy, land, food insecurity, and climate change could contribute to that dynamic, as in the Syrian example discussed in Chapter 2.

Another domain that has been addressed systemically is *corruption*. It is essential in managing resources across the nexus, as it can undermine the effectiveness of technical interventions and policy decisions. One example of using system dynamics to model corruption is provided by Ullah (2012), who offers an excellent literature review of models of corruption and a framework to model corruption, specifically in Pakistan.

Since 2010, there has been a strong interest in integrating systems thinking and tools into conflict analysis and management (Jones, 2015; CDA, 2016). Before any conflict analysis can be carried out, it is essential to assess the actors involved in the conflict, their connections, the effects of the conflict, the factors driving it, and the conflict boundaries. Because conflicts tend to be complex, systems tools such as those of SD have been proposed to analyze conflict (Coleman et al., 2007; USAID, 2011; Ricigliano,

2011, 2012; Schirch, 2013; Usenik and Turnsek, 2016; BenDor and Schreffan, 2019; among others). The tools are used to (i) analyze the results of conflict assessment, (ii) predict how conflicts may evolve, (iii) identify places to intervene in the conflict, and (iv) propose meaningful interventions leading to peace and stability. With minor exceptions, many of these studies use qualitative CLDs rather than quantitative stock and flow diagrams.

System dynamics tools have also been used to analyze the impact of climate change on specific issues such as water, agriculture, energy, etc. More complex models have been proposed to look at how climate change impacts various socioeconomic and natural systems at different scales and explore climate policy options to mitigate the impacts (Fiddaman, 2002; Huerta et al., 2011; Sterman et al., 2012; Sohofi et al., 2016; Melkonian et al., 2017; Redivo, 2021; Moon et al., 2021; Ganji and Naseri, 2021; Egerer et al., 2021; Bozorg-Haddad et al., 2022, among others).

Among these studies, the SD model of Moon et al. (2021) stands out in analyzing the impact of climate change on environmental, economic, and social systems in urban and rural environments at the country scale of Korea while considering the existing dynamic interactions among these systems. Figures 7.7 shows a causal loop diagram for this study. Additional stock and flow graphs and quantitative analyses

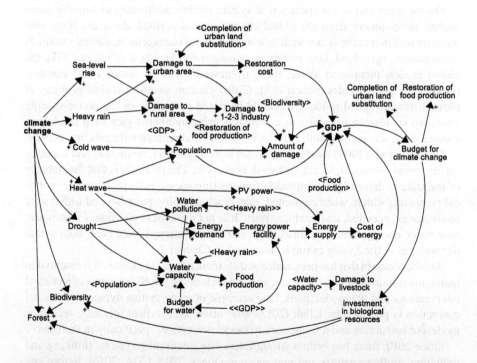

FIGURE 7.7   Causal loop diagram of the climate change impact model of Moon et al. (2021). The original chart has been redrawn using the STELLA software of isee systems. <.> and <<.>> are ghosts.

Source: Moon et al. (2021). Creative Commons Attribution 4.0 International License.

were developed by Moon et al. (2021) to estimate the impact of climate change on Korea's GDP, which was the study's primary goal.

7.3 THE SYSTEM DYNAMICS MODELING PROCESS

The general modeling guidelines discussed in Chapter 6 also apply to SD modeling. In general, system dynamics models are built in steps of increasing complexity. A rule of wisdom that appears quite often in the SD modeling literature is to start with simple (not simplistic) models and ensure that they pass a series of tests recommended in the literature (Sterman, 2000; Forrester and Senge, 1980). They include boundary adequacy, structure assessment, dimensional consistency, parameter assessment, extreme conditions, behavior analysis and reproduction, surprise behavior, sensitivity analysis, and policy analysis. These tests help build confidence in the models. As the models become more robust, sophistication can always be added to them in due time. It should be remembered that system dynamics modeling is *both an art and a science*; it involves systems thinking, which, as noted by Vaughan (2013) and discussed in Chapter 5, consists of balancing critical and creative thinking.

Several road maps have been proposed to build SD models, including the five steps of Sterman (2000) discussed in Chapter 6. Figure 7.8 shows another road map presented by Ford (2010). It consists of eight steps combined into six key activities once a problem has been identified. They include (i) problem familiarization, (ii) problem definition, (iii) model formulation by constructing stock and flow diagrams and CLDs, (iv) parameter estimation, (v) simulation to explain the problem being addressed, and (vi) simulation analysis consisting of sensitivity analysis (step 7) and policy analysis (step 8). Figure 7.8 shows the cyclical nature of the road map and its many feedback loops.

Figure 7.8 also shows that system dynamics modeling is divided into qualitative and quantitative parts. The first four steps in Ford's map can be interpreted as the qualitative and conceptual components of system dynamics modeling. Steps 5–8 emphasize the quantitative dimension of that modeling. Whether qualitative or quantitative modeling is used depends mainly on the system analysis, the availability of data and information about the system components, and the participating audience (Wolstenholme, 1990).

As remarked by Amadei (2019), one way to summarize all the recommendations available in the literature to model complex issues with the tools of system dynamics is to make sure that the models are:

- The right ones for the context and scale of interest and those who will benefit from the decisions based on the models
- Done right from an SD modeling point of view
- Created for the right reasons for the issues being addressed with the appropriate level of comprehensiveness, simplicity, and usefulness

Finally, an overarching recommendation of SD modeling is ensuring that each step of Figure 7.8 involves the participation of multiple stakeholders, including the intended

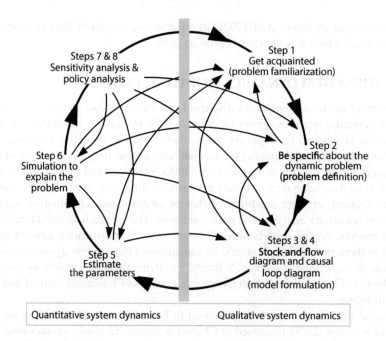

FIGURE 7.8 Cyclical nature of system dynamics modeling.

Source: Ford (2010), used by permission of Island Press.

Note: The components are divided into those involved in qualitative modeling (right-hand side) and those involved in quantitative modeling (left-hand side).

audience(s). Group model building (GMB) has been proposed as a participatory decision-making process that uses system dynamics tools (Vennix, 1996; Andersen et al., 1997). Variations of that method include the *Community-Based System Dynamics* (CBSD) method (Hovmand, 2014) and the *Participatory System Dynamics* method (Stave, 2010).

Within the context of complex adaptive systems such as communities, it is clear that GMB provides an exciting value proposition in engaging various stakeholders in collaboratively making decisions and coming up with a "shared reality" that they can all agree on (Vennix, 1996). The outcome of that process is limited by the uncertainty and complexity involved in all the systems interacting in the landscape of Figure 5.1 and by how ill-defined problems are. The outcome is also limited by the group participants' bounded rationality regardless of their culture. Notably, it is challenging to communicate and explore the sheer complexity of the landscape in Figure 5.1 and how peace, sustainability, and climate security interact and unfold in that landscape.

In general, GMB requires (i) a high level of coordination from the decision-making team and (ii) a willingness of all groups of stakeholders to participate in the shared reality and be engaged. Whether participatory system dynamics is successful is hard to identify. BenDor and Scheffran (2019, p. 107) review several success criteria and assessment questions proposed in the literature related to environmental decision-making. The criteria address (i) individual and collaborative learning; (ii) the potential to involve the public and stakeholders; (iii) the inclusion of stakeholder values, assumptions, and preferences; (iv) the increasing of decision quality; (v) the fostering of trust in institutions; (vi) the reduction of stakeholder conflict; and (vii) cost-effectiveness.

It should be noted that the scenario of well-functioning model-building teams holding to a fixed, long-term shared reality is highly improbable. More often than not, there is a good chance that the assumptions and pre-conditions in that scenario will not be met, and unexpected events are more likely to occur. The stakeholders are more likely to hold different opinions and have difficulty reaching some form of consensus, let alone agreeing on a system model of the problems they are experiencing. The shared reality of group modeling should be seen as a dynamic concept that needs to be revisited regularly through reflection-in-action.

7.4   THE ABM METHOD

7.4.1   VALUE PROPOSITION

Besides the SD method, other methods, such as ABM, have been used to model conflict or the effect of climate change on human and environmental systems. Compared to system dynamics, ABM is more appropriate when it is necessary to account for less abstraction and low levels of aggregation, as indicated in Figure 7.1. Generally, ABM modeling follows steps similar to those described above for SD modeling.

A value proposition of agent-based modeling (ABM) tools is to capture the dynamics between multiple autonomous individual agents and heterogeneous groups of agents interacting in a system (Wilensky and Rand, 2015). This feature is particularly beneficial when capturing network-based processes and agent interactions involved in conflict/peace, sustainability, and climate security practices at the community scale. The agents may include social agents (people, institutions, organizations, partners) or non-social agents (e.g., services or components of infrastructure systems).

In the ABM method, the agents have individual discrete behavior and can act according to their own rules and objectives (Billari et al., 2006). They may exhibit learning and adaptive behaviors, and their interactions may be complex, nonlinear, or discontinuous. The agents' behavior is defined by logic and a set of rules the user selects. Moreover, the exchange may change with time and location. A significant advantage of ABM is its ability to capture emergent evolutionary phenomena and self-organization at the global system level that may only unfold through local agent interaction while considering their evolving behavior in a specific environment (Scholl, 2001; Rahmandad and Sterman, 2008; Borshchev, 2013; Glenn, 2014, Grigoryev, 2016). Examples of applications of ABM using the commercial *NetLogo* software (Wilensky and Rand, 2015) and *AnyLogic* (Borshchev, 2013) can be found on the web.

ABM can be a singular modeling tool or complement system dynamics modeling (Borshchev and Filippov, 2004). It can be used, for instance, to consider the heterogeneity in the behavior of individual components within a system dynamics stock or reservoir representing a specific population, a group, or an institution. Finally, ABM can help explain how an SNA social network is generated and how it could be modified if new rules (e.g., rules of behavior change) were introduced in systems or subsystems that are part of that network.

ABM has been used, for instance, to model societal, environmental, and resource management issues (Berger and Troost, 2013) and different types of conflict dynamics (Epstein, 2002; Kennedy et al., 2010; Masad, 2016; Lemos, 2018; Akhbari and Grigg, 2013). BenDor and Schreffan (2019, pp. 121–123) provide a detailed list of authors who have applied ABM to analyze different forms of conflict. ABM has also been used to assess the effect of climate adaptation and mitigation practices on human development and security issues (Hailegiorgis et al., 2010; Troots et al., 2012; Berger and Troots, 2013; Hassani-Mahmooei, 2017).

7.4.2 Illustrative Example

An example of the application of ABM is presented below using the agent-based tool in the *AnyLogic* software (Personal Learning Edition, version 8.7.6). The conceptual model shown in Figure 7.9 simulates a conflict between groups of individual agents, A and B, sharing different opinions about peace, sustainability, climate security, etc. It is an adapted version of the model "AB Market and SD supply chain" available on the AnyLogic software website and discussed in the book by Borshchev (2013, Example 7.5 in Section 7.6). The model captures the adoption and diffusion of two groups with competing ideas.

The narrative behind the model of Figure 7.9 is as follows. Groups A and B compete to recruit agents from an existing pool of susceptible members. The agents can

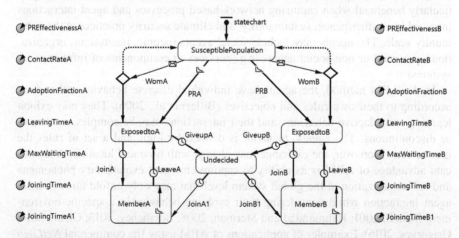

FIGURE 7.9 A statechart showing the different states the recruited agents could experience.

Note: This is an adapted version of the model "AB Market and SD supply chain" available on the AnyLogic software website.

experience different states whose dynamics are represented using the so-called "statechart" of Figure 7.9. The AnyLogic version of AB modeling uses statecharts that "define internal states, reactions to external events, and the corresponding transitions of a particular object: a person, a physical device, an organization, a project, etc. At any given moment in time, a statechart is in exactly one simple state" (Borshchev, 2013).

The members in A and B are recruited through public relations (*PRA, PRB*) with daily effectiveness (*PREffectivenessA, PREffectivenessB*). Members are also recruited by word of mouth (*WomA, WomB*) efforts triggered by a message sent by a random person in each group to a certain number of people (*ContactRateA, ContactRateB*). Having received that message, a person may join the *ExposedtoA* or *ExposedtoB* groups with an adoption probability (*AdoptionFractionA, AdoptionFractionB*). Otherwise, the person returns to the *SusceptiblePopulation* state (dotted lines). A person moves from the states *ExposedtoA* to *MemberA* or *ExposedtoB* to *MemberB* at a fixed rate (*JoiningTimeA* or *JoiningTimeB*).

Once agents become members of A or B, some leave these groups after some time (*LeavingTimeA, LeavingTimeB*). They then rejoin the *ExposedtoA* and *ExposedtoB* states. Once in these states, members may give up, join the *Undecided* state, and choose to switch groups after some time (*MaxWaitingTimeA, MaxWaitingTimeB*). Members may choose to rejoin A or B after some time (*JoiningTimeA1, JoiningTimeB1*). The dynamic of Figure 7.9 may take place over days, months, or years.

A numerical example is presented in Figure 7.10 for the input data listed in Table 7.2. It shows the variation of groups A and B over 100 days for 1000 initially susceptible people. In this example, groups A and B have the same levels of effectiveness, contact rates, and fractions of adoption. They differ in how long the members remain in each group before leaving or rejoining, with longer times for group B. Hence, group B ends up with a larger population than A. Both populations stabilize quickly.

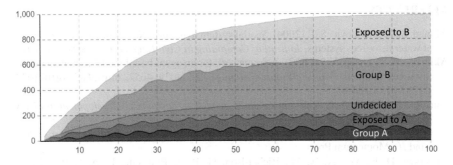

FIGURE 7.10 Distribution of the population in the five states of Figure 7.9 over 100 days for the input data of Table 7.2.

TABLE 7.2
Input Data for the ABM Model in Figure 7.9

Group A		Group B	
PREffectiveness A	0.02/day	PREffectiveness B	0.02/day
Contact rate A	5/day	Contact rate B	5/day
Adoption fraction A	0.015	Adoption fraction B	0.015
Leaving time A	2 days	Leaving time B	5 days
Maxwaiting time A	2 days	Maxwaiting time B	7 days
Joining time A	2 days	Joining time B	5 days
Joining time A1	2 days	Joining time B1	5 days

7.5 CONCLUDING REMARKS

The hard modeling tools presented in this chapter complement those described in the previous chapter. Qualitative or quantitative, the tools allow us to explore the intra- and inter-dynamics of systems. More specifically, they capture the relationship between the structural and behavioral patterns of systems and the overall dynamic of the iceberg model of Figure 1.1. The SD and ABM methods "function as 'virtual laboratories' where we can create controlled experiments to understand uncertainty and system organization" (BenDor and Scheffran, 2019). Both methods require following several steps, from problem identification to modeling with or without sensitivity analysis. Quantitative modeling is challenging as it involves data selection for all system components and their interactions. Uncertainty can be explored by conducting sensitivity analyses.

NOTE

1 https://exchange.iseesystems.com/public/bernardamadei/pscgoalseeking

REFERENCES

Ahmad, S., & Simonovic, S. P. (2004). Spatial system dynamics: New approach for simulation of water resources systems. *Journal of Computing in Civil Engineering, 18*(4), 331–340.

Akhbari, M., & Grigg, N.S. (2013). A framework for an agent-based model to manage water resources conflicts. *Water Resource Manage, 27*, 4039–4052. https://doi.org/10.1007/s11269-013-0394-0

Amadei, B. (2015). *A systems approach to modeling community development projects.* Momentum Press.

Amadei, B. (2019). *A systems approach to modeling the water-energy-land-food nexus* (Vols. *I* and *II*). Momentum Press.

Andersen, D. F., Vennix, A. M., Richardson, G. P., & Rouwette, E. A. (1997). Group model building: problem structuring, policy simulation, and decision support. *Journal of Operational Research Society, 58*(5), 691–694. https://doi.org/10.1057/palgrave.jors.2602339

Bazilian, M., Rogner, H., Howells, M., Hermann, S., Arent, D., Gielen, D., Steduto, P., Mueller, A., Komor, P., Tol, R. S. J., & Yumkella, K. K. (2011). Considering the energy, water, and food nexus: Towards an integrated modeling approach. *Energy Policy*, *39*, 7896–7906. https://doi.org/10.1016/j.enpol.2011.09.039

BenDor, T., & Scheffran, J. (2019). *Agent-Based modeling of environmental conflict and cooperation*. CRC Press, Taylor & Francis.

Berger, T., & Troost, C. (2013). Agent-based modeling of climate adaptation and mitigation options in agriculture. *Journal of Agricultural Economics*, *65*(2), 323–348. https://doi.org/10.1111/1477-9552.12045

Billari, F. C., Fent, T., Prskawetz, A., & Scheffran, J. (2006). *Agent-based computational modeling: Applications in demography, social, economic, and environmental sciences*. Springer.

Borshchev, A. (2013). *The big book of simulation modeling. Multimethod modeling with AnyLogic 6*. AnyLogic North America.

Borshchev, A., & Filippov, A. (2004). From system dynamics and discrete event to practical agent-based modeling: Reasons, techniques, tools. *Proceedings 22nd International Conference of the System Dynamics Society*, July 25–29, Oxford, England.

Borshchev, A., & Grigoryev, I. (2020). The big book of simulation modeling. Multimethod modeling with anylogic 8, AnyLogic North America. Chapter 1. https://www.anylogic.com/upload/books/new-big-book/1-modeling-and-simulation-modeling.pdf

Bossel, H. (2007a). *System Zoo 1 simulation models*. Books on Demand, GmbH.

Bossel, H. (2007b). *System Zoo 2 simulation models*. Books on Demand, GmbH.

Bossel, H. (2007c). *System Zoo 3 simulation models*. Books on Demand, GmbH.

Bozorg-Haddad, O., Dehghan, P., Zolghadr-Asli, B., Singh, V. P., Chu, X., & Loáiciga, H. A. (2022). System dynamics modeling of lake water management under climate change. *Scientific Reports*, *12*, 5828. https://doi.org/10.1038/s41598-022-09212-x

Choucri, N., Electris, C., Goldsmith, D., Mistree, D., Madnick, S. E., Morrison, J. B., Siegel, M. D., & Sweitzer-Hamilton, M. (2005). Understanding and modeling state stability: Exploiting system dynamics. IEEAC paper #1278, version 5, 1–11. http://web.mit.edu/smadnick/www/wp/2006-02.pdf

Collaborative for Development Action (CDA). (2016). *Designing strategic initiatives to impact conflict systems: Systems approaches to peacebuilding. A resource manual*. CDA Collaborative Learning Projects.

Coleman, P. T., Vallacher, R. R., Nowak, A., & Bui-Wrzosinska, L. (2007). Intractable conflict as an attractor. *American Behavioral Scientist*, *50*(11), 1454–1475. https://doi.org/10.1177/0002764207302463

Dale, L. L., Karali, N., Millstein, D., Carnall, M., Vicuña, S., Borchers, N., Bustos, E., O'hagan, J., Purkey, D., Heaps, C., Sieber, J., Collins, W. D., & Sohn, M. D. (2015). An integrated assessment of water-energy and climate change in Sacramento, California: How strong is the nexus. *Climate Change*, *132*, 223–235. https://doi.org/10.1007/s10584-015-1370-x

Davies, E. G. R., & Simonovic, S. P. (2011). Global water resources modeling with an integrated model of the social-economic-environmental system. *Advances in Water Resources*, *34*, 684–700. https://doi.org/10.1016/j.advwatres.2011.02.010

Egerer, S., Cotera, R. V., Celliers, L, & Costa, M. M. (2021). A leverage points analysis of a qualitative system dynamics model for climate change adaptation in agriculture, *Agricultural Systems*, *189*, 103052, https://doi.org/10.1016/j.agsy.2021.103052

Elms, D. G., & Brown, C. B. (2012). Decisions in a complex context: A new formalism? *Proceedings of the International Forum on Engineering Decision Making*, 6th IFED, Lake Louise, Canada.

Epstein, J. M. (2002). Modeling civil violence: An agent-based computational approach. *PNAS*, *99*(3), 7243–7250. https://doi.org/10.1073/pnas.092080199

Fiddaman, T. (2002). Exploring policy options with a behavioral climate-economy model. *System Dynamics Review, 18*, 243–267. https://doi.org/10.1002/sdr.241

Ford, A. (2010). *Modeling the environment*. Island Press.

Forrester, J. W. (1969). *Urban dynamics*. Productivity Press.

Forrester, J. W. (1971). *World dynamics* (2nd ed. in 1973). Productivity Press.

Forrester, J. W. (1997). System dynamics in the elevator. https://www.ventanasystems.co.uk/forum/viewtopic.php?p=1964#p1964

Forrester, J.W. & Senge, P.M. (1980). Tests for building confidence in system dynamics models. *TIMS Studies in the Management Sciences*, 14, 209–228.

Ganji, F., & Nasseri, M. (2021). System dynamics approaches to assess the impacts of climate change on surface water quality and quantity: A case study of Karoun River, Iran. *Environmental Science and Pollution Research, 28*, 31327–31339. https://doi.org/10.1007/s11356-021-12773-5

Ghosh, A. (2017). *Dynamic systems for everyone: Understanding how our world works* (2nd ed.). Springer.

Glenn, J. C. (2009). Introduction to futures research. In *Introduction to the futures methods research series*. Futures research methodology, V3.0, The Millennium Project, Washington, DC. https://www.millennium-project.org/publications-2/futures-research-methodology-version-3-0/

Grigoryev, I. (2016). *AnyLogic7 in three days. A quick course in simulation modeling* (3rd ed.). CreateSpace Independent Publishing Platform.

Hailegiorgis, A., Kennedy, W. G., Balan, G. C., Bassett, J. K., & Gulden, T. (2010). An agent-based model of climate change and conflict among pastoralists in East Africa. *International Congress on Environmental Modelling and Software. 69.* https://scholarsarchive.byu.edu/cgi/viewcontent.cgi?article=2420&context=iemssconference

Hannon, B., & Ruth, M. (2001a). *Modeling dynamic biological systems*. Springer.

Hannon, B., & Ruth, M. (2001b). *Dynamic modeling*. Springer.

Hargrove, J. L. (1998). *Dynamic modeling in health science*. Springer.

Hassani-Mahmooei, B. (2017). Agent-based modeling of sustainable development in a changing climate: A security perspective. Monash University. Doctoral thesis. https://doi.org/10.4225/03/58a650207592b

Hermann, S. (2012). Finding CLEWS. Exploring sustainable energy developments: Looking at Climate-Land-Energy-water interactions methodology and components. Presentation at joint ICTP-IAEA workshop on sustainable energy development, October 1–5, 2012. Trieste, Italy. http://indico.ictp.it/event/a11197/session/40/contribution/30/material/0/0.pdf

Hovmand, P. S. (2014). *Community-based system dynamics*. Springer.

Howells, M., Hermann, S., Welsch, M., Bazilian, M., Segerström, R., Alfstad, T., Gielen, D., Rogner, H., Fischer, G., Van Velthuizen, H., Wiberg, D., Young, C., Roehrl, R. A., Mueller, A., Steduto, P., & Ramma, I. (2013). Integrated analysis of climate change, land-use, energy, and water strategies. *Nature Climate Change, 3*, 621–626. https://doi.org/10.1038/nclimate1789

Huerta, J. M., Esquivel-Longoria, M. I. & Arellano-Lara, F. (2011). A system dynamics approach to examine climate change impact: The case of the state of Guanajuato, Mexico. In *Proceedings of the 29th International Conference of the System Dynamics Society*. https://archives.albany.edu/downloads/fj236k096?locale=en

Hughes, B. B. (2016). International Futures (IFs) and integrated, long-term forecasting of global transformations. *Futures, 81*, 98–118. https://doi.org/10.1016/j.futures.2015.07.007

Jones, D. (2015). Conflict resolution: Wars without end. *Nature, 519*, 148–151. https://doi.org/10.1038/519148a

Kennedy, W. G., Gulden, T., Hailegiorgis, A. B., Bassett, J., Coletti, M., Balan, G. C., Clark, M., & Cioffi-Revilla, C. (2010). An agent-based model of conflict in East Africa and the effect of the privatization of land. *Proceedings 3rd World Congress on Social Simulation*, September 6–9, Kassel, Germany.

Lemos, C. M. (2018). *Agent-based modeling of social conflict: From mechanism to complex behavior*. Springer.

Masad, D. P. (2016). Agents in conflict: Comparative agent-based modeling of international crises and conflict. Doctoral dissertation, George Mason University, Fairfax, VA.

Meadows, D. (2008). *Thinking in systems*. Chelsea Green Publishing.

Meadows, D. L., Behrens, W. W. III., Meadows, D. H., Naill, R. F., Randers, J., & Zahn, E. K. O. (1974). *The dynamics of growth in a finite world*. Wright-Allen Press, Inc.

Meadows, D. H., Meadows, D. L., Randers, J., & Behrens, W. W. III. (1972). *The limit to growth*. Universe Book, Inc.

Meadows, D. H., Meadows, D. L. & Randers, J. (1992). *Beyond the limit, global collapse or a sustainable future*. Earthscan Publications Limited.

Meadows, D. H., Randers, J., & Meadows, D. (2004). *Limits to growth: The 30-year update*. Chelsea Green Publishing.

Moon, T. H., Chae, Y., Lee, D. S., Kim, D. H., & Kim, H. (2021). Analyzing climate change impacts on health, energy, water resources, and biodiversity sectors for effective climate change policy in South Korea. *Scientific Reports*, *11*, 18512. https://doi.org/10.1038/s41598-021-97108-7

Moyer, J. D., & Hedden, S. (2020). Are we on the right path to achieve the sustainable development goals? *World Development*, 127. https://doi.org/10.1016/j.worlddev.2019.104749

Pasqualino, R., Jones, A. W., Monasterolo, I., & Phillips, A. (2015). Understanding global systems today: A calibration of the World3-03 model between 1995 and 2012. *Sustainability*, *7*, 9864–9889. https://doi.org/10.3390/su7089864

Pasqualino, R., & Jones, A. W. (2020). *Resources, financial risk and the dynamics of growth*. Routledge.

Perdercini, M., Arquitt, S., & Chan, D. (2020). Integrated simulation for the 2030 agenda. *System Dynamics Review*, *36*(3), 333–357. https://doi.org/10.1002/sdr.1665

Peters, D. H. (2014). The application of systems thinking in health: Why use systems thinking? *Health Research Policy and Systems*, *12*(51), 166–171. https://doi.org/10.1186/1478-4505-12-51

Pidd, M. (2004). *Computer simulation in management science* (5th ed.). John Wiley & Sons.

Pruyt, E. (2013). Small system dynamics models for big issues: Triple jump towards real-world dynamic complexity. Version 1.0, TU Delft Library, Delft, the Netherlands.

Rahmandad, H., & Sterman, J. (2008). Heterogeneity and network structure in the dynamics of diffusion: Comparing agent-based and differential equation models. *Management Science*, *54*(5), 998–1014. https://doi.org/10.1287/mnsc.1070.0787

Rastetter, E. B., King, A. W., Cosby, B. J., Hornberger, G. M., O'Neill, R. V., & Hobbie, J. E. (1992). Aggregating fine-scale ecological knowledge to model coarse-scale attributes of ecosystems. *Ecological Applications*, *2*, 55–70. https://doi.org/10.2307/1941889

Redivo, F. (2021, July 19). System dynamics for climate change mitigation. In *System Dynamics Blog*. https://systemdynamics.org/system-dynamics-for-climate-change-mitigation/

Richardson, G. P. (1999). *Feedback thought in social science and systems theory*. Pegasus Communications.

Richardson, G. P., & Andersen, D.F. (2010). Systems thinking, mapping, and modeling in group decision and negotiation. In D. Kilgour and C. Eden (eds.), *Handbook of Group Decision* and *Negotiation. Advances in Group Decision* and *Negotiation* (Vol. *4.*, pp. 313–324). Springer. https://doi.org/10.1007/978-90-481-9097-3_19

Richmond, B. (2004). *An introduction to systems thinking, STELLA software*. isee Systems, Inc.

Richmond, J., Lees Stuntz, L., Richmond, K., and Egner, J. (eds.), (2010). *Tracing connections: Voices of systems thinkers*. isee Systems, Inc.

Ricigliano, R. (2011). A systems approach to peacebuilding. In *Paix sans frontieres: Building peace across borders*. http://www.c-r.org/accord-article/systems-approach-peacebuilding

Ricigliano, R. (2012). *Making peace last: A toolbox for sustainable peacebuilding*. Paradigm Publishers.

Robinson, W. A. (2001). *Modeling dynamic climate systems*. Springer.

Rotmans, J., & deVries, B. (eds.). (1997). *Perspectives on global change: The TARGETS approach*. Cambridge University Press.

Sachs, J., Schmidt-Traub, G., Kroll, C., LaFortune, G., & Fuller, G. (2019). Sustainable development report 2019; Bertelsmann Stiftung and Sustainable Development Solutions Network (SDSN): New York. https://www.sustainabledevelopment.report/reports/sustainable-development-report-2019/

Schieritz, N., & Milling, P. M. (2003). Modeling the forest and modeling the trees: A comparison of system dynamics and agent-based simulation. *Proceedings of the 21st International Conference of the System Dynamics Society*, July 20–24. New York City.

Schirch, L. (2013). *Conflict assessment & peacebuilding planning*. Kumarian Press.

Scholl, H. J. (2001). Agent-based and system dynamics modeling: A call for cross-study and joint research. *Proceedings of the 34th Hawaii International Conference on System Sciences* January 6, Maui, HI, USA, (p. 8). https://doi.org/10.1109/hicss.2001.926296

Senge, P. (1994). The fifth discipline: The art & practice of the learning organization. Doubleday.

Sohofi, S. A., Melkonyan, A., Karl, C. K., & Krumme, K. (2016). System archetypes in the conceptualization phase of water-energy-food-nexus modeling. *34th International Conference of the System Dynamics Society: Black Swans and Black Lies: System Dynamics in the Context of Randomness and Political Power-play*, Delft, Netherlands, Vol 34.

Stave, K. (2010). Participatory system dynamics modeling for sustainable environmental management: Observations from four cases. *Sustainability*, 2(9), 2762–2784. https://doi.org/10.3390/su2092762

Sterman, J. (2000). *Business dynamics: Systems thinking and modeling for a complex world*. McGraw Hill.

Sterman, J., Fiddaman, Franck, T., Jones, A., Mccauley, S., Rice, P., Sawin, E., & Siegel, L. (2012). Climate interactive: The C-ROADS climate policy model. *System Dynamics Review*, 28(3), 295–305. https://doi.org/10.1002/sdr.1474

Stroh, D. P. (2015). *Systems thinking for social change*. Chelsea Green Publishing.

The World in 2050 (TWI2050). (2020). Innovations for sustainability. Pathways to an efficient and post-pandemic future. Report prepared by The World in 2050 initiative. International Institute for Applied Systems Analysis (IIASA), Laxenburg, Austria. www.twi2050.org

Troost, C., Calberto, G., Berger, T., Ingwersen, J., Priesack, E., Warrach-Sagi, K., & Walter, T. (2012). Agent-based modeling of agricultural adaptation to climate change in a mountainous area of Southwest Germany. *International Congress on Environmental Modelling and Software*. 126.

Ullah, M. A. (2012). Enhancing the understanding of corruption through system dynamics modeling: A case study analysis of Pakistan. Doctoral dissertation. University of Auckland, New Zealand.

U.S. Agency for International Development (USAID). (2011). *Systems thinking in conflict assessment: Concepts and application*. USAID. https://usaidlearninglab.org/sites/default/files/resource/files/Systems%20Thinking%20Concept%20Note.pdf

Usenik, J., & Turnsek, T. (2016). Modeling conflict dynamics: System dynamic approach. In T. Krambeger, V. Potocan, and V. M. Ipavek (eds.), *Sustainable Logistics and Strategic Transportation Planning* (pp. 273–294). IGI Global. https://doi.org/10.4018/978-1-5225-0001-8.ch013

Vaughan, M. (2013). *The thinking effect.* Nicholas Brealey Publishing.

Vennix, J. A. M. (1996). *Group model building: Facilitating team learning using system dynamics.* Wiley.

Welsch, M., Hermann, S., Howells, M., Rogner, H. H., Young, C., Ramma, I., Bazilian, M., Fischer, G., Alfstad, T., Gielen, D., Le Blanc, D., Röhrl, A., Steduto, P., & Müller, A. (2014). Adding value with CLEWS: Modeling the energy system and its interdependencies for Mauritius. *Applied Energy, 113*, 1434–1445. https://doi.org/10.1016/j.apenergy.2013.08.083

Wilensky, U., & Rand, W. (2015). *An introduction to agent-based modeling: Modeling natural, social, and engineered complex systems with NetLogo.* The MIT Press.

Wolstenholme, E. F. (1990). *System inquiry: A system dynamics approach.* John Wiley & Sons.

Zadeh, L. (1973). Outline of a new approach to the analysis of complex systems and decision processes. *IEEE Transactions on Systems, Man, and Cybernetics, SMC-3*(10), 28–44. https://doi.org/10.1109/TSMC.1973.5408575

8 Systems Archetypes

8.1 INTRODUCTION

As mentioned in the discussion on complex adaptive systems in Chapter 3, out of all the systems at play in the landscape where the PSC nexus unfolds, human social systems (e.g., populations, households, communities, institutions) are the most complex to analyze. It is not easy to infer the structure responsible for the observed behavior patterns of human systems as they interact among themselves and with other systems (natural, infrastructure, and economic). However, the complexity of this form of reverse analysis can be reduced by considering *systems archetypes*, sometimes called *generic structures* (Senge, 1994), that may emerge in social systems and create recurring shared behavior patterns. Etymologically, an archetype is a "model, first form, original pattern from which copies are made" (https://www.etymonline.com/). This chapter deals with story archetypes and not character archetypes.

Senge (2006) noted that archetypes "reveal an incredibly elegant simplicity underlying the complexity of management issues... [They allow us] to see more places where there is leverage in facing difficult challenges, and to explain these opportunities to others." Archetypes have been discussed extensively in the systems literature (Goodman and Kleiner, 1994; Senge et al., 1994; Kim, 2000; Braun, 2002; Stroh, 2015; among others) and have been shown to help tremendously in the reverse analysis of human systems' behavior patterns.

Archetypes are unique qualitative systems thinking diagnoses and decision-making tools. They help identify the dynamics that relate systems structure to behavior (Meadows, 2008).

> A system to a large extent causes its own behavior. Once we see the relationship between structure and behavior, we can begin to understand how systems work, what makes them produce poor results, and how to shift them into better behavior patterns.

They can be interpreted as traps or grooves forcing a system to produce the same answer (intended or unintended) under the same conditions. They can also be construed as creating *attractors* of various strengths, i.e., levels where systems tend to return after changing. In short, archetypes create *habits* (good or bad) that define the system's character and destiny. Recognizing archetypes allows decision-makers to identify places of second-order change and leverage points in systems where changing structures and habits may cause the systems to adopt new behavior patterns over time (Meadows, 2008).

The rationale for using archetypes in analyzing human social systems is that, despite being seemingly complex, the patterns of behavior of these systems are not always completely random. For instance, recurring (generic) practices have been found to manifest themselves in different cultures and contexts. Archetypes allow recognizing and differentiating generic patterns from non-generic ones that depend

DOI: 10.1201/9781003435006-8

on scale and context. Both generic and non-generic patterns of human behavior are often found at play side by side in community development.

Although archetypes have traditionally been used to qualitatively model various forms of dynamics among human systems or between them and other systems, they can also be applied to model multiple forms of dynamics at play in each sector of the nexus or across the sectors of the PSC nexus. For example, Zhang et al. (2016) considered the interaction among the sustainable development goals (SDGs) and identified several archetypes at play in it.

In general, selecting the archetype(s) that best matches the issues being addressed requires first identifying the story that underlies these issues. Several archetypes can be considered through trial and error, which "can reveal whole new insights" (Kim and Anderson, 2007). As noted by Sterman (2000), that selection can be aided by using reference behavior over time graphs describing how the issues change over time and whether they show trends such as (i) linear growth or decay, (ii) exponential growth or decay that can be modeled by a single reinforcing (for growth) or balancing (for decay) loop, (iii) goal-seeking that can be modeled using a single balancing loop, (iv) oscillation which can occur when a delay is combined with a balancing loop, and (v) delays. Other higher forms of behavior can be obtained by combining the aforementioned basic modes, such as S-shaped growth (sequence of reinforcing and balancing loops), S-shaped growth with overshoot and oscillation, or overshoot and collapse (i.e., a series of multiple reinforcing and balancing with or without delay).

The SD reinforcing and balancing types of feedback described in Chapter 7 are fundamental archetypes that contribute to more complex archetypes. Ten archetypes are described below, with illustrative examples related to one, two, or three sectors of the PSC nexus. Various authors have proposed specific causal loop diagrams (CLDs) and behavior over time graphs to represent the dynamic behind each archetype and for different domains of application (Senge et al., 1994; Kim, 2000; Braun, 2002; Kim and Anderson, 2007; Stroh, 2015). The Waters Center for Systems Thinking (WCST, n.d.) offers an online course that describes the dynamics behind nine systems archetypes in more detail (www.waterscenterst.org).

8.2   FIXES THAT FAIL OR BACKFIRE

A symptom of a problem begs for a resolution. The implementation of a solution promptly alleviates the symptom. The problem symptom returns to its prior level or perhaps worsens due to the solution's unexpected consequences after some delay. Due to this development, the same (or a comparable) remedy must be reapplied (Kim and Anderson, 2007).

The corresponding CLD is shown in Figure 8.1. Both the problem symptom and unintended consequences increase over time. This archetype calls for (i) paying particular attention to the nature of the quick fix and its possible long-term consequences once the problem symptoms have been identified and (ii) analyzing how past actions to address the problem have been performed. In the short term, consider applying the fix while developing a symptom solution (Braun, 2002).

> Example 1: Peacemaking and peacekeeping activities are deployed to fix conflict (symptom). But the actions create division (unintended consequences) in the distribution of humanitarian aid, creating more conflict. The Bosnia example

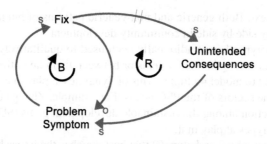

FIGURE 8.1 Dynamics of the fixes that fail or backfire archetype. Legend: s, same direction; o, opposite direction; R, reinforcing loop; B, balancing loop.

Source: © 2020 Waters Center for Systems Thinking, WatersCenterST.org Adapted from archetype described in *The Fifth Discipline*, Senge (2006) and by Innovation Associates, Inc.

comes to mind. Another example is the spread of cholera attributed to the presence of UN troops in Haiti following the 2010 earthquake.

Example 2: Farming is introduced to revive the sluggish economy (problem symptom). Deforestation (fix) is considered to create farming land. The fix creates a division between farmers and forest people and contributes to climate change. Conflict and climate change negatively affect the economy. See the example of the CMRT reserve in Chapter 6.

Example 3: About how to effectively transform civil conflicts (symptom), Hayden (2018) remarked how peacekeeping and humanitarian aid (fix) to communities rely on principles of neutrality, which is contrary to making structural changes necessary to transform the conflict. As a result, the conflict is not altered.

Example 4: Conflict exists between a host community and refugees/IDPs. A quick fix is to create a camp to host the refugees/IDPs. This action, in turn, brings more people to the area. Another dynamic suggested by CDA (2016) reads as follows: "The politicians representing the [refugee/] IDP ethnic communities are eager to exploit these camps as symbolic of their group's suffering, making the camps a tool in the partisan struggle and reducing the political will to find a more permanent resolution to the suffering caused by displacement. Also, various groups will benefit from the funding provided to the camps, establishing an incentive for perpetuating them."

8.3 SUCCESS TO THE SUCCESSFUL

To be successful, two or more people, organizations, projects, campaigns, etc., are vying for a small pool of resources. One of them tends to attract more resources and hence has a higher chance of continuing to succeed if it becomes more successful (or has historically been more successful) than the others. Even though the other alternatives might be superior, its first success justifies investing more resources while removing possibilities from the other alternatives to create its success (Kim and Anderson, 2007).

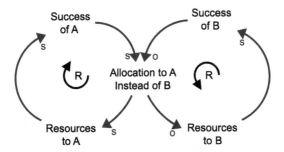

FIGURE 8.2 Dynamics of the success to the successful archetype.Legend: s, same direction; o, opposite direction; R, reinforcing loop; B, balancing loop.

Source: © 2020 Waters Center for Systems Thinking, WatersCenterST.org Adapted from archetype described in *The Fifth Discipline*, Senge (2006) and by Innovation Associates, Inc.

The corresponding CLD is shown in Figure 8.2. The performance of A increases and that of B decreases. This archetype calls for paying particular attention to (i) how slight differences in initial resource distribution, dominance, favoritism, corruption, and privilege can create a self-fulfilling prophecy of division and conflict and more dominance and privilege; (ii) both parties' definitions of success; and (iii) and whether both parties require the same initial level of resources to be successful.

Example 1: A development or humanitarian aid agency prioritizes services to one group (A) and not another (B). This decision, in turn, creates conflict. An example is a dynamic between refugees (outsiders) moving into a region (insiders). Humanitarian aid to the outsiders and a lack of coherence between insiders and outsiders create conflict and resentment.

Example 2: The Belgian colonial authorities supported Tutsis as the ruling class over Hutus in Rwanda in the 1930s (McNamee, 2021).

Example 3: Corruption is rampant and benefits one group (class, cast, etc.)

Example 4: The "Battle for the Streets" in Hong Kong in 2019 involved citizen protest and government crackdown. Figure 8.3 shows a zero-sum interaction between protesters and a dictator, "where one side gains in a thing only because the opposite side has lost something in return" (Clancy, 2020). This figure represents how the conflict in Hong Kong started in February 2019. As shown by Clancy (2020), the dynamic of the conflict evolved until October 2019 and included more feedback loops and archetypes, as discussed below in Section 8.12.

8.4 LIMITS TO GROWTH OR SUCCESS

Growing efforts are initially successful, which motivates even more of these efforts. However, over time, the system runs into constraints, which slows down the rate of

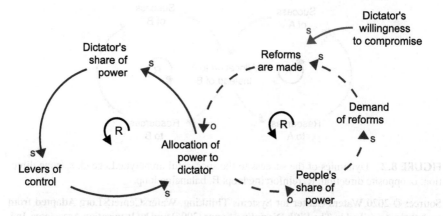

FIGURE 8.3   The dictator's dilemma battle for governing institutions: Success to the successful archetype. Legend: R, reinforcing loop; B, balancing loop. Dictator's view (solid lines), People's view (dotted lines).

Source: Clancy (2020). Used by permission of the author. Redrawn using the STELLA software.

progress in the outcomes. As success triggers off the limiting action and performance drops, the tendency is to concentrate even more on the initial growing actions (Kim and Anderson, 2007).

The corresponding CLD is shown in Figure 8.4. This archetype calls for paying particular attention to the constraint to growth (removal or limiting), especially before the limits are reached.

> Example 1: A population's health, well-being (performance), and economic growth (efforts) form a reinforcing loop. Drought related to climate change limits the amount of water for irrigation available for agriculture, negatively affecting food production and health. This trend creates a balancing loop that restricts any unlimited growth.

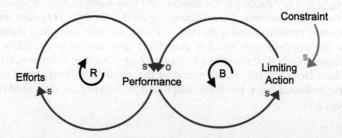

FIGURE 8.4   Dynamics of the limits to growth or success archetype. Legend: s, same direction; o, opposite direction; R, reinforcing loop; B, balancing loop.

Source: © 2020 Waters Center for Systems Thinking, WatersCenterST.org Adapted from archetype described in *The Fifth Discipline*, Senge (2006) and by Innovation Associates, Inc.

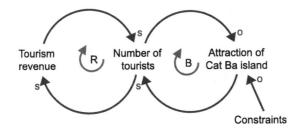

FIGURE 8.5 Limits to growth dynamics for the Cat Ba biosphere in Vietnam. Legend: s, same direction; o, opposite direction; R, reinforcing loop; B, balancing loop.

Source: Nguyen and Bosch (2013). Reproduced with permission from Wiley & Sons. Redrawn using the STELLA software.

> Example 2: Economic growth increases the standard of living. The latter requires an increase in resources for production and services. But the available resources are finite.
>
> Example 3: In the Cat Ba biosphere example described in Chapter 12, a limit to growth dynamics was used to identify how limiting constraints (pollution, overcrowding, lack of fresh water, and poor service quality) prevented sustainable tourism development on the island (Figure 8.5).

8.5 ESCALATION

One party (A) responds to a perceived threat by acting. The opposite party (B) then interprets these behaviors as causing an imbalance in the system, which makes them feel threatened. B then reacts to close the gap which from A's perspective leads to an imbalance, and so on. With the two balancing loops in this archetype, the dynamic of two parties striving to find a sense of "safety" turns into an overall reinforcing process that increases tension on both sides (Kim and Anderson, 2007).

The corresponding CLD is shown in Figure 8.6. This archetype calls for special attention to defining what represents a threat for each party, addressing insecurity, and bringing it under control without delay. Another option is to consider a larger goal that encompasses the desires of each party (Braun, 2002).

> Example 1: Reduced resources associated with climate change creates competition between two groups interested in natural resources—water conflict between the northern and southern parts of Yemen (Glass, 2010).
>
> Example 2: The Israeli-Palestinian conflict follows this archetype. Escalation occurs as violence by one side engenders a more intense response by another. The escalation stops after someone's collapse.
>
> Example 3: The civil war in Yemen between the Yemeni government and the Houthis follows the escalation archetype, as shown in Figure 8.7. Over time, it transformed into a proxy war between the Saudi coalition and Iran.

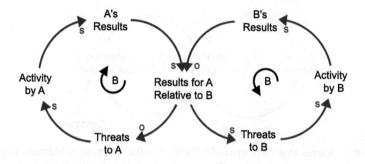

FIGURE 8.6 Dynamics of the escalation archetype. Legend: s, same direction; o, opposite direction; R, reinforcing loop; B, balancing loop.

Source: © 2020 Waters Center for Systems Thinking, WatersCenterST.org Adapted from archetype described in *The Fifth Discipline*, Senge (2006) and by Innovation Associates, Inc.

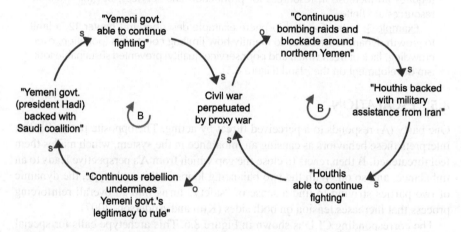

FIGURE 8.7 Escalation archetype between the Yemeni government and Houthis.

Source: Pulley (2021), reproduced with permission from the author. Redrawn using the STELLA software.

8.6   SHIFTING THE BURDEN

Applying a symptomatic treatment or a more fundamental solution can address a problem symptom. The urge to implement a more fundamental remedy is lowered when a symptomatic solution is implemented since the problem symptom is diminished or goes away. The symptom returns over time, and another round of symptomatic treatments are applied in a vicious, reinforcing figure-8 cycle. The side effects of the symptomatic solutions frequently serve to further detract from more basic ones (Kim and Anderson, 2007).

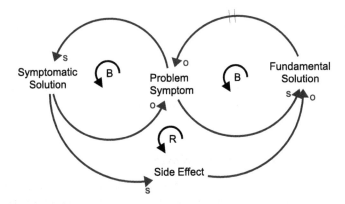

FIGURE 8.8 Dynamics of the shifting the burden archetype. Legend: s, same direction; o, opposite direction; R, reinforcing loop; B, balancing loop.

Source: © 2020 Waters Center for Systems Thinking, WatersCenterST.org Adapted from archetype described in *The Fifth Discipline*, Senge (2006) and by Innovation Associates, Inc.

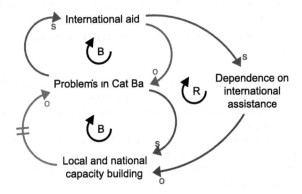

FIGURE 8.9 Shifting the burden dynamic for the Cat Ba biosphere in Vietnam. Legend: s, same direction; o, opposite direction; R, reinforcing loop; B, balancing loop.

Source: Nguyen and Bosch (2013). Reproduced with permission from Wiley & Sons. Redrawn using the STELLA software.

The corresponding CLD is shown in Figure 8.8. This archetype calls for paying particular attention to (i) how easy it is to become addicted to symptomatic solutions and avoid addressing the problem symptom faced and (ii) shifting attention as soon as possible from symptomatic solutions to fundamental solutions. However, the symptomatic solution may be used for some time to develop the fundamental solution (Braun, 2002).

Example 1: Quick fixes to some service infrastructure without considering long-term performance create more problems in the long term than fixing the infrastructure well at the outset.

Example 2: In the Cat Ba biosphere example described in Chapter 12, a shifting the burden dynamics (Figure 8.9) was used to model the unintended consequences of relying on financial assistance from international organizations (symptomatic solution) to address the island's local issues (threatened Golden-Headed Langur species, poverty, waste accumulation, and pollution).

The assistance created more dependence (side effect) on outside help. Short of building capacity and resilience (fundamental solution), many of the original problems in Cat Ba Island remain because the core issues (less noticeable or visible) have not been addressed.

8.7   DRIFTING OR ERODING GOALS

It is possible to close the performance gap between desired performance and actual performance by either reducing the goal or taking corrective measures to achieve the goal. A steady lowering of the goal frequently closes the gap. The degree of performance likewise declines over time. The organization may not even be aware of the impact of this drift because it may occur so gradually and even without intentional action (Kim and Anderson, 2007).

The corresponding CLD is shown in Figure 8.10. This archetype calls for paying particular attention to the nature of the corrective actions and how goals erode over time. The goals may be externalized from the dynamic of Figure 8.9. A reality check between the actual situation and desired goals needs to be considered as soon as possible (Braun, 2002).

> Example 1: Eroding of the goal of democracy due to "creeping authoritarianism," whereby specific corrective actions (e.g., efforts to intimidate the media, state surveillance, manipulating elections) become gradually more pronounced and accepted (Walt, 2017).
> Example 2: A community identifies high goals for itself. Over time, the goals cannot be met because (i) goals were too complex and ambitious to start with and did not match the capacity of the community, and (ii) the community's interest in reaching the goals erodes with time.

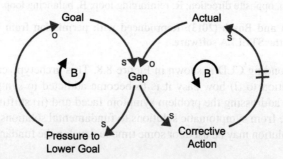

FIGURE 8.10 Dynamics of the drifting and eroding goals archetype. Legend: s, same direction; o, opposite direction; R, reinforcing loop; B, balancing loop.

Source: © 2020 Waters Center for Systems Thinking, WatersCenterST.org Adapted from archetype described in *The Fifth Discipline*, Senge (2006) and by Innovation Associates, Inc.

Example 3: External assistance and services to a community decrease over time due to a decreasing commitment from government and community leaders.

8.8   TRAGEDY OF THE COMMONS

In the tragedy of the commons (Hardin, 1968, 2008), individuals use common resources for their own benefit without considering how their actions would affect others. All parties involved eventually lose out because of the "commons" becoming overburdened by the cumulative effects of all individual actions. The commons' resources might even be depleted (Kim and Anderson, 2007).

The corresponding CLD is shown in Figure 8.11. This archetype calls for special attention to the management (regulation and coordination) of finite resources, collaboration, the monitoring and evaluation of resources, and the need to develop common ground. Another option is to explore substituting or renewing the resources available to both parties before depletion (Braun, 2002).

Example 1: Overusing shared natural resources, overgrazing, fishing, fertilizers, and deforestation. There is no agreement as to how to share the resources.

Example 2: In the Cat Ba biosphere example described in Chapter 12, a tragedy of the commons dynamics was used to model conflict between the island's tourism industry and agricultural industry (Figure 8.12). The tourism industry (owners of hotels and restaurants, tour operators) wants to gain more revenue from tourism. Similarly, the agricultural sector (farmers) wants more income from agriculture. Both increase the total investment activities in the system. However, the system has limited carrying capacities and resilience due to the lack of fresh water, electricity, trained staff, land for cultivation, etc. These issues ultimately reduce the revenue for each industry. The leverage point is better management of the commons through education and self-regulation and developing an integrated island master plan.

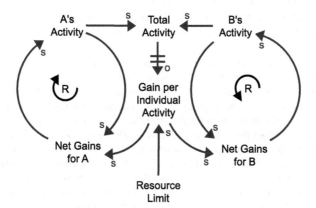

FIGURE 8.11   Dynamics of Tragedy of the Commons archetype. Legend: S, same direction; O, opposite direction; R, reinforcing loop; B, balancing loop.

Source: © 2020 Waters Center for Systems Thinking, WatersCenterST.org Adapted from archetype described in *The Fifth Discipline*, Senge (2006) and by Innovation Associates, Inc.

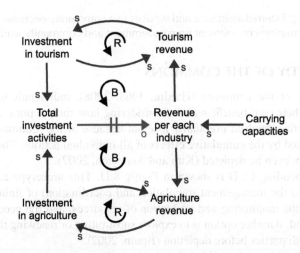

FIGURE 8.12   The tragedy of the commons dynamic for the Cat Ba biosphere in Vietnam. Legend: s, same direction; o, opposite direction; R, reinforcing loop; B, balancing loop.

Source: Nguyen and Bosch (2013). Reproduced with permission from Wiley & Sons. Redrawn using the STELLA software.

8.9   ACCIDENTAL ADVERSARIES

"When teams or parties in a working relationship misinterpret the actions of each other because of misunderstandings, unrealistic expectations or performance problems, suspicion, and mistrust erode the relationship. If mental models fueling the deteriorating relationship are not challenged, all parties may lose the benefits of their synergy" (Braun, 2002).

The corresponding CLD is shown in Figure 8.13. This archetype calls for special attention to creating awareness of how each party's message and behavior influence the other party. One option is to develop collaborative work upfront (Braun, 2002).

Example 1: Conflict emerges during development projects between two groups (communities, NGOs, institutions, or mixed) that are expected to work together. Because of a lack of initial shared vision and capacity to adapt to change, group A takes the lead, which the other group B sees as a threat. Group B retaliates, which upsets group A, which in turn retaliates. Conflict resolution was not envisioned in the joint project to handle such conflict. This conflict results in a lose-lose situation.

Example 2: This example is a modified version of the dynamic between water, energy, and food proposed by Sohofi et al. (2016) and applied to the PSC nexus. The success of each sector of the nexus is allowed to increase and decrease. Since the three sectors are interdependent, one sector's success contributes to the other two's success. A goal-seeking process is at play for each sector to reduce the gap between its current level of success and some desired value. But the action to narrow the gap of one sector creates unintended consequences that reduce the success of the other sectors. In other words, an increase in the state of peace may negatively affect sustainability and climate security if it creates unintended consequences. The same reasoning could be applied to sustainability or climate security as a starting point.

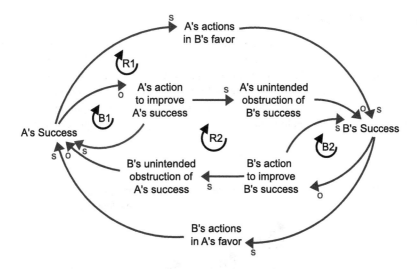

FIGURE 8.13 Dynamics of the Accidental Adversaries archetype. Legend: s, same direction; o, opposite direction; R, reinforcing loop; B, balancing loop.

Source: © 2020 Waters Center for Systems Thinking, WatersCenterST.org Adapted from archetype described in *The Fifth Discipline*, Senge (2006) and by Innovation Associates, Inc.

8.10 REPRESSION AND REVOLUTION

"Official policies are perceived as repressive, and members of an oppressed group join together to act defiantly" (WCST). The corresponding CLD is shown in Figure 8.14. This archetype calls for mediation and reaching a joint ground agreement.

Example 1: The US Revolutionary War between British authorities and colonists in the late eighteenth century

Example 2: Nonviolent resistance movements in India (Gandhi) and the US (Martin Luther King)

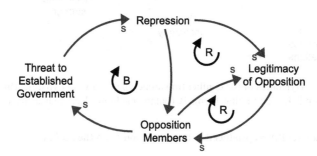

FIGURE 8.14 Dynamics of repression and revolution archetype. Legend: s, same direction; o, opposite direction; R, reinforcing loop; B, balancing loop.

Source: © 2020 Waters Center for Systems Thinking, WatersCenterST.org Adapted from archetype described in *The Fifth Discipline*, Senge (2006) and by Innovation Associates, Inc.

8.11   THE CONFLICT TRAP

This archetype was suggested by Hayden (2018) to explain the dynamic of civil conflict in countries such as Somalia. Figures 8.15.a and 8.15.b depict two CLDs: one showing the original conflict trap and one showing how security and aid interventions affect the conflict trap. Figure 8.15.a shows how the reinforcing nature of the trap negatively affects human security and economic development. In Figure 8.15.b, the reinforcing cycle is broken by introducing security, peace operations, and aid.

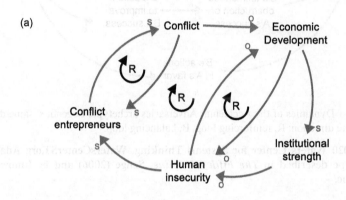

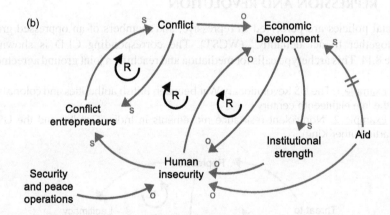

FIGURE 8.15   Dynamics of the conflict trap archetype. (a) Initial dynamic; (b) After interventions. Legend: R (reinforcing loop); B (balancing loop). Redrawn using the STELLA software.

Source: Hayden (2018). Reproduced with permission from the author.

8.12 ARCHETYPES DYNAMICS

8.12.1 SIMULTANEOUS ARCHETYPES

It is not unusual for multiple archetypes to play simultaneously in community development (Sohofi et al., 2016; Turner et al., 2016; Zhuang, 2014, among others). A case study is discussed in Chapter 12 regarding the development of Cat Ba Island in Vietnam. In that case, three archetypes were found to coexist. Their dynamics are presented in Figures 8.5, 8.9, and 8.12.

Figure 8.16 shows an example proposed by Sohofi et al. (2016), where different archetypes play a role in addressing the effect of climate change on the water-energy-food-land nexus.

In Figure 8.16, the *limits to success* archetype can be found in the loop combinations (R1, B1) for energy production, (R2, B2) for water production, and (R3, B3, and B4) for agriculture production. A less apparent archetype, the *accidental adversaries* archetype, is also at play in Figure 8.16. It deals with competition and associated trade-offs related to simultaneously trying to increase water, energy, and agriculture production (R1, R2, and R3) when these three sectors depend on each other, and the success of one of them negatively affects the success of the other two.

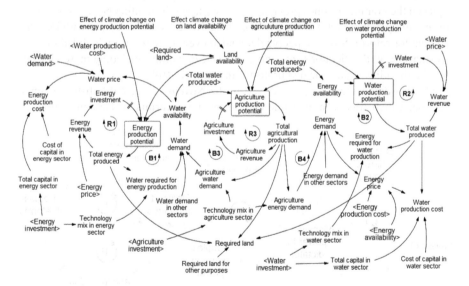

FIGURE 8.16 Causal loop diagram illustrating the limits to success dynamic across the water, energy, and agriculture sectors of the nexus. Legend: R, reinforcing loop; B, balancing loop. Redrawn using the Vensim software.

Source: Sohofi et al. (2016), used by permission of the System Dynamics Society.

8.12.2 Changing Archetypes

In other cases, the dominant archetype(s) may change over time. An illustrative example of that dynamic is the conflict in Hong Kong in 2019, described in detail in Clancy's Dictator's Dilemma paper (2020). In that paper, the author broke down the conflict between the Hong Kong Police, the Hong Kong Chief Executive, and China (defined as the Dictator) on one side and the residents of Hong Kong (defined as the People) on the other side into three stages.

The conflict started in February 2019 when the Hong Kong Chief Executive proposed a new reform to deport any arrested Hong Kong citizens to China. This proposal led to the conflict dynamic of Figure 8.3, where a "success for the successful" archetype best represented the conflict between the dictator and the people. From February to June 2019, the conflict evolved, as shown in Figure 8.17, to include a "fixes that fail" archetype to capture the effect of the refusal of reforms and compromise from the Hong Kong Chief Executive. This decision led to more unmet demands from the people that extended to issues beyond the original reform.

Figure 8.18 shows the following conflict dynamic between July and October 2019. The dominant archetype was an escalation and a broadening of the conflict that became more aggressive and violent between police and the population (arms race archetype). The occupation of Hong Kong's international airport from August 12–14, 2019, led to brief declining support for the conflict by the people. Periodic protests replaced the continuous ones previously followed, but the conflict between the dictator and the people remained strong. The Hong Kong Chief Executive withdrew the demand for reform. Still, the people demanded even more reform which led to more resistance from the dictator's side and aggressive dynamics, including more violence and the shooting of an unarmed protestor in October 2019.

The pro-democracy camp fared well in the November 24, 2019, district council election, which was seen as a referendum on the government. Demonstrations of

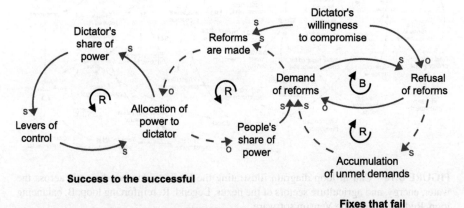

FIGURE 8.17 Conflict dynamics showing the "success to the successful" and "fixes that fail" dynamics in Hong Kong for February to June 2019. Legend: R, reinforcing loop; B, balancing loop. Dictator's view (solid lines), People's view (dotted lines).

Source: Clancy (2020). Used by permission of the author. Redrawn using the STELLA software.

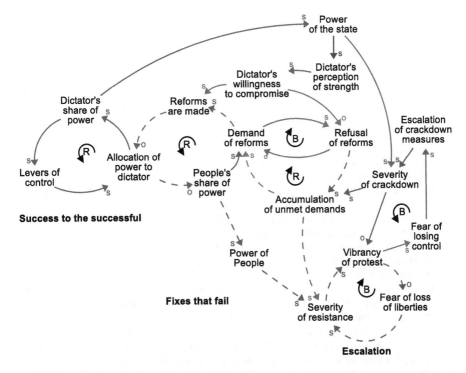

FIGURE 8.18 Conflict dynamics showing "success to the successful," "fixes that fail," and "escalation (arms race)" dynamics in Hong Kong for July to October 2019. Legend: R, reinforcing loop; B, balancing loop. Dictator's view (solid lines), People's view (dotted lines).

Source: Clancy (2020). Used by permission of the author. Redrawn using the STELLA software.

lesser intensity continued until February 2020, putting pressure on the government. They dwindled due to the COVID pandemic in March 2020.

8.13   CONCLUDING REMARKS

Archetypes help in making sense of the relationship between system structure and behavior. Once identified, places of leverage can be selected, and the where and when of interventions can be outlined. As seen in this chapter, multiple archetypes can be at play at the community level, either simultaneously or sequentially. Hence, several places of preferred interventions are possible. Questions remain as to (i) which leverage points to address first and (ii) whether different places of intervention are synergistic or require trade-offs.

REFERENCES

Braun, W. (2002). *The system archetypes*. University at Albany. http://www.albany.edu/faculty/gpr/PAD724/724WebArticles/sys_archetypes.pdf
Clancy, T. (2020, March 30). The dictator dilemma: Hong Kong case study. https://infomullet.com/2020/03/30/dictatorsdilemma/

Collaborative for Development Action (CDA). (2016). *Designing strategic initiatives to impact conflict systems: Systems approaches to peacebuilding. A resource manual*. CDA Collaborative Learning Projects.

Glass, N. (2010, June). The water crisis in Yemen: Causes, consequences, and solutions. *Global Majority E-Journal, 1*(1), 17–30. https://www.american.edu/cas/economics/ejournal/upload/glass_accessible.pdf

Goodman, M., & Kleiner, A. (1994). The archetype family tree. In P. M. Senge (ed.), *The fifth discipline field book: Strategies and tools for building a learning organization*. Doubleday.

Hardin, G. (1968). The tragedy of the commons. *Science, 162*, 1243–1248. https://doi.org/10.1126/science.162.3859.1243

Hardin, G. (2008). The tragedy of the unmanaged commons: Population and the disguises of providence. http://billtotten.blogspot.com/2008/09/tragedy-of-unmanaged-commons.html

Hayden, N. K. (2018). *Balancing belligerents or feeding the beats: Transforming conflict traps*. CISSIM Policy Brief, The University of Maryland Center for International and Security Studies. https://drum.lib.umd.edu/bitstream/handle/1903/20654/Hayden-Balancing%20belligerents%20or%20feeding%20the%20beasts_022618.pdf

Kim, D. H. (2000). *Systems archetypes I and II*. Nabu Press.

Kim, D. H., & Anderson, V. (2007). *System archetypes basics: From story to structure*. Pegasus Communications.

McNamee, T. (2021). Such a long journey: Peacebuilding after genocide in Rwanda. In T. McNamee and M. Muyangwa, (eds.), *The State of Peacebuilding in Africa*. Palgrave Macmillan. https://doi.org/10.1007/978-3-030-46636-7_21

Meadows, D. H. (2008). *Thinking in systems*. Chelsea Green Publishing.

Nguyen, N. C., & Bosch, O. J. H. (2013). A systems thinking approach to identify leverage points for sustainability: A case study in the Cat Ba Biosphere Reserve, Vietnam. *System Research and Behavioral Science, 30*(2), 104–115. https://doi.org/10.1002/sres.2145 Wiley Blackwell.

Pulley, K. (2021). A systems approach to understanding the Yemen civil war and humanitarian crisis. Term paper, CVEN 5837, University of Colorado, Boulder.

Senge, P. (1994). *The fifth discipline: The art & practice of the learning organization*. Doubleday.

Senge, P. (2006). *The fifth discipline: The art & practice of the learning organization* (Revised & Updated edition). Doubleday.

Senge, P., Kleiner, A., Roberts, C., Ross, R. B., & Smith, B. J. (1994). *The fifth discipline field book: Strategies and tools for building a learning organization*. Doubleday.

Sohofi, S. A., Melkonyan, A., Karl, C. K., & Krumme, K. (2016). System archetypes in the conceptualization phase of water-energy-food-nexus modeling. *In 34th International Conference of the System Dynamics Society: Black Swans and Black Lies: System Dynamics in the Context of Randomness and Political Power-play*, 17-21 July, Delft, Netherlands, Volume *34*.

Sterman, J. (2000). *Business dynamics: Systems thinking and modeling for a complex world*. McGraw Hill.

Stroh, D. P. (2015). *Systems thinking for social change*. Chelsea Green Publ.

Turner, B. L., Menendez, H. M., Gates, R., Tedeschi, L. O., & Atzori, A. S. (2016). System dynamics modeling for agricultural and natural resource management issues: A review of some past case and forecasting future roles. *Resources, 5*(40). https://doi.org/10.3390/resources5040040

Walt, S. (2017, July 27). https://foreignpolicy.com/2017/07/27/top-10-signs-of-creeping-authoritarianism-revisited/

Waters Center for Systems Thinking (WCST). (n.d.). https://waterscenterst.org/

Zhang, Q., Prouty, C., Zimmerman, J. B., & Mihelcic, J. R. (2016). More than target 6.3: A systems approach to rethinking sustainable development goals in a resource-scarce world. *Engineering, 2*, 481–489. https://doi.org/10.1016/J.ENG.2016.04.010

Zhuang, Y. (2014). *A system dynamics approach to integrated water and energy resources management*. Graduate Theses and Dissertations. http://scholarcommons.usf.edu/etd/5164

9 A System-Based Methodology

9.1 INTRODUCTION

As noted by Seelos (2020), "system work is not about solutions: it's about discovering and steering pathways for change at a pace appropriate for our ability to learn and for what local communities can enact and absorb." Recognizing the need to use a systematic approach to address how community development and the peace–sustainability–climate (PSC) nexus unfold is necessary but insufficient: it also needs to be operational. The process must be incorporated into a methodology that guides decision-makers to map, identify, and rank problems; find forms of leverage; develop strategies; implement holistic solutions and interventions; and propose coherent governance and policies in the short and long term. Among other things, to be effective, the methodology requires (i) a clear understanding of the community landscape and the problems/issues that need to be addressed (i.e., the power of the story and mental models) and how to bridge the gap between current and desired community development states, (ii) an ability to use multiple modeling tools, (iii) participatory involvement of different categories of stakeholders/actors, and (iv) flexibility and adaptability to change.

The methodology presented below builds on the one proposed by the author to address the water–energy–land–food nexus at the community level (Amadei, 2019). The method is setting-specific and depends on the context and scale of the community development landscape in which the PSC nexus unfolds.

9.1.1 STAKEHOLDER PARTICIPATION

One characteristic of the methodology is that it emphasizes participation by the stakeholders/actors involved in community development and the three sectors of the PSC nexus. The stakeholders include all individuals and groups (i.e., critical, primary, and secondary) who can make or influence decisions about the nexus, even those who may not have a voice in the matter but will be impacted by how the nexus unfolds (Caldwell, 2002). As shown in Figure 9.1, they can be divided into three types. Some people, such as community members, contribute to bottom-up solutions, whereas others who are part of governmental organizations offer top-down solutions. Outsiders are a third group that contributes to outside-in solutions. Examples of outsiders include NGOs, donors, commercial sector groups, civil society, etc. Figure 9.1 further shows that three degrees of causality must be considered when addressing the PSC nexus and community development: upward, downward, and outside-in.

The three categories of stakeholders play a critical role in making decisions across the PSC nexus as they contribute a diversity of perspectives, trade-offs, knowledge,

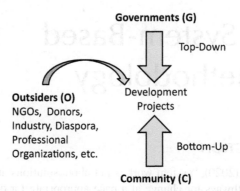

FIGURE 9.1   Stakeholder dynamics involve a combination of bottom-up, top-down, and outside-in contributions from community members, governments, and outsiders.

skills, and attitudes through relational practices. Individuals or group members can influence each other positively or become sources of tension when confronted with different perspectives, experiences, and expertise.

In an ideal situation, community members are uniquely positioned to identify and address development issues regarding conflict, provide services and goods, and adapt to and mitigate climate change. They understand their situations better than the other two groups and are more accountable. Community members are also better positioned to decide on the relevance and effectiveness of interventions, own and implement solutions, operate and maintain the solutions, and choose how and when to scale up if necessary.

Likewise, governmental institutions can play different top-down roles, such as enablers, service providers, or regulators/controllers (GWP, 2000). They may scale up solutions, provide support, develop standards, etc. Finally, outsiders can facilitate and support outside-in roles (e.g., financial, technical, and policy).

One cannot emphasize the need for collaboration and synergy between these three groups of stakeholders enough. When seeing community development as a three-legged stool, its stability or success depends on the strength of all three groups of stakeholders simultaneously; a weak leg of the seat makes it unstable and development unsuccessful. As noted by Flammini et al. (2014) for the food–energy–water nexus, the effectiveness of the dynamics between different groups of stakeholders depends on many factors, such as (i) the willingness of all groups to participate in dialogue and decision-making, (ii) their capacity to make meaningful contributions, and (iii) their availability for dialogue and decision-making toward a shared vision. The same relational factors apply to the PSC nexus.

Another possible structural distribution of stakeholders to address complex systems proposed by the Omidyar Group (2017) is to divide them into three teams with representatives of the three groups of Figure 9.1: (i) a small executive core team, (ii) a medium-sized extended team to support the core team, and (iii) a much larger group of participants who provide knowledge and experience as required. The three teams play different roles in each methodology step presented below. For instance, all three teams may contribute to the community appraisal, whereas the first two teams may contribute to all efforts leading to scenarios of intervention and implementation.

Another category of stakeholders could be added to Figure 9.1 to capture the particular case when displaced and migrating populations (e.g., refugees and Internally Displaced People (IDPs)) move into an existing community landscape. Many development and humanitarian aid case studies demonstrate the importance of considering the dynamic between host communities and displaced populations to prevent conflict. This complex integration creates demands on displaced people and the hosting community. Coherence between these two groups is necessary to avoid conflict, ensure sustainable community development, provide resilience to adverse events, and ensure climate security (Moore, 2014; Mowjee et al., 2015; OECD, 2017).

9.1.2 THE STORYLINE

The proposed methodology requires having at the outset a *community development story* with a narrative and script outlined by the three categories of stakeholders in Figure 9.1. In the present case, the story must incorporate several sectors of the PSC nexus. The story also acknowledges that different stakeholders may have different opinions based on different perceptions. Hjorth and Bagheri (2006) best summarized that stories represent a powerful way to engage people (e.g., stakeholders) in doing something once they realize they are part of the stories and can control their future.

Among all three groups of Figure 9.1, community members are better positioned to oversee the community story. The story is based on a shared vision that clearly outlines the community development landscape (context, scale, and boundary) and what systemic changes to the community are desired, starting with its current level of development, conflict/peace, and response to climate change (i.e., its baseline). The current and desired levels involve two narratives, each with its specific mental models, structure dynamics, patterns of behavior and trends, and manifesting events. The story must also describe how the PSC nexus unfolds at the current level and may develop at the desired level.

The driving forces that keep the dynamic going from a current level to a desirable level of community development, peace, sustainability, and climate security can be interpreted as what Senge (2006, p. 140) calls "creative tension." Thus, interventions in human development and security can be construed as pulling the reality of the current level toward the desirable one. For this emerging transformation to occur, the three groups of stakeholders shown in Figure 9.1 need to partner and collaborate on defining the current and desirable levels of community development, "hold steady to the [shared] vision" (Senge, 2006), develop strategies, formulate interventions, and assess progress through monitoring and evaluation. This approach must occur at all levels of the iceberg model in Figure 1.1 (i.e., in the mental models, structural and behavioral patterns, and events). Without these tasks, not much change will occur, and most interventions will be short-lived.

More specifically, the community development story can be narrated (and scripted) as follows:

1. A community in a specific landscape (context, scale, and boundary) is currently at a certain level or *stage of development.* In some cases, such as in marginalized communities, that level is not advanced. It operates

based on specific mental models (habits, belief systems, etc.) in that state. Various social, infrastructure, environmental, and economic systems are at play, and specific policies and regulations provide services (e.g., energy, water, food, and transportation), and livelihood. The overall state of well-being, health, peace, prosperity, sustainability, and resilience of the community emerges from the interaction of these systems and their respective structure. The level of community development is limited by the community's capacity to reach some goals and provide services and ensure an adequate level of development, security, and resilience. The limiting capacity can be institutional, financial, technical, environmental, educational, or social/cultural. It can be identified with the analysis presented in Chapter 5. Consequently, the community experiences a certain level of peace, sustainability, and climate security in its current reality.

2. Out of its desire or as suggested by other stakeholders such as governmental institutions and outsiders, the community is interested in progressing and transitioning to a more advanced stage of development over time, which can be interpreted as a desired or aspirational level. In some instances, the community aims to reach a higher level of sustainability, peace, and climate security in the short and long term. A new mindset is required, new mental models must be endorsed, a new community structure must be reconsidered, new behavior patterns must be accepted, and systemic change must be embraced. As the community experiences changes and adapts to new levels of development through capacity building, it may experience greater well-being, peace, prosperity, and resilience. This outcome may have expected or unexpected consequences. The changes can be at different levels ranging from transformational, reform, or incremental (Kehrer et al., 2020). There is also the possibility that the changes are limited or nothing happens.

3. A team of outside advisors has been called to work in a participatory manner with the community and governmental organizations to lay out a methodology that can (i) identify and map current conflict issues, the vulnerability of the community to climate change, and unstainable forms of community livelihood and security; (ii) address these issues; and (iii) propose an integrated plan of action (strategy and operations) as the community moves from one level of development to the next. Because of the stakeholder dynamic shown in Figure 9.1, the community hopefully benefits from its new level of development, and the government is now engaged and plays an active role in supporting and scaling projects and developing policies to ensure peace, sustainability, and security at the local, regional, and national scales and over time.

In general, the dynamic of community development systemic change mentioned above in the development story depends on the state of development the community is starting with (i.e., its development baseline with its initial conditions of peace, sustainability, and climate security). The higher the baseline, the faster the transition rate is, and the more resilient the community will react to change over time. This dynamic is explored in one of the SD models in Chapter 10.

Community development stories have unique characteristics. They are not always straightforward and linear; they are systemic and consist of many plots with twists and turns and feedback mechanisms. Parts of these stories can be simple, complicated, or complex and sometimes create confusion because of their uncertainties. The stories may require those who hear, read, or experience them to be flexible and adaptive in their thinking, be willing to change their beliefs and perceptions, and have imagination.

Another characteristic of stories is that they do not always end well or as expected. Some approaches to community development can backfire with unintended consequences when, for instance, stories are imposed on populations or when these populations are coerced into adopting others' stories. Problems also arise when community stakeholders or different stakeholder groups do not share the same narrative, are in conflict, and cannot reach some compromise and consensus in addressing joint issues and selecting appropriate interventions.

9.2   METHODOLOGY STAGES

This section describes various stages of a systems-aware methodology to help decision-makers and practitioners forge scenarios of community development interventions to address peace, sustainability, and climate security issues at the community scale. Having a methodology to address community development is not new and has been embraced by multiple development agencies. New herein is the idea that systems thinking and tools must be integrated into all methodology stages. More details about the value proposition of integrating a systems approach into the different steps in the management of community development intervention can be found in Amadei (2015).

In addition, to be systemic, the proposed methodology combines the participatory action research (PAR) techniques of community appraisal discussed in Chapter 5, the various systems modeling and analysis tools described in Chapters 6 and 7, and some decision-making tools. The road map of the methodology consists of ten stages, as shown in Figure 9.2:

1. *Defining the situation space.* This preliminary stage is about gaining clarity about the context, scale, boundaries, and overall landscape/setting where the PSC nexus and community development unfold. As discussed in Chapter 5, describing the situation space can be seen as conducting a systems-aware *pre-appraisal* or *pre-feasibility* of the community landscape and deciding whether to proceed with the next stage (i.e., the appraisal). It includes gathering preliminary information about community livelihood, resources management, resource allocation, critical issues, etc. It is also about determining whether the community landscape is experiencing or has been dealing with challenges, such as past conflicts, and whether climate change has impacted the community and for how long. The pre-appraisal represents an opportunity for decision-makers to get global insights about the community's current reality (the mindset, structure, and behavior patterns of Figure 1.1) and frame questions (e.g., why the community is the

FIGURE 9.2   Ten stages of the systems-aware methodology.

way it is? what accounts for its current state?). It is also about developing relationships with its constituents, creating shared understanding, inviting participation, building trust and relationships, and identifying a core group that will represent the community. All this information will help dictate the type of appraisal to be carried out, what areas to focus on, and the resources (material and human) necessary to carry out the assessment. An appraisal team with the appropriate qualifications, skills, and diversity is also selected to match the situation space best. Another aspect of this stage is for outsiders to decide on their capacity to pursue any intervention alone or in partnership with other organizations.

2. *Defining the community baseline.* Systems mapping and visualization tools are essential to creating a baseline community profile. As discussed in Section 5.4, participatory appraisal methods such as PAR follow an inductive systems-aware process to acquire information about the current structure of the community landscape, including the human, natural, infrastructure, and economic systems at play in the community and their interaction. Population, education, economic, environmental, political, cultural, and infrastructure profiles are laid out (Grassroots Collective, n.d.). Systems mapping also identifies the community's mental models, behavior, and structural patterns. Additional data are also collected about the capacity of the community to reach development and security goals and

provide services, its vulnerability, its resilience to adverse events, and its current levels of peace and climate security. Stakeholder/actor, partner, gender, capacity, risk, conflict, SWOT/C, and leverage analyses are carried out. At the end of this stage, broad intervention goals are outlined.

3. *Defining the problem space.* At the end of the appraisal, a *baseline profile* of the community is established, and issues are outlined and ranked (Section 5.6). Community issues are gaps between current and desired states, and their dynamic hypotheses are systemically outlined and categorized. Possible theories are suggested to explain how these issues unfold (i.e., possible explanations that relate mental models to structure and behavior). Preliminary conceptual mental models are proposed to explain the community development and security state, its deep structure (Omidyar group, 2017), and how the PSC nexus unfolds in the community landscape. Historical analysis of the landscape (including how the community coped and adapted to past stressors, risks, and drivers) is also required to assess the community's response to future threats and how those risks could affect the security of the sectors of the PSC nexus.

4. *Understanding the landscape dynamics.* The soft system modeling tools of Chapter 6 (i.e., concept maps, problem and solution tree causal analysis, cross-impact analysis, and network analysis) are used to analyze further the issues identified in the problem space and, more specifically, their root causes, impact and dependence, and relationships. An outcome of the landscape dynamics is identifying the objectives to address the issues (goals) and strategic development themes.

5. *Modeling the landscape dynamics.* The qualitative and quantitative system simulation modeling tools (SD, ABM, or a combination of both) in Chapter 7 are used to reproduce, as accurately as possible, the current scenario at play across the community landscape and the PSC nexus and the deep structures that may explain the current issues, behavior patterns, and trends observed across the nexus and at the community level.

6. *Exploring alternative intervention scenarios.* Possible places to intervene in the landscape are formulated and conceptualized. Several alternative peace, development, and climate security intervention and pathway scenarios that could best address the issues faced by the community over the short and long term are outlined. This process is done using a deductive and formative approach with criteria, such as intervention relevance, feasibility (economic, time, skills, experience), and sustainability (long-term performance) (Grassroots Collective, n.d.). Systems-based tools are used to (i) model and simulate alternative interventions; (ii) assess whether and to what extent the peace, development, and climate security issues are addressed; and (iii) explore possible impacts and unintended consequences.

7. *Making decisions and formulating a theory of change (ToC).* Appropriate multiobjective decision-making tools such as the Multiple Criteria Decision Analysis (Delp et al., 1977; DCLG, 2009) or Multi-Criteria Utility Assessment method (Caldwell, 2002) are used to select satisfactory peace, development, and climate security-related intervention strategies by

evaluating and ranking whether the interventions meet specific goals and objectives. Leverage opportunities are identified, and leverage hypotheses and impact are outlined for each selected intervention strategy. A ToC can be formulated in terms of a cause-and-effect statement for each intervention strategy to visualize steps for long-term changes: if x [pre-conditional activity], then y [expected change and outcome] because z [rationale]. The ToC can be at the individual or the group level (CDA, 2016) and operate at different levels among the three categories of stakeholders in Figure 9.1. Over time, decisions are made about reducing the gap between current and desired capacity. The building blocks toward peace, sustainability, and climate security and their interaction are outlined.

8. *Intervention strategy and operation.* A logistical and tactical plan is developed to implement stepwise the most satisfactory/appropriate peace, climate security, and development-related intervention strategies across the community. The plan includes indicators, performance metrics, and verification methods to (i) monitor and evaluate the progress and effectiveness of the proposed interventions, including potential risks, and (ii) decide whether the proposed interventions can be scaled up and what strategies and policies must be put in place to ensure their long-term performance and benefits. A systems-aware logical framework approach (Amadei, 2015) is required here as a strategic executive summary and road map where (i) intervention inputs, activities, outputs (objectives), goals (effects, purpose), and impact (outcome and aim) are clearly outlined in a systemic and logical (horizontal and vertical) manner and (ii) assumptions (sources of risks) and modes of verification are defined. A successful strategy requires the different categories of stakeholders to align around a common purpose, even though they may share different agendas (Stroh, 2015).

9. *Intervention implementation and exit strategy.* During project implementation, it is likely that logistical and tactical changes and vice versa will dictate changes in operational decisions. This feedback mechanism extends beyond project closure, although the intensity of the feedback is much less after project closing than before. At this framework stage, the project managers may have gained enough understanding to (i) predict the project's medium- to long-term performance, (ii) suggest alternatives if conditions change or the project does not perform as planned, and (iii) foresee any future intervention if the needs arise. An exit strategy is outlined.

10. *Reflective practice on the action.* Following the implementation of the interventions, it is a good practice to reflect on action. Community development practitioners must reflect on a project once it has been completed. This *reflection-on-action*, or "debriefing" process, represents a valuable learning exercise in identifying what has worked and not worked in a project. It helps incorporate changes in future projects and explore areas of potential improvement. Reflective practice is also valuable for practitioners as it promotes self-learning, enhances skills and knowledge, increases confidence and understanding, self-motivation, and professionalism. The reflective practice may also give some insights into the applicability of systems tools and provide possible changes for future interventions.

Project sustainability (i.e., its long-term performance) must be ensured once the project has ended (post-evaluation). The project must be able to continue delivering benefits to the target community, which requires measures and processes to be in place should problems arise and decisions need to be made (e.g., *reflection-post-action*). Projects should also be evaluated for replicability and scaling up (i.e., expanding the project scope and implementation toward a more significant impact within the community or other communities). Scalability in a complex and uncertain setting is challenging. Like many forms of behavior in systems, it emerges when the right conditions are in place and a "tipping point" has been reached. All parties involved in development projects can contribute to making the environment fertile for that tipping point to sprout and grow.

The ten stages of Figure 9.2 are not independent and form a *road map* from collecting data about the community landscape and the PSC nexus to developing an action plan to address issues raised by analyzing the data. Furthermore, feedback mechanisms are at play between the ten stages, as decisions made in any given stage may require a reassessment of those in previous ones. Unlike linear causality, this type of reciprocal causality provides a way to re-examine assumptions and acquire more information if necessary. It should be noted that the system modeling stage 5 described above represents a critical transition between understanding the community landscape and its issues and developing a support system necessary to decide on interventions across the PSC nexus at the community level.

Chapter 10 presents a series of system dynamics models that are useful in stages 5, 6, and 7 of the methodology presented above.

9.3   CONCLUDING REMARKS

Addressing complex human development and security issues and exploring the mutual interaction between development and the three sectors of the PSC nexus is not a random process. The methodology presented in this chapter provides a *learning roadmap* to address issues in each sector of the PSC nexus and across the nexus while considering how the sectors interact with the social, economic, environmental, and infrastructure community systems. Systems thinking is embedded in each step of the road map.

The learning roadmap of Figure 9.2 is practical for decision-makers working at a specific scale. It becomes more complicated if decisions are made across different development scales, from the individual to the community or regional scales. In that case, decisions made in each of the ten methodology stages at one scale, say a large scale, must be synchronized with those at more minor scales. This cross-decision-making is likely to be challenging.

REFERENCES

Amadei, B. (2015). *A systems approach to modeling community development projects.* Momentum Press.

Amadei, B. (2019). *A systems approach to modeling the water-energy-land-food nexus.* Vols. *I* and *II*. Momentum Press.

Caldwell, R. (2002). *Project design handbook.* Cooperative for Assistance and Relief Everywhere (CARE), Atlanta, GA. CARE's Project Design Handbook I Food Security and Nutrition Network (fsnnetwork.org)

Collaborative for Development Action (CDA). (2016). *Reflecting on peace practice (RPP) basics. A resource manual.* CDA Collaborative Learning Projects.

Delp, P., Thesen, A., Motiwalla, J., & Seshadri, N. (1977). *Systems tools for project planning.* International Development Institute.

Department for Communities and Local Government. (DCLG). (2009). *Multi-criteria analysis: A manual.* Communities and Local Government Publications, U.K. 1132618.pdf (publishing.service.gov.uk)

Flammini, A., Puri, M., Pluschke, L., & Dubois, O. (2014). *Walking the nexus talk: Assessing the water-energy-food nexus in the context of sustainable energy for all initiatives.* Environment and Natural Resources Working Paper No. 58, FAO, Rome. Walking the nexus talk: assessing the water-energy-food nexus in the context of the sustainable energy for all initiative (fao.org)

Global Water Partnership. (GWP). (2000). *Integrated water resources management.* TAC Background No 4 (gwp.org)

Grassroots Collective. (n.d.). Tools for Planning Community Development Projects | Grassroots Hub (thegrassrootscollective.org)

Hjorth, P., & Bagheri, A. (2006). Navigating towards sustainable development: A system dynamics approach. *Futures, 38,* 74–92.

Kehrer, K., Flossmann-Kraus, U., Ronco Alarcon, S. V., Albers, V., & Aschmann, G. (2020). Transforming our work: Getting ready for transformational projects. Deutsche Gesellschaft für Internationale Zusammenarbeit (GIZ), Bonn, Germany. Transformation Guidance_GIZ_02 2020.pdf

Moore, L. V. (2014). Resilience and conflict prevention in West Darfur. Summer 2014 Insights Newsletter - Resilience | United States Institute of Peace (usip.org)

Mowjee, T., Garrasi, D., & Poole, L. (2015). *Coherence in conflict: Bringing humanitarian and development aid streams together,* DANIDA, Ministry of Foreign Affairs of Denmark. coherence_in_conflict_web_1.pdf (humanitarianoutcomes.org)

OECD. (2017). *Humanitarian development coherence.* https://www.oecd.org/development/humanitarian-donors/docs/coherence-oecd-Guideline.pdf

Senge, P. (2006). *The fifth discipline: The art & practice of the learning organization.* Doubleday.

Seelos, C. (2020). Changing systems? Welcome to the slow movement. *Stanford Social Innovation Review, Winter,* 40–47.

Stroh, D. P. (2015). *Systems thinking for social change.* Chelsea Green Publishing.

The Omidyar Group. (2017). *Systems practice workbook.* Systems Practice Workbook - Observatory of Public Sector Innovation (oecd-opsi.org)

10 Illustrative Examples— Part 1

10.1 INTEGRATED CAPACITY ANALYSIS

As discussed in Chapter 5, capacity analysis is essential to determine the ability of community stakeholders to (i) reach specific goals such as recovering from conflict, absorbing displaced populations, handling crises and emergencies related to particular adverse events and hazards, and adapting and coping with climate change and (ii) provide services to community members to meet their basic needs such as water and sanitation, hygiene, food, shelter, transportation, education, health, telecommunication, the management of critical infrastructure, and the prevention of violence and injury. Capacity analysis is essential in stage 5 (i.e., modeling the landscape dynamics and its current capacity) and stage 6 (i.e., exploring intervention scenarios, including capacity building) of the methodology shown in Figure 9.2.

In this chapter, we consider, as an illustrative example, the seven capacity categories of the University of Virginia, Charlottesville (UVC) framework proposed by Bouabid and Louis (2015): institutional, human resources, technical resources, economic and financial, energy, environmental, and social–cultural capacity. Each category has context- and scale-specific requirements (see Table 5.4). The analysis presented in this chapter applies to other types of capacity frameworks.

Although the seven capacity categories likely depend on each other in community development, the UVC framework falls short of quantifying their interdependencies. Furthermore, the capacity categories are also assumed to be static. An integrated capacity analysis requires exploring the different capacity categories, their connections, and how they change over time. This section shows how to combine cross-impact analysis and system dynamics (SD) to capture such characteristics. It is assumed that all seven categories of capacity and their respective requirements are interconnected and contribute to the overall ability of a community to provide a specific service or reach a particular goal. The service might provide security, water, energy, food resources, transportation, telecommunication, health, etc. The goal might be to determine the capacity of a community to ensure sustainable peace, develop specific sustainable practices toward resource security, or guarantee climate security, or all three at the same time.

10.1.1 MAPPING CAPACITY INTERACTIONS

Before an integrated SD model of the capacity linkages can be created, it is essential to map how the seven capacity categories of the UVC framework interact when reaching a specific goal or providing some service. One way of doing so is to map their respective influence and dependence using the cross-impact analysis mentioned

TABLE 10.1

Cross-Impact Analysis Among Seven Categories of Capacity: Inst. (Institutional), HR (Human Resources), Tech. (Technical), Econ. (Economic/Financial), and Env. (Environmental)

	Inst.	HR	Tech.	Econ.	Energy	Env.	Social	Net Influence
Inst.	0	2	3	3	3	3	3	17
HR	1	0	3	3	1	1	2	11
Tech.	1	2	0	2	2	2	2	11
Econ.	2	2	2	0	3	3	3	15
Energy	1	2	2	3	0	2	3	13
Env.	1	0	3	2	2	0	3	8
Social	3	3	3	2	2	2	0	15
Net Dependence	9	11	13	15	13	13	16	90
Average Dependence	1.28	1.57	1.86	2.14	1.86	1.86	2.28	

Source: Amadei (2020), open-access journal.

in Section 6.3. Table 10.1 summarizes an example of a cross-impact matrix Amadei (2020) proposed.

In this example, semi-quantitative scores were assigned to describe the strength (*enabling influence*) between interacting categories of capacity, two at a time. The scores ranged between 0 for no influence, 1 for low enabling influence, 2 for medium enabling influence, and 3 for strong enabling influence. It should be noted that the scores in Table 10.1 are not associated with any actual case study, only guessed based on the author's experience with small-scale low-income communities such as the one in Morocco considered in Appendix B. Ideally, actual values (or a range of values) at the community level would have to be selected in a participatory manner by groups of stakeholders (see Figure 9.1) with different types of expertise during community appraisal as discussed in Chapter 5. Another remark about Table 10.1 is that it involves a high level of aggregation because, as discussed in Table 5.4, each capacity category contains multiple requirements whose interdependencies are not considered here.

Figure 10.1 shows how the different capacity categories plot on an influence-dependence diagram divided into four sectors. In this illustrative example, with high influence and low dependence (sector 1), the institutional capacity has higher leverage and dominance among all types of capacity for the considered service or goal. The high influence and dependence of social, economic, and energy capacity (sector 3) make these forms of capacity more challenging to address for the service or goal being considered because their influence and dependence cannot be separated through feedback mechanisms.

On the other side of the dependence versus influence spectrum in Figure 10.1 are the low-influence and high-dependence (sector 4) categories of capacity that are

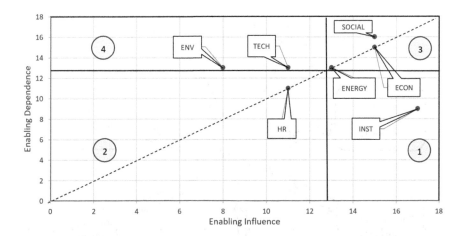

FIGURE 10.1 Graph showing the degrees of direct net influence and dependence for all seven categories of capacity: INST (Institutional), HR (Human Resources), TECH (Technical), ECON (Economic), ENERGY, ENV (Environmental), and SOCIAL (Social/Cultural). The graph consists of four sectors defined by the average values (12.85) of the net influence and dependence of Table 10.1.

Source: Amadei (2020), open-access journal.

the outputs of other capacity interactions. They include environmental capacity and technical capacity. Finally, the human resources capacity is in the low-influence and low-dependence sector 2 in Figure 10.1. As such, it does not seem as significant to the service delivery as the other capacity categories but should not be ignored. By being located on the first diagonal of Figure 10.1, the effect of the other seven capacity categories on HR is the same as that of HR on these types of capacity.

10.1.2 System Dynamics Analysis

Once the interaction between the seven capacity categories has been identified, a SD model can be created. The SD model of Figure 10.2 consists of seven satellite modules, one for each category of capacity considered in this example.

An interactive user interface of the SD model shown in Figure 10.2 can be found on the web.[1] Each module tracks how each capacity factor CF_i ($i = 1 - 7$), defined in eq. (5.1), changes with time, starting with an initial value, CF_{io}, and at a rate, dCF_i/dt. The central module in Figure 10.2 calculates the net influence and dependence scores of each capacity category (see Table 10.1). It also determines the community capacity assessment C_A defined by eq. (5.2) and relates it to some community capacity (development) level selected by the modeler (e.g., Table 5.5).

Figure 10.3 shows the *goal-seeking* structure of the technical capacity module; all other modules in Figure 10.2 have the same structure. The rate of change of the capacity factor is calculated as the product between (i) a basic adjustment rate, (ii) the gap between the current value of the capacity factor and the desired value

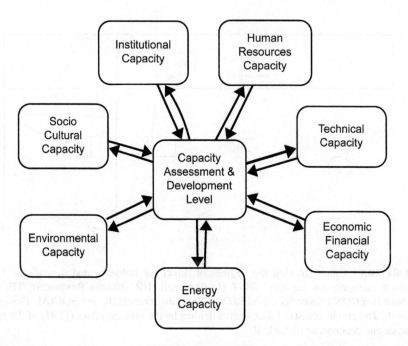

FIGURE 10.2 The SD capacity model consists of seven satellite modules and a central module.

Source: Amadei (2020), open-access journal.

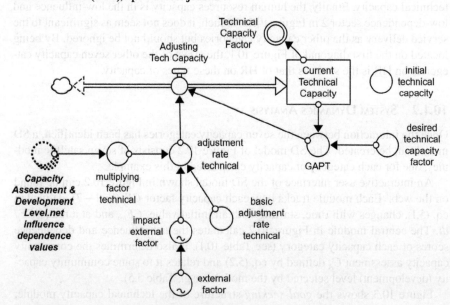

FIGURE 10.3 Stock and flow diagram of the technical capacity module.

Source: Amadei (2020), open-access journal.

to meet a goal or provide a service, (iii) a time-dependent external factor, and (iv) the average dependence (sensitivity) of each capacity factor on the other ones (see the bottom row in Table 10.1). A biflow is used in Figure 10.3 to account for possible increases or decreases in the capacity factor over time. The "external factor" converter varies between -4 (strong negative influence), 0 (neutral influence), and 4 (strong positive influence). Its impact varies between -0.5 and 2.5. For instance, a value of the external factor greater than one could be used to model the enabling influence of peace or climate security measures. A value less than one would capture the possible constraining impact of adverse events, such as climate change, conflict, etc., on each capacity category; a negative value could also be used to model a reduction in capacity.

As a numerical example, the SD capacity model was applied to the case study proposed by Bouabid and Louis (2015), which analyzes the capacity of a community in Morocco to provide wastewater and sewage treatment services. The input data for this example can be found in Appendix C. The initial values of the capacity factors, CF_{io}, were selected from the table in Appendix B; all desired capacity factors were taken equal to 100; and all basic capacity adjustment rates are equal to 0.01/ year. No adverse external events were considered. Figure 10.4 shows the variation of the community capacity assessment C_A and the community capacity (development) level CCL defined in Table 5.5 over 50 years. Without dependency between the capacity categories, C_A remains constant and equal to its initial value of 24. The community capacity level (CCL) is equal to 2 (i.e., only limited local services could be provided). If the capacity dependency is considered, the capacity assessment rises to a value of 64 over 50 years, and the community acquires the capacity to manage community-based systems ($CCL=3$) from years 12 to 41 and to serve multiple communities from a centralized system ($CCL=4$) until year 50. As the capacity of the community to provide a service increases, better technologies can be used to that effect (Ahmad, 2004).

Figure 10.4 shows that accounting for the enabling influence among the different capacity types in the analysis gives a more optimistic picture of how the community can quickly provide services. This conclusion is not surprising because all components in the double capacity matrix of Table 10.1 are enabling, and the "impact external factor" is constant and equal to 1. In the present formulation, the *enabling* influence increases the actual adjustment rates of all capacity categories even though their basic adjustment rates are constant.

For comparison, an additional capacity analysis was carried out to explore the constraining effect of an adverse event. The "external factor" is now equal to -3 and constant over 50 years for all capacity categories. Figure 10.5 shows the resulting reduction in the capacity assessment C_A from an initial value of 24 to 15 over 50 years. Likewise, the CCL decreases from 2 to 1 after 22 years. In other words, the community is losing its capacity to manage the service because of the ongoing adverse event.

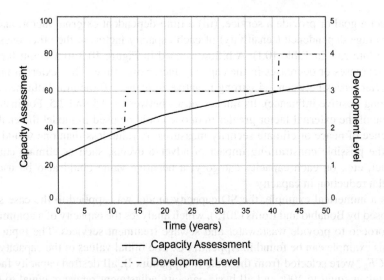

FIGURE 10.4   Capacity assessment and community capacity level over time.

Source: Amadei (2020), open-access journal.

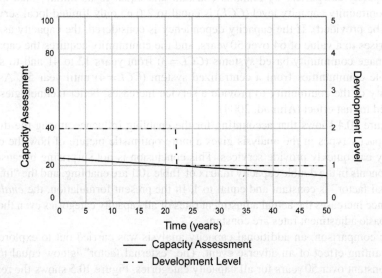

FIGURE 10.5   Variation of community capacity assessment and community capacity (development) level with time for a constraining environment.

Source: Amadei (2020), open-access journal.

10.1.3 REMARKS

The analysis presented above shows how soft and hard systems tools can be combined to explore the dynamic of community capacity and identify priorities in capacity building. A more detailed but challenging analysis would require considering the linkages between the requirements of the different capacity categories.

The above numerical examples show that adding the interdependence between the seven types of capacity proposed in the UVC framework when identifying the weakest capacity C_A and level of development CCL can account for possible enabling and constraining factors affecting every capacity type. The numerical examples show that an enabling influence between the capacity types gives a more optimistic perspective of what the community can handle over time. On the other hand, any constraining influence is more pessimistic. Additional numerical examples could be run where the influence scores between capacity types in Table 10.1 change in time and vary between positive enabling and negative constraining values. This dynamic can be explored using the user interfaces of the models available on the web.

The approach presented above is also limited to one type of service or goal. It becomes more challenging when several interdependent types of service need to be provided or goals met simultaneously. In that case, the community capacity assessment C_A needs to be determined first for each service or goal of interest while considering various forms of influence and dependence among the categories of capacity supporting that service or contributing to the goal (Table 10.1). In doing so, there is no guarantee that the same capacity category would be the limiting factor for all services or goals and that the corresponding CCLs would be the same. For instance, a community may manage relatively well community-based water supply systems ($CCL = 3$). Yet it might not manage telecom, transportation services, or climate security adaptation and mitigation ($CCL = 1$) due to a different type of limited capacity.

Furthermore, in other cases, managing one type of service well or meeting a goal may directly or indirectly affect delivering a different service or meeting another purpose. Hence, this dilemma requires trade-offs by decision-makers. An example would be prioritizing water resources for electricity production instead of agriculture or vice versa. Likewise, the community may decide on peace-building and climate security efforts that could negatively affect community development and livelihood.

Accounting for all the linkages at play in providing multiple services or reaching some goals at the community level requires policymakers and practitioners to adopt advanced systems-based decision-making. One approach would be determining the limiting capacity, C_A, and CCL, for each type of service or goal. The service or goal with the lowest CCL value is first addressed (leverage point) by considering its dependence and influence on the other service types and other community-related limiting factors. Another approach would be to conduct a cross-impact analysis for all services or goals combined. Consider, for instance, two services that depend on the same seven capacity categories. The integrated cross-impact matrix for both interconnected services would be (14×14) in size. Two interrelated stock and flow diagrams, like Figure 10.2, would have to be created per service of interest.

Regardless of the multi-service or goal approach, deciding which service or goal and which capacity to address first will impact the choice of community interventions (technical or non-technical). Over time, any change in community capacity creates changes in the range of interventions to provide the service or meet the goal. When considering several service types or goals, the different interventions must be coordinated, preferably synergistically, and not create unintended consequences for each other.

10.2   FROM CAPACITY TO RESILIENCE

Community resilience is closely related to capacity building, as resilience requires capacity. The higher the initial capacity of the community, the more resilient the community is likely to cope and adapt over time when faced with adverse events. Both capacity and resilience are critical in preventing a decline in human development and security, descending into crises and conflict, avoiding socioeconomic instability, and adapting to climate change. According to the NRC (2012), resilience is defined as "the ability [of individuals, groups, communities] to prepare and plan for, absorb, recover from, or more successfully adapt to [actual or potential] adverse events." Resilience in community development is often described as an *acquired capacity* to cope with and adapt to various forms of stress and shock associated with adverse natural and non-natural events of different intensities. According to Folke (2016), resilience is about "cultivating the capacity to sustain development in the face of expected and surprising change and diverse pathways of development and potential thresholds between them."

Regardless of the initial level of acquired capacity, events will likely reverse some community development progress, which may have been built over several years or decades. Services, such as water, energy, food supply, transportation, telecommunication, and security, may be reduced quickly due to adverse events and take a long time to be back in operation. To illustrate that statement, let's consider Figure 10.6, which shows how the overall capacity of a community $C(t)$ to provide multiple services or reach some goals varies with time following an adverse event or stressor.

Immediately after the event, the overall community capacity drops from its initial value of C_o to a lower level of C_{min} at time t_{min}. The drop's magnitude and rate depend

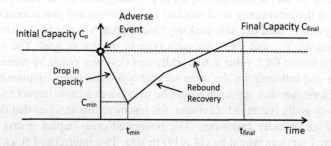

FIGURE 10.6   Variation of community capacity following a disaster or crisis, not to scale.

Source: Amadei (2020), open-access journal.

on many factors, such as the severity of the stressor, its duration, and its surprising effect on the community. If some capacity-building measures are available, the decline is followed by some response and several periods of recovery (new normal conditions), coping, and adaptation, which hopefully leads, after a certain amount of time t_{final}, to a final capacity C_{final} larger than the initial one. This value becomes the new initial community-acquired capacity for the next event. The ratio C_{final}/C_o could be interpreted as a possible measure of resilience.

The initial community capacity affects, to a great extent, the size of the immediate capacity drop, the recovery time, and the recovery rate dC/dt. The larger the initial acquired capacity C_o (i.e., the more resilient the community is initially) and the better prepared a community is with its awareness, adaptation, and mitigation plans, the lower the drop, the faster the recovery, and the steeper the rebound. In developing societies, where the initial resilience (acquired capacity) is usually insufficient to start with, the drop in capacity will likely be significant, the time to recover will be extensive, and the rebound rate will be low, flat, or even negative. In that case, the response curve in Figure 10.6 must not go below minimum standards (The Sphere Project, 2018).

Other factors besides the initial capacity level may control the curve's overall shape in Figure 10.6. They include the risk of secondary disasters, the clarity of policy and direction, collective motivation, good communications, technical assistance, the availability of funds to reboot the economy, cash flow, and the reusing of salvaged material, among others.

It should be noted, however, that even though a community may possess all the positive attributes of peace-building, adaptation and mitigation, preparedness, response, and recovery, it is likely that the recovery part of Figure 10.6 may consist of a series of up and down "new normal" conditions, especially when faced with unusual events (Norris et al., 2008). Furthermore, a community may show all the resilience signs, yet some parts may be more prepared than others. The opposite is true, as some community parts may be resilient, yet the entire community is not. Like capacity, resilience is scale (physical and temporal) and context-dependent.

Figure 10.7 shows a SD stock and flow diagram that attempts to reproduce the dynamic of Figure 10.6. It consists of two (7×1) arrayed stocks: a base capacity and a built capacity. Each stock represents how the seven types of capacity (measured in capacity units, cu) considered herein change with time (in months), starting from some initial values. Following an event at time $t = 0$ and before capacity building even begins, all seven types of *base capacity* are assumed to drop exponentially at a specific rate (per unit of time), which can be constant, time-dependent, or dependent on the initial base capacity value. This trend simulates how a community quickly loses capacity without any capacity-building interventions. Examples would be decreasing security as a conflict persists or the impact of climate change without community adaptation or mitigation measures in place.

For each capacity type, *capacity building* starts at a time selected by the user. It is defined in Figure 10.7 by a (7×1) array "capacity-building starting time" expressed in the present example in fractions of a month following the event. The capacity-building interventions start at different times. The total capacity is the sum of the decreasing base capacity and the increasing built capacity at any given time.

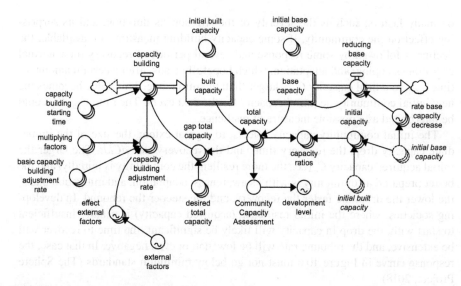

FIGURE 10.7   Stock and flow system dynamics representation of the dynamic of Figure 10.6.

Source: Amadei (2020), open-access journal.

For each capacity type, the built capacity is assumed to increase at a rate that is the product between a basic capacity-building adjustment rate and the difference between desired and current total capacity. The rate is the product of a basic value and a multiplying factor equal to the average dependence (sensitivity) of each capacity factor on the others (see the bottom row of Table 10.1). A converter, "external factors," plays the same role as in Figure 10.3 and could account for the enabling or constraining effect of time-dependent beneficial or adverse events on the seven types of capacity building.

An interactive user interface of the SD model shown in Figure 10.7 can be found on the web.[2] A numerical example was conducted with the input data listed in Appendix C. Figure 10.8 shows the variation of the community capacity assessment C_A (weakest capacity type) and community development level CCL over six years (72 months) for the wastewater and sewage service input data listed in Appendix B and Table 10.1. As recovery occurs, the community can manage more sophisticated community-based systems, because its level of development varies from not initially having the capacity to manage the service (level 1) to managing community-based systems (level 3) after about 40 months.

Figure 10.9 shows the variation of the ratios between the current total capacities and their initial values with time. These ratios can be interpreted as a measure of resilience for each capacity category. Not all types of capacity recover at the same time. In this example, the social–cultural and environmental capacities take longer (48 months) for the capacity ratios to reach a value of 1.

A final scenario considers the impact of an additional external event between months 30 and 40. During that interval, the "external factors" converter in Figure 10.7

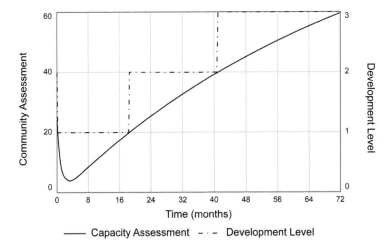

FIGURE 10.8 Variation of community capacity assessment and community development over 72 months (six years), assuming capacity dependency and an enabling environment.

Source: Amadei (2020), open-access journal.

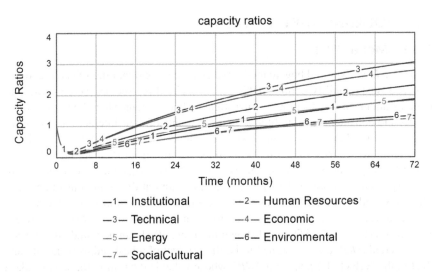

FIGURE 10.9 Variation of the current and initial capacity ratio for all seven capacity types over 72 months (six years).

Source: Amadei (2020), open-access journal.

equals −4 for all seven capacity types. Figure 10.10 shows the variation in the community capacity assessment and community development level over 72 months. Compared to Figure 10.8, the external event impacts the development level, which drops from 2 to 1 and increases to 2 following the impact.

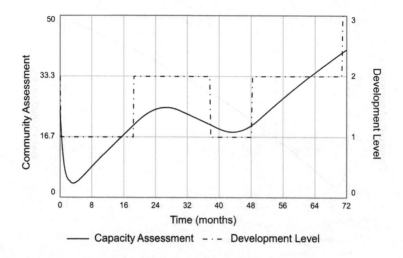

FIGURE 10.10 Variation of community capacity assessment and community development over 72 months (six years), assuming capacity dependency and an adverse event between months 30 and 40.

10.3   MODELING THE PSC NEXUS

10.3.1   MODEL PSC1

In Chapter 7, we explored how to model the goal-seeking dynamics of each sector of the peace–sustainability–climate (PSC) nexus. The three sectors were assumed to be independent. In this section, we investigate what happens when the three sectors interact and consider semi-qualitative measurements of their interaction. As shown in Figure 10.11, there are now three stocks defined as P (peace), S (sustainability), and C (climate security) that vary with time, starting from their initial values P_o, S_o, and C_o, respectively. The three states, $P(t)$, $S(t)$, and $C(t)$, adjust over time toward their respective desirable values DP, DS, and DC and at different adjustment rates ARP, ARS, and ARC. The current state of each sector is assumed to influence the adjustment rates of the other two (e.g., ~ effect of P on ARC and ARS). An interactive user interface of the SD model shown in Figure 10.11 can be found on the web.[3]

The actual ARP rate is assumed to be the product of a basic adjustment rate and a factor, the "effect of S and C on ARP," whose value is the minimum (e.g., weakest link) between the effect of the current sustainability and climate security states on peace. Likewise, the actual ARS rate is assumed to be the product of a basic rate and a factor, the "effect of P and C on S," whose value is the minimum between the effect of the current peace and climate security states on sustainability. Finally, the actual ARC rate is assumed to be the product of a basic rate and a factor, the "effect of P and S on C," whose value is the minimum between the effect of the current peace and sustainability on climate security. The three adjustment rates also depend on some "external factors" to account for the enabling or constraining effect of specific time-dependent beneficial or adverse events on peace, sustainability, and climate security.

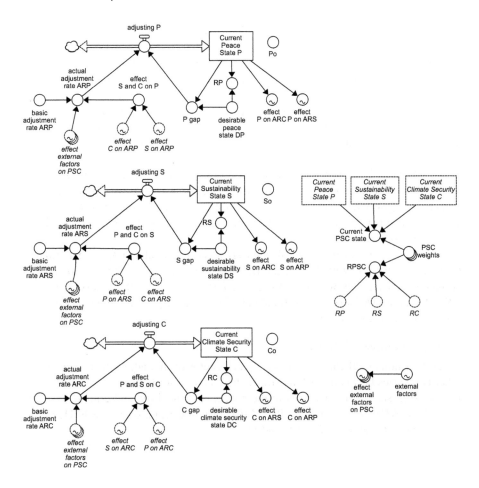

FIGURE 10.11 A stock and flow diagram accounts for the interdependence between the three sectors of the PSC nexus.

In Figure 10.11, the change of the stock, *P*, over time ("adjusting *P*") is equal to

$$\frac{dP}{dt} = ARP \times (DP - P) \tag{10.1}$$

Likewise, the change of the stock, *S*, over time ("adjusting *S*") is equal to

$$\frac{dS}{dt} = ARS \times (DS - S) \tag{10.2}$$

Likewise, the change of the stock, *C*, over time ("adjusting *C*") is equal to

$$\frac{dC}{dt} = ARC \times (DC - C) \tag{10.3}$$

Solving these three nonlinear first-order differential equations with (P_o, S_o, C_o) as initial conditions would give an expression for $P(t)$, $S(t)$, and $C(t)$ if we knew the functional forms of *ARP*, *ARS*, and *ARC* and the different functions (~) in Figure 10.11. The three biflows in Figure 10.11 capture possible increases or decreases in each stock. Each state may decrease, for instance, if the adjusting rate becomes negative. In that case, the peace, sustainability, or climate security states would degrade over time. Figure 10.11 also determines the weighted average "current PSC state" and ratio *RPSC* of the peace, sustainability, and climate security states.

As in Chapter 7, we will assume that (P, DP), (S, DS), and (C, DC) can be expressed respectively in generic peace units (pu), sustainability units (su), and climate security units (cu) ranging over some [0–100] scales (Table 7.1). These units are *arbitrary* and are introduced here as semi-quantitative adequate measures of peace, sustainability, and climate security.

As an illustrative example, an SD analysis was carried out assuming that initially (i) peace is very low with $P_o = 20$ pu; (ii) sustainability is low with $S_o = 30$ su; (iii) climate security is low with $C_o = 50$ cu; (iv) $DP = DS = DC = 100$; and (v) the basic *ARP*, *ARS*, and *ARC* = 0.01/year. Input data for the subsequent three numerical runs can be found in Appendix C.

10.3.1.1 Numerical Run 1

In the first numerical run, the effect of each sector on the adjustment rates of the other two varies between −0.2 and 1.2 as the sector varies between 0 and 100 units. Figure 10.12 shows the increases in the peace, sustainability, and climate security ratios $RP = P/DP$, $RS = S/DS$, and $RC = C/DC$ over 100 years. In Figure 10.11, *RPSC* is the weighted average of *RP*, *RS*, and *RC*.

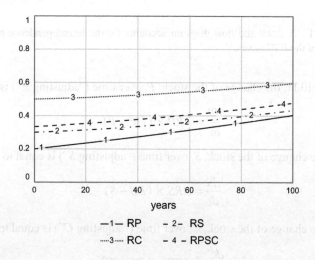

FIGURE 10.12 Variation of $RP = P/DP$, $RS = S/DS$, $RC = C/DC$, and *RPSC* over 100 years.

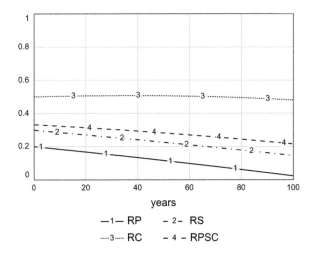

—1— RP   – 2– RS
·····3····· RC   – 4 – RPSC

FIGURE 10.13 Variation of $RP = P/DP$, $RS = S/DS$, $RC = C/DC$, and $RPSC$ over 100 years demonstrating the unintended consequences of climate practices on sustainability and peace.

10.3.1.2 Numerical Run 2

The second numerical example simulates the negative effect of climate security on peace and sustainability. The effect of climate security on ARS and ARP has a constant value of -0.2 to simulate some unintended constraining consequences of climate practices on sustainability and peace. The corresponding variation of $RP = P/DP$, $RS = S/DS$, and $RC = C/DC$ over time is shown in Figure 10.13. Because of the causal links between sustainability, peace, and climate security, all three states decrease from low to very low values.

10.3.1.3 Numerical Run 3

A final scenario considers the effects of the time-dependent external factors on one or several adjustment rates. For instance, let's assume that some conflict arises between years 20 and 50, during which the external factors converter in Figure 10.11 is equal to -4. Figure 10.14 shows that the conflict affects all three states with no recovery after year 60.

10.3.2 Model PSC2

The three P, S, and C stocks are arrayed with several components, as shown in Figure 10.15. All components can have different desirable states, initial values, and adjustment rates. They can be expressed in generic peace units (pu), sustainability units (su), and climate security units (cu), ranging over a [0–100] scale. The scale can be broken down into several achievement-level groups for each component using a semi-quantitative rating scale, similar to that in Table 7.1.

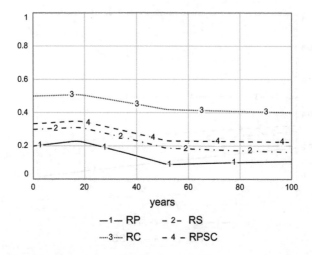

FIGURE 10.14   Variation of $RP = P/DP$, $RS = S/DS$, $RC = C/DC$, and $RPSC$ over 100 years demonstrating the unintended consequences of conflict between years 20 and 50.

Three peace sectors P_i ($i = 1 - 3$) (e.g., positive, negative, and cultural peace) are assumed to interact with four sustainability sectors S_i ($i = 1 - 4$) (e.g., people, planet, prosperity, and partnerships) and two climate security sectors C_i ($i = 1 - 2$) (e.g., adaptation and mitigation). In Figure 10.15, layered stocks represent the current peace, sustainability, and climate security states as three-, four-, and two-dimensional arrays. An interactive user interface of the SD model shown in Figure 10.14 can be found on the web.[4]

Compared to Figure 10.11, the converters "~effect P on ARS" and "~effect P on ARC" are now 3×4 and 3×2 functions that describe the effect of positive, negative, and cultural peace on the four sustainability and the two climate security adjustment rates. The average effects of the three components of peace P on ARS and ARC are determined.

The same approach is used for the converters "~effect S on ARP" and "~effect S on ARC," which are 4×3 and 4×2 functions that describe the effect of people, planet, prosperity, and partnerships on the three peace and two climate security adjustment rates. The average effects of the four components of sustainability S on ARP and ARC are determined.

Finally, the converters "~effect C on ARP" and "~effect C on ARS" are 2×3 and 2×4 functions that describe the effect of the two climate security components on the three peace and four sustainability adjustment rates. The average effects of the two components of climate security C on ARS and ARP are determined.

The actual adjustment rates ARP_i ($i = 1 - 3$) for each peace sector P_i are calculated as the product between the basic peace adjustment rates and a 3×1 "effect external factors on peace," the effect S and C on ARP, whose values are the minimum (e.g., weakest link) between the effect of the current sustainability and climate security states on peace. Likewise, the actual adjustment rates ARS_i ($i = 1 - 4$) for each

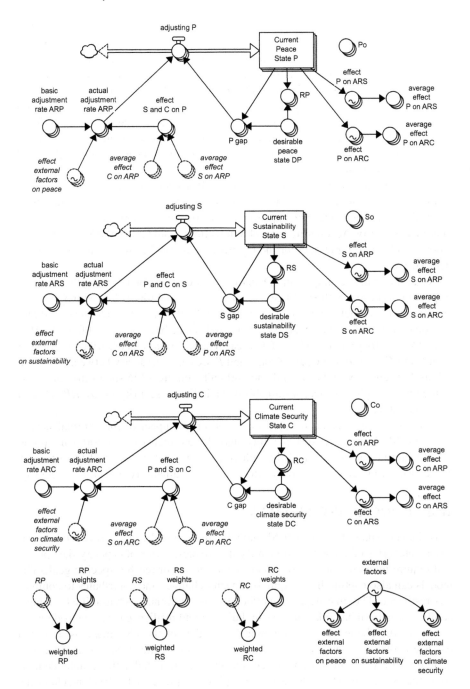

FIGURE 10.15 SD model of the *PSC* nexus. Three sectors of peace, four sectors of sustainability, and two sectors of climate security are considered.

sustainability sector S_i are calculated as the product between the basic sustainability adjustment rates and a 4×1 "effect external factors on sustainability," the effect P and C on S, whose value is the minimum between the effect between the current peace and climate security states on sustainability. The actual adjustment rates ARC_i ($i = 1 - 2$) for each climate security sector C_i are calculated as the product between the basic climate security adjustment rates and a 2×1 "effect external factors on climate security," the effect of P and S on C, whose value is the minimum between the effect of the current peace and sustainability on climate security. Figure 10.14 also determines the weighted RP, RS, and RC ratios of the peace, sustainability, and climate security states.

It should be noted that the model of Figure 10.15 does not account for the interaction among the four dimensions that define the state of sustainability, the three dimensions that define the state of peace, and the two dimensions that define the state of climate security. Accounting for such interactions would make the SD model even more complicated. Input data for the following numerical example can be found in Appendix C.

As an illustrative example, an SD analysis was carried out assuming that initially (i) peace is very low with P_o (40, 30, 30 pu); (ii) sustainability is low with S_o (60, 40, 30, 20 su); (iii) climate security is low with C_o (60, 40 cu); (iv) all DP_i, DS_i, and DC_i are equal to 100 pu, su, and cu, respectively; and (v) the basic $ARP_i = 0.003/0.02/0.01/$year, $ARS_i = 0.01$/year, and $ARC_i = 0.04$/year. The functions that describe the effect of P on S and C, S on P and C, and C on S and P are linear and vary between -0.2 and 1.2, as P, S, and C vary between 0 and 100 units. Figure 10.16 shows the variations of the three weighted peace, sustainability, and climate security ratios, RP, RS, and RC, over 100 years.

Two cases are considered based on the level of impact of the external factors in Figure 10.15 on peace, sustainability, and climate security over 100 years: (a) no effect (external factors $= 0$) and (b) high constraining effect (external factors $= -3$). The constraining factors negatively affect peace, sustainability, and climate security.

10.4 CONCLUDING REMARKS

This chapter explored how simple SD models can capture the interaction between different categories of capacity and identify the weakest forms of capacity (i.e., places that require intervention first to provide some service or reach a specific goal). The models can also capture how acquired capacity changes and contributes to community resilience. The time-dependent effect of adverse events, such as climate change, conflict, or natural hazards, on capacity building and resilience is also considered.

One of the challenges of developing SD models of the PSC nexus is finding a balance between simplicity and a realistic depiction of the structural mechanisms underlying the problem being analyzed. The models presented in this chapter demonstrate that SD models do not have to be complex to capture the feedback mechanisms between the three sectors of the PSC nexus.

A significant challenge in all the SD models is keeping models simple and comprehensive at the same time without considering too many details that could lead to "paralysis in analysis." Another challenge related to the previous one is finding data

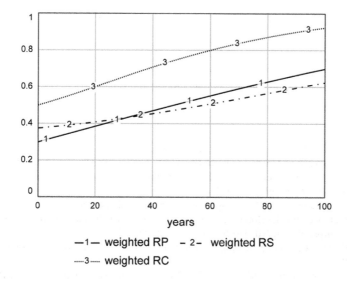

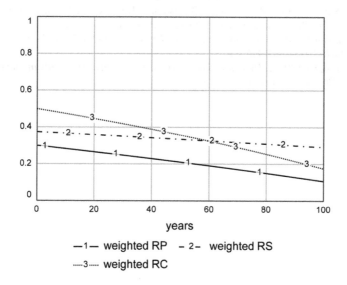

FIGURE 10.16 Variations of the three weighted peace, sustainability, and climate security ratios, *RP*, *RS*, and *RC*, over 100 years: 10.16.a, no external effects; 10.16.b, high constraining external effects.

sources to estimate the model parameters and their linkages. The PSC models presented in this chapter are generic and can be used to conduct parametric studies on how changes in one sector of the nexus could impact other sectors. The models use fictitious units to semi-quantify changes that need to be backed up with metrics. Chapter 11 will explore how to model the PSC nexus dynamics as it interacts with community systems.

NOTES

1 https://exchange.iseesystems.com/public/bernardamadei/capacity
2 https://exchange.iseesystems.com/public/bernardamadei/resilience-capacity
3 https://exchange.iseesystems.com/public/bernardamadei/psc1
4 https://exchange.iseesystems.com/public/bernardamadei/psc2

REFERENCES

Ahmad, T. T. (2004). *A classification tool for selecting sanitation service options in lower-income communities*. MS dissertation, University of Virginia, Charlottesville, VA, USA.

Amadei, B. (2020). A systems approach to community capacity and resilience. *Challenges*, *11*(2), 28. https://doi.org/10.3390/challe11020028

Bouabid, M., & Louis, G. (2015). Capacity factors for evaluating water and sanitation infrastructure choices for developing communities. *Journal Environmental Management*, *161*, 335–343. https://doi.org/10.1016/j.jenvman.2015.07.012

Folke, C. (2016). Resilience. *Ecology and Society*, *21*(4), 44. https://www.jstor.org/stable/26269991

National Research Council. (NRC). (2012). *Disaster resilience: A national imperative*. The National Academies Press. https://doi.org/10.17226/13457

Norris, F., Stevens, S.P., Pfefferbaum, B., Wyche, K.F., & Pfefferbaum, R.L. (2008). Community resilience as a metaphor, theory, set of capacities, and strategy for disaster readiness. *American Journal of Community Psychology*, *41*(1-2), 127–150. https://doi.org/10.1007/s10464-007-9156-6

The Sphere Project. (2018). *Humanitarian charter and minimum standards in humanitarian response*. Practical Action Publ.

11 Illustrative Examples – Part 2

11.1 INTRODUCTION

As emphasized in Chapter 2, peace, sustainability, and climate security are interdependent states that emerge from the interaction of multiple systems in community development. At the same time, these three states affect community systems through various feedback mechanisms. Simply put, the three PSC nexus sectors (and their opposites) are *entangled* and cannot be modeled in isolation (i.e., decoupled) and independently from the community landscape and the multiple systems with which they interact. This chapter explores how to model that entanglement using system dynamics tools.

The two PSC models (PSC1 and PSC2) presented in Chapter 10 were self-contained. They assumed that the three nexus sectors interacted and could be evaluated semi-quantitatively using arbitrary peace units, sustainability units, and climate security units ranging over a [0–100] scale (Table 7.1). Using this approach in practice requires metrics to describe each level of achievement as was done, for instance, with the ISI project sustainability framework discussed in Section 2 (see Table 2.3). The two PSC models in Chapter 10 also assumed that the interactions between the three states could be expressed in functional forms.

The three models, PSC3, PSC4, and PSC5, presented in this chapter differ from those in the previous one as they go deeper into modeling how the three sectors of the PSC nexus interact with some of the systems involved in the community landscape of Figure 5.1. The models use the STELLA Architect (version 3.2) platform's unique feature to capture interactions between variables using user-specified equations or converters with built-up graphical functions.

11.2 EXAMPLE 1—MODEL PSC3

The stock and flow diagram of the first example is shown in Figure 11.1. It captures, in an aggregated manner, the dynamics at play between a population and the community resources upon which it depends for livelihood. These two variables are dynamic and are impacted by the state of the community, which may vary over time. Model PSC3 can be run using the online interactive user interface on the web.[1]

The "PSC module" in Figure 11.1 incorporates the model of Figure 10.11 and determines the values of the peace, sustainability, and climate security states starting from their initial values. The overall "state of the community" is the weighted average of the peace (P), sustainability (S), and climate security (C) states. The three states are assumed to be interdependent and change toward some desired states.

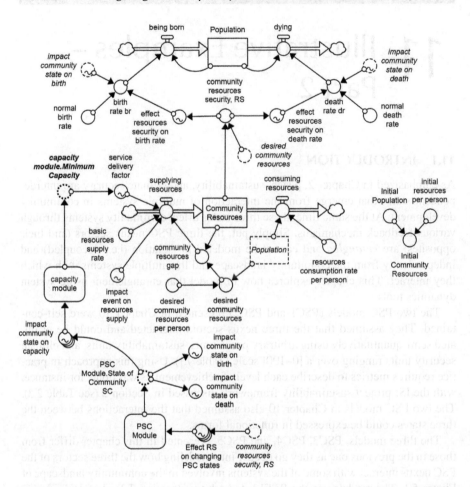

FIGURE 11.1 Dynamics at play between a population and the community resources it depends on for its livelihood.

Figure 11.2 shows the peace component of the PSC module only; the sustainability and climate security states have the same dynamics.

The state of the community and the states of peace, sustainability, and climate security vary over a spectrum ranging from 0 (most constraining) to 100 (most enabling). They can be divided into levels with 10 or 20 units each, as shown in Table 11.1.

Births add to the population (a reinforcing loop) and create a compounding (exponential growth) behavior. Likewise, deaths decrease the population size (a balancing loop) and create a draining (exponential decline) behavior. The overall increase or decrease in the population depends on the birth and death rates, their relative values, and the current population size. In the population part of the stock and flow diagram, the dominant loop dictates the population's behavior—growth or decay.

The dynamic of the population in Figure 11.1 can be expressed in a mathematical form as follows. Let $P(t)$ be the population variable (with an initial value P_o), and *br*

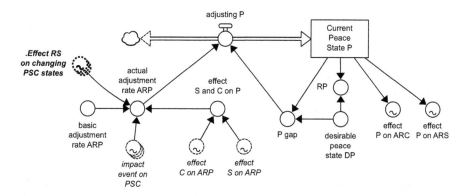

FIGURE 11.2 Dynamics of the peace state component of the PSC module.

TABLE 11.1

The State of the Community Ranges from Most Constraining to Most Enabling Regarding Peace (P), Sustainability (S), and Climate Security (C)

Ranking	State of Community	P, S, or C are
0–20	Most constraining	Unlikely
20–40	Constraining – reducing	Possible but restricted
40–50	Constraining – limiting	Possible but limited
50–60	Enabling – allowing	Possible and allowed
60–80	Enabling – supporting	Possible and supported
80–100	Most enabling	Likely

---

and *dr* are the birth and death rates, respectively. The change in the population with time is equal to

$$\frac{dP}{dt} = (br - dr)P. \tag{11.1}$$

Both *br* and *dr* depend on the value of the *community resources security* ratio, *RS*, between the current amount of community resources and the desired amount. This ratio varies between 0 and 1. Built-up graphical functions (~) defined as the "effect of resources security on birth and death rate" are used in Figure 11.1 to model the possible effect of resource security on the growth or decay of the population. The "impact community state on birth and death" are functions that simulate the time-dependent enabling or constraining influence of the state of the community (i.e., peace vs. conflict, sustainability vs. unsustainability, climate security vs. vulnerability) on birth and death.

In the community resources part of Figure 11.1, the resources are assumed to be supplied at a specific rate by some unspecified processes. The consumption rate of the resources depends on the population size and the consumption rate per person. The population is seeking a desired level of available resources per person.

The dynamic of the community resources can be expressed mathematically as follows: Let $R(t)$ be the community resources state variable. Its initial value is equal to R_o. Let a denote the rate of "supplying resources," and b represent the rate of "consuming resources" (the product of population and resources consumption rate per person). Finally, let K denote the desired resources (i.e., the product of the population and the desired resources per person) assumed to be larger than R. Accordingly, the rate of change of R is equal to:

$$\frac{dR}{dt} = a(K - R) - b. \tag{11.2}$$

The "supplying resources" rate in Figure 11.1 depends on a "basic resources supply rate" and a "service delivery factor" related to the community's capacity (or ability) to provide the resources. The capacity module in Figure 11.1 contains the seven capacity types shown in Figure 10.2 and accounts for their mutual interactions as described in Table 6.3.

The capacity module shown in Figure 11.3 determines the "minimum capacity" for resource delivery (i.e., C_A defined in eq. (5.2)). The service delivery factor in Figure 11.1 varies between 0 and 1.2 as the minimum capacity varies between 0 (no capacity) and 100 (total capacity) (i.e., from no capacity to full capacity of providing resources to the population). The impact of the state of the community on each capacity category is accounted for using build-up functions. The impact varies non-linearly between −2 and +2 as the state of the community varies between 0 and 100 (see Table 11.1).

An overall feedback structure is at play in the model. In the PSC module (Figure 11.2), the rates of change of peace, sustainability, and climate security depend on the value of the resource security factor, RS. The rates increase with the community resources security level. The rates also depend on the time-dependent impact of possible events, such as crises, wars, or climate change effects (e.g., droughts, floods, and heatwaves). The converter "impact event on resources supply" in Figure 11.1

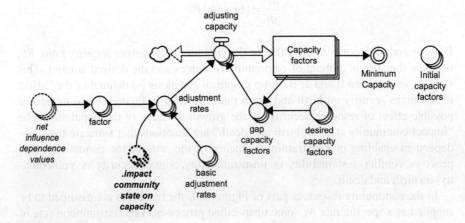

FIGURE 11.3   Details of the capacity module.

accounts for the impact of such events on the supply of resources. Events may trigger changes in the community from peace to conflict, sustainability to unsustainability, or climate security to vulnerability. Events may also impact the supply of resources, impacting peace, sustainability, and climate security. Or both dynamics could happen simultaneously.

The two differential equations (11.1) and (11.2) can be solved for $P(t)$ and $R(t)$ using the STELLA system dynamics software (version 3.2). The mathematical alternative would be to solve the two nonlinear first-order differential equations analytically, which is not trivial.

Input data for an illustrative example of the application of the PSC3 model can be found in Appendix D. Figure 11.4 shows the variation of the community resources security, RS, the population, P, and the average state of the community, SC, over 50 years for four initial levels of the P, S, and C states ranging between 20 and 80. The desired P, S, and C states are equal to 100. In this example, the community state is assumed to impact the *institutional capacity* only. This limited impact was selected since, according to Figure 10.3, the institutional capacity influences most other capacity types in the present example. Figure 11.4 shows some delays before the effect of a change in the community state on the security of the resources is felt. As the initial values of peace, sustainability, and climate security states increase, the community resources security, population, and the community state increase with time.

The model of Figure 11.1 assumes that the resources and their supplying process are aggregated. This limitation could be overcome by introducing, for instance, a chain of stocks and flows describing the different steps in the supplying process. In the case of water supply, for example, the steps would include source, procurement, storage, treatment, distribution, and disposal of wastewater. In the food sector, the steps would range from the production of crops and livestock raising to food consumption and waste disposal. The impact of the state of the community is likely to differ for each step.

11.3   EXAMPLE 2—MODEL PSC4

The stock and flow diagram for this second example is shown in Figure 11.5. It explores the dynamic between a population and some of the finite resources it depends on for livelihood, such as water, energy, and food/agriculture. These three resources depend on each other as part of a WEF nexus dynamic (Amadei, 2019). The SD model of Figure 11.5 consists of four modules, one module for the population and three interacting modules for the resources.

Figure 11.6 shows the population module. Its dynamic is described by eq. (11.1). The birth rate (*br*) and death rate (*dr*) depend on an overall *community resources security* (*RS*), which is now the weighted average of three resources securities (current resources amount/desired resources amount). It varies between zero and one. Built-up graphical functions (~) defined as the "effect resources security on birth and death" are used in Figure 11.6 to model the possible effect of the overall community

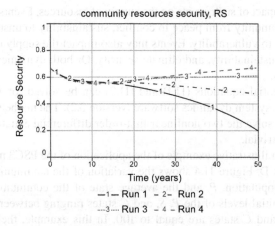

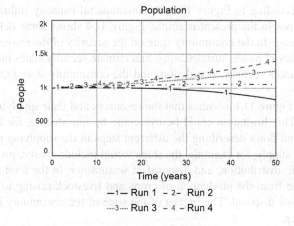

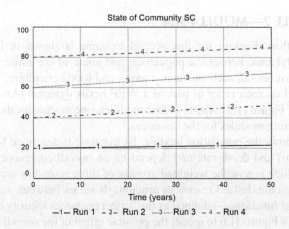

FIGURE 11.4 Variation of community resources security, RS, population, and community state, SC, with time for four initial and equal levels of P, S, and C states: Run 1 (20), Run 2 (40), Run 3 (60), Run 4 (80).

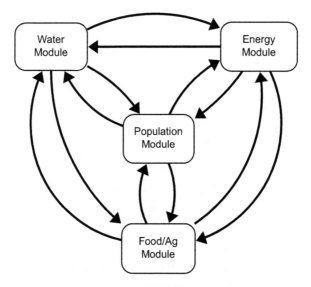

FIGURE 11.5 Modular stock and flow diagram showing the dynamic between a population and three types of interacting resources upon which it depends.

resources security on the growth or decay of the population. Model PSC4 can be run using the online interactive user interface on the web.[2]

As in the previous example, the overall state of the community is calculated in the PSC module and is the weighted average of the peace, sustainability, and climate security states starting from some initial values. The three states depend on the community resources security, *RS*. The converters "impact community state on water, food, and energy" are introduced in the water, energy, and food capacity modules as in Figure 11.3.

Figure 11.7 shows a detailed representation of the food module; the other two resource modules have the same structure. The capacity analysis is carried out for each resource type using the model in Figure 11.3. A minimum capacity is identified, and a service delivery factor is calculated. The service delivery factor varies between 0 and 1.2 as the minimum capacity varies between 0 (no capacity) and 100 (total capacity) (i.e., from no capacity to full capacity of providing each resource to the population.) An "impact event on food supply" converter is included to account for the effect of a possible event on supplying food, affecting the water, energy security, and the community state. The resource dynamic is described using three interdependent differential equations like eq. (11.2).

The interactions between water, energy, food, and land are included using converters such as "effect of...on..." in each module of Figure 11.5. The following interactions are considered: (i) the effect of water resources on producing energy and food and (ii) the effect of energy resources on producing water and food. Energy consumption depends on the energy demand per person and the water and food demands. Similarly, water consumption depends on the water demand per person and the food and energy demands. Finally, food resource consumption depends on the population's needs. If necessary, other direct and indirect interactions between sectors could be considered and added to the model.

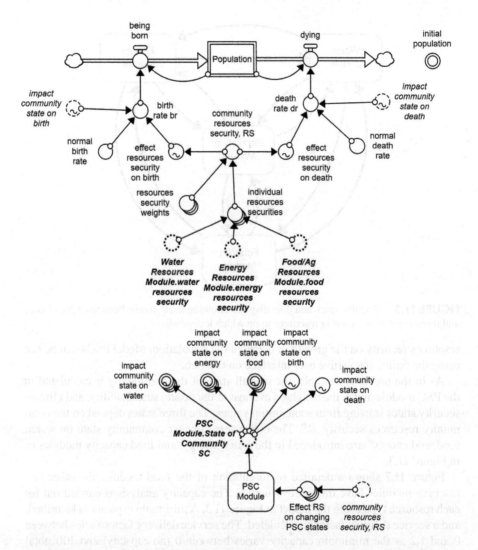

FIGURE 11.6 Population module and calculation of the community resources security.

The model could be expanded further to include, for instance, how different consumptions of water, energy, land, and food resources (e.g., domestic, agricultural, and industrial/commercial) affect each other and interact with the population. For instance, household water consumption may be further broken down into drinking, cleaning, laundry, flushing toilets, and washing. Likewise, agricultural water consumption could be broken down into water consumption for specific crop and livestock types. Finally, industrial/commercial water consumption could be divided into consumptions in the so-called take-make-waste industrial process.

In summary, this model provides a way to capture the dynamic of how (i) three types of resources contribute to population birth and death, (ii) population growth or decay affects the consumption of the resources, (iii) the different types of the

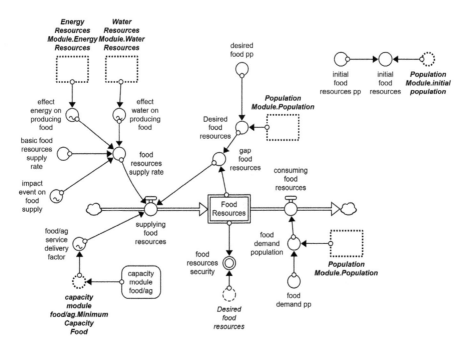

FIGURE 11.7 Nuts and bolts of the food module (all other modules have the same structure).

capacity of the community to deliver services affect the availability of resources, and (iv) each resource security and the overall community resource security change over time. The model also captures the time-dependent influence of the peace, sustainability, and climate security states and the overall weighted average of the state of the community, SC, on community development and the different types of capacity for each resource. It also includes an overall feedback structure where the peace, sustainability, and climate security states and the overall community state change due to an event that impacts resource security over time. As in the previous model, this would be, for instance, when events such as a crisis, war, or climate change (e.g., droughts, floods, heatwaves) affect the security of the resources and could trigger a change in the community state from peace to conflict, sustainability to unsustainability, or climate security to insecurity.

Input data for the two illustrative examples of the PSC4 model application presented below can be found in Appendix D. Figure 11.8 shows the variation of the weighted community resources security, *RS*, and the population, *P*, over 50 years for four initial levels of the peace, sustainability, and climate security states state ranging between 20 and 80. The desired *P*, *S*, and *C* states are equal to 100. Figure 11.8 also shows the variation of the water, energy, and food security ratios when the initial peace, sustainability, and climate security states equal 80. As these initial states become more enabling, the community resources security and population increase with time.

As a second example, Figure 11.9 shows the same three plots when a limited amount of water supply is available from years 10 to 15 and 30 to 35 ("impact event on water supply"=0.01 instead of 1) due to some unspecified constraining event.

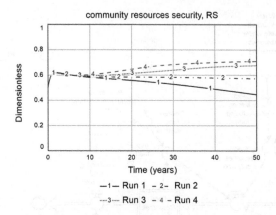

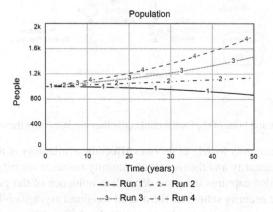

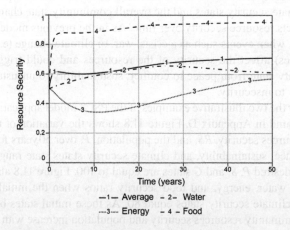

FIGURE 11.8   Variation of (a) the weighted community resources security and (b) population over 50 years for four levels of the initial peace, sustainability, and climate security states: Run 1 (20), Run 2 (40), Run 3 (60), and Run 4 (80). The variation of the water, energy, and food security when the initial peace, sustainability, and climate security states = 80, or most enabling, is shown in Figure (c).

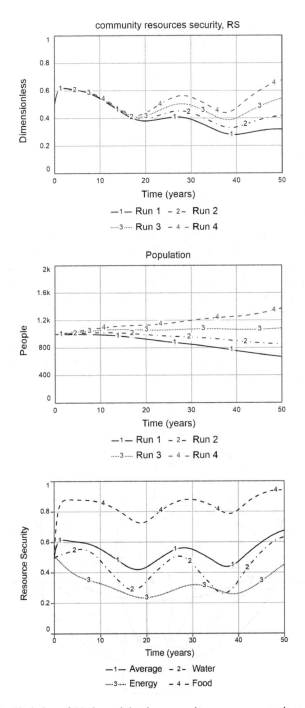

FIGURE 11.9 Variation of (a) the weighted community resources security and (b) population over 50 years for four equal levels of the initial community state: Run 1 (20), Run 2 (40), Run 3 (60), and Run 4 (80). The variation of the water, energy, and food security when the initial peace, sustainability, and climate security states = 80 is shown in figure (c). Limited water supply is available from years 10 to 15 and 30 to 35.

Due to the WEF nexus connections, the reduced water supply impacts energy and food resources security and the population that depends on the availability of water resources. As in the previous example, the community resources security and population increase with the values of the initial peace, sustainability, and climate security states.

As in the previous example, the model can be extended further to include the various processes involved in the supply of water, energy, and food and the effect of events on these processes. One step in making the model more complex is considering these processes and the various water, energy, and food consumption types mentioned above.

11.4   EXAMPLE 3—MODEL PSC5

The third and final model examines how the PSC nexus unfolds in multiple aspects of community development. This more detailed model builds on the WELF-G model proposed by Amadei (2019, p. 85) to analyze the numerous dynamic interactions at play across the water, energy, land/soil, and food sectors of the WELF nexus and how these sectors interact with components of the various social, natural, infrastructure, and economic systems at the community level. The model, called PSC5, presented in this section integrates two types of nexuses: the PSC and WELF nexuses. It can be run using the online interactive user interface on the web.[3]

This model shown in Figure 11.10 represents one of many possible constructs that can capture the dynamics and behavior of a community as its development story unfolds and the links between water, energy, land, and food resources on the one

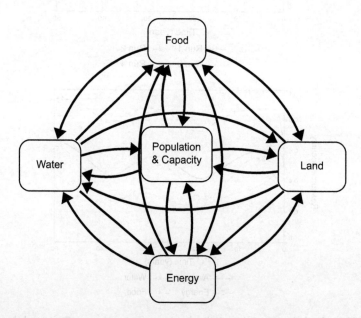

FIGURE 11.10   Modular stock and flow diagram showing the dynamic between a population and four types of resources upon which it depends. Each module consists of several submodules.

hand and peace, sustainability, and climate security on the other. For that reason, the model was purposely designed to be *generic* by including key modules and sub-modules that are more likely to be important when making decisions in the management and allocation of WELF resources in the context of communities that could be subject to enabling events (e.g., peace, climate security) or constraining possibilities (e.g., conflict, climate vulnerability).

The model consists of five interacting modules, each with several submodules. Community development is assumed to unfold over a landscape with a fixed boundary and a surface area divided into five land sectors: residential, pasture, arable (crops), wild (partially forested), and industrial/commercial. Variables, parameters, and endogenous rules within the selected boundary are considered in the model. They are assumed to explain, as thoroughly as possible, the landscape dynamic (i.e., the mental models, structural and behavioral patterns, and trends of the iceberg of Figure 1.1) that needs to be modeled.

The five modules are described in detail in the book by Amadei (2019), and their description is not repeated here. Only modifications to the original modules and submodules are discussed below.

The narrative of the mental model reads as follows:

- The peace, sustainability, and climate security states are interrelated in the capacity submodule of the "population and capacity module" in Figure 11.10. They change with time at different rates toward some desired values. The states may depend on current water, food, energy resources, and health. Time-dependent climate change may also impact the three states and the resources.
- The weighted averages of peace, sustainability, and climate security define the state of the community, SC. The latter impacts birth, death, migration, the workforce, land, vegetation growth, removal, forestation, land productivity, etc. SC also affects seven types of capacity to provide different services such as (i) the supply of water, energy, and food (plant-based and meat-based); (ii) the provision of education and health services; (iii) construction; and (iv) the production of arable and pasture land. The influence/dependence between the seven capacity categories is assumed to be the same for all services and is defined in Table 10.1. This approach provides a way to account in an *aggregated* manner for the effect of the state of the community in its ability to deliver different community services.
- Various service delivery factors are introduced in the water resources, food resources, land resources, and energy resources modules of Figure 11.10.
- Irrigation and non-irrigation water ratios are determined in the water resources module. The food resources module determines crop and livestock unit (LU) ratios. The energy resources module determines several energy ratios in three areas: (i) water uses (non-irrigation and irrigation water, wastewater treatment); (ii) agriculture (crops, pasture, livestock units); and (iii) other uses (households, residential land, industry/commerce land, and wildland). A health ratio is also calculated. These ratios are the

proportions between current water energy, food, and health resources and their respective desired values.

- These ratios allow users to analyze the feedback effects of water, energy, and food security on peace, sustainability, and climate security states. The users select the ratios that are deemed to affect the three states. The water ratio is only considered in the present model.
- The impact of climate change is included in the modules of Figure 11.10. It can trigger a shift from peace to conflict, sustainability to unsustainability, or climate security to vulnerability.

11.4.1 THE POPULATION AND CAPACITY MODULES

11.4.1.1 Demography

As in the original WELF-G model, the population module consists of three submodules: demography, health, and workforce/employment. The demography part of the population module calculates the male and female population in five age groups: 0–4, 5–15, 16–39, 40–59, and ≥ 60, the total male and female populations, and the entire population. It also keeps track of male and female literacy. The size of the population changes due to deaths, births, and migration (immigration and emigration). Different factors related to the availability of water, food, energy, population density, and health affect birth and death. The time-dependent impact of the state of the community on birth, death, migration, workforce, land productivity, livestock productivity, and land characteristics is now included using several "impact community state on..." converters. These new converters are determined in the capacity submodule and depend on the enabling or constraining aspect of the state of community SC.

Men's and women's literacy depends on the capacity of the community to provide educational services. The capacity submodule determines the ability to offer such services. The educational service delivery factor varies between 0 and 1.5 as the minimum capacity for education varies between 0 (no ability) and 100 (total capacity) (i.e., from no to full capacity of providing educational services to the population).

11.4.1.2 Health

The health part of the population module differs from that used in the original WELF-G model. Health is an integrated state that changes toward the desired value with time. The rate of change of health depends on climate change and the capacity of the community to provide health services. The health service delivery factor varies between 0 and 1.5 as the minimum capacity for health varies between 0 (no ability) and 100 (total capacity) (i.e., from no to full capacity of providing health services to the population). The effect of health on birth, death, education, and the workforce is determined.

11.4.1.3 Workforce and Employment

The workforce/employment part of the population module keeps track of the distribution of jobs and labor among the 16–59 age group in three main areas: agriculture (livestock and crops), construction, and other activities (e.g., government, industry, commerce, self-employment). Health and the community state, SC, affect the workforce size.

11.4.1.4 Capacity

The capacity analysis is carried out for each community service of interest. A minimum capacity is determined, and a service delivery factor is calculated using the same approach as in the last two examples.

11.4.2 THE FOOD RESOURCES MODULE

Plant-based and animal-based food cover the specified diet of the community (plant-based, meat-based, or mixed). The plant-based food demand of the community is met with three types of crops: grains, vegetables, and fruits. Three different unspecified livestock types meet the community's meat-based food demand. Livestock is fed with forage originating from the pastureland. If insufficient forage is available, a supplement in grains (fodder) must be provided to the livestock, which reduces the amount of grain available for human consumption.

The capacity to provide agricultural services affects farmland productivity (crop and pasture) and livestock. A capacity analysis determines the minimum ability to provide plant- and animal-based food in the capacity module. The minimum capacity controls the efficiency (ranging from 1–10 for crops and 1–20 for livestock) of converting crops and livestock into plant-based and animal-based food, respectively. The higher the capacity, the more efficient the conversion, and the lower the demand for crops and livestock to meet the food demand.

Two time-dependent converters, "effect climate change on land productivity and adding LUs," are introduced in the food resources module. The impact of the community state on agricultural land productivity and adding LUs is also included.

11.4.3 THE LAND RESOURCES MODULE

The land over the landscape area is divided into five unequal sectors: wild (partially forested), arable (to grow crops such as grains, vegetables, and fruit), pasture (for livestock grazing and feeding), residential (for people's living), and industrial/commercial. The land resources module is divided into one submodule for each sector and a land zoning submodule. Unlike the WELF-G model, the present model assumes no land redistribution (rezoning) over time.

- In the soil/vegetation submodule, converters have been added to account for the impact of the community state on the rates of soil erosion, vegetation cover growth, and removal. The converters are both 5×1 arrays, as the community state may affect the five soil types differently. Two additional converters were added to model the effect of climate change on vegetation cover growth and desertification.
- In the agricultural land submodule, the capacity to provide rural services affects crops and pasture productivity, adding livestock and the loss of pasture and arable land.
- In the industrial/commercial land submodule, one converter is included to account for the impact of the community state on losing land for industrial and commercial purposes.

- In the residential land submodule, the capacity to provide construction services influences the building rate of homes and infrastructure, home repairs, home removal, and the availability of construction materials. The ability to deliver construction services follows the same model for education, literacy, and health in the population module. The construction service delivery factor varies between 0.8 and 2, from no to total capacity of providing construction services to the population.
- In the wildland submodule, two converters are included to account for the impact of the community state and climate change on the death of mature trees and the loss of new trees, thus affecting the timber industry.

11.4.4 THE WATER RESOURCES MODULE

The water module consists of three submodules that interact with each other and deal with water balance, water demand, and wastewater. Compared to the WELF-G model, the present model does not incorporate wastewater in the water balance submodule and does not include the contribution of spring water.

11.4.4.1 Water Balance

In the water balance submodule, a capacity analysis determines the minimum ability to provide water services for irrigation and non-irrigation. The water service delivery factor varies between 0 and 10 as the minimum water capacity varies between 0 (no ability) and 100 (total capacity), i.e., from no to full capacity of providing water services to the population. The impact of the community state on each water (irrigation and non-irrigation) service capacity category is included. Two time-dependent converters, "impact climate change on precipitation" and "impact climate change on evaporation," are introduced in the water balance submodule.

11.4.4.2 Water Demand

In the water demand submodule, a time-dependent converter, "impact climate change on water demand," is introduced. It is the same for all types of water demand.

11.4.4.3 Wastewater

In the wastewater submodule, the impact of the community state on wastewater service capacity is included. The wastewater service delivery factor varies between 0 and 1.2 as the minimum capacity for wastewater handling varies between 0 (no ability) and 100 (total capacity), i.e., from no to full capacity of providing wastewater services to the population.

11.4.5 THE ENERGY RESOURCES MODULE

The energy module consists of two submodules. The energy demand submodule tallies the demand for energy from the different sectors included in the model.

The impact of the community state on renewable and non-renewable service capacity is included. The energy service delivery factor varies between 0 and 10 as the minimum capacity for energy supply varies between 0 (no ability) and 100 (total capacity) (i.e., from no to full capacity of providing energy services to the population).

11.4.6 Numerical Example

Input data for the illustrative example of the PSC5 model application presented below can be found in Appendix E. The model can be run using the online interactive user interface on the web.

This example considers the dynamic of Figure 11.10 for two cases: (i) no climate change effect and (ii) increasing effect of climate change in reducing the precipitation amount. The level of climate change varies gradually and nonlinearly from 0 (no impact) to 4 (high impact) over 50 years, as shown in Figure 11.11.

Figure 11.12, a, b, c, and d compares the variations of the population, health, crops (grains), and water over 50 years for the two cases considered. Figure 11.13 shows the variation of peace, sustainability, and climate security for the two cases considered.

The model captures the adverse effects of climate change. As it takes place, health decreases, resulting in more deaths and fewer births, thus reducing the population. Fewer precipitation events result in more irrigation and non-irrigation water demand and less plant-based and meat-based food produced. Climate change decreases the states of peace, sustainability, and climate security from possible to unlikely, according to the classification of Table 11.1.

11.5 SENSITIVITY ANALYSIS

In modeling the current landscape dynamics and the impact of possible interventions, it is crucial to conduct a sensitivity analysis to explore how the model outputs depend on the variability of each input parameter. Exploring the "what-if" and "what-happens-if" in any model helps to decide whether and to what extent a model is more sensitive to specific parameters than others and their respective uncertainty. It can also help to identify more critical parameters, which, if prioritized, could become leverage points in deciding on intervention scenarios. In general, sensitivity analysis takes time and is often a "chicken-and-egg" process since it is not always obvious which parameters, even those with high leverage, are more critical than others until a sensitivity analysis is conducted and deemed satisfactory.

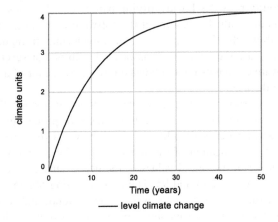

FIGURE 11.11   Variation of climate change level with time from 0 (no impact) to 4 (maximum impact).

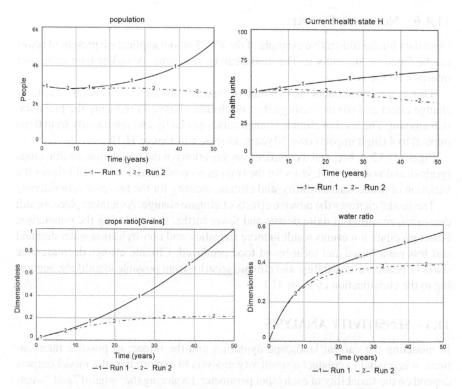

FIGURE 11.12 Variation of the population, health, water ratio, and crop ratio (grains) over 50 years. Run 1: no climate change, Run 2: progressive climate change of Figure 11.11.

The *STELLA Architect* dynamic modeling software platform (version 3.2) contains a helpful sensitivity analysis capability that allows the user to vary several interlinked model parameters incrementally over a specific range selected by the users. This capability provides for identifying parameters that most affect specific model trends. Another valuable feature of the software is the possibility of assigning specific probability distributions (e.g., normal, lognormal, triangular, or uniform distributions) to capture the uncertainty associated with one or several parameters. Finally, the software computes the confidence levels and scatter of any output variable of interest to the user.

As an illustrative example, an analysis was carried out for the PSC4 model to explore its sensitivity to variations in the initial states of peace, sustainability, and climate security when water availability is limited between years 10–15 and 30–35. Figure 11.14 shows the variation of the water, energy, food security, and resource security with time when the initial values of the peace, sustainability, and climate security states vary between 15 and 95. The corresponding 50, 75, and 100% confidence levels and the mean values for water, energy, food, and resource security are shown. Food and energy security shows the most sensitivity to the initial states, whereas water security is less sensitive.

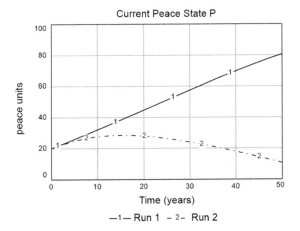

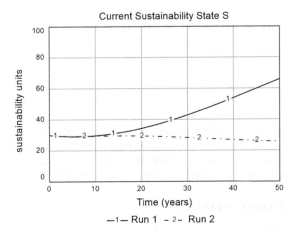

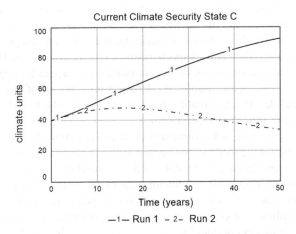

FIGURE 11.13 Variation of the peace, sustainability, and climate security states over 50 years. Run 1: no climate change, Run 2: progressive climate change of Figure 11.11.

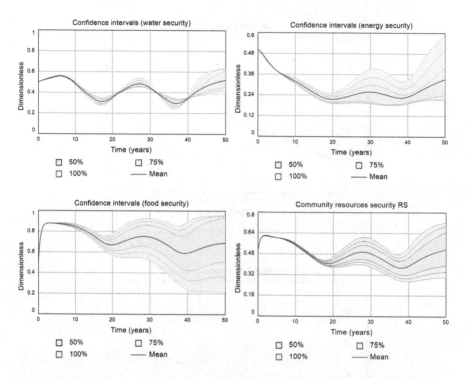

FIGURE 11.14 Variation of individual resource securities and RS for 11 values of the initial peace, sustainability, and climate security states in Figure 11.4 ranging from 15 to 95. The 50 (Inner Bounds), 75 (Middle Bounds), and 100% (Outer Bounds) confidence limits and mean values are shown. Limited water supply is assumed from years 10 to 15 and 30 to 35.

11.6   CONCLUDING REMARKS

The three SD models presented in this chapter represent a sample of possible conceptual representations of different dynamics unfolding between various systems in a community landscape and the sectors of the PSC nexus. It must be remembered that SD models such as those proposed herein are not designed to reproduce all possible activities, especially feedback mechanisms, expected to occur in the landscape where the PSC and community development unfold; this would be impossible. The system dynamics models are simplified constructs (or replicas) of the complex and adaptive PSC and development reality. They are designed to be flexible and customizable for a specific context at a given scale.

A unique characteristic of the three models presented above is that they account, to a certain extent, for the feedback interaction between community development and livelihood on the one hand and the state of the community (i.e., peace vs. conflict, sustainability vs. unsustainability, climate security vs. vulnerability) on the other. Both depend on time and each other. For example, peace vs. conflict, sustainability vs. unsustainability, or climate security vs. vulnerability are community states that enable vs. constrain community development and livelihood. Favorable conditions such as peace, sustainability, and climate security increase the capacity of the community to provide services such as water, food, energy, education, health, etc. Conversely, conflict, unsustainability, and climate vulnerability decrease that capacity. On the other side of the feedback interaction, community development and livelihood impact how peace, sustainability, and climate security unfold. For instance, poor livelihood is likely to trigger conflict, unsustainability, and climate vulnerability. The three models also account for the time-dependent impact of specific possible events (e.g., crisis, war, climate change) on community systems.

The three SD models can be extended to include more than peace, sustainability, and climate security. For instance, the states of education, health, physical safety, and others can be added to the models. The state of the community is then defined as a weighted average of multiple interdependent states contributing to community development and livelihood.

The development of system dynamics models such as those presented above can be a challenging and intimidating process. Once a mental model of the landscape dynamics is adopted, the process requires considerable resources (time, personnel, and funding) to collect and analyze input data in the appraisal stage (stage 2) of the methodology shown in Figure 9.2. For the models to be used for quantitative decision-making, all parameters (stocks, converters, and links) involved in the models must be estimated quantitatively or semi-quantitatively. The estimation can quickly become complex and demanding as more variables, parameters, interactions, and different build-up functionalities are included and require input values.

Modeling landscape dynamics is critically located as stage 5 in Figure 9.2. The goal is to reproduce and calibrate, as accurately as possible, the current scenario(s) at play across the community landscape and the PSC nexus and the deep structures that may explain the issues, behavior patterns, and trends observed across the nexus and at the community level. This so-called behavior reproduction process is not easy. It requires modelers and decision-makers to conduct multiple rounds of iteration and re-evaluate some of the input parameters until the model is deemed satisfactory. This process does not, however, guarantee the model's uniqueness in reproducing the observed behavior patterns.

Once the models are deemed acceptable, various possible intervention(s) scenarios can be proposed for each issue, and decisions can be made about implementing these interventions (stage 6 in Figure 9.2). Once in place, the SD models can be used to analyze these interventions' merits and their unintended consequences. This approach will be discussed further in Chapter 13.

NOTES

1 https://exchange.iseesystems.com/public/bernardamadei/psc3
2 https://exchange.iseesystems.com/public/bernardamadei/psc4
3 https://exchange.iseesystems.com/public/bernardamadei/psc5

REFERENCE

Amadei, B. (2019). *A systems approach to modeling the water-energy-land-food nexus* (Vols. *I* and *II*). Momentum Press.

12 Cases Studies

12.1 THE CAT BA BIOSPHERE RESERVE

The Cat Ba Biosphere Reserve (CBBR) in Vietnam is an excellent example illustrating the complex dynamics between different conservation and sustainable development factors. Nguyen and Bosch (2009), Bosch et al. (2013), and Nguyen and Bosch (2013) described in detail how they proposed a systems approach (using causal loops) and the four levels of thinking of the iceberg model of decision-making shown in Figure 1.1 to develop a road map and intervention strategies for the Cat Ba Island. A similar analysis was proposed by another group of researchers, Mai and Smith (2015, 2018), who focused on the tourism aspect of the CBBR.

The project in Hai Phong City in northeast Vietnam focuses on "the interconnectedness of the environment, the livelihood of people and economic benefits, and the adoption of policies and processes by the government and management bodies to ensure that long-term sustainable management is ongoing." It also involved the participation of a wide range of stakeholder groups, including senior politicians from the district to the central government, academics, donor organizations, field officers, and managers at various levels of the government, as well as villagers and commune residents. As noted by Bosch et al. (2013) and Nguyen and Bosch (2013), the approach used in the CBBR can serve as a decision template for developing and conserving other biospheres in the world.

The biosphere reserve is located on Cat Ba Island in northeast Vietnam (context, scale, and boundary). The island is a UNESCO biosphere reserve recognized for its unique biodiversity (see Figure 12.1) and has attracted tourism, which is the most significant contributor to its economy. It is occupied by 16,000 people living in six communes and one town. Poor economic development on the island has forced people to encroach on the reserve, the primary source of tourism income. In addition to environmental degradation, threats to wildlife, and marine pollution, the island faces multiple human development and security issues. A longitudinal study of Cat Ba Island was carried out by Bosch et al. (2013) and Nguyen and Bosch (2013) and consisted of the following steps.

12.1.1 IDENTIFYING ISSUES

Two workshops were conducted in 2007 with a range of stakeholders to gather their *mental models* on critical issues faced by Cat Ba Island, including "waste treatment, pollution, the high number of floating farms, overuse of underground water, strong growth in tourism, lack of fresh water and electricity (especially in the summer—tourist season), lack of skilled labor for the tourism industry, uncontrolled tourism development, insufficient infrastructure, lack of access to suitable markets for locally produced products, encroachment on conservation areas, lack of integrated planning, lack of capacity, environmental degradation, and poverty." These issues represent the

DOI: 10.1201/9781003435006-12

FIGURE 12.1   The Cat Ba bio reserve.

Source: Vinh, Q. N. (2021, January 5). *Birds Eye View of Cat Ba Island · Free Stock Photo.* Pexels. https://www.pexels.com/photo/birds-eye-view-of-cat-ba-island-6348812/

events in the iceberg model in Figure 1.1. The stakeholders developed mental models and behavior-over-time (BOT) graphs for each issue identified. Both activities involve the thinking level in the bottom tier in the iceberg of Figure 1.1 and are driven by values, beliefs, and assumptions that people have about each issue.

12.1.2   BUILDING CAPACITY

With the problem articulation and mental models in mind, a two-month system thinking and capacity-building program was conducted for a group of policymakers, managers, and technical officers from different levels of government, agencies, and NGOs. At this thinking level (the second tier from the bottom of the iceberg of Figure 1.1), possible systemic structures were proposed to explain the issues.

12.1.3   DEVELOPING STRUCTURAL MODELS

During the two-month capacity-building programs, the issues previously identified by the stakeholders were integrated into a preliminary big-picture systems model that shows patterns, interdependencies, and feedback structures. Dynamic hypotheses were formulated. A causal loop diagram (CLD) of the model is shown

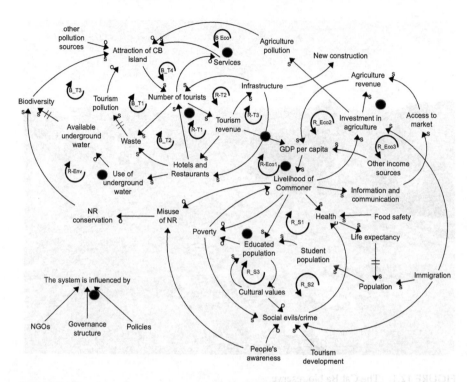

FIGURE 12.2   A current systems model of the CBBR in Vietnam. Legend: s (same direction); o (opposite direction); R (reinforcing loop); B (balancing loop); T (tourism); Eco (Economic); Env (environment); S (social); 1, 2, and 3 refer to loop number, e.g., R_T1 (reinforcing loop no.1 of tourism); Black dots are identified areas for systemic interventions. Redrawn using the STELLA software.

Source: Nguyen et al. (2013), used by permission of John Wiley & Sons.

in Figure 12.2 and includes reinforcing (R) and balancing (B) feedback loops. As Nguyen and Bosh (2009) described, the loops are regrouped into *six sectors*. They include (i) tourism development reinforcing loops (R_Tx), (ii) tourism development balancing loops (B_Tx), (iii) environmental development loops (R_Env), (iv) economic development reinforcing loops (R_Econx), (v) economic development balancing loops (B_Ecox), and (vi) social development reinforcing loops (R_Sx). Individual CLD loops and their combinations were used to identify structural and behavior patterns (past and current trends) shared by different groups of stakeholders (third tier from the bottom of the iceberg of Figure 1.1). These patterns have the potential to influence future trends. Additional CLDs focusing on tourism were proposed by Mai and Smith (2015).

12.1.4   Identifying Leverage Areas and Systemic Interventions

As part of another participatory workshop in 2009, leverage areas and systemic interventions were identified in the system model of Figure 12.2 (see black dots).

They included "cross-sectional collaboration; development and implementation of government plans; capacity building for decision-makers, managers, and local people; waste management and treatment; people's awareness; conservation of endangered species; investment for agriculture; improving the livelihood of commoners; and tourism development" (Bosch et al., 2013).

These leverage areas were identified from four interdependent systems archetypes at play in Figure 12.2 (Nguyen and Bosch, 2013). In the *limit to growth* archetype (Figure 8.5), leverage resides in reducing constraints preventing sustainable tourism development, such as pollution, lack of fresh water, and poor service quality, instead of adding more tourism irrespective of the current conditions and future impact (reinforcing R_T1,2,3 loops vs. balancing B_T3,4 loops in Figure 12.2). If not addressed, the constraints could collapse tourism growth over time due to the reduced capacity of the island to accept more tourists. At the same time, zoning and capping tourism were suggested to limit the footprint of tourism infrastructure, thus putting less pressure on the island's carrying capacity (Mai and Smith, 2015).

For the *fixes that fail* archetype (Figure 8.1), the leverage resides in maintaining a long-term focus on tourism development rather than applying short-term fixes (e.g., building more hotels and facilities to attract more tourists) such as converting conservation land to hotels and roads which would release more untreated waste, create pollution, and worsen the island conditions (reinforcing R_T1–3 loops vs. balancing B_T1–2 loops in Figure 12.2). This approach requires managers and decision-makers to focus long-term on the sustainable development of the CBBR. At the same time, they also need to develop short-term measures to prevent long-term unintended consequences (Mai and Smith, 2015). A CLD of that dynamic was proposed by Mai and Smith (2015) and is shown in Figure 12.3.a.

Another *"fixes that fail"* archetype dynamic suggested by Mai and Smith (2015, 2018) illustrated in Figure 12.3.b relates to unemployment and poverty. Tourism creates more local agriculture and fishery jobs. Still, some of these jobs are taken by

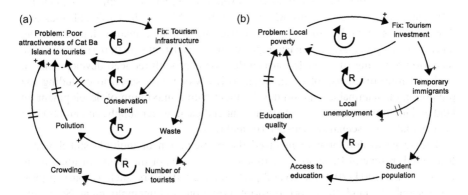

FIGURE 12.3 Two *fixes that fail* archetype examples for the Cat Ba Island. 12.3a relates to tourism infrastructure, 12.3b relates to unployment and poverty.

Source: Mai and Smith (2015), used by permission of Informa UK Ltd.

outsiders to the island who compete "with the local people for jobs and also cause environmental pollution problems through the proliferation of floating fish farms." The outsiders also create demand for lodging and education, thus "overwhelming local schools and reducing access to education for local children." Fewer available jobs to the local people create more poverty and encroachment on the reserve for their livelihood.

The *tragedy of the commons* archetype (Figure 8.11) models a dynamic between the tourism industry and agriculture (R_Eco2 vs. B_Eco and R_Eco1 vs. B_T3–4 loops in Figure 12.2). Both sectors are trying to maximize their revenue while not realizing that they are both limited by the "lack of fresh water, lack of electricity (and costs), lack of trained staff, and lack of land for cultivation, etc." The leverage resides in developing a master plan for the island that balances the tourism industry and agriculture while reducing poverty and protecting biodiversity and natural resources.

Finally, the *shifting the burden* archetype (Figure 8.8) emphasizes the importance of prioritizing local capacity building over depending on international assistance and aid. The leverage reduces outside dependence while building local capacity over time. This recommendation requires better-trained local professionals responsible for managing the CBBR.

12.1.5 DEVELOPING INTERVENTION SCENARIOS

Bosch et al. (2013) suggested strategies and policies for implementing systemic interventions in Cat Ba Island. They included enhancing the rangers' ability to manage the National Park effectively; carrying out a social welfare study regarding community development in the CBBR; creating an annual report card on the health of the Cat Ba Ecosystem; forming community partnerships for the management and protection of natural resources; and moving the floating farms away from popular tourist destinations and out of the national marine protected areas.

Models were constructed to rank and develop short and long-term action plans for different systemic interventions. Mai and Smith (2018) used the CLD and stock and flow tools of system dynamics to explore five intervention scenarios for sustainable tourism development: (i) a scenario representing the current situation, (ii) a best-case scenario promoting sustainable tourism development with reduced development on land and minimized use of clean water, (iii) a worst-case scenario excluding the promotion of sustainable tourism development with a maximum of development on land and no improvement in waste treatment and clean water supply, (iv) and (v) two intermediate case scenarios between (ii) and (iii).

The scenario development involved the participation of multiple stakeholders. It resulted in several Behavior-over-time (BOT) graphs of the future of tourism on Cat Ba Island 2004–2050 for several performance indicators, such as tourism jobs, water supply/demand, the resort footprint, pollution, and unemployment. Stock and flow models were developed for the tourism economic sector, the population sector, the natural resources sector (Figure 12.4), and the environmental sector. It was concluded that the present scenario was not sustainable and that the two intermediate scenarios mentioned above were more likely to be implemented in the future.

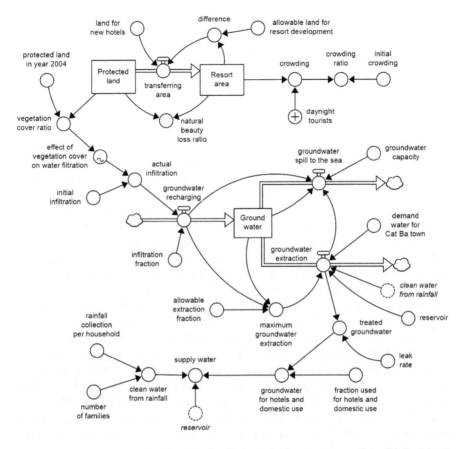

FIGURE 12.4   Stock and flow diagram for the natural resources sector of the Cat Ba Island.

Source: Mai and Smith (2018), used by permission of Elsevier.

12.1.6   REMARKS

The Cat Ba Island case study emphasizes the interconnectedness between sustainable development and conservation and the complexity of using trade-offs and synergies in community development. It provides an excellent illustration of how a systems approach can be used to explore the dynamic equilibrium between people and their environment, which, as discussed in Chapter 2, is key to sustainability. In the case of Cat Ba Island, the driving force of the island's economy, tourism, must be controlled and sensitive to the carrying capacity of the island's natural resources and ensure community livelihood.

12.2   THE SYRIAN CONFLICT

12.2.1   BACKGROUND

Many countries in the Middle East and North Africa (MENA) and the Sahel region of Africa have increasingly experienced civil unrest and conflict over the past

10 years. This upheaval has been attributed to multiple interdependent issues related to environmental degradation, significantly reduced water resources due to climate change, unsustainable agricultural practices, poor management of resources, corruption, and political instability. Many of these case studies illustrate the complexity of the dynamic between peace/conflict, sustainability/unsustainability, and climate security/vulnerability and how these three sectors interact in human development and security. The Syrian conflict is used in this section as an illustrative example of that complex dynamic.

Civil unrest and the uprising in Syria started during the Arab Spring in March 2011. From March to July 2011, multiple protests across Syria demanded democratic and economic reforms, accountable governance, human rights, and political freedoms, including press, speech, and assembly. They quickly became violent as the regime tried to suppress them with military lead attacks on protesters using tactics ranging from arrests to gunfire, torture, murder, and other human rights violations, such as the water supply interruption (Arab Spring, 2020). In July 2011, the protesters retaliated using firearms (Vox, 2017). In 2012, the violence continued into a full-blown civil war as more repression tactics were used, further legitimizing the revolution. A timeline of the escalating conflict since 2011 can be found on the web (UNICEF, n.d.).

The climate security literature is divided as to the reasons that led to the Syrian conflict in the first place (Peters et al., 2020). There is a strong opinion that it began following the worst recorded drought in Syria and Middle East Fertile Crescent history 2006–2010 (Kelley et al., 2015). That assumption has been disputed by Selby et al. (2017) and others who claimed that the climate change-related drought was not the only driver of the Syrian conflict. Other factors have been proposed to explain social unrest, violent conflict, and civil war starting in 2011 (Gleick, 2014, 2019; Vidal, 2016; Suter, 2017). They include weak country governance, poverty, economic liberalization, a lack of environmental and agricultural policymaking, land tenure issues, political insecurity, and corrupt water management.

Following the Arab Spring in 2011, about 1.5 million rural workers migrated into informal settlements from rural to urban areas. Unfortunately, the urban areas were not equipped to absorb the excess population due to limited infrastructure and livelihood resources, which resulted in a humanitarian crisis, poverty, protests, and an oppressive and violent response from the Syrian government. This dynamic, in turn, fueled the country's civil war, which became a multi-sided proxy war for other countries, forced the migration of refugees fleeing the violence, and fed the refugee crisis in Europe starting in 2015 with an estimated 5.6 million people (Amnesty International, 2021; UNHCR, 2022). Today, the conflict "has shifted into a seemingly unsolvable regional crisis, leaving a country scarred by terror and instability" (Shelter Box, n.d.) and the collapse of its economy.

An attempt at summarizing the dynamic between climate change, human development and security, and civil unrest in Syria with a simple CLD was proposed in Figure 2.1. This section explores further the detailed aspects of CLD. It is based on a report by Whitworth (2021), who analyzed the dynamic of various interdependent variables involved in the Syrian conflict 2010–2020 in greater depth. They include climate, water, agriculture, energy, corruption, liberalization, socio-political issues, and human insecurity. The dynamics of these factors and their interdependence are illustrated in more detail in the CLDs of Figures 12.5 and 12.6. Both figures use the

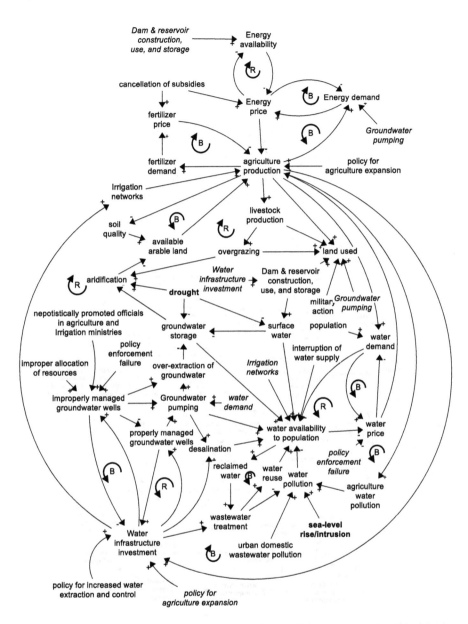

FIGURE 12.5 Causal loop diagram showing the effect of climate change and drought on Syria's water system and on energy, agriculture, and land sectors.

Source: Withworth (2021). Used by permission of the author.

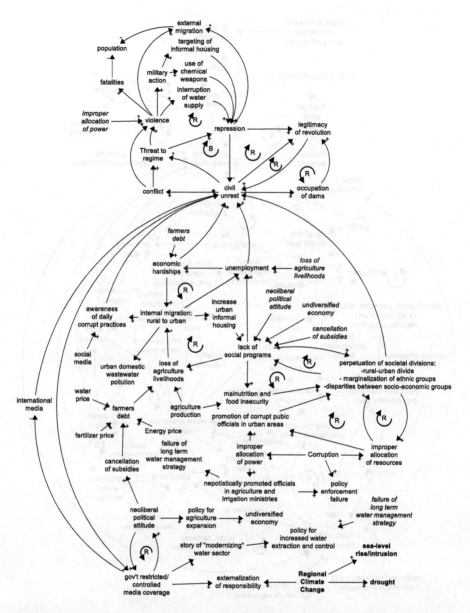

FIGURE 12.6 Causal loop diagram showing the dynamic among government actions, socioeconomic consequences, and media influence sectors involved in the collapse of Syrian agriculture and the migration of people.

Source: Withworth (2021). Used by permission of the author.

ghost functionality of the STELLA software that allows a variable to appear at different locations in CLDs for clarity's sake. The variables shown in these figures are discussed below. It is important to note that the analysis carried out by Whitworth is confined to the geographical boundaries of Syria.

12.2.2 CLIMATE AND WATER

The water demand in Syria is primarily divided into domestic, agricultural, and industrial uses. The agricultural sector consumes most of the freshwater resources. Surface water comes from seven main water basins; some are shared with neighboring countries such as Turkey and Iraq. Surface water is also available from major artificial lakes and reservoirs. Syria's groundwater resources are essentially fossil groundwater systems with slow recharge rates and are connected to groundwater systems in Lebanon, Turkey, Israel, the West Bank, and Golan Heights. Reclaimed water is another source of freshwater in Syria. Due to reduced rainfall from 2006 to 2010, some parts of Syria became water scarce, with reduced water resource availability for rural and increasing urban populations.

Figure 12.5 shows the effect of climate change and associated drought on Syria's water system climate change-induced drought decreases surface waters and groundwater recharge. Climate change-induced sea level rise creates saltwater intrusion into fresh groundwater resources and water pollution along the coast. The dam and reservoir systems increase the control of surface waters. The water demand increases with the population. Water reclamation and reuse after treatment contribute to the water available to the population. Water resources depend on other factors, such as water infrastructure investment, irrigation methods, groundwater pumping, water well management, pollution, and water price.

12.2.3 AGRICULTURE AND ENERGY

Agriculture has been the largest industry in Syria and, therefore, the largest consumer of freshwater in the country. The major crops include wheat, cotton, barley, lentils, and chickpeas, two-thirds of which are produced in the northeastern region. Between 1978 and 2007, 24% of Syrian land was used to cultivate these crops, and any increase in cultivated land was due to increased irrigation (Kelley et al., 2015; Mourad and Berndtsson, 2011). Traditionally, the crops were irrigated by rainfall, and even with improved irrigation networks, 67% of all agricultural land was still rain-fed as of 2015 (Weinthal et al., 2015). During the drought, which affected the northeastern region the most, most of Syria received less than 8 inches (203 mm) of annual rainfall necessary for rainfall-irrigated agriculture. Soil erosion increased, and harvests, crops, seeds, and livestock were lost, resulting in a 17% decrease in agricultural shares, loss of livelihoods, and ultimately an internal migration of 1.5 million people from rural to urban areas (Gleick, 2014). The dynamic is depicted in the CLD of Figure 12.6.

Other interdependent factors shown in Figures 12.5 and 12.6 contributed to the collapse of Syrian agriculture and the migration of people. Among others, they can be attributed to (i) unsustainable governmental policies in drought conditions to boost agricultural market expansion and water extraction and control, (ii) the attempted liberalizing of the economy with a neo-liberal political attitude, (iii) the cancellation of fuel and fertilizer subsidies creating challenging market conditions in the rural sector, (iv) the poor management of irrigation systems, (v) the increased investment in water infrastructure systems with the digging of thousands of unlicensed water wells, as well as over-extraction of groundwater resources, (vi) overgrazing, and (vii) the degradation of soil conditions including salinization and nitrate contamination.

Furthermore, corrupt bribery, cronyism, and nepotism by the ruling regime and officials in power (mostly Alawites in the dominant Suni population) resulted in an improper allocation of resources such as water, energy, and food. The regime failed to enforce liberal government policies (Gersh, 2017), which fueled mistrust and frustration from the rural population. Disparities and tensions between socioeconomic groups, ethnic groups, and regional inequalities created tension between rural and urban people (Figure 12.6). All these factors already started before the drought forced many farmers into unemployment and disintegrated the agriculture market. Syria had to import wheat in 2008 despite having been historically a wheat exporter. Between 2006 and 2009, an estimated 1.3 million rural people in eastern Syria were affected (Gleick, 2014). The farmers' debt, loss of livelihoods, unemployment, economic hardships, and lack of social programs in place are shown in Figure 12.6.

The large population influx to cities created additional problems and pressures on infrastructure and services, as the cities were unprepared and unsupported to respond to informal settlements. Additionally, the lack of domestic and industrial wastewater treatment plants exacerbated the water crisis in urban areas and increased urban domestic wastewater pollution (Mourad and Berndtsson, 2011). Due to limited economic opportunities in cities and the lack of social programs, the poverty rates increased rapidly in urban areas in Syria between 2004 and 2009. Faced with the crisis, the government attempted to discourage the growth of informal settlements and urban populations by incentivizing internally displaced people to return to rural areas in the northern and eastern regions with cash handouts, transport assistance, and food aid upon return to the region. Still, few migrants chose to do so (Châtel, 2014). The internal migration pattern toward urban areas and the subsequent increase in informal settlements and urban regions increased domestic wastewater pollution and unsanitary conditions. In 2022, cholera outbreaks were reported in displaced population encampments (ABC News, 2022). The loss of livelihoods, income, and, more directly, the loss of wheat production resulted in malnutrition and food insecurity despite the distribution of food by the regime that benefitted some privileged sections of the population.

12.2.4   THE SYRIAN MEDIA

Figure 12.6 also shows the media's role in diffusing the importance of the Syrian crisis. Climate change was conveniently used to outsource the blame and, therefore, the regime's responsibility, as they claim Syria is a "naturally water-scarce country" (Châtel, 2014). The government failed to acknowledge or address the mismanagement and its impact. Through media and international relations, the regime tried to depict the drought and subsequent humanitarian crisis as an international affair, using climate change and the lack of international financial support as its scapegoat.

Rather than addressing the decreasing rainfall and worsening drought conditions, the state-owned media, the Syrian Arab News Agency (SANA), focused on the increased crop production and efforts to modernize Syria's water infrastructure and even denied local water shortages (Weinthal et al., 2015; Châtel, 2014). As conditions worsened, only online and international news covered the economic dislocation and migration to urban areas. Still, SANA continued omitting the drought coverage and the economic and social situations. The drought was only covered in global or regional climate change reporting, despite other neighboring countries, such as Turkey and Iraq, managing it better and not experiencing the same economic decline and social repercussions (Kelley et al., 2015).

12.2.5 A Geopolitical Conflict

Since 2010, the conflict in Syria has involved a wide range of individuals and groups along ethnic and religious lines that reflect the complexity of the Syrian population. These groups have different agendas in the conflict. They include the Kurds who span the borders between Turkey, Syria, and Iraq and aspire to autonomy and sovereignty. Several other groups, smaller in population, including the (i) Turkmen, who are strongly associated with Turkey; (ii) Assyrians, a Christian group that is highly discriminated against because of their religion; (iii) Druze, a subsect of Shi'a Islam; and (iv) small populations that identify as Armenian and Circassian (Kannike, 2021). The leading players within the Syrian conflict are the regime-lead Shi'a, the Rebels, mainly consisting of Sunni Muslims, the Kurds, who have fought with the Rebels at times and independently at others, and, previously (most active 2013–2017), the Islamic State (Glenn et al., 2019; Vox, 2017). The Syrian Democratic Forces, formed in 2015, are a rebel group composed mainly of Kurdish, Sunni, and Assyrian militias (Glenn et al., 2019).

The Syrian civil war can also be seen as a proxy war involving groups such as Al-Qaeda and ISIL and countries such as Turkey, the Gulf states, including Saudi Arabia, and the Sunni majority, with Qatar, Jordan, and the United States supporting the rebels. The Syrian regime has been supported by the Shi'a majority of Iran, and Hezbollah in Lebanon, which is backed by Iran and Russia (Vox, 2017).

Over the years, the conflict in Syria has resulted in even more limited access to resources. Between 2010 and 2018, Syria lost 943,000 hectares of cultivated land because of military actions, displacement of agriculture workers, mismanagement of resources, and other costs from the conflict, including changes in controlling land as various fronts moved in (Human Rights Watch, 2021). The additional land loss was due to airstrikes, specifically from the Syrian-Russian military alliance, which became more involved in 2015 (Human Rights Watch, 2021) and 2019. The loss of arable land and the destruction of bakeries exacerbated the issue of food insecurity. The regime again destroyed "systematically depopulat[ing]" areas that housed internally displaced populations, and informal settlements, perpetuating the housing crisis and targeting those already disenfranchised by the regime's actions (Weinthal et al., 2015). Figure 12.6 depicts the effects of military action on land in the agriculture subsystem and the targeting of informal housing settlements.

The water crisis was also exacerbated and has been weaponized throughout the conflict. Gleick (2014) cited the "intentional and incidental targeting of water systems" throughout the war in Syria. The occupation of land coincides with the occupation of the water resources within those territories. The occupation of hydro-electric dams stifled the water resources behind the dams and the energy resources that they produced.

12.2.6 REPRESSION AND REVOLUTION ARCHETYPE

In Figure 12.6, civil unrest was brought about by numerous factors, including the perpetuation of societal divisions, unemployment, and economic hardships. The awareness of the corrupt practices spurred it on, and international media resulted in conflict in the form of protests, which was seen as a threat to the Syrian regime.

The top part of Figure 12.6 shows a repression and revolution archetype (Figure 8.13): civil unrest increases the danger to the established government, which uses repression to subdue, but by doing so, proves the legitimacy of the revolution. The legality of the revolution incited more civil unrest, creating a reinforcing loop. More specifically, in Syria's case, some forms of civil unrest included the occupation of dams, which resulted in a decreased energy supply in areas outside of the territory of the occupied dam, and the threat of interrupting the water supply, reinforcing the legitimacy of the revolution. The violent political and military decisions on behalf of the regime include the targeting of informal housing, water supply interruption, and chemical weapons, all of which are easily considered war crimes. The water supply interruption had many impacts: increasing internal migration, expanding the use of improperly managed wells, increasing domestic wastewater pollution, and decreasing the available water supply. The nepotistic and improper allocation of power potentially resulted in increased violence from the regime. Violence has generally resulted in external migration and fatalities, decreasing the population. The loss of life is compounded by malnutrition and food insecurity in the country, reinforced by the military actions that occupy land once used for agricultural production.

12.2.7 FINDING LEVERAGE

Despite the complex and unsolvable nature of the Syrian conflict, there are several places in the CLDs of Figures 12.5 and 12.6 where interventions could have positive outcomes. Of course, not all interventions are feasible due to the levels of destruction and corruption at the country level, which are still prevalent 11 years after the Arab Spring. Whitworth (2021) considered several leverage points in Figures 12.7 and 12.8. Some are new, while others were already included in Figures 12.5 and 12.6. These leverage points could lead to solutions contributing to reducing the conflict over time if combined:

- Water scarcity and management could be improved by considering new methods of water provisioning, such as rainwater collection, desalination, and wastewater treatment and reuse. Cultivating less water-demanding crops combined with drip irrigation techniques could reduce agricultural water consumption.

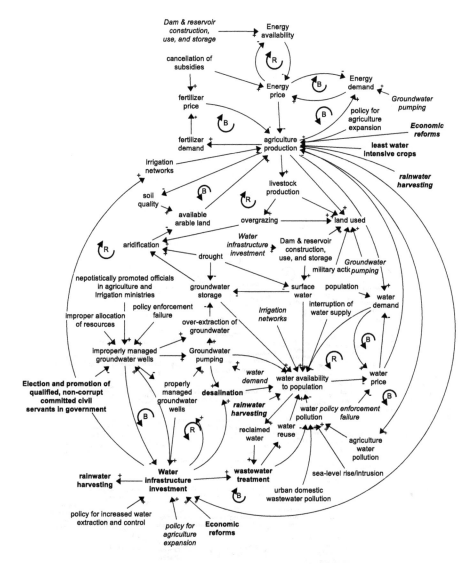

FIGURE 12.7 Leverage points of intervention (in bold letters) in the dynamics of Figure 12.5.

Source: Withworth (2021). Used by permission of the author.

- Investment in water infrastructure and economic reforms could improve the country's capacity to store and provide clean water, treat wastewater, produce hydroelectricity, and increase agricultural production.
- Substantial leverage exists in addressing the root causes of social unrest. Pursuing a democratic path with human rights, freedom of speech, press, and assembly is necessary for the election and promotion of qualified, not corrupt, and committed civil servants. This change, in turn, would promote social programs, reduce social unrest, and improve water and energy

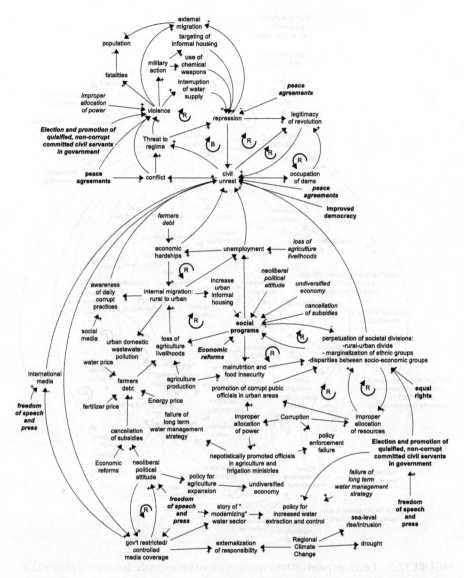

FIGURE 12.8   Leverage points of intervention (in bold letters) in the dynamics of Figure 12.6.

Source: Withworth (2021). Used by permission of the author.

infrastructure performance. It requires that trust is regained between the population and the government.

- Increase resilience by promoting social and ecological connectedness and cohesion.
- The repression and revolution archetype could be addressed through conflict resolution and peace agreements.

12.2.8 A STOCK AND FLOW MODEL

An attempt at creating a stock and flow model of the dominant dynamics of Figures 2.1 and 12.5 to 12.8 is shown in Figures 12.9 (a, b, and c). It is based on the generic structures of overshoot and collapse available in the SD literature (see models of Breierova, 1997). The model PSC6 can be run using the online interactive user interface on the web.[1]

The first part of the model is shown in Figure 12.9.a. It was designed to capture the overshoot and collapse of the rural population as it runs out of resources due to gradual climate change, poor resource management, and other factors (local, national, and regional). As the pool of rural resources decreases from some initial value, the rural population collapses, and migration from rural to urban occurs. Several "other resources limiting factors" affect the production of pastoral resources (e.g., water, energy, food, etc.). They may include weak governance, human insecurity, liberalization of the economy, a lack of environmental and agricultural policymaking, corrupt water management personnel, overgrazing, digging unauthorized water wells, over-extraction of groundwater, and the degradation of soil conditions due to salinization and nitrate contamination.

Any interventions that reduce the impact of these factors, such as providing better resource management, investing in infrastructure (e.g., water collection and wastewater treatment, desalination), and reducing the effects of climate change through adaptation and mitigation measures would produce more rural resources and reduce the overall internal migration rate.

The second part of the model is shown in Figure 12.9.b. It captures the straining impact of migration on urban livelihood. Another overshoot and collapse structure

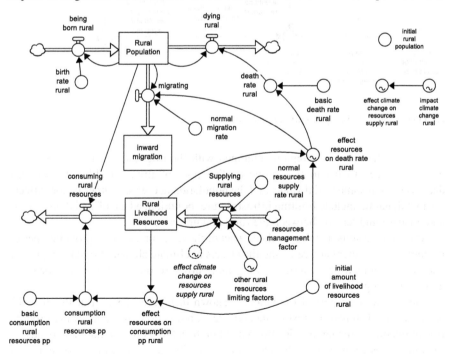

FIGURE 12.9A Rural population dynamics.

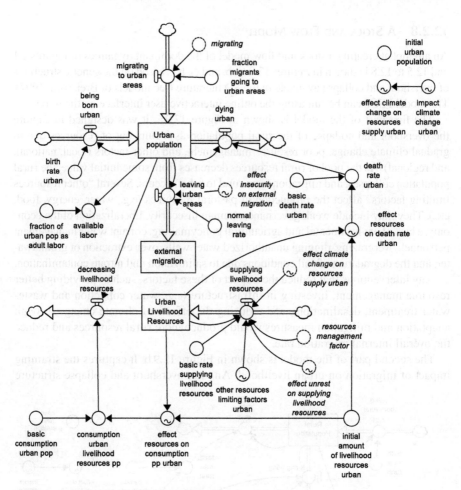

FIGURE 12.9B   Urban population dynamics.

shows how the urban population combined with the migrant population consumes more resources than can be produced. The pool of urban livelihood resources decreases from some initial value, and the population decreases. Other factors affecting that dynamic include limiting infrastructure, pollution, a lack of social programs, and mistrust and tension between the rural and urban people.

Any interventions that reduce the impact of these factors, such as providing better resource management and reducing the effects of climate change through adaptation and mitigation measures, would produce more urban resources and reduce the overall external migrating rate.

Finally, the third part of the model is shown in Figure 12.9.c. It deals with different forms of unrest. Unrest disincentivizes job creation and reduces the production of livelihood resources. Unemployment in the adult labor population depends on the ratio between available jobs and adult labor. The latter is assumed to be a fixed percentage of the total urban population and varies with time. The level of labor

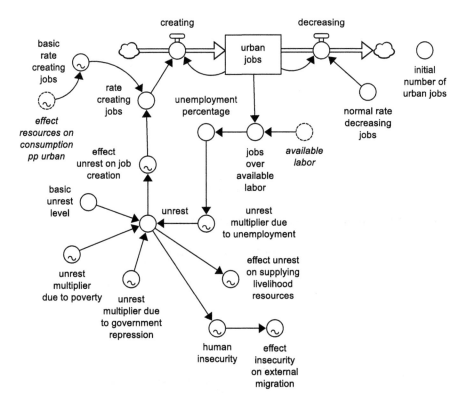

FIGURE 12.9C   Unrest and oppression dynamics.

decreases as the population declines due to reduced livelihood resources. Poverty and unemployment create more unrest, threatening the government and creating more violent repression and human insecurity. As a result, external migration increases.

Any interventions that reduce unrest by introducing economic reforms, promoting the election and training of qualified non-corrupt decision-makers, developing peace agreements, and implementing democratic measures (i.e., equal rights and freedom of speech and press) could result in increasing urban resources and jobs, thus reducing unemployment, and reducing human insecurity and outward migration.

A numerical example of the PSC6 model is presented in Appendix F. The data used in this example are based on rough data available in the literature about Syria's dynamic 2020–2020 (Withworth, 2021). Among all variables in Figures 12.9.a–c, the time-dependent effect of climate change and the level of resources management for rural and urban conditions strongly influence the urban and rural resources and internal and external migration. To illustrate that dependence, the effect of climate change is assumed to increase over 20 years, as shown in Figure 12.10. The resources management factor is assumed to be the same for the rural and urban settings, constant, and ranges between 1 (no management) and 5 (good management). A parametric study was carried out using the data listed in Appendix F.

Figures 12.11 and 12.12 show the variation in rural and urban livelihood resources and migration over 20 years. As expected, with better resource management through,

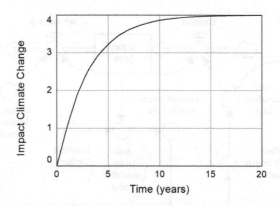

FIGURE 12.10   Assumed level of climate change with time.

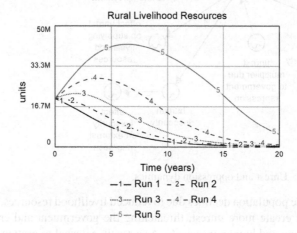

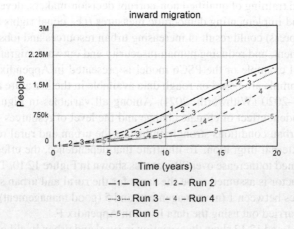

FIGURE 12.11   Time-dependent variation of rural livelihood resources and inward migration for different levels of rural resources management ranging between 1 (Run 1) and 5 (Run 5).

for instance, climate practices (adaptation and mitigation), more resources are available, and migration to urban areas decreases. Similarly, the same trend can be seen for the urban conditions in Figure 12.12. Finally, Figure 12.13 shows how better management of resources reduces urban unemployment and unrest levels.

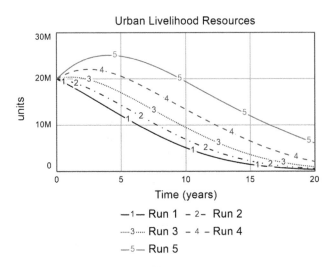

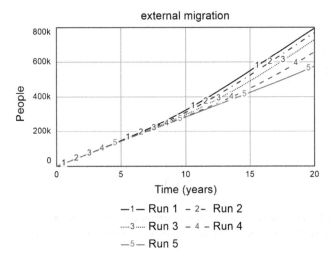

FIGURE 12.12   Time-dependent variation of urban livelihood resources and outward migration for different levels of urban resources management ranging between 1 (Run 1) and 5 (Run 5).

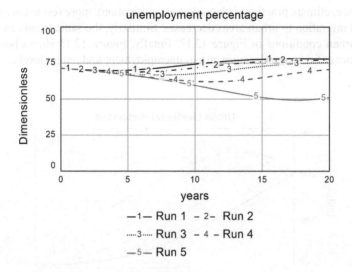

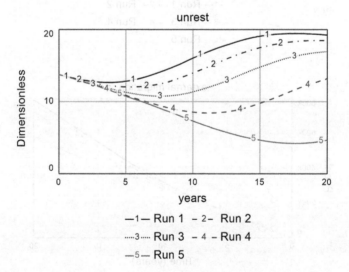

FIGURE 12.13 Time-dependent variation of urban unemployment and unrest for different levels of urban resources management ranging between 1 (Run 1) and 5 (Run 5).

12.3 CONCLUDING REMARKS

The case studies presented in this chapter demonstrate the value proposition of SD in exploring the dynamics of complex systems using CLDs and stock and flow tools. Both show the complex dynamic of sustainable community development. The Syrian case explored the linkages between sustainability, peace, and climate security.

The archetypes in both case studies help identify areas of intervention and leverage points. Multiple scenarios involving different groups of stakeholders are possible and need to be planned, evaluated, ranked, and implemented. Chapter 13 provides guidelines on how to do so.

NOTE

1 https://exchange.iseesystems.com/public/bernardamadei/psc6

REFERENCES

ABC News. (2022, November 5). Lebanon, Syria, and Iraq face growing cholera outbreaks driven by conflict, climate change, and poverty. https://www.abc.net.au/news/2022-11-06/middle-east-cholera-outbreak/101621178

Amnesty International. (2021). The World's refugee in numbers. https://www.amnesty.org/en/what-we-do/refugees-asylum-seekers-and-migrants/global-refugee-crisis-statistics-and-facts//

Arab Spring: A Research & Study Guide: Syria. (2020). *Cornell University library*. https://guides.library.cornell.edu/arab_spring/Syria

Bosch, O. J. H., Nguyen, N. C., Maeno, T., & Yasui, T. (2013). Managing complex issues through evolutionary learning laboratories. *Systems Research*, *30*, 116–135. http://doi.org/10.1002/sres.2171

Breierova, L. (1997). Generic structures: Overshoot and collapse. https://ocw.mit.edu/courses/15-988-system-dynamics-self-study-fall-1998-spring-1999/e8bd0c07ef2848b39e55fc8ff52dcb88_generic3.pdf

Châtel, F. D. (2014). The role of drought and climate change in the Syrian Uprising: Untangling the triggers of the revolution. *Middle Eastern Studies*, *50*(4), 521–535. http://doi.org/10.1080/00263206.2013.850076

Gersh, N. (2017, February 6). The role of corruption in the Syrian War. https://globalanticorruptionblog.com/2017/02/06/the-role-of-corruption-in-the-syrian-civil-war/

Gleick, P. H. (2014) Water, drought, climate change, and conflict in Syria. *American Meteorological Society*, *6*, 331–340. https://doi.org/10.1175/WCAS-D-13-00059.1

Gleick, P. H. (2019). Water as a weapon and casualty of armed conflict: A review of recent water-related violence in Iraq, Syria, and Yemen. *WIREs Water*. https://doi.org/10.1002/wat2.1351

Glenn, C., Rowan, M., Caves, J., & Nada, G. (2019, October 28). *Timeline: The rise, spread, and fall of the Islamic State*. Wilson Center. https://www.wilsoncenter.org/article/timeline-the-rise-spread-and-fall-the-islamic-state

Human Rights Watch. (2021, March 21). Syria: Bread crisis exposes government failure. https://www.hrw.org/news/2021/03/21/syria-bread-crisis-exposes-government-failure

Kelley, C. P., Mohtadi, S., Cane, M. A., Seager, R., & Kushnir, Y. (2015). Climate change in the Fertile Crescent and implications of the recent Syrian drought. *Proceedings of the U.S. National Academy of Sciences*, *112*(11), 3241–3246. https://doi.org/10.1073/pnas.1421533112

Mai, T., & Smith, C. (2015). Addressing the threats to tourism sustainability using systems thinking: A case study of Cat Ba Island, Vietnam. *Journal of Sustainable Tourism*, *23*(10), 1504–1528. https://doi.org/10.1080/09669582.2015.1045514

Mai, T., & Smith, C. (2018). Scenario-based planning for tourism development using system dynamics modeling: A case study of Cat Ba Island, Vietnam. *Tourism Management*, *68*, 336–354. https://doi.org/10.1016/j.tourman.2018.04.005

Mourad, K. A., & Berndtsson, R. (2011). Syrian water resources between the present and the future. *Air, Soil, Water Research, 4*(1), 93–100. https://doi.org/10.4137/ASWR.S8076

Nguyen, N. C., & Bosch, O. J. H. (2013), A Systems thinking approach to identify leverage points for sustainability: A case study in the Cat Ba Biosphere Reserve, Vietnam. *System Research and Behavioral Science, 30*(2), 104–115. https://doi.org/10.1002/sres.2145 Wiley Blackwell.

Nguyen, N. C., Bosch, O. J. H., & Maani, K. E. (2009). The importance of systems thinking and practice for creating biosphere reserves as learning laboratories for sustainable development. http://journals.isss.org/index.php/proceedings53rd/article/view/1161/398

Peters, K., Dupar, M., Opitz-Stapleton, S., Lovell, E., & Cao, Y. (2020). Climate change, conflict, and fragility; An evidence review and recommendations for research and action. https://odi.org/en/publications/climate-change-conflict-and-fragility-an-evidence-review-and-recommendations-for-research-and-action/

Selby, J., Dahi, O.S., Fröhlich, C., & Hulme, M. (2017). Climate change and the Syrian civil war revisited. *Political Geography, 60*, 232–244. https://doi.org/10.1016/j.polgeo.2017.05.007

Shelter Box. (n.d.). https://shelterbox.org/syria/the-syrian-conflict-explained/?_gl=1%2Azfiwv%2A_ga%2AMTgwMTUwMzM1Ny4xNjc4MjkzNjYy%2A_ga_C73VTN624G%2AMTY3ODI5MzY2NS4xLjEuMTY3ODI5MzcxMS4wLjAuMA.

Suter, M. (2017, September 12). Running out of water: Conflict and water scarcity in Yemen and Syria. https://www.atlanticcouncil.org/blogs/menasource/running-out-of-water-conflict-and-water-scarcity-in-yemen-and-syria

UN Children's Fund (UNICEF). (n.d.) A timeline of the Syrian civil war and refugee crisis. https://www.unicef.ie/stories/timeline-syrian-war-refugee-crisis/#:~:text=A%20Timeline%20of%20the%20Syrian%20Civil%20War%20and,Jordan%20close%20to%20the%20Syrian%20border.%202013%20

UN High Commission of Refugees (UNHCR). (2023, April 6). https://data.unhcr.org/en/situations/syria

Vidal, J. (2016, September 7). Water supplies in Syria deteriorating fast due to conflict, experts warn. https://www.theguardian.com/environment/2016/sep/07/water-supplies-in-syria-deteriorating-fast-due-to-conflict-experts-warn

Vox. (2017). Syria's war: Who is fighting and why [video]. https://www.youtube.com/watch?v=JFpanWNgfQY

Weinthal, E., Zawarhi N., & Sowers, J. (2015). Securitizing water, climate, and migration in Israel, Jordan, and Syria. *International Environmental Agreements, 15*, 292–307. https://doi.org/10.1007/s10784-015-9279-4

Whitworth, H. (2021). Understanding the Syrian conflict through a system less. Term paper, CVEN 5837, University of Colorado, Boulder.

13 Systemic Interventions

13.1 INTRODUCTION

System dynamics (SD) models were introduced in Chapters 10–12 to capture the complex interaction among the peace–sustainability–climate (PSC) nexus's three sectors and other systems in the community landscape of Figure 5.1. These structural models were purposely kept generic to show the range of applications of SD in modeling complex nexus and human development and security issues. There are, of course, multiple ways to model the systems of Figure 5.1 and how the three sectors of the PSC nexus interact with these systems.

Modeling the PSC nexus and the landscape dynamics of Figure 5.1 corresponds to stage 5 in Figure 9.2. In that stage, the goal is to reproduce in a satisfactory (satisficing) manner and as accurately as possible (i) the current scenario(s) at play across the community landscape and the PSC nexus; (ii) the deep structures that may explain the issues, behavior patterns, and trends observed across the nexus and at the community level; and (iii) the dynamic hypotheses formulated at the end of the appraisal phase discussed in Chapter 5. This so-called behavior reproduction process is *inductive* and not easy. But, once established, it creates *baseline scenario*(s), which is (are) the foundation of dynamic scenario planning, as discussed below. It helps, in a *deductive* manner, to formulate, model, select, plan, and implement possible interventions to address the issues. Creating a baseline scenario was illustrated in the two case studies in Chapter 12. The progression from formulating intervention scenarios to implementing solutions and, eventually, developing policy plans corresponds to stages 6–10 in Figure 9.2.

Several factors must be acknowledged before using SD tools to reproduce the baseline scenario(s) and model possible interventions. First, as discussed in Chapter 6, all models are simplified simulations, interpretations, and explanations of reality. Second, the models do not necessarily provide unique renditions of the issues being addressed, nor should they be expected to propose concrete solutions for each issue. One of the benefits of SD modeling is, however, to be able to recognize the complex and adaptive nature of learning about the PSC nexus and community-related issues at stake, their variability, their sensitivity to different initial and ongoing conditions, their interconnections, and the fact that cause and effect may be separated in time and space (de Geus, 1998). In general, SD models help decision-makers make more intelligent decisions when selecting various intervention scenarios than purely subjective ones or decisions focusing on only one sector of the nexus or a specific community issue.

Third, one of the consequences of the ill-structured and messy nature of the issues at play across the PSC nexus and the community landscape is that, because of their uncertainty and unpredictable behavior, the behavior reproduction process inherent to SD modeling must be done in a reflective and iterative, incremental, and trial-and-error manner involving multiple feedbacks as shown in Figure 7.8. This learning process also requires incorporating the input of individuals and multidisciplinary opinions from the three groups of stakeholders described in Figure 9.1. It is also vital that all participants involved in developing the baseline scenario(s) and proposing intervention scenarios are at least knowledgeable of the systems thinking skills and habits discussed in Section 4.6.

Fourth, the behavior reproduction process requires that qualitative and quantitative data are available. This process becomes challenging when dealing with dominantly qualitative social and human systems variables. As discussed in Chapters 10–12, it is necessary to introduce proxies, determinants, indicators, and metrics. Recall that in the models presented in these chapters, peace, sustainability, and climate security were semi-quantified using arbitrary peace units (pu), sustainability units (su), and climate security units (cu) that varied over a 0–100 range broken down into several levels of achievement (Table 7.1). Using this approach in practice requires metrics to describe each level of achievement.

Once the models are deemed acceptable, various possible intervention scenarios can be proposed for each issue identified, and decisions can be made about implementing these interventions (stage 6 in Figure 9.2). The SD models are used again to analyze the merits of these interventions and their intended and unintended consequences.

Interventions are generally designed to bridge the gaps between the current and desired PSC states and community development levels. This transition process must be done in a systems-aware manner, keeping in mind that issues across the nexus and in the community are already interrelated in their current and desired states and that addressing one of them may have intended or unintended consequences on the others. Meeting that challenge depends on (i) the current levels of peace, sustainability, climate security, and community development and (ii) the path the community is willing to take to reach higher levels, as summarized in the *community development story* discussed in Section 9.1.

The transition process also implies that the community welcomes change and has a reasonable idea of the desired development state and its indicators related to peace, sustainability, climate security, well-being, health, prosperity, poverty reduction, etc. These emerging states can be interpreted as multiple strategic objectives. In addition, the community must have the resources and skills necessary to increase its capacity over time to reduce the gaps. In general, the higher the community's capacity to perform specific functions, the greater the potential for the community to reach higher levels of peace, sustainability, climate security, and development sooner, assuming no unexpected events would derail capacity building. If such events occur, communities with higher initial capacity will likely be more resilient and recover more quickly, as discussed in Section 10.2.

13.2 DYNAMIC SCENARIO PLANNING AND FORMULATION

13.2.1 Definitions

Scenario planning, or scenario analysis, is an essential tool in *Futures Research* (Glenn and Gordon, 2009). Essentially, scenarios help to "systematically explore, create, [anticipate], and test possible and desirable future pathways to improve decisions"

(Glenn, 2009). They do not predict the future but describe *possibilities* (projections) in complex settings (Weimer-Jehle, 2010), some being more credible, relevant, and probable than others.

In the context of decision-making across the sectors of the PSC nexus and community development, intervention scenarios might be helpful to decision-makers in (i) envisioning alternative hypothetical futures and changes in each sector of the nexus or across the nexus; (ii) exploring possible pathways of transitioning from a current to a desired community development state and levels of peace, sustainability, and climate security; (iii) assessing the implications of possible actions and policy decisions in an uncertain environment over the long term; (iv) creating new decisions or reframing old ones; (v) establishing benchmarks and targets to monitor change; and (vi) identifying key assumptions and preconditions, which, if not met, could lead to risks and unintended consequences in the short and long term.

Scenario planning represents a transitional mode of decision-making between making short-term predictions and speculating over the long term (Zurek and Henrichs, 2007). It can follow forward or backward pathways (Robinson, 1982). *Forecasting* is the most commonly used forward approach to tackle complex problems. It takes the present state and, at times, historical data as the starting point and justification to meet future goals and seeks to determine the likelihood of reaching those goals. One of the limitations of forecasting is that predictions are based on extrapolating past and current trends to predict the future, which usually works well, but only for short-term (less than 20 years) futures (Dreborg, 1996). Forecasting is not good at predicting the future in situations of high uncertainty that are likely to change unpredictably over the long term.

Compared to forecasting, *backcasting* starts with the end or outcome in mind (e.g., alternative desired development levels or specific PSC states). It considers a series of possible/plausible futures from the desired state(s) to the current state, not just in terms of likelihood but preferably in terms of desirability (e.g., socioeconomic, environmental), feasibility (i.e., based on capacity); and other criteria, such as security, prosperity, health, and well-being (Robinson, 2003). Dreborg (1996) noted that backcasting is appropriate to address complex societal problems involving multiple systems for which uncertainty is present, change is a constant, and the "time horizon is long enough to allow considerable scope for deliberate choice."

A strong value proposition of backcasting is testing complex systems and seeing their possible responses and robustness to different situations, with some being more probable than others and some more constraining than others. In return, this helps identify the appropriateness of current policies to address such situations and what it would take to develop, in an uncertain environment, and assess (monitor and evaluate) new future policies. Hence, backcasting represents a powerful approach for exploring interventions across the PSC nexus and at the community level in the medium- to long-term future (i.e., 20–50 years or more). Forecasting can still be incorporated into an overall backcasting approach to scenario planning when, for instance, trying to predict an evident trend or developing a blueprint to address a specific issue in the short term.

Dynamic scenario planning combines the normative aspects of scenario analysis, focusing on what is *desirable*, and SD concentrating on what is *possible* (Ward and

Schriefer, 1998). Various corporate entities and government agencies have used it to make strategic planning decisions and explore the most likely futures in various complex and uncertain situations at different scales. The reader will find several examples of the application of scenario planning in the texts by Georgantzas and Acar (1995), Fahey and Randall (1998), and Ritchie-Dunham and Rabbino (2001).

13.2.2   EXAMPLES OF SCENARIO ANALYSIS FRAMEWORKS

Examples of scenario analysis frameworks incorporating systems thinking are available in the development literature. They are primarily policy tools to simulate national, regional, or global transformations and predictions into the future (e.g., mid to end of the twenty-first century):

- The World3-03 "world model" looks at different scenarios or pathways of world development by considering the links between economic growth and the environment (Meadows et al., 2004). The framework has evolved since its original versions, World 2 and 3, starting at MIT in the 1970s. Updated versions of that framework have been proposed in the literature (Bossel, 2007). It has been recalibrated using more recent data from 1995 to 2002 around industrial and service output, population, birth rate, life expectancy, and arable land (Pasqualino et al., 2015).
- The Pardee Center for International Futures (IFs) framework accounts for links between various systems and subsystems related to economics, agriculture, population, energy, education, health, environment, infrastructure, and socio-political systems (Hughes, 2016; Moyer and Hedden, 2020). The latest version of the IF framework (August 2022) is available online (https://korbel.du.edu/pardee/).
- Frameworks to model and forecast changes associated with human–environment interactions and global environmental changes include the TARGETS framework (*Tool to Assess Regional and Global Environmental and Health Targets for Sustainability*) developed by Rotmans and deVries (1997). It consists of five interacting dynamic submodels covering the areas of population and health, energy, land and food, water, and biogeochemical cycles (see Figure 2.5). Another framework called ANEMI, developed by Davies and Simonovic (2010, 2011), considers "eight [interacting] sectors of the society-biosphere-climate system—climate, carbon cycle, land use, population, surface water flow, water use, water quality, and the economy" (Davies and Simonovic, 2010).
- *The Integrated Sustainable Development Goals* (iSDG) framework uses an integrated SD modeling methodology to explore development scenarios linking strategies and policy as a country progresses toward reaching the 17 SDGs. It was built on the *Threshold 21* (T21) model (Barney, 2002; Pedercini et al., 2018). As shown in Figure 5.5, it involves 78 SDG indicators divided into ten social, ten economic, and ten environmental sectors, each consisting of interconnected stocks (variables) and flows with possible feedback processes (Pedercini et al., 2020). The latest version of the software is available on the Millennium Institute website (www.isdgs.org).

- The CLEWS framework, which stands for *Climate-Land-Energy-Water Strategy* (Bazilian et al., 2011), uses an integrated approach to develop intervention scenarios and carry out policy analysis around water, energy, and land resources and the impact of climate on these resources (www. osimosys.org). The framework allows the resources to interact where one module's output becomes another's input. The CLEWS framework allows for scenario-based analysis around energy, water, and food shortages while considering climate effects. Examples of the application of this framework can be found in Hermann (2012), Hermann et al. (2012), Howells et al. (2013), Welsch et al. (2014), and Dale et al. (2015).
- Examples of integrated assessment modeling frameworks and scenario analysis tools can be found on the International Institute of Applied Systems Analysis (IIASA) website (www.iiasa.ac.at).

It should be noted that the global frameworks mentioned above were designed to handle high levels of decision-making around complex interacting issues. They possess two general features. First, they have been mainly used to model the complex and integrated dynamics of change and development at the global, regional, or country scale with high aggregation. Second, they all acknowledge the difficulty in obtaining data to quantify the links considered in the frameworks. This second shortcoming is often mentioned in complex systems models of nexus issues.

Besides the global scenario analyses mentioned above, others have focused on specific issues such as water, energy, land, food, health, population, etc. (see review in Amadei, 2019). Although sector-specific, the analyses often include other socio-economic and environmental factors that interact with the sector of interest. A good example, among many others, is the CanadaWater system dynamic model proposed by Simonovic and Rajasekaram (2004). Although focusing on water, the model uses a decision-making process involving 12 scenarios to "investigate policy options in the areas of freshwater availability, wastewater treatment, economic growth, population growth, energy production, and food production" for Canada.

13.2.3 FORMULATING INTERVENTION SCENARIOS

In complex settings such as the landscape of Figure 5.1, it is impossible to formulate the best intervention scenarios that would (i) address issues involving one or several sectors of the PSC nexus and (ii) include the different systems the nexus interacts with at the community level. Multiple intervention scenarios are possible for different contexts and scales. Despite that limitation, scenario formulation is not just a random and intuitive process. A review of the literature (Amadei, 2019) shows that *good-enough intervention scenarios* must have narratives and storylines with the following characteristics:

1. *Be clear about the vision, outcome, and desirable future state(s).* The predictive impact of possible interventions and pathways must be compatible with reducing the gap between current and desired conditions. That vision must be formulated as part of a theory of change (ToC) narrated in terms of all three sectors of the PSC nexus and the future development and security

of the community. Reasonable and challenging assumptions and preconditions must be identified for each intervention scenario to unfold successfully. The predictive community outcome and desirable future states need to be (i) expressed in terms of definite fundamental changes in peace versus conflict, sustainability versus unsustainability, climate security versus vulnerability, and changes in livelihood and other systems and (ii) supported by preferably measurable performance indicators that are technically feasible, reliable, valid, relevant, sensitive to change, cost-effective, and timely (Caldwell, 2002), but also specific, easy to understand, and data-supported (Winograd and Farrow, 2011). More specifically, the vision includes framing which sectors of the PSC nexus and community systems and subsystems need to be considered: in what context, within what boundaries (environmental, political, and socioeconomic) and constraints, for what different levels of uncertainty and acceptable risk, and over what temporal and physical scales.

2. *Define the present baseline condition.* Scenario planning requires that the present is clearly defined regarding the nexus and the community. More specifically, there is a need to identify the baseline scenario mentioned earlier in this chapter. It describes (i) the current dynamics at play in each sector of and across the nexus, (ii) the various systems the nexus interacts with, (iii) existing constraints and stressors across the landscape and whether those are likely to be relevant in the future, (iv) the capacity and vulnerability of the community, and (v) what exogenous relevant factors (e.g., socioeconomic or political surprises or crises) are currently affecting the landscape or could affect it in the future.

3. *Select mental models.* Ideally, each intervention scenario must have a foundational narrative and storyline built on solid mental models. As discussed with the iceberg model in Figure 1.1, addressing practical issues and events is driven by mental models and structural and behavioral patterns.

4. *Lay out credible alternative scenarios.* Once the vision and future community state(s) have been identified, credible alternative scenarios (usually 3–4 scenarios) with solid narratives, mental models, documentation, and dynamic hypotheses must be clearly articulated to account for uncertainty. To be considered credible, the scenarios must possess attributes/indicators of success and stakeholder participation while also being adaptive to possible changes, stressors, and constraints over time, which could affect the effects of the interventions in the short and long term and, subsequently, the systems affected by these interventions. Furthermore, scenarios must show the potential to limit trade-offs and increase synergies across the nexus sectors. In practice, however, there are no precise requirements for the number of scenarios that should be considered. Robinson (1990) noted that the challenge for decision-makers is to "choose between exploring a wide range of options with multiple scenarios and exploring one scenario in more depth."

5. *Envision a logical strategic framework for each scenario.* A logical strategic framework or logframe must be outlined for all alternative credible intervention scenarios. This strategic planning approach, common in managing development projects (see review by Amadei, 2014), requires a clear

understanding of the scenarios' impacts/outcomes, goals, objectives/outputs, activities, and inputs. Meeting the goals and objectives contributes to the desired end state and reinforces the vision and ToC discussed in the first guideline proposed above.

6. *Synchronize the scenarios.* When multiple interventions are envisioned, which is more likely the case (as in the case studies in Chapter 12), a challenge is synchronizing the inputs/activities/outputs/goals/impacts among all interventions. Another challenge is synchronizing interventions at different physical scales (local, regional, and global) and time-scale (short-, medium-, and long-term). Synchronization requires considering some trade-offs and synergies across sectors. The effect of physical and time scales on synchronizing interventions was discussed in Section 5.2.2.

These six guidelines generally do not guarantee optimum or even promising interventions. They are necessary but insufficient to eliminate, at least in part, the randomness of a purely intuitive or empirical decision-making approach (based on experience, for instance). Nevertheless, they provide a much-needed structure involving the stakeholders of Figure 9.1 when defining possible pathways at the crossroads between the three sectors of the PSC nexus.

Table 13.1 provides a *non-exhaustive* list of components that can be assembled to create intervention storylines and narratives. Because of the uncertainty involved in peace versus conflict, sustainability versus unsustainable practices, and climate security versus vulnerability and community development in general, it is recommended to create a range of narratives representing the best-case to less-than-best-case intervention scenarios. That ranking can be based on several criteria, such as (i) the confidence in the quality and quantity of core and sector-specific data about the sectors of the PSC nexus and the systems of the community landscape, (ii) the importance and value of some sectors and systems versus the others, (iii) the strength

---

TABLE 13.1

Possible Storyline Components in Scenario Planning

Areas of Interest	Possible Storyline Components...
Population-Related	• Changes in demographics, diet, fertility, migration, education, group empowerment • Occurrence of natural and non-natural hazards and effects on population dynamics • Changes in institutional capacity (governance, the rule of law, etc.) • Desired changes in health, labor, income, and distribution • Gender equality • Justice, equity, diversity, and inclusion (JEDI) issues • Current and target education (traditional and technical) by gender • Desired employment level by sector (agriculture, construction, tourism, etc.), jobs versus labor

(Continued)

TABLE 13.1 (Continued)
Possible Storyline Components in Scenario Planning

Areas of Interest	Possible Storyline Components…
Peace-Related (Positive, Negative, Cultural)	• Current versus desired positive peace domains: well-functioning government, sound business environment, equitable distribution of resources, acceptance of the rights of others, good relations with neighbors, free flow of information, high levels of human capital, and low levels of corruption • Current versus desired negative peace domains: ongoing domestic and international conflict, societal safety and security, and militarization • Current versus desired cultural peace • Transitioning from conflict to peace through peacebuilding, peacemaking, and peacekeeping • Addressing conflicts between different resources and service users • Addressing recurring conflict issues
Community Livelihood-Related	• Current versus desired community resource security (WASH, energy, land/veg, food, agriculture) • Community resources consumption • Current versus desired management of resources and services • Current versus desired levels of community capacity • Effect of mismanagement of resources, aging infrastructure, and overexploitation of resources • Effect of behavior change on livelihood demands • Pollution and toxic contamination • Current versus desired capacity and effect of capacity level on community livelihood and development • Effect of resources supply, prices, and regulations on peace/conflict • Impact of future community growth on resource security • Consumption • Governance and the rule of law
Climate Security-Related	• Effect of climate change on livelihood resources (e.g., water, land, food, and energy supply) and community services (e.g., transportation, telecom, health, etc.) • Effect of climate change on environment and ecosystems • Current versus desired levels of climate change awareness, adaptation, and mitigation practices at different scales • Current versus desired community resilience to climate change and other natural and non-natural hazards • Nature and effectiveness of climate actions • Resilience to single and multiple adverse events • Response to past events and addressing vulnerabilities

(Continued)

TABLE 13.1 (*Continued*)
Possible Storyline Components in Scenario Planning

Areas of Interest	Possible Storyline Components...
PSC Nexus-Related	• Potential dynamic interactions between sectors of the nexus over time.
	• Managing trade-offs and synergies related to peace, sustainability, and climate security
	• How to provide more efficient and resilient resource delivery
	• Current versus desired interaction between the three PSC sectors
	• Effect of future population growth on peace, livelihood, and climate change
	• Impact of providing more efficient infrastructure to supply livelihood resources
	• Manage trade-offs between the PSC nexus sectors
	• Identify leverage points and create synergy between sectors of the nexus
	• Education and empowerment of stakeholders
	• Capacity building across sectors
	• The cumulative effect of climate change and conflicts over time.
	• Where and when the dynamic between peace, sustainability, and climate security (or their opposites) starts and ends?
	• Causal chains (i.e., pathways) between the three sectors (i.e., how one or two sectors may trigger the others) and how diverse development and security areas may start a state of peace versus conflict, sustainability versus unsustainability, and climate security versus vulnerability

of the stakeholder dynamics of Figure 9.1, and (iv) the capacity of the community to deliver specific services in the short and long term and its resilience to adverse events, as discussed in Section 5.4.

13.3 EVALUATING AND SELECTING INTERVENTION SCENARIOS

Regardless of how solid and comprehensive the scenario narratives are, the next question is about which intervention scenario(s) to select and pathways to follow to reduce the gaps between current and desired states of peace, sustainability, climate security, and overall community development. Some credible intervention scenarios identified and formulated are likely better suited than others to address the gaps. Therefore, decision support systems based on a multiobjective evaluation and selection process are required to identify the most desirable scenarios and consider them in further detail to move toward possible implementation. The process can be based strictly on decision-makers' intuition, judgment, and experience (not considered here) or involve a combination of subjective decision-making tools supported by analytical and numerical methods. The decision science literature (Decision Sciences Institute, 2013) and Futures Research literature (Glenn and Gordon, 2009) have proposed multiple methods and tools of decision-making that are worth considering in the evaluation and selection of intervention scenarios.

Regardless of the tools used to evaluate and select intervention scenarios, it is essential to realize that it is impossible to know with certainty (i.e., optimally and most desirably) that an intervention is "best" compared to the others because all are likely to have some benefits and restrictions and require some forms of compromise. As noted by Simon (1978), "omniscient rationality" is not possible in a realistic world (such as the landscape of Figure 5.1 in which the PSC nexus unfolds) that is characterized by uncertainty, complexity, nonlinearities, and feedback mechanisms. Hence, only *satisficing* (i.e., good enough) interventions can be outlined, not optimum ones. This remark creates constraints regarding the range of tools used to evaluate and select scenarios.

13.3.1 SHARED SOCIOECONOMIC PATHWAYS SCENARIOS

O'Neill and coworkers (Kriegler et al., 2012; O'Neill et al., 2014; 2017) proposed an interesting framework for framing intervention scenarios around shared socioeconomic pathways (SSP). Pathways are defined as alternative future scenarios of socioeconomic development associated with mitigation and adaptation to climate change at the country or regional scale. Figure 13.1 shows five pathway narratives and storylines proposed by O'Neill and coworkers "representing different combinations and challenges to mitigation and adaptation" to climate change.

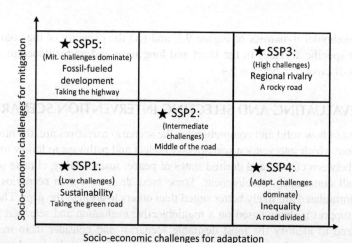

FIGURE 13.1 Five SSP pathways represent mitigation challenges and climate change adaptation.

Source: O'Neill et al. (2017). Used by permission of Elsevier.

The pathways are briefly described as follows (O'Neill et al., 2017):

- SSP 1: low socioeconomic challenges to adaptation and mitigation because of solid institutions, significant income growth, a decline in inequality, and a long-term, sustained value shift that puts sustainability first.
- SSP 2: middle-of-the-road challenges to adaptation and mitigation.
- SSP 3: high socioeconomic challenges to adaptation and mitigation because of slow technical advancement, poor investment in human capital, slow income growth, and weak institutions.
- SSP 4: no difficulty in mitigation because of modest economic growth, access to technology, and knowledge in the sector of the economy where power is concentrated. The challenges to adaption are high for the section of the population with low levels of income and limited access to effective institutions.
- SSP 5: no difficulty in adaptation because of high economic growth allowing for the quick completion of various development goals. The challenges to mitigation are high because of rapid economic growth that relies on fossil fuels.

The different pathways represent storylines with specific mental models and assumptions on "demographics, human development, economy and lifestyles, policies and institutions (excluding climate policies), technology, and environment and natural resources." The pathways indicators, variables, and metrics are primarily *qualitative* and based on expert opinions, statistical and probabilistic projections, and forecasting narratives available in the literature (e.g., IPCC) about climate change's past and plausible future effects at the country or regional level.

The concept of SSP has been extended to explore future scenarios combining socioeconomic development and conflict involvement associated with mitigation and adaptation to climate change at the country or regional scale (Hegre et al., 2016). As mentioned in Section 2.5, opinions are divided in the literature on how peace/conflict, sustainability/unsustainability, and climate security/vulnerability affect each other and contribute to human development and security. Hegre and coworkers considered pathways with specific indicators and variables related to economic growth (GDP per capita), population growth, and educational attainment. The authors concluded that "investing in a sustainable future [i.e., following a pathway such as SSP 1 in Figure 13.1] is fully consistent with an ambition of global stability and peace while simultaneously having comparatively low barriers to climate change mitigation and adaptation." Improvement in education contributes to that trend.

A limitation of the pathway approach is that it provides socioeconomic projections of the effect of climate change (and conflict) at the regional, national, and even sub-national levels (Mariya Absar and Preston, 2015) but not at the community level. Another limitation of the SSP approach is its subjective nature. Its effectiveness could be enhanced by integrating it into dynamic scenario planning and combining it with SD tools and some of the narrative components (qualitative and quantitative) listed in Table 13.1.

Another type of pathway analysis involving climate change and adverse events was proposed by Randers et al. (2019), which looked at the possible influence of 14 socioeconomic SDGs on three environmental SDGs and well-being until 2050.

Different pathways were considered, including a business-as-usual pathway where decision-making has been made using the traditional socioeconomic mindset since 1980. They concluded that in a "business-as-usual scenario from 2018 to 2050, human societies become richer, in the sense that people live in countries with higher GDP per person, but they live in more unequal societies and in an environment that is increasingly damaged by human activity."

13.3.2 Multi-Criteria Decision Analysis

Multi-criteria decision analysis (MCDA) or multi-criteria decision making (MCDM) was already mentioned in Section 5.6 as a tool to rank *retrospectively* issues identified at the end of the community appraisal. It requires selecting critical criteria or objectives deemed essential in the decision process. The same method can be used *prospectively* to rank intervention scenarios with clear goals. The challenge is to choose criteria specific to each sector of the PSC nexus and criteria that cut across all three sectors. Once the criteria are selected, an MCDA performance matrix is created. Subjective scores and weights (values of importance) are assigned for different scenarios, final ratings are calculated as the sums of the scores times weights, and sensitivity analyses are carried out to see how the ratings vary.

A fictitious example is summarized in Table 13.2, where three individual alternative scenarios and three combined alternative scenarios are considered. The weights

TABLE 13.2

Fictitious Example of an MCDA Performance Matrix for a Community Project

Criteria	Weight	Scenario 1		Scenario 2		Scenario 3		Combined Scenarios 1		Combined Scenarios 2		Combined Scenarios 3	
		Score	Score x Weight	Score	Score x Weight	Score	Score x Weight	Score	Score x Weight	Score	Score x Weight	Score	Score x Weight
Cost-Effectiveness	3	2	6	1	3	1	3	2	6	2	6	3	9
Social Acceptability	5	3	15	1	5	2	10	2	10	2	10	3	15
O&M Feasibility	4	2	8	1	4	2	8	2	8	1	4	2	8
Environmental Sustainability	5	1	5	3	15	2	10	3	15	3	15	2	10
Community Participation	4	3	12	2	8	2	8	3	12	2	8	3	12
Impact on Community Health	4	2	8	2	8	1	4	2	8	1	4	2	8
Economic Impact	3	3	9	2	6	1	3	2	6	2	6	3	9
Number of People Impacted	4	2	8	2	8	2	8	2	8	3	12	3	12
Ratings			71		57		54		73		65		83

vary from 1 to 5, with scores varying from 1 to 3. In this example, the combined scenarios three option tallies the highest weighted score and may want to be considered first. However, the other options may still need to be considered if the combined scenario three option is limiting upon extra investigation.

The MCDA represents a valuable tool to filter prospectively alternative interventions and retain those that meet critical criteria. However, its main limitation resides in its subjective nature because the weights and scores are only intelligent guesses that decision-makers make based on their intuition and experience. It is crucial that these decision-makers and stakeholders from the three groups shown in Figure 9.1 are qualified individuals, possess the necessary expertise, are systems thinkers, and are aware of their personal biases. The inherent subjectivity can also be reduced by embedding the MCDA criteria of evaluation that are objective (e.g., cost-effectiveness, health impact, economic impact, and impacted population in Table 13.1) into SD models to analyze their relative importance. Nonobjective criteria, such as community participation and social acceptability in Table 13.1, can also be embedded in the models once semi-quantitative proxies have been selected. This process can help account for possible interdependencies among criteria not usually accounted for in the MCDA analysis.

13.3.3 CROSS-IMPACT BALANCE ANALYSIS

The Cross-Impact Balance (CIB) method was proposed by Weimer-Jehle (2006, 2010). It resembles the cross-impact analysis discussed in Section 6.3 but goes beyond scoring the direct influence and dependence of two variables at a time. Its main value proposition is to handle multiple variables' impact and sensitivity and determine whether a given scenario involving the variables is consistent with their assumed rules of interaction. The variables include interacting states, social entities (individuals, groups, institutions), and project-specific components such as infrastructure.

As an illustrative example of CIB analysis, let's consider in an aggregated manner the peace, sustainability, and climate security sectors of the PSC nexus. The sectors' interactions can be high, medium, or low. Using the approach proposed by Weimer-Jehle (2010), their interaction matrix is assumed to be represented as summarized in Table 13.3. Each state can influence or impact the other two states in an enabling/promoting or constraining/inhibiting way. Decision-makers use a scoring range to conduct the cross-impact judgment between the three states. Weimer-Jehle (2006) uses the following scale: −3 (strong inhibiting influence), −2 (inhibiting influence), −1 (slightly inhibiting influence), 0 (no influence), +1 (slightly promoting influence), +2 (promoting influence), and +3 (strong promoting influence). The scoring selected in Table 13.3 is arbitrary.

Table 13.3 consists of six 3×3 sub-tables (sub-matrices) that define the rules of how the three PSC sectors could *"possibly"* agree or disagree as they influence each other; the diagonal sub-tables are left empty. The term "possibly" is essential here because, as remarked by Weimer-Jehle, not all decision scenarios are consistent with the rules of how the three sectors are assumed to interact. In practice, these rules can be determined during participatory appraisal with the stakeholders in Figure 9.1.

TABLE 13.3

Example of Cross-Impact Balance Analysis: High (H), Medium (M), and Low (L)

		Peace			Sustainability			Climate Security		
		H	M	L	H	M	L	H	M	L
Peace	H				2	1	−3	2	1	−3
	M				1	2	−3	1	0	−1
	L				−2	0	2	−2	0	2
Sustainability	H	2	1	−3				2	−1	−1
	M	1	0	−1				1	1	−2
	L	−2	0	2				−2	−1	3
Climate Security	H	2	0	−2	2	1	−3			
	M	1	1	−2	1	0	−1			
	L	−2	0	2	−2	0	2			
Total + or −		+4	1	−5	+4	2	−6	+4	0	−4

A scenario must be selected before determining whether a decision scenario is consistent with the rules specified in Table 13.3. For instance, let's assume a high peace, high sustainability, and high climate security (HHH) scenario, where the term "high" needs to be described by specific context- and scale-specific indicators. The question is whether that scenario is even possible for the rules selected in Table 13.3.

Following the methodology of Weimer-Jehle (2006, 2010), the three shaded rows of Table 13.3 corresponding to the selected HHH scenario are identified first. The corresponding scores are added for each one of the nine columns. The values at the bottom of Table 13.3 show each state's dependence (sensitivity) on the other two for the selected scenario. For a scenario to be consistent with the rules, the highest values at the bottom of the table must be associated with the states that match those of the selected scenario state. In this example, +4, +4, and +4 match the HHH scenario. Hence, that scenario is *consistent* with the rules of agreement and influence. Another consistent scenario is low peace, sustainability, and climate security (LLL). If the scenario were inconsistent, a new one would need to be selected among all $3 \times 3 \times 3 = 27$ possible system scenarios or revised scores would need to be laid out. Note that multiple scenarios could match a set of rules.

13.3.4 Optimization Methods

As discussed by the author regarding scenario evaluation and ranking for the water–energy–land–food nexus (Amadei, 2019), single-objective and multiple-objective optimization tools combined with sensitivity analysis can help formulate, evaluate, and select intervention scenarios. These mathematical tools can manage complex issues and multiple variables, such as those addressed in this book.

This section briefly reviews these methods and presents some illustrative examples using the STELLA Architect software platform (version 3.2). It contains a unique functionality that can be used to conduct single or multiobjective optimization (combined with sensitivity analysis) once an SD model has been built and objective functions and constraints for key variables have been selected. Two webinars demonstrating this functionality can be found on the web (https://www.iseesystems. com/resources/webinars/). The numerical examples mentioned below use the input data listed in Appendices C, D, and E.

13.3.4.1 Single Objective Optimization

The goal of single objective (or criteria) constrained optimization is to find, among various alternatives, an optimum solution to a complex problem with multiple variables once an objective (also called goal or utility) function and associated constraints have been established. Mathematically speaking, this amounts to solving the following (Venter, 2010):

$$\text{Optimize: } f(\mathbf{x})$$

$$\text{Subject to: } g_j(\mathbf{x}) \leq 0 \quad j = 1, M$$

$$h_k(\mathbf{x}) = 0 \quad k = 1, P$$

$$x_{iL} \leq x_i \leq x_{iU} \, i = 1, N \tag{13.1}$$

where $f(\mathbf{x})$ is the objective function of a vector $\mathbf{x}$ of decision variables x_i ($i= 1,N$). In eq. (13.1), $g_j(\mathbf{x})$ and $h_k(\mathbf{x})$ represent inequality ($j=1, M$) and equality ($k=1, P$) constrained functions, respectively. The N variables x_i vary over a domain defined by their respective upper bound x_{iU} and lower bound x_{iL}. Constrained optimization consists of finding the vector of variables x that results in an optimum solution for $f(\mathbf{x})$ while satisfying all the conditions listed in eq. (13.1). The different functions in eq. (13.1) can be linear or nonlinear. For problems in which a satisficing solution, rather than an optimum one, is sought, the same approach can be used to determine the vector $\mathbf{x}$ that yields a *satisficing* value of $f(\mathbf{x})$ rather than an *optimum* (best) value.

An example of single objective optimization is, for instance, trying to optimize the overall security of a community, S, which is believed to depend on three variables as follows:

$$S = f(P, SU, CS) \tag{13.2}$$

In this equation, P, SU, and CS are peace, sustainability, and climate security measures, respectively. These measures depend on many variables constrained between specified upper and lower bounds. The goal is to find the combination of variables that optimizes security or a good enough security value.

Four illustrative examples of single objective optimization are presented below using the SD models in Chapters 10 and 11.

Example 1

As a first example, let us consider the PSC1 model of Figure 10.11. The single objective consists of finding out what combination of basic peace, sustainability, and climate security adjustment rates per year ARP [0.01–0.02/year], ARS [0.01–0.05/year], and ARC [0.01–0.05/year] would result in a maximum value of the average RPSC ratio at year 100. The optimization analysis (using the Differential Evolution Method with x_i [$i = 1,3$]) gives a value of that ratio equal to 0.89 for the three highest values of the adjustment rates as expected, i.e., ARP=0.02/year and ARS=ARC=0.05/year.

A second analysis was conducted for the case shown in Figure 10.14, simulating a conflict between years 20 and 50. In this case, the maximum value of RPSC at year 100 is equal to 0.22 for ARP=ARS=ARC=0.01/year. The algorithm allows exploring what would happen if optimization were sought at specific times between 0 and 100 years. For instance, if, for the example of Figure 10.14, optimization is aimed at year 30, the maximum value of RPSC at that time is equal to 0.31 for ARP=ARS=ARC=0.01/year, but the value of RPSC at year 100 is equal to 0.22.

A similar illustrative example could be developed for the PSC2 model of Figure 10.15, where three basic adjustment rates for peace, four for sustainability, and two for climate security are considered. In that case, x_i ($i = 1,9$) in eq. (13.1). The goal would be to optimize the average of the three RP, RS, and RC ratios for constrained values of the nine adjustment rates. Another option is considering a multiobjective optimization for the three weighted RP, RS, and RC ratios, as discussed below.

Example 2

As a second illustrative example, let us consider the dynamic of Figure 10.7, showing how community capacity drops after an adverse event and increases because of capacity building. Multiple variables could be used in the optimization analysis. In this example, the single objective is to optimize the community capacity assessment (hence the development level) for (i) values of the seven capacity-building adjustment rates ranging between 0.01 and 0.05/month and (ii) values of the capacity-building starting times ranging between 1 and 4 months. This single objective optimization example consists of x_i ($i = 1,14$) variables. The optimization results are listed in Tables 13.4 and 13.5 at 12 and 72 months of recovery after an adverse event. Both tables indicate that the adjustment rates and starting times for all types of capacity do not have to be identical if the objective is to optimize community capacity assessment and the development level.

TABLE 13.4

Values of Capacity Basic Adjustment Rates (/month) to Optimize Community Capacity Assessment at 12 and 72 Months After an Event

Time (Months)	Inst.	HR	Technical	Econ.	Energy	Env.	Socio-Cultural	Community Capacity Assessment
12	0.05	0.05	0.05	0.05	0.05	0.05	0.05	50.15
72	0.05	0.05	0.04	0.04	0.04	0.05	0.03	98.93

Inst. (Institutional), HR (Human Resources), Econ. (Economic/Financial), and Env. (Environmental)

TABLE 13.5

Values of the Capacity-Building Starting Times (in Months) to Optimize Community Capacity Assessment at 12 and 72 Months After an Event

Time (Months)	Inst.	HR	Technical	Econ.	Energy	Env.	Socio-Cultural	Community Capacity Assessment
12	1	2	2	2	3	3	4	50.15
72	1	3	3	2	2	1	2	98.93

Inst. (Institutional), HR (Human Resources), Econ. (Economic/Financial), and Env. (Environmental)

Example 3

A third example considers the PSC3 model of Figure 11.1. The goal is to find a combination of factors that would maximize the state of the community, SC, at time $t = 50$ years. The following eight variables were considered: (i) the seven basic capacity adjustment rates in the capacity module ranging from 0.001 to 0.003/year and (ii) the basic resources supply rate ranging from 0.5 to 0.8/year. Assuming that the states of peace, sustainability, and climate security carry the same weights (1/3 each), the maximum value of SC is equal to 27.1 for a basic resources supply rate of 0.8/year, and the following values of the capacity adjustment rates (per year): 0.001 for institutional capacity, 0.001 for human resources capacity, 0.003 for technical capacity, 0.0025 for economic/financial capacity, 0.0025 for energy capacity, 0.002 for environmental capacity, and 0.002 for socio-cultural capacity. In this example, the basic adjustment rates $ARP = ARS = ARC = 0.01$/year.

Example 4

Finally, the fourth example considers model PSC5 shown in Figure 11.10. The goal is to find the values of (i) basic arable land yield (grains) [10–30 t/ha/year], (ii) basic pasture land yield [30–50 t/ha/year], (iii) basic rate of adding livestock units

TABLE 13.6

Values of Five Variables to Optimize the Peace State at Year 20 Without and With Climate Change Effect

	Basic Arable Land Yield (t/ha/year)	Basic Pasture Land Yield (t/ha/year)	Basic Rate Adding LUs (/year)	Fraction of Allocated GW for Irrigation	Fraction of Allocated SW for Irrigation	Peace State P
No Climate Change	30	30	0.7	0.008	0.3	47.6
With Climate Change	20	50	0.9	0.008	0.3	26.7

(livestock 1) [0.7–0.9/year], (iv) fraction allocated as GW for irrigation [0.004–0.008/year], and (v) fraction allocated as SW for irrigation [0.1–0.3/year] to maximize the state of peace at year 20 without climate change and with the progressive climate change effect of Figure 11.11. The results are shown in Table 13.6.

13.3.4.2 Multiobjective Optimization

Constrained optimization becomes more complicated when the decision process involves multiple objectives that may or may not compete and depend on each other. In this case, $f(x)$ in eq. (13.1) becomes a multiobjective function $f(\mathbf{x}) = (f_1(\mathbf{x}), f_2(\mathbf{x})\dots f_k(\mathbf{x}))^T$ where k is the number of objective functions. In the case of the PSC nexus, a good example would be to consider an objective function for each of the three nexus sectors. Each function would depend on a vector $\mathbf{x}$ of indicators specific to peace, sustainability, and climate security.

Several evolutionary-based multiobjective (or multicriteria) optimization techniques have been proposed to handle multiple objective problems. Among them, *evolutionary Pareto-based algorithms* have been found to provide the most robust and rapid search algorithms to determine "near-optimal solutions" to complex multiobjective optimization problems involving continuous or discrete/integer variables and linear and nonlinear objective functions and constraints (Coello Coello, 1999; Lampinen and Zelinka, 2000; Collette and Siarry, 2003). Chichakly (2013) demonstrated a strong value proposition for using *Differential Evolution* (DE), which is a type of evolutionary multiobjective optimization algorithm initially proposed by Storn and Price (1997).

In general, when using multiobjective Pareto-based optimization algorithms, the objective functions $(f_1(\mathbf{x}), f_2(\mathbf{x})\dots f_k(\mathbf{x}))$ cannot all be optimized at the same time. The focus becomes determining a set of *feasible* nondominated solutions, where "a non-dominated solution is defined as one that outperforms each of the other identified solutions in at least one objective" (Chichakly, 2013). The algorithms produce a so-called Pareto solution set, i.e., a set of solutions that fall on a k-dimensional trade-off surface, sometimes called a Pareto front (Miettinen, 1999). Several solutions are possible and linked: if one objective is met, another may not be completed entirely. Decision-makers require additional subjective preferences and trade-offs to select an appropriate solution to the optimization problem among all possible Pareto optimal solutions. Pareto-based methods apply primarily to complex issues with a limited number of objective functions (Chichakly, 2013).

In the context of this book, a multiple objective optimization example is, for instance, trying to optimize peace (P), sustainability (SU), and climate security (CS), each being dependent on various variables as follows

$$P = f(PPI, GPI, CPI)$$

$$SU = g(people, planet, prosperity)$$

$$CS = h(awareness, adaptation, mitigation) \tag{13.3}$$

The first function in eq. (13.3) depends on the positive, negative, and cultural peace indices discussed in Section 2.3. The second function involves the 3Ps of sustainability, which depends on some of the 17 SDGs (Table 2.1). Finally, the third function depends on three CS practices.

Two illustrative examples of multiple objective optimizations are presented below using the SD models in Chapters 10 and 11.

Example 5

The multiobjective constrained optimization problem selected in this example relates to Figure 10.11 and the PSC1 model. Unlike the first example, the multiobjective consists of finding out what combination of basic peace, sustainability, and CS adjustment rates per year ARP [0.01–0.02], ARS [0.01–0.05], and ARC [0.01–0.05] would result in maximum values of the peace, sustainability, and CS states at year 100. The analysis gives the following values: 78.4 for peace, 93.3 for sustainability, and 95.2 for CS when ARP = 0.02/year and ARS = ARC = 0.05/year.

Example 6

This example considers model PSC5. The *multiobjective* constrained optimization problem selected here is to determine what combination of (i) basic arable land yield (grains) x_1 [10–30 t/ha/year], (ii) basic pasture land yield x_2 [30–50 t/ha/year], (iii) basic rate of adding livestock units x_3 (livestock 1) [0.7–0.9/year], (iv) fraction allocated as GW for irrigation x_4 [0.004–0.008/year], and (v) fraction allocated as SW for irrigation x_5 [0.1–0.3/year] would result in maximum values of the peace, sustainability, and CS states at year 20 for two scenarios: no climate change and linearly increasing climate change. The results of the optimization analysis (using the Differential Evolution Method) are listed in Table 13.7.

TABLE 13.7

Values of Five Variables to Maximize the Peace, Sustainability, and Climate Security States at Year 20 With No Climate Change Effect and a Linearly Increasing Climate Change Effect From 0 to 4 Over 50 Years

	Basic Arable Land Yield (t/ha/year)	Basic Pasture Land Yield (t/ha/year)	Basic Rate Adding LUs (/year)	Fraction of Allocated GW for Irrigation	Fraction of Allocated SW for Irrigation	Peace State P	Sustainability State S	Climate Security State C
No Climate Change	30	30	0.7	0.008	0.3	47.6	79.6	96.1
With Climate Change	30	50	0.9	0.008	0.3	41.9	38.4	65.6

13.3.5 Remarks

The combination of decision-making methods (MCDA or optimization) with SD provides a way to explore (i) to what extent alternative intervention scenarios address the issues and dynamic hypotheses outlined at the end of the appraisal, (ii) whether the scenarios are compatible with physical constraints and requirements (present and future), and (iii) whether specific goals and objectives necessary to address these issues are met. The analysis may reveal that some constraints and requirements could be released to address critical issues. In other instances, the goals and objectives may be too restrictive for some selected interventions and need to be revised.

Another filter that can be used to choose among interventions is to simulate how they are likely to *impact* the sectors of the nexus and the systems and subsystems of Figure 5.1 and identify possible intended and unintended consequences. Technical or socioeconomic-political values may be used to describe that impact. Examples of values include benefit-cost or effectiveness-cost, the risk level associated with uncertainties, environmental and human effects, short- or long-term benefits and consequences, and so on. Positive and negative impacts must be considered along with their degrees (high, medium, and low) of likelihood and importance. Methods to evaluate these effects must be in place along with a risk management strategy (Smith and Merritt, 2002).

In summary, the decision process for evaluating and selecting interventions necessitates considering a series of feedback mechanisms in the systems-based methodology of Figure 9.2 until an intervention is deemed robust enough to be considered for its implementation and performance in the short, medium, and long term and when subject to predictable and extreme situations.

13.4 DECISION-MAKING AND THEORY OF CHANGE

13.4.1 Challenges of Decision-Making

The decision-making process involved in the formulation, simulation, and selection of alternative interventions (stages 7–10 in Figure 9.2) is not easy because, as emphasized in the previous chapters, the issues at stake across the PSC nexus and at the community level are often ill-defined, messy, and complex. When faced with such problems, decision-makers are more inclined to think first in a more straightforward linear and deterministic way than in a systemic manner (Forrester, 1971; Simon, 1972; Georgantzas and Acar, 1995; Ghosh, 2017).

The more straightforward approach will likely create unintended negative consequences and unexpected results, some more critical than others. This conclusion has been reached in many natural and social sciences fields for which dealing with ill-defined, messy, and complex issues and their uncertainty is the norm rather than the exception. It must be remembered that only approximate solutions to such problems are possible (Zadeh, 1973; Dijksterhuis et al., 2006; Rodrigues-Nikl and Brown, 2012; Elms and Brown, 2012).

Because of the different levels of complexity in the issues involved at the crossroads of peace/conflict, sustainability/unsustainability, and climate security/vulnerability, decision methods used by decision-makers will likely vary. In their paper, "Decisions in a Complex Context—a New Formalism," Elms and Brown (2012) advocated for deciding ill-defined/structured complex problems using a combination of *objective/rational* tools when the situations are straightforward and predictable and *subjective/intuitive* tools in more complex and uncertain situations. Objective tools are the tools of choice in directive planning decision-making, where critical/rational thinking and deductive reasoning are the norms (Axelrod, 1997; Nolan, 1998). In community development, they may address technical issues in the infrastructure and economic systems of the landscape. On the other hand, subjective tools are the preferred tools of creative self-reflective decision-makers who use interactive planning to deal with uncertain, flexible, and adaptive systems and situations (Schön, 1983; Nolan, 1998; Ostrom, 2007). In community development, subjective tools are better suited to make decisions for the social and environmental systems in the landscape.

In general, the challenge is for decision-makers to (i) select methods that best match the context in which decisions must be made and (ii) decide when to think in a critical/rational manner versus creatively (see Table 4.2). Choosing between directive and interactive planning, on the one hand, and critical/rational and creative thinking, on the other, in community development requires decision-makers to have acquired a certain level of situational awareness and decision-making maturity. These skills are more likely found in individuals with the systems thinking habits discussed in Section 4.6.

13.4.2 COMPREHENSIVENESS VERSUS IMPACT

Interventions at the crossroads between peace, sustainability, and climate security must balance comprehensiveness and impact. Rodrigues-Nikl and Brown (2012) noted that decision-makers would likely be confronted by two opposite desires when formulating, evaluating, and selecting interventions from multiple systemic alternatives. On the one hand, they want interventions encompassing a wide range of factors and constraints and meeting goals and objectives within system boundaries that are as inclusive as possible. On the other hand, these boundaries must be limited enough that tangible decisions can be made and interventions with meaningful impacts implemented. A guiding principle suggested by Rodriguez-Nikl and Brown (2012) reconciling this dilemma is the so-called decision invariance criterion, which states that in deciding whether the desired result has been reached,

> the system should be large enough that any subsequent extension of the system boundary does not change the decision. If the decision is maintained with an extension of the system boundary, then a likely limit to the decision system has been attained.

A situation may also arise when none of the alternative interventions considered, as comprehensive as they may be, yield the desired impact. In that case, the consequences of this shortcoming must be reanalyzed (Figure 9.2) in a participatory manner with the stakeholders of Figure 9.1 to consider potential trade-offs.

13.4.3 Trade-offs, Benefits, and Synergies

Because of the entanglement of the different sectors of the PSC nexus; the sectors' connections to the social, environmental, economic, and infrastructure systems in the landscape of Figure 5.1; and each system's intra-connections (Figure 6.3), it is likely that any intervention somewhere in the landscape will positively or negatively impact something else. SD tools help analyze such trade-offs or their opposites, called synergies.

Synergy occurs, for instance, when making decisions across the three sectors of the PSC nexus instead of considering each sector in isolation. Synergistic choices create solutions at the nexus level that yield outcomes more significant than the sum of the effects of each sector since a decision in one sector enhances another sector. An example would be a community where peace, sustainability, and CS are in place and of priority to the community stakeholders. Where can synergy in community development and security be found?

Synergistic choices in decision-making by practitioners and policymakers are likely to arise once *leverage points* in the community landscape of Figure 5.1 have been identified (i.e., where intervention is most likely to yield more effective and efficient returns on the investment or action taken). Leverage points, sometimes called tipping points, can differ in community development. For instance, they include identifying what already works in the community, existing community capacity, and resiliency. Another alternative is to find and empower individuals inside and outside a community who are doing better than others under the same conditions and scaling up their solutions to the community as a whole (Pascale et al., 2010). Another example might be considering issues that can quickly be addressed first (i.e., the low-hanging fruit) that will help build community confidence and resilience over time.

Another example that creates synergy is changing the community's mindset and finding common ground about specific issues and their interconnectedness (Meadows, 1997). Changing the mindset can also be interpreted as creating *second-order* change rather than *first-order* (Watzlawick et al., 1974), as discussed in Section 4.4.3. A PSC nexus-related example of first-order solutions would be focusing on one sector of the nexus without considering how it interacts with the others. On the other hand, second-order solutions have a broader impact than first-order ones, transforming the system entirely by using a new strategy or mindset or reframing what the system can or cannot do. The integrated approach for community development involving all three sectors of the PSC nexus presented in this book creates second-order change.

The leverage points can be identified by recognizing the variables that influence the others most. For instance, this identification can be made using cross-impact analysis of the variables involved in the peace, sustainability, and climate security sectors. Recall Table 6.3 and Table 10.1, showing the interaction between different types of capacity and semi-qualitative indicators to measure their respective dependence and influence. Figures 6.8 and 10.1 show that leverage in the cross-impact analysis is usually found for variables with high influence/impact and low reliance on others.

Another way of defining leverage points is to complement the results of the cross-impact analysis with those of the network analysis. As discussed in

Section 6.4, network analysis maps how various agents (e.g., social, infrastructure, and economic) interact. Using different network measures such as centrality, critical agents that contribute the most to the network, whether in influence or dependence, can be identified.

Finally, the leverage points can be identified from possible archetypes that may be able to explain, at least in part, some behavior patterns at the landscape, system, subsystem, or nexus level. Archetypes were discussed in Chapter 8, where the leverage point of each one was identified. For instance, the leverage point in a system showing a *limit to success [growth]* archetype (e.g., Figure 8.4) is to reduce the effect of the balancing process. Likewise, the leverage point in a system showing a *shifting the burden* archetype (e.g., Figure 8.8) (i.e., addressing symptoms instead of causes of a problem) is to focus on causes first. Finally, a system showing a *tragedy of the commons* archetype (e.g., Figure 8.11) may require better management of shared resources among users. A combined analysis of these three archetypes in the Cat Ba Island case study described in Chapter 12 helped identify the intervention places shown in Figure 12.2.

13.4.4 Developing a Theory of Change

A Theory of Change (ToC) is "a method commonly used to understand the strategy and approach of an intervention" (TIPC, 2021). It can be formulated as a cause-and-effect pathway that reads as follows: if x [pre-conditional activity], then y [expected change and outcome] because z [rationale]. ToC is a dynamic and strategic living tool that may change during the life cycle of an intervention and can consist of several steps.

Although theories of change can be formulated in different ways, they all emphasize the importance of adopting a strategic combination of steps and an *intervention logic*. The latter clearly defines an intervention's vision, mission, goals, and objectives. The intervention logic includes targets and uses verifiable indicators (measurements) to qualify and quantify the progress of the interventions and addresses the assumptions and risks involved. Figure 13.2 shows an example of a ToC pathway proposed by the Transformative Innovation Policy Consortium (TIPC). Progress from inputs to impact involves multiple feedback mechanisms. As explained in the *Logic Model Workbook* by the Innovation Network (2013), a logical model can support many intervention activities, including planning, management, communication, consensus-building, and fundraising.

In the development field, a *Logical Framework Approach (LFA)* (or logframe) is often used to create a logical pathway in project planning and management. Bakewell and Garbutt (2005) reviewed logframes used by 18 development agencies and emphasized the value proposition that logframes provide a common platform for understanding and communication between different project stakeholders. As noted by INTRAC (2017), LFA has its share of strengths (e.g., logical progression and feedback) and weaknesses (e.g., rigidity, linearity, static nature, etc.).

Using the logical framework methodology, a ToC requires first identifying the intervention's transformative outcome, impact, or overarching long-term goal(s) that define the success story. Once established, a downward analysis is used to identify (i) the preconditions to meet the goals in terms of objectives, (ii) the outputs (i.e., results)

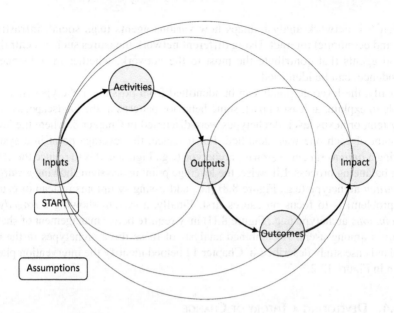

FIGURE 13.2 Components of the theory of change for a specific intervention. The lines show possible feedback connections between the different steps.

Source: TIPC (2021), Creative Commons y 4.0.

necessary to meet the objectives, (iii) the activities necessary to create the outputs, and (iv) the inputs or elements that need to be mobilized to carry out the activities. Each step of the pathway from input to impact requires identifying objectively verifiable indicators of success, means of verification, and outlining the assumptions necessary for success.

The logframe can also be considered upward, as shown in Figure 13.3. The IF-AND-THEN logic in that figure captures the essence of the ToC. The "impact" or "outcome" represents the end state and the overall tangible changes the intervention is expected to make. Notably, the terminology used to describe the components in the LFA logic can vary from one institution to the other (Mercy Corps, 2003; INTRAC, 2017). Despite those differences, the underlying concept is always to have a structured approach to an intervention that is articulated and can be understood by all stakeholders. Furthermore, it is an approach that can be communicated to partners and donors.

A systems approach to the ToC with a built-in logical framework requires exploring the logic of each intervention and the logic of multiple simultaneous interventions. For the PSC nexus, the approach must describe changes in each sector, how changes in each sector affect changes in the other two, and changes in human development and security in the context and scale of interest. In addition, for each intervention, multiple feedback mechanisms can occur between the different components of the logical approach, as shown by the dotted line in Figure 13.2.

A built-in logical framework or logframe in a ToC represents the *strategic* component of intervention planning. Once in place, it provides the necessary

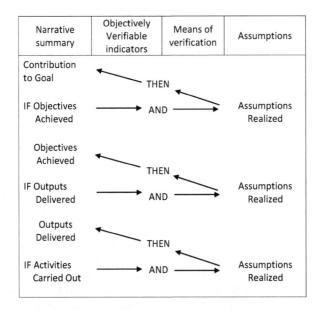

Narrative summary	Objectively Verifiable indicators	Means of verification	Assumptions
Contribution to Goal			
IF Objectives Achieved			Assumptions Realized
Objectives Achieved			
IF Outputs Delivered			Assumptions Realized
Outputs Delivered			
IF Activities Carried Out			Assumptions Realized

FIGURE 13.3 The logic of the LFA using a bottom-up approach.

Source: INTRAC for Civil Society (2017), open-access *Resources Archive – INTRAC*.

information to develop the intervention *logistics, tactics,* and *planning.* They define the activities and resources required for the interventions and the corresponding action and resource delivery time frames.

13.5   FROM SELECTING TO IMPLEMENTING INTERVENTIONS

Upon selection of specific interventions in each sector of the PSC nexus and across the nexus for the context and scale of the landscape in which peace, sustainability, and climate security unfold, and as the last step before their implementation, decision-makers must focus on the details of these interventions and define their logistics and tactics. More specifically, once the *what* and *why* of each intervention have been identified, the next issue is *who*, among the stakeholders of Figure 9.1, should oversee the planning, design, implementation, and monitoring and evaluation phases of these interventions based on the stakeholders' existing skills, expertise, capacity, and willingness to learn new skills.

The *when* and *where* are about developing a timeline (e.g., Gannt chart) and scale for implementing the interventions, including evaluation benchmarks and possible delays. Finally, the *how* and *how much* go into envisioning, among other things, (i) the enabling and constraining dynamic of each sector of the nexus; (ii) the peacebuilding, sustainable development, and climate security practices; (iii) strategies for resource allocation, including possible benefits and trade-offs; (iv) how potential technical and nontechnical solutions match the community level of development; (v) how community well-being and prosperity are enhanced; (vi) how capacity-building resources are allocated in different socioeconomic sectors and how policy decisions are enforced; and (vii) how potential risks might be managed. The *how* is also about monitoring and evaluating implemented interventions and their long-term performance, deciding on their scalability, and identifying possible unintended consequences.

The last step in the overall methodology for addressing the peace, sustainability, and climate security nexus at the community level presented in this book (stage 10 in Figure 9.2) is to develop a detailed implementation (operational) plan for the one (or maybe, at best, two) intervention alternative(s) selected in the process discussed in this chapter. Like for all community development projects, the plan must include a breakdown of all activities (and possible alternatives), resources, costs, benefits, and risks, as well as provisions for assessing (monitoring and evaluating) the impact of the interventions, potential scaling, and their long-term performance and benefits. Contingency plans must also be considered if required. Using the terminology from Amadei (2014), this can be regarded as *reflection before action*.

Reflection-in-action is necessary while executing the implementation plan and deciding whether the actual implementation performance compares to the desired corrective actions required to get back on target. Following completion, *reflection-after-action* helps to identify what has worked, what could have been better, and whether scaling the interventions should be considered. This reflection, in turn, may help inform policy choices (i.e., deciding on selected courses of action that could significantly benefit many people in the same context and at the same scale). Lessons learned in one context and at a given scale may also inform policies that could be implemented in different environments.

REFERENCES

Amadei, B. (2014). *Engineering for sustainable human development: A guide to successful small-scale development projects*. ASCE Press.

Amadei, B., (2019). *A systems approach to modeling the water-energy-land-food nexus*. Vols. *I* and *II*. Momentum Press.

Axelrod, R. (1997). Advancing the art of simulation in the social sciences. *Complexity*, *3*(2), 16–22. https://doi.org/10.1007/978-3-662-03366-1_2

Bakewell, O., & Garbutt, A. (2005). *The use and abuse of the logical framework approach*. Swedish International Development Cooperation Agency, Stockholm, Sweden. http://www.intrac.org/data/files/resources/518/The-Use-and-Abuse-of-the-Logical-Framework-Approach.pdf

Barney, G. O. (2002). The global 200 report to the President and the threshold 21 model: Influences of Dana Meadows and system dynamics. *System Dynamics Review*, *18*(2), 123–136. https://doi.org/10.1002/sdr.233

Bazilian, M., Rogner, H., Howells, M., Hermann, S., Arent, D., Gielen, D., Steduto, P., Mueller, A., Komor, P., Tol, R. S. J., & Yumkella, K.K. (2011). Considering the energy, water, and food nexus: Towards an integrated modeling approach. *Energy Policy*, *39*, 7896–7906. https://doi.org/10.1016/j.enpol.2011.09.039

Bossel, H. (2007). *System Zoo 3 simulation models*. Books on Demand, GmbH.

Caldwell, R. (2002). *Project design handbook*. Cooperative for Assistance and Relief Everywhere (CARE), Atlanta, GA. CARE's Project Design Handbook | Food Security and Nutrition Network (fsnnetwork.org)

Chichakly, K. (2013). Multiobjective design and innovation of robust stormwater management plans. Doctoral dissertation. University of Vermont, VT.

Coello Coello, C. A. (1999). A comprehensive survey of evolutionary-based multiobjective optimization techniques. *Knowledge and Information Systems*, *1*(3), 269–308. https://doi.org/10.1007/BF03325101

Collette, Y., & Siarry, P. (2003). *Multiobjective optimization: Principles and case studies*. Springer.

Dale, L. L., Karali, N., Millstein, D., Carnall, M., Vicuña, S., Borchers, N., Bustos, E., Hagan, J., Purkey, D., Heaps, C., Sieber, J., Collins, W. D., & Sohn, M. D. (2015). An integrated assessment of water-energy and climate change in Sacramento, California: How strong is the nexus. *Climate Change*, *132*, 223–235. https://doi.org/10.1007/s10584-015-1370-x

Davies, E. G. R., & Simonovic, S. P. (2010). ANEMI: A new model for integrated assessment of global change. *Interdisciplinary Environmental Review*, *11*(2/3), 127–161. http://doi.org/10.1504/IER.2010.037903

Davies, E. G. R., & Simonovic, S. P. (2011). Global water resources modeling with an integrated model of the social-economic-environmental system. *Advances in Water Resources*, *34*, 684–700. https://doi.org/10.1016/j.advwatres.2011.02.010

De Geus, A. (1998). Planning as learning. *Harvard Business Review*, March Issue. Retrieved April 1, 2023, from Planning as Learning (hbr.org).

Dijksterhuis, A., Bos, M. W., Nordgren, L. F., & van Baaren, R. B. (2006). On making the right choice: The deliberation-without-attention effect. *Science*, *311*, 1005–1007. https://doi.org/10.1126/science.1121629

Dreborg, K. H. (1996). Essence of backcasting. *Futures*, *28*(9), 813–828. https://doi.org/10.1016/S0016-3287(96)00044-4

Elms, D. G., & Brown, C. B. (2012). Decisions in a complex context: A new formalism? Proc. International Forum on Engineering Decision Making, 6th IFED, Lake Louise, Canada.

EuropeAid. (2002). *Project cycle management handbook* (version 2.0). PARTICIP GmbH, Fribourg, Germany. introduction (kalidadea.org).

Fahey, L., & Randall, R. M. (eds.). (1998). *Learning from the future: Competitive foresight scenarios*. John Wiley & Sons.

Forrester, J. W. (1971). Counterintuitive behavior of social systems. *MIT Technology Review*, *73*(3), 52–68. https://doi.org/10.1016/S0040-1625(71)80001-X

Georgantzas, N. C., & Acar, W. (1995). Scenario-driven planning: Learning to manage strategic uncertainty. Quorum Books.

Glenn, J. C. (2009). Introduction to futures research. In *Introduction to the futures methods research series*. Futures research methodology, V3.0, The Millennium Project, Washington, DC. Futures Research Methodology - Version 3.0 - The Millennium Project (millennium-project.org)

Glenn, J. C., & Gordon, T. J. (2009). Futures research methodology - Version 3.0, AC/UNU The Millennium Project, Washington DC. Futures Research Methodology - Version 3.0 - The Millennium Project (millennium-project.org)

Ghosh, A. (2017). *Dynamic systems for everyone: Understanding how our world works*. (2nd ed.). Springer.

Hegre, H., Buhaug, H., Calvin, K. V., Nordkvelle, J., Waldhoff, S. T., & Gilmore, E. (2016). Forecasting civil conflict along the shared socioeconomic pathways. *Environmental Research Letters*, *11*, 054002. https://doi.org/10.1088/1748-9326/11/5/054002

Hermann, S. (2012). Finding CLEWS. Exploring sustainable energy developments: Looking at climate-land-energy-water interactions methodology and components. Presentation at joint ICTP-IAEA workshop on sustainable energy development, Oct. 1–5, 2012. Trieste, Italy. Retrieved Nov. 15, 2017, from http://indico.ictp.it/event/a11197/session/40/contribution/30/material/0/0.pdf

Hermann, S., Welsch, M., Ericsdotter Segerstrom, R., Howells, M.I., Young, C., Alfstad, T., Rogner, H.H., & Steduto, P. (2012). Climate, land, energy, and water (CLEW) interlinkages in Burkina Faso: An analysis of agricultural intensification and bioenergy production. *Natural Resources Forum*, *36*, 245–262. https://doi.org/10.1111/j.1477-8947.2012.01463.x

Howells, M., Hermann, S., Welsch, M., Bazilian, M., Segerström, R., Alfstad, T., Gielen, D., Rogner, H., Fischer, G., Van Velthuizen, H., Wiberg, D., Young, C., Alexander Roehrl, R., Müller, A., Steduto, P., & Ramma, I. (2013). Integrated analysis of climate change, land use, energy, and water strategies. *Nature Climate Change*, *3*, 621–626. https://doi.org/10.1038/nclimate1789

Hughes, B. B. (2016). International Futures (IFs) and integrated, long-term forecasting of global transformations. *Futures*, *81*, 98–118. https://doi.org/10.1016/j.futures.2015.07.007

Innovation Network. (2013). *Logic model workbook*. Retrieved Oct. 1, 2013, from http://www.innonet.org/client_docs/File/logic_model_workbook.pdf

INTRAC for Civil Society. (2017). *The logical framework* The-Logical-Framework.pdf (intrac.org).

Kriegler, E., O'Neill, B. C., Hallegatte, S., Kram, T., Lempert, R. J., Moss, R. H., & Wilbanks, T. (2012). The need for and use of socio-economic scenarios for climate change analysis: A new approach based on shared socio-economic pathways. *Global Environmental Change*, *22*, 807–822. https://doi.org/10.1016/j.gloenvcha.2012.05.005

Lampinen, J., & Zelinka, I. (2000). *Mixed variable non-linear optimization by differential evolution*. Proc. 5th Int. Conf. On Soft Computing, *Proc.*, Nostradamus. 99.

Mariya Absar, S., & Preston, B. L. (2015). Extending the shared socioeconomic pathways for sub-national impacts, adaptation, and vulnerability studies. *Global Environmental Change*, *33*, 83–96. https://doi.org/10.1016/j.gloenvcha.2015.04.004

Meadows, D. H. (1997). Places to intervene in a system in increasing order of effectiveness. *Whole Earth, Winter*, 78–84.

Meadows, D. H., Randers, J., & Meadows, D. (2004). *Limits to growth: The 30-year update*. Chelsea Green Publishing.

Mercy Corps. (2003). *Design, monitoring and evaluation guidebook*. Mercy Corps, Portland, OR. DM&E FINAL Guidebook 3.5.03 (fsnnetwork.org)

Miettinen, K. (1999). Nonlinear multiobjective optimization. Springer.

Moyer, J. D., & Hedden, S. (2020). Are we on the right path to achieve the sustainable development goals? *World Development*, 127. https://doi.org/10.1016/j.worlddev.2019.104749

Nolan, R. (1998). *Projects that work: Context-based planning for community change*. Unpublished report. Department of Anthropology, Purdue University, West Lafayette, IN.

O'Neill, B. C., Kriegler, E., Riahi, K., Ebi, K. L., Hallegatte, S., Carter, T. R., Mathur, R., & van Vuuren, D. P. (2014). A new scenario framework for climate change research: The concept of shared socioeconomic pathways. *Climate Change*, *122*, 387–400. https://doi.org/10.1007/s10584-013-0905-2

O'Neill, B. C., Kriegler, E., Ebi, K.L.,Kemp-Benedict, E., Riahi, K., Rothman, D.S., van Ruijven, B. J., van Vuuren, D. P., Birkmann, J., Kok, K., Levy, M., & Solecki, W. (2017). The roads ahead: Narratives for shared socioeconomic pathways describing world futures in the twenty-first century. *Global Environmental Change*, *42*, 169–180. https://doi.org/10.1016/j.gloenvcha.2015.01.004

Ostrom, E. (2007). A diagnostic approach for going beyond panaceas. *Proceedings of the National Academy of Sciences*, *104*(39), 15181–15187. https://doi.org/10.1073/pnas.0702288104

Pascale, R., Sternin, J, & Sternin, M. (2010). *The power of positive deviance: How unlikely innovators solve the world's toughest problems*. Harvard University Review Press.

Pasqualino, R., Jones, A.W., Monasterolo, I., & Phillips, A. (2015). Understanding global systems today: A calibration of the World3-03 model between 1995 and 2012. *Sustainability*, *7*(8), 9864–9889.

Pedercini, M., Zuellich, G., Dianati, K., & Arquitt, S. (2018). Toward achieving the sustainable development goals in Ivory Coast: Simulating pathways to sustainable development. *Sustainable Development*, *26*, 588–595. https://doi.org/10.1002/sd.1721

Pedercini, M., Arquitt, S., & Chan, D. (2020). Integrated simulation for the 2030 agenda. *System Dynamics Review*, *36*, 333–357. https://doi.org/10.1002/sdr.1665

Randers, J., Rockström, J., Stoknes, P., Goluke, U., Collste, D., Cornell, S., & Donges, J. (2019). Achieving the 17 sustainable development goals within 9 planetary boundaries. *Global Sustainability*, *2*, e24. https://doi.org/10.1017/sus.2019.22

Ritchie-Dunham, J. L., & Rabbino, H. T. (2001). *Managing from clarity: Identifying, aligning, and leveraging strategic resources*. John Wiley & Sons.

Robinson, J. B. (1982). Energy backcasting: A proposed method of policy analysis. *Energy Policy*, *10*(4), 337–344. https://doi.org/10.1016/0301-4215(82)90048-9

Robinson, J. B. (1990). Futures under glass: A recipe for people who hate to predict. *Futures*, *22*(8), 820–842. https://doi.org/10.1016/0016-3287(90)90018-D

Robinson, J. B. (2003). Future subjunctive: Backcasting as social learning. *Futures*, *35*(8), 839–856. http://doi.org/10.1016/S0016-3287(03)00039-9

Rodriguez-Nikl, T., & Brown, C. B. (2012). A systems approach to civil engineering decisions. *ASCE Journal of Professional Issues in Engineering Education and Practice*, 138(4), 257–261.

Rotmans, J., & deVries, B. (eds.). (1997). *Perspectives on global change: The TARGETS approach*. Cambridge University Press.

Schön, D.A. (1983). *The reflective practitioner: How professionals think in action*. Basic Books.

Simon, H. A. (1978). *Rational decision-making in business organizations*. Nobel Memorial Lecture. Retrieved April 30, 2018, from Herbert A. Simon - Prize Lecture (nobelprize.org)

Simonovic, S. P., & Rajasekaram, V. (2004). Integrated analyses of Canada's water resources: A system dynamics approach. *Canadian Water Resources Journal*, *29*(4), 223–250. http://dx.doi.org/10.4296/cwrj223

Smith, P. G., & Merritt, G. M. (2002). *Proactive risk management*. Productivity Press.

Storn, R., & Price, K. (1997). Differential evolution - a simple and efficient heuristic for global optimization over continuous spaces. *Journal of Global Optimization*, *11*, 341–359. http://doi.org/10.1023/A:1008202821328

Transformative Innovation Policy Consortium. (TIPC). (2021). Motion handbook: Developing a transformative theory of change. Motion Handbook: Developing a Transformative Theory of Change - TIPC (Tipconsortium.Net)

Venter, G. (2010). Review of optimization techniques. In R. Blockley and W. Shyy (eds.), *Encyclopedia of Aerospace Engineering*. John Wiley & Sons.

Ward, E., & Schriefer, A. E. (1998). Dynamic scenarios: System thinking meets scenario planning. In L. Fahey & R. Randall (eds.), Learning *from* the *Future*: Competitive *Foresight Scenarios* (pp. 79–94). John Wiley.

Watzlawick, P., Weakland, J. H., & Fisch, R. (1974). *Change: Principles of problem formation and problem resolution*. W.W. Norton.

Weimer-Jehle, W. (2006). Cross-impact balances: A system-theoretical approach to cross-impact analysis. *Technological Forecasting & Social Change*, *73*(4), 334–361. https://doi.org/10.1016/j.techfore.2005.06.005

Weimer-Jehle, W. (2010). Introduction to qualitative systems and scenario analysis using cross-impact balance analysis. *Interdisciplinary research unit on risk governance and sustainable technology development*, University of Stuttgart. http://www.cross-impact.de/Ressourcen/Guideline percent20No percent201.pdf

Welsch, M., Hermann, S., Howells, M., Rogner, H. H., Young, C., Ramma, I., Bazilian, M., Fischer, G., Alfstad, T., Gielen, D., Le Blanc, D., Röhrl, A., Steduto, P., & Müller, A. (2014). Adding value with CLEWS: Modeling the energy system and its interdependencies for Mauritius. *Applied Energy*, *113*, 1434–1445. https://doi.org/10.1016/j.apenergy.2013.08.083

Winograd, M., & Farrow, A. (2011). Sustainable development indicators for decision making: Concepts, methods, decisions, and uses. In *Dimensions of sustainable development, UNESCO-Encyclopedia of Life Support Systems*, Paris France.

Zadeh, L. (1973). Outline of a new approach to the analysis of complex systems and decision processes. *Trans. Institute of Electrical and Electronics Engineers, SMC-3*(10), 28–44. https://doi.org/10.1109/TSMC.1973.5408575

Zurek, M. B., & Henrichs, T. (2007). Linking scenarios across geographic scales in international environmental assessments. *Technology Forecasting & Social Change, 74*(8), 1282–1295. https://doi.org/10.1016/j.techfore.2006.11.005

14 Conclusions

14.1 A COMPLEXITY- AND SYSTEMS-AWARE APPROACH

This book looks at the triple nexus between peace, sustainability, and climate security (PSC) at the community level. A conclusion reached in this book is that the nexus, like all nexuses, must be considered an integral part of the community development story. Its narrative describes how community members envision progress from a current state to a desired one of development and security. This dynamic creates a "creative tension" (Senge, 2006) necessary for community development. Without it, communities stagnate.

This book starts with the hypothesis that there is no place in a community where PSC or their opposites (i.e., conflict, unsustainability, and climate vulnerability) reside. All three do not exist as boxes that can be extracted and manipulated by well-intentioned academics and decision-makers. Instead, PSC security are states that emerge from mutual interactions and interactions with the systems and subsystems upon which the community depends. Community development affects PSC security, and vice versa, through multiple feedback mechanisms. These states are entangled, dynamic, change over time, and are context- and scale-specific. A challenge in addressing the three sectors of the PSC nexus and their interaction is to (i) handle them using an integrated approach that embraces complexity and uncertainty and (ii) accept that only good enough solutions, and not the best ones, are possible.

Since the Enlightenment 400 years ago, humans have been obsessed with organized simplicity, where problems are solved one at a time and in a compartmentalized manner by experts, individuals, or groups making decisions based on simplified models of reality with limited understanding, perceptions, perspectives, beliefs, feelings, emotions, experiences, expertise, and habits (Dörner, 1997). The organized simplicity of the reductionistic and deterministic approach has dominated Western culture and is embedded in our institutions. It has often led to solutions creating unintended consequences. The history of science and engineering contains many examples where more harm than good was done because of poorly designed, planned, and implemented interventions (Amadei, 2014). In human development and security, reductionist decision-making has often resulted in poorly executed interventions with no long-term benefits, resulting in diminished livelihoods, conflicts, and divided communities.

Simply put, combined with positivism, which adds that reality can only be explained rationally and is devoid of choice, values, and consciousness, reductionism has been used to address issues of a world that does not resemble the real one. Yet, it is still dominant in science, engineering, and technology. Because of its tunnel vision, reductionism can only capture a small fraction of the web-like nature of reality. It must be supplemented (but not substituted) with a systems- and complexity-aware approach. This book makes a case for using the latter to address human development and security and the entanglement between the three sectors of the

PSC nexus. It recognizes that traditional reductionist thinking is not wrong per se; it is simply not right all the time, especially in dealing with real-world complexity, wholeness, and multiple ill-defined problems, messy and sometimes referred to as wicked by Rittel and Weber (1973). Issues in the peace versus conflict, sustainability versus unsustainability, and climate security versus vulnerability spectrum fall into that category of problems.

Adopting a systems approach to dealing with actual reality is part of a new mindset for societal transformation, which is more comprehensive than the ones that created the problems starting in the last centuries. The iceberg model discussed in Chapter 1 represents an excellent metaphor for understanding that community issues do not change by placing external band-aids on them. Instead, they require changing the underlying mindset and creating different structures and behavior patterns that ultimately affect the problems and their outcomes. Changing the mindset is necessary to address conflict, unsustainability, and climate vulnerability. It requires looking at the world differently, which can best be illustrated by the quote of Arthur Schopenhauer

> Thus, the task is not so much to see what no one yet has seen but to think what nobody yet has thought about that which everybody sees.

Although changing the mindset has been recognized by some as a leverage place for community development change, many roadblocks still exist in being adopted by different constituencies. As discussed in Chapter 3, the jury is still out about the components of the new mindset at scales ranging from the local to the global. It is clear that the mindset must encompass the inner and outer dimensions of decision-makers and that a change in mindset must also be accompanied by higher levels of leadership and compassion than has been the case in the past. A question facing our planet today is whether it is possible to mobilize enough "better angels" to create a world where *all* humans have fulfilling lives, meet their basic needs, and live with dignity and peace. The answer is yes if there is a willingness to do so and those who talk about change walk the talk. It is a matter of human choice (UNDP/HDR, 2022).

Changing the mindset requires looking at the PSC nexus, community development, and security differently. The approach necessitates decision-makers among the three groups of stakeholders considered in this book (i.e., community members, governments, and community outsiders) to acquire a systems thinking perspective and habits (Table 4.2) and to be able to distinguish between different levels of complexity using a reflective practice when confronted with community issues. The decision-makers must also be familiar with and able to use appropriate decision-making methods that may range from directive methods with strong objectivity to interactive ones that are more subjective (Elms and Brown, 2012). For example, objective and rational tools are preferred when critical thinking and deductive reasoning are the norms. In community development, these tools are more likely to address dominantly complicated technical issues that unfold in the infrastructure and economic systems of the landscape. On the other hand, subjective tools are preferred by creative self-reflective decision-makers faced with uncertain, flexible, and adaptive systems and situations. In community development, these tools are better suited to make decisions for the social and environmental systems in the landscape.

This book emphasizes that deciding on interventions across the peace–sustainability nexus and community development and security is not random. As discussed in Chapter 9, there is a need to follow a methodology with a road map consisting of multiple stages. Appropriate reductionistic or systemic modeling and decision tools must be selected for each stage. The road map starts with understanding the context, scale, and boundaries of the community environment (landscape) in which the nexus unfolds. This initial phase of defining the situation space is followed by (i) the collection and analysis of data about the nexus and its environment, (ii) the formulation and ranking of nexus-related and landscape-related issues, (iii) the modeling of the issues, (iv) the selection and ranking of possible interventions to address these issues, and (v) the development of an intervention plan. Following the plan, solutions are implemented, monitored, and evaluated. A systems- and complexity-aware approach must be included at each methodology stage. In other words, appraisal of the landscape must be done in an integrated manner, as should the identification, formulation, and ranking of issues. Intervention scenarios must also be formulated, evaluated, and ranked using an integrated approach. Finally, the methodology calls for considering multiple feedback mechanisms at play between the different stages of the methodology roadmap.

In the methodology mentioned above, nexus- and landscape-related issues and interventions can be modeled and interpreted using complementary soft systems qualitative tools (e.g., concept maps, cross-impact analysis, and network analysis) and hard systems tools (e.g., system dynamics, agent-based modeling, and hybrid methods), as discussed in Chapters 6 and 7. This book looked more specifically at system dynamics, a powerful hard system modeling tool that, when combined with soft tools such as network analysis, multi-criteria decision analysis, cross-impact analysis, capacity analysis, and scenario planning, can be used to reproduce, at least in part, the past and current complex dynamics of the landscape in which the PSC nexus unfolds. System dynamics can handle very complex dynamics qualitatively with causal loop diagrams or quantitatively using stock and flow diagrams. Once calibrated, system dynamics models can help to conduct "what-if" and "what-happens-if" simulations, sensitivity analysis, and optimization.

A variety of system dynamics models of the PSC nexus were presented in Chapters 10 and 11. The rationale for developing these models was to propose generic structures most likely found in different community settings and to demonstrate various ways of connecting PSC security to development. Most of these models assumed a goal-seeking dynamic between current and desired community development states. The dynamic gaps between these states represent issues that must be addressed with changes in behavior and structural re-patterning. Those impacted by the events preferably define the desired states.

All models in this book acknowledge that PSC security are not quantitative commodities. Hence, qualitative and semi-quantitative indicators, proxies, and performance metrics are required to characterize, monitor, and evaluate these three states and their nexus over time. The challenge is measuring the states that emerge from the interaction of multiple systems and subsystems of different levels of complexity, uncertainty, and adaptability, operating under various constraints (e.g., geopolitical, environmental, cultural, etc.).

The numerical examples presented in this book used semi-quantitative measures of PSC security expressed in generic peace units (pu), sustainability units (su), and climate security units (cu). These units are *arbitrary* and range over three [0–100] scales, which can be broken down into several achievement-level groups from very low to very likely using a semi-quantitative rating scale (see Table 7.1). Each group is specific to the context in which the PSC nexus analysis is carried out.

For completeness, metrics and indicators must be introduced to describe each level of achievement for (i) positive, negative, and cultural peace; (ii) people, planet, prosperity, and partnership components of sustainability; and (iii) awareness, adaptation, and mitigation components of climate security as done, for instance, with the Envision® project sustainability framework (ISI, 2018) discussed in Chapter 2. Table 14.1 could be constructed for each component of the PSC security sectors utilizing a structure like that of Table 2.3. Indicators from the list in Table 2.8 can be used to define the A to F conditions.

Finally, Table 14.1 must be supplemented with metrics and indicators across sectors of the PSC nexus, such as those listed in Table 2.8. For example, questions may arise about what crossover indicators best capture the sectors' interaction. As for many types of nexuses, databases are required and are lacking in the literature.

Another challenge in modeling the PSC nexus is to find cross-sector indicators that link quantitative technical measures with nontechnical (socioeconomic) ones that tend to be more qualitative. Socioeconomic indicators are often more challenging to measure than technical ones related to infrastructure, despite being equally important in understanding the nexus dynamics. As the author (Amadei, 2019) emphasized regarding the water–energy–land–food (WELF) nexus, the lack of metrics linking technical and nontechnical issues is a limiting factor in developing comprehensive models to capture the dynamic across all nexus types mentioned in the literature.

Dynamic scenario analysis (i.e., a combination of system dynamics modeling and backcasting from the field of Futures Research) was reviewed in Chapter 13 and suggested as an approach to decide on alternative modes of intervention to bring a community from its current state of development to a desired/satisfactory level of

TABLE 14.1

Metrics Used to Determine the Achievement Level for Any Peace, Sustainability, and Climate Security Component

Very Low	Low	Somewhat Possible	Very Possible	Very Likely
0–20	21–40	41–60	61–80	81–100
A + B	A + B + C	A + B + C + D	A + B + C + D + E	A + B + C + D + E + F
(A) ...				
(B) ...				
(C) ...				
(D) ...				
(E) ...				
(F) ...				

development and address issues across the landscape. In dynamic scenario analysis, system-level interventions are formulated, simulated, evaluated, and ultimately selected using a multiobjective approach that captures the connections and constraints across the landscape. It should be noted that system tools do not negate traditional deterministic tools but are instead complementary. Deterministic tools are, for instance, more appropriate to analyze community infrastructure and economic systems but are less helpful in dealing with social and environmental systems.

As emphasized in this book, it must be remembered that systems tools and models generally do not model the actual reality and provide only an interpretation that resides in the brains of the modelers and decision-makers. Furthermore, it is impossible to model everything, which would likely lead to paralysis in analysis. More specifically, the challenge in modeling complex systems can best be summarized as "[producing] simple, balanced, and elegant models at an appropriate level of aggregation in time and space to be useful" (Wolstenholme, 1999). The models of the PSC nexus must be simultaneously comprehensive and simple enough to be understood by different stakeholders. As noted by Costanza et al. (1993) and Costanza and Ruth (1998), another challenge is to apply an appropriate trade-off between model "realism, precision, and generality." That trade-off depends mainly on the model's purpose. There may be situations when, in addressing the PSC nexus, there is a need to produce general models to build consensus, others where realism for a specific sector is required, and still others where precision is essential to quantify a particular issue. However, it should be noted that generality, realism, and accuracy cannot be maximized simultaneously (Costanza and Ruth, 1998). Only two out of consensus, authenticity, and precision can be selected once the model purpose has been defined.

In the methodology described in Chapter 9, models play a critical role in representing the current community situation once data have been collected and analyzed and defining how to achieve some desired configuration. Models are beneficial in deciding which interventions are of a higher priority than others and exploring "what would happen if" regarding community peace, livelihood, and climate security. Models are also helpful in policy interventions by studying the effect and cost of unusual events such as climate change and hazards on human development and security and the most likely essential variables.

Regardless of the models used, scenarios of intervention and proposed solutions are context and scale-dependent: geography is vital in defining the context. It is hard to translate a set of solutions from one scale to another because of nonlinearities. The solutions in the landscape must match the landscape characteristics.

The two case studies in Chapter 12 show the complexity of the interaction between PSC security at different scales. Understanding the various aspects of the interactions requires decision-makers to be system thinkers and be able to identify archetypes at play at the community level. At times, several archetypes may be at play and interact. Recognizing archetypes helps to identify leverage points of intervention.

Finally, one last conclusion that can be drawn from this book is that addressing the PSC nexus and community landscape requires collaboration between three groups of stakeholders (Figure 9.1) and should not be left in the hands of experts only. Community members contribute to bottom-up solutions, representatives of governmental institutions (local to national) provide top-down solutions, and outsiders (e.g.,

NGOs, private sector actors, professional organizations, etc.) contribute outside-in solutions (Figure 9.1). As discussed in Section 13.3.3, cross-impact balance analysis can determine whether intervention scenarios are consistent with the stakeholders' rules of interaction.

An integrated approach to the nexus implies that the three categories of stakeholders influence and depend on each other. As community members may be the closest to the actual community needs, they can influence government representatives and outsiders, and vice versa. That complex dynamic needs to be mapped, understood, and assessed. Social network analysis is an appropriate tool to understand and map stakeholder dynamics, as it may help identify individuals, groups, or institutions that may block or facilitate change. It may also help identify individuals and groups that have already solved problems that most community members still face. A systems approach to the nexus should not be interpreted as excluding the role of experts. These experts are still necessary—but not sufficient—to guarantee meaningful interventions.

14.2 PSC NEXUS CHALLENGES

As the author (Amadei, 2019) discussed regarding the WELF nexus, a systems- and complexity-aware approach to any nexus does not come without its share of challenges and questions. These challenges apply to the PSC nexus as well. One of them, which traditional development practitioners and decision-makers often find hard to accept, is that it is impossible to come up with concrete and optimum solutions to the complex and uncertain issues at play in the nexus sectors and community landscape. However, multiple *good enough* solutions, some better than others, are possible. Thus, decision-makers must recognize that addressing PSC security and community development is more about satisfying than optimizing (Simon, 1972), while deciding on potential trade-offs and synergies across all nexus sectors as comprehensively as possible. Many open-ended questions are yet to be answered, such as: How can consensus about solutions across the PSC sectors be reached among stakeholders? How can deal with conflicting opinions? How can we monitor and evaluate interventions after implementation? How can we scale up successful interventions and guarantee their success and benefits over time? How are intervention scenarios consistent with the rules of interaction between the nexus sectors and among the stakeholders? Ultimately, what represents successful PSC security interventions?

An integrated approach to community PSC security generates multiple questions and challenges about the what, why, who, where, when, and how aspects of the nexus. For instance, where does the PSC nexus start in the community landscape, and what are the initial PSC security conditions? An integrated approach also requires a detailed mapping and understanding of the nexus and landscape structure, including its components (i.e., systems, subsystems, and sub-subsystems), links, and feedback mechanisms among these components. Such an approach also requires modelers to select an appropriate study scale in a given context and proper boundary conditions that dictate what is exogenous and endogenous to the study being carried out. To that list, one can add a need to identify and formulate appropriate indicators of PSC security and to select values (or a range of values) for these indicators if quantitative system modeling is carried out.

Another challenge in developing integrated models of the PSC nexus is the selection and collection of data about the nexus sectors, their interactions, and their interactions with community systems for different contexts and scales. Such data are usually missing in the nexus literature, regardless of the nexus considered. More specifically, missing in the literature is an understanding of the causal chains (i.e., pathways) between the three sectors (i.e., how some sector(s) may trigger the other(s)) and how diverse development and security areas may trigger a state of peace versus conflict, sustainability versus unsustainability, and climate security versus vulnerability (Peters et al., 2020). Which combination of input parameters and linkages to select? Which mechanisms and variables are the most relevant to describe the issues? Understanding that dynamic and answering those questions may help in climate impact assessment, climate- and hazard-related risk management, capacity building, and planning adaptation and mitigation interventions ahead of adverse events. All these challenges are not easy to overcome, especially when dealing with transboundary and geopolitical factors.

Finally, the literature has not comprehensively explored the nuts and bolts of how to meet the challenges mentioned above in different contexts and scales (where and when). Even more importantly, the value proposition of a nexus approach to community PSC security has not yet been operationally demonstrated enough in practice and conveyed to development practitioners and decision-makers in a comprehensive and nonacademic enough manner for them to use it. A growing challenge is operationalizing the PSC nexus and developing a portfolio of well-documented past, revised past, and current case studies that demonstrate the value proposition of using a nexus approach instead of a silo approach in different contexts and at different scales. The different contexts may be associated with various climatic groups and rural, urban, or refugee camp settings. The scales may range from local to national or regional.

REFERENCES

Amadei, B. (2014). *Engineering for sustainable human development: A guide to successful small-scale development projects*. ASCE Press.

Amadei, B. (2019). *A systems approach to modeling the water-energy-land-food nexus*. Vols. *I* and *II*. Momentum Press.

Costanza, R., & Ruth, M. (1998). Using dynamic modeling to scope environmental problems and build consensus. *Environmental Management, 22*(2), 183–195. https://doi.org/10.1007/s002679900095

Costanza, R., Wainger, L., Folke, K., & Mäler, K-G. (1993). Modeling complex ecological economic systems: Toward an evolutionary, dynamic understanding of people and nature. *BioScience, 43*(8), 545–555. https://doi.org/10.2307/1311949

Dörner, D. (1997). *The logic of failure: Recognizing and avoiding error in complex situations*. Perseus Books.

Elms, D. G., & Brown, C. B. (2012). Decisions in a complex context: A new formalism? Proc. International Forum on Engineering Decision Making, 6th IFED, Lake Louise, Canada.

Institute for Sustainable Infrastructure. (ISI). (2018). Envision® sustainable infrastructure framework guidance manual. https://sustainableinfrastructure.org/wp-content/uploads/EnvisionV3.9.7.2018.pdf

Peters, K., Dupar, M., Opitz-Stapleton, S., Lovell, E., & Cao, Y. (2020). Climate change, conflict, and fragility; An evidence review and recommendations for research and action. Climate change, conflict, and fragility: An evidence review and recommendations for research and action | ODI: Think change

Rittel, H., & Webber, M. (1973). Dilemmas in a general theory of planning. *Policy Science*, *4*, 155–169. https://doi.org/10.1007/BF01405730

Senge, P. (2006). *The fifth discipline: The art & practice of the learning organization.* Doubleday.

Simon, H. (1972). Theories of bounded rationality. In C. B. McGuire and R. Radner (eds.), *Decision and Organization* (pp. 161–176). Amsterdam: North-Holland.

UNDP Human Development Report (UNDP/HDR) (2022). *The human development report 2021/2022. Uncertain times, and unsettled lives, shaping our future in a transforming world.* Human Development Report 2021/2022 | United Nations Development Programme (undp.org)

Wolstenholme, E. F. (1999). Qualitative vs. quantitative modeling: The evolving balance. *Journal of the Operational Research Society*, *50*(4), 422–428. https://doi.org/10.2307/3010462

Appendix A

Source: Amadei, B. (2019). *A systems approach to modeling the water-energy-land-food nexus.* Vols. I and II. Momentum Press. Reproduced with permission from Momentum Press.

HUMAN SYSTEMS

Human (Social) Systems	Categories and Variables
	Demography
	Population (total and by gender)
	Population by group (ethnicity, caste, marginal, religion, language, age, marital status, etc.)
	Birth rate by group
	Death rate and life expectancy by group
	Vulnerability by group
	Immigration by group
	Emigration by group
	Population in extreme poverty
	Education
	Literacy level
	Educational attainment
	Education level by population group
	Distance and time to educational services
	Health
Populations	Fertility by group
	Disease types
	Diseases by population group
	Maternal mortality
	Child mortality
	Distance and time to health services
	Level of health and hygiene education
	Level of immunization
	Employment
	Population in agriculture (sector, gender, age)
	Population in the industry (sector, gender, age)
	Population in administration (sector, gender, age)
	Self-employed population (gender, age)
	Unemployed population (gender, age, reasons)
	Child labor
	Distance and time to employment
	Others
	Beliefs and practices

(Continued)

347

Human (Social) Systems	Categories and Variables
Community	**Households/Families**
	Number of households
	Household distribution
	People per household
	Language being spoken per household
	Modes of livelihood
	Lifestyles and diet
	Income and expenses (annual and by type)
	Land per household
	Education, health, religion, and employment levels
	Land security level (local indicators)
	Water security level (local indicators)
	Energy security level (local indicators)
	Food security level (local indicators)
	Transportation level (local indicators)
	Physical security level (local indicators)
	Debt level
	Loan access level
	Access and use of toilets, sanitation, and hygiene
	Level of participation in community affairs
	Social networks strength
	Groups
	Political (needs, impact, effectiveness)
	Neighborhood (needs, impact, effectiveness)
	Co-ops (needs, impact, effectiveness)
	Cultural (needs, impact, effectiveness)
	Special interest (needs, impact, effectiveness)
	Others
	Conflict dynamics
	Marginalized and vulnerable groups
	Gender equality
	Violence and oppression
	Human rights
Institutions	**Social**
	Education (schools, teachers)
	Health (services, infrastructure, workforce)
	Religious
	Economic and Financial
	Banks (impacts, service level, access)
	Commercial organizations (impacts, service level, access)

(Continued)

Human (Social) Systems	Categories and Variables

Governance
Legislation level
Regulation's level
The rule of law level
Corruption level
Stability level
Accountability level
Participation level

Public Services
Different levels of institutional services (local, regional)

NATURAL/ENVIRONMENTAL SYSTEMS

Natural Systems	Variables
Water	Precipitation
	Rainfall intensity and distribution
	Evaporation
	Rivers and springs
	Groundwater
	Water supply and withdrawal
	Runoff level
	Pollution level
	Seasonal variations
	Ecosystem services (many)
Land/Soil	Type and distribution
	Ecosystem functioning and diversity
	Erodibility level
	Sources of minerals
	Hazards from soil and rock minerals
	Level of pollution
	Soil thickness and depth to bedrock
	Soil compaction level
	Soil porosity
	Soil fertility and productivity level
	Soil saturation level
	Topography and slope
	Rock versus soil cover distribution
	Soil and rock permeability
	Land quality
	Degraded and wasteland

(Continued)

Natural Systems	Variables
Biota	Forest coverage (private vs. community)
Animal and Plant Life	Growth and decay rate
	Biodiversity level
	Extinction level
	Transpiration
	Carbon sequestration
Air	Pollution level
	Wind and humidity level
Natural Disasters and Adverse Events	Risks of drought, landslides, and floods
	Occurrence of changes in weather patterns
	Hazards from geological processes
Waste (Air, Liquid, Solid)	Amount
	Environmental release
	Treated/untreated
	Pollution level

INFRASTRUCTURE SYSTEMS

Engineered Systems	Categories
Water	Water harvesting systems (ponds, tanks, fog collection, rooftop)
	Water supply chain facilities (procurement, storage, treatment, distribution, disposal)
	Freshwater source protection systems
	Water treatment systems and technology
	Wastewater collection and treatment systems and technology
	Water drainage and irrigation systems
	Sanitation systems
Energy	Sources of energy (primary and backup)
	Energy supply chain facilities (from sources to consumers)
	Systems used for cooking and heating
	Renewable energy systems
	Centralized and off-grid systems
Agriculture/Food	Use of fertilizer
	Irrigation systems (quality, quantity, access)
	Mechanized systems
	Food supply chain facilities (source to consumers)
Education	Schools (number, locations, conditions)

(Continued)

Engineered Systems	Categories
Transportation	Transportation modes
	Transportation infrastructure
Healthcare	Health infrastructure (centralized, decentralized)
	Sanitation facilities
Others	Telecommunication
	Material consumption
	Emissions

ECONOMIC SYSTEMS

Economic Systems	
Agriculture	Crop production and value-added
	Livestock production and value-added
	Fisheries production and value-added
	Forest production and value-added
	Crops and livestock diversity
Industry	Productivity
	Capital and Labor
Others	GDP
	Investment
	Production, distribution, and trade

Appendix B

Example of a wastewater and sewage treatment capacity assessment for a small village in Southern Morocco. Bold letters apply to the case study being analyzed. *Source*: Bouabid, M., & Louis, G. (2015). Reproduced with permission from Academic Press.

Capacity Types	Requirements	1 – 20	21– 40	41 – 60	61 – 80	81 – 100	Score
Service level	Gap (l/d/c)	< 20	**21 – 40**	41 – 60	61 – 80	> 80	40
				Capacity factor			**40**
Institutional	Body of legislation	None	**Basic**	Intermediate	Complete	Advanced	30
	Associated regulations	None	**Basic**	Intermediate	Complete	Advanced	30
	Administrative agencies	None	National	**Regional**	State	Local	50
	Administrative processes	None	**Basic**	Intermediate	Complete	Advanced	25
	Governance	None	**Basic**	Regional	State	Local	25
				Capacity factor			**32**
Human Resources	Professionals	**None**	Collection supervisor	Collection supervisor, Treatment supervisor	Engineer, Chemist, Admin. Collection treatment supervisor	Engineer, Chemist, Admin. manager, Collection treatment manager	15
	Skilled labor	None	**Mechanics, Clerk**	Lab. technician, Mechanics, Clerk, Electrician	Lab. technician, Maintenance technician, Operator, Admin. assistant	Lab. technician, Maintenance technician, Operator, Admin. assistant, IT technician	40

(Continued)

Capacity Types	Requirements	1 – 20	21 – 40	41 – 60	61 – 80	81 – 100	Score
	Unskilled labor	None	**Maintenance worker**	Maintenance worker, Plant worker	Maintenance assistant, Operator assistant		30
	Illiterate labor	None	**Caretaker**	Maintenance helper			30
				Capacity factor			29
Technical	Operations	None	**Individual disposal**	Collection, Pumping, Prelim. treatment	Collection, Pumping, Complete treatment, Bacteriological analysis	Monitoring pumping station, Monitoring treatment, Bacteriological analysis, Chemical/ biological analysis	30
	Maintenance	**None**	Sceptic tank pump	Clean collector systems, Maintain pumps	Collector systems, Station pumps, Treatment equipment	Collector systems, Station pumps, Treatment equipment, IT systems	10
	Adaptation	None	**Rarely**	Occasionally	Usually	Frequently	25
	Supply chain	None	**National supplier**	Regional supplier	National manufacturer, Regional distributor	National manufacturer, Local distributor	30
				Capacity factor			24
Economic/ Financial	Private sector %	None	International	**National**	Regional	Local	50
	Bonds rating	**None**	National	Regional	State	Local	10
	User fees	None	**Uniform flat rate**	Single block rate	Increasing block rate	Increasing block rate	30
	Budget	None	**Basic accounting**	Annual	Tracked annually	Tracked quarterly	30
	Asset values	None	**Real estate**	Real estate, Equipment	Real estate, Equipment, Cash	Real estate, Equipment, Cash, Stocks	30
	Debt rating	**None**	(ccc)	(bb)	(bbb)	(a-aa)	10
				Capacity factor			27

(*Continued*)

Capacity Types	Requirements	1 – 20	21 – 40	41 – 60	61 – 80	81 – 100	Score
Energy	Primary source	None	Non-conventional	**Conventional**	Mid-voltage source	High-voltage source	50
	Back up	**None**	Generator <20 HP	Generator <40 HP	Generator <60 HP	Generator >60 HP	10
	% of budget	Very high	High	**Moderate**	Low	Very low	50
	Outage rate	Very high	High	**Moderate**	Low	Very low	50
				Capacity factor			**40**
Environmental	Quality and sensitivity	Very low	Low	**Moderate**	High	Very high	50
	Quantity	Very low	Low	Moderate	**High**	Very high	65
				Capacity factor			**57.5**
Social/ Cultural	Communities	Very low	Low	**Moderate**	High	Very high	50
	Stability	Very low	Low	**Moderate**	High	Very high	50
	Equity	Very low	Low	Medium	**High**	Very high	65
	Castes	Very high	High	Medium	Low	**Very low**	85
	Participation of women	Very low	Low	**Moderate**	High	Very high	50
				Capacity factor			**60**

For example, the community has a CCL of 2 because technical capacity is the limiting factor in the capacity assessment, with a value of 24. In other words, until technical issues related to wastewater and sewage treatment service are addressed first, the community only has the capacity to "manage systems for small collections of residential units," and a limited level of local service can be provided. Once addressed, human resources and economic and financial capacity will be managed next.

REFERENCE

Bouabid, M., & Louis, G. (2015). Capacity factors for evaluating water and sanitation infrastructure choices for developing communities. *Journal of Environmental Management*, *161*, 335–343. https://doi.org/10.1016/j.jenvman.2015.07.012

Appendix C
Input Data for the Examples in Chapter 10

C.1 CAPACITY ANALYSIS

A user-friendly interactive user interface can be found on the website: https://exchange.iseesystems.com/public/bernardamadei/capacity

Capacity Type	Initial Value	Desired Value	Basic Adjustment Rate/Year
Institutional	32	100	0.01
Human	29	100	0.01
Technical	24	100	0.01
Econ/Financial	28	100	0.01
Energy	40	100	0.01
Environmental	55	100	0.01
Sociocultural	60	100	0.01

Time unit: years
The effect each capacity type has on the others is described in Table 10.1.
Example 1 (Figure 10.4): All impact external factors = 1.
Example 2 (Figure 10.5): All impact external factors = −3.

C.2 CAPACITY AND RESILIENCE

A user-friendly interactive user interface can be found on the website: https://exchange.iseesystems.com/public/bernardamadei/resilience-capacity

Capacity Type	Initial Base Capacity	Initial Built Capacity	Desired Capacity	Basic Building Capacity Adjustment Rate/Month	Multiplying Factors	Capacity Building Starting Time (Months)
Institutional	32	0	100	0.01	1.28	1
Human	29	0	100	0.01	1.57	1
Technical	24	0	100	0.01	1.86	1
Econ/ Financial	28	0	100	0.01	2.14	1
Energy	40	0	100	0.01	1.86	1
Environmental	55	0	100	0.01	1.86	1
Sociocultural	65	0	100	0.01	2.28	1

Time unit: Months
Rate base capacity decrease: 1/month
Example 1 (Figures 10.8 and 10.9): All impact external factors = 1.
Example 2 (Figure 10.10): All impact external factors = −4 between months 30 and 40.

C.3   MODELING THE PSC NEXUS

C3.1   MODEL PSC1

A user-friendly interactive user interface can be found on the website: https://exchange.iseesystems.com/public/bernardamadei/psc1

States	Initial Values	Desirable Values	Basic Adjustment Rate/Year
Peace	20 pu	100 pu	0.01
Sustainability	30 su	100 su	0.01
Climate security	50 cu	100 cu	0.01

Time units: years.
External factors ranging between −4 and 4.
Effect external factors on PSC: $1 + 0.375 \times$ external factor.
The effect of each sector on the adjustment rates of the other two varies linearly: $y = 0.014x - 0.2$.

- Run 1 (Figure 10.12).
- Run 2 (Figure 10.13): The effect of climate security on the rate of change of peace and sustainability is equal to −0.2.
- Run 3 (Figure 10.14): Some conflict arises between years 20 and 50 where the external factors are equal to −4 between years 20 and 50.

C3.2   MODEL PSC2

A user-friendly interactive user interface can be found on the website: https://exchange.iseesystems.com/public/bernardamadei/psc2

Peace State (pu Units)	Initial Values	Desirable Values	Basic Adjustment Rate/Year	RP Weights
P1	40	100	0.03	1/3
P2	30	100	0.02	1/3
P3	20	100	0.01	1/3

Sustainability State (su Units)	Initial Values	Desirable Values	Basic Adjustment Rate/Year	RS Weights
S1	60	100	0.01	1/4
S2	40	100	0.01	1/4
S3	30	100	0.01	1/4
S4	10	100	0.01	1/4

Climate State (cu Units)	Initial Values	Desirable Values	Basic Adjustment Rate/Year	RC Weights
C1	60	100	0.04	1/2
C2	40	100	0.04	1/2

External factors ranging between -4 and 4.

Effect external factors on PSC: $1 + 0.375 \times$ external factor.

The effect of each sector on the adjustment rates of the other two varies linearly: $y = 0.014x - 0.2$. Case (a): all external factors $= 0$; Case (b): all external factors equal to -3.

Appendix D

Input Data for the Examples in Chapter 11

MODEL PSC3

A user-friendly interactive user interface can be found on the website: https://exchange.iseesystems.com/public/bernardamadei/psc3

Initial population: 1000 people

Normal birth rate: 0.01/year

Normal death rate: 0.01/year

Initial resources pp: 10 units/pp

Resources consumption rate pp: 1 unit/year/person

Resources supply rate: 0.45/year

Desired community resources pp: 15 units/pp

Effect resources security on birth rate: $0.2 + 1.8 \times$ (community resource security)

Effect resources security on death rate: $2 - 1.8 \times$ (community resource security)

Service delivery factor: [0 to 1.2]

Impact community state on birth: $0.8 + 0.004 \times$ (community state)

Impact community state on death: $0.8 - 0.004 \times$ (community state)

PSC initial values range from 20 to 80

Event magnitude: from -4 to 4

Impact event on PSC: $1 + 0.375 \times$ event magnitude

Effect RS on changing PSC state: $4 \times$ (community resource security)

Influence-dependence capacity matrix: See Table 10.1

D.1.1 RESOURCES CAPACITY MODULE

Capacity Type	Initial Values	Desired Values	Basic Adjustment Rate/Year	Impact CS On Capacity
Institutional	32	100	0.003	Nonlinear [−2,2]
Human	29	100	0.003	1
Technical	24	100	0.003	1
Financial	28	100	0.003	1
Energy	40	100	0.003	1
Environmental	55	100	0.003	1
Sociocultural	60	100	0.003	1

D.1.2 PSC Module

States	Initial Values	Desirable Values	Basic Adjustment Rate /Year
Peace	20 – 80 pu	100 pu	0.005
Sustainability	20 – 80 su	100 su	0.005
Climate security	20 – 80 cu	100 cu	0.005

The effect of each sector on the adjustment rates of the other two varies linearly: $y = 0.014x - 0.2$.

MODEL PSC4

A user-friendly interactive user interface can be found on the website: https://exchange.iseesystems.com/public/bernardamadei/psc4

Initial population: 1000 people

Normal birth rate: 0.01/year

Normal death rate: 0.01/year

Effect resources security on birth rate: $0.2 + 1.8 \times$ (community resource security)

Effect of resources security on death rate: $2 - 1.8 \times$ (community resource security)

Impact current state on birth: $0.8 + 0.007 \times$ (community state)

Impact current state on death: $0.8 - 0.007 \times$ (community state)

PSC initial values range from 20 to 80

Impact community state on water: nonlinear from −2 to 2

Impact community state on energy: nonlinear from −2 to 2

Impact community state on food: nonlinear from −2 to 2

Effect RS on changing PSC (peace and sustainability) state: $4 \times$ (community resource security)

Event magnitude: from −4 to 4

Impact event on PSC: $1 + 0.5 \times$ event magnitude

Initial water resources per person: 10^4 water units (e.g., m³)

Initial energy resources per person: 10^5 energy units (e.g., MWh)

Initial food resources per person: 10^7 food units (e.g., kJ)

Desired water resources per person: 2×10^4 water units (e.g., m³)

Desired energy resources per person: 2×10^5 energy units (e.g., MWh)

Desired food resources per person: 2×10^7 food units (e.g., kJ)

Basic WEF resources supply rates (1/year): 0.4, 0.4, 0.9

WEF demand (pp/year): 8 m³, 10 MWh, 3.65×10^6 kJ

Resource security weights: 1/3, 1/3, 1/3

Energy demand per food unit: 0.001 energy unit/food unit/year

Energy demand per water unit: 0.1 energy unit/water unit/year

Water demand per energy unit: 0.01 water unit/energy unit/year

Water demand per food unit: 10^{-6} water units/food units/year

Interaction across WEF sectors:

- Effect water on producing food $= 2 \times 10^{-7} \times$ water resources
- Effect water on producing energy $= 0.4 + 1.3 \times 10^{-7} \times$ water resources
- Effect energy on producing food $= 0.2 + 3.8 \times 10^{-8} \times$ energy resources
- Effect energy in producing water $= 0.2 + 10^{-8} \times$ energy resources

Service delivery factors: [0–1.2] depend on minimum community service capacities for water, energy, and food.

Influence-dependence capacity matrix: See Table 10.1.

D.2.1 CAPACITY MODULE WATER

Impact current state on energy: [−2,2] for state ranging from −10 (constraining) to 10 (enabling).

Basic adjustment rate: 0.0008/year

Capacity Type	Initial Values	Desired Values
Institutional	32	100
Human	29	100
Technical	24	100
Financial	28	100
Energy	40	100
Environmental	55	100
Sociocultural	60	100

D.2.2 CAPACITY MODULE ENERGY

Impact current state on energy: [−2,2] for state ranging from −10 (constraining) to 10 (enabling).

Basic adjustment rate: 0.0005/year

Capacity Type	Initial Values	Desired Values
Institutional	22	100
Human	19	100
Technical	14	100
Financial	18	100
Energy	30	100
Environmental	45	100
Sociocultural	50	100

D.2.3 CAPACITY MODULE FOOD

Impact current state on food: [−2,2] for state ranging from −10 (constraining) to 10 (enabling).

Basic adjustment rate: 0.0005/year

Capacity Type	Initial Values	Desired Values
Institutional	27	100
Human	24	100
Technical	19	100
Financial	23	100
Energy	35	100
Environmental	50	100
Sociocultural	55	100

D.2.4 THE PSC MODULE

States	Initial Values	Desirable Values	Basic Adjustment Rate /Year
Peace	20 – 80 pu	100 pu	0.004
Sustainability	20 – 80 su	100 su	0.004
Climate security	20 – 80 cu	100 cu	0.004

The effect of each sector on the adjustment rates of the other two varies linearly: $y = 0.014x - 0.2$.

Run 1 (Figure 11.8). The PSC initial values range from 20 to 80.
Run 2 (Figure 11.9). Same as in run 1, but impact event on water supply $= 0.01$ instead of 1 from years 10–15 and 30–35.

Appendix E
The PSC5 Model

A user-friendly interactive user interface can be found on the website: https://exchange.iseesystems.com/public/bernardamadei/psc5

E.1 POPULATION MODULE

E.1.1 DEMOGRAPHY

Variables	Initial Values
Pop. 0–4 (M/F)	400,400
Pop. 5–15 (M/F)	400,400
Pop. 16–39 (M/F)	400,400
Pop. 40–59 (M/F)	200,200
Pop. ≥ 60 (M/F)	100,100
Input Parameters (red)	**Values**
Normal death rate 0–4 (M/F)	0.01,0.01
Normal death rate 5–15 (M/F)	0.01,0.01
Normal death rate 16–39 (M/F)	0.01,0.01
Normal death rate 40–59 (M/F)	0.01,0.01
Normal death rate ≥ 60 (M/F) (life expectancy of 85 years)	0.04,0.04
Migration by age group (5 groups)	0,0,0,0,0
Average home size (people)	7
Fraction (16–39) female childbearing	0.8
Births per (16–39) female per year	0.5
Fraction male/female birth	0.5,0.5
Fraction male/female literacy (16–59)	0.5,0.5
Basic energy consumption per home	5000 kWh/year
Functions (green)	**Range**
Effect of plant-based food on birth	0.8–1.2
Effect of meat-based food on birth	0.8–1.2
Effect energy on birth	1–1.1
Effect of water on birth	0.5–1.5
Effect of plant-based food on death	1.2–0.8
Effect of meat-based food on death	1.2–0.8
Effect energy on death	1.2–1
Effect water on death	1.2–0.5
Effect of population density on death	1–1.2

New variables, input, functions (pink)	Range
Level of climate change	0–4
Impact of climate change on house energy consumption	1–1.1
Impact community state on migration	From E.2
Impact community state on birth	From E.2
Impact community state on death	From E.2
Minimum capacity education	From E.2
Service delivery factor education	0–1.5
Effect of health on the death rate	See health
Effect of health on the birth rate	See health

E.1.2   HEALTH

Variables	Initial Values
The current state of health	50
Input Parameters (red)	**Values**
Desired state of health	100
Basic adjustment rate ARH (per year)	0.01
Multipliers (green)	**Range**
Effect of health on birth rate	0.5–1
Effect of health on death rate	1.2–1
Effect of health on education	0.8–2
Effect of health on workforce	1.0–1.2
New variables, input, functions (pink)	**Range**
Minimum capacity health	From E.2
Service delivery factor health	0–1.5
Impact of climate change on health	1 to −1

E.1.3   WORKFORCE AND EMPLOYMENT

Variables	Initial Values
Input Parameters (red)	**Values**
Fraction labor in agriculture, construction, and others	0.4,0.4,0.2
Fraction workforce 16–59	0.8
Fraction livestock labor	0.5
Fraction ag labor per livestock type (3 types)	1/3,1/3,1/3
Normal employment per livestock unit (LU)	2,2,2
Fraction farmland labor (crops and pasture)	0.25,0,25,0,25,0,25
Normal employment per 1000 tons of crop	1,1,1
Forage required jobs	5
Construction jobs required per home	100
Other construction jobs required	100
Jobs required for other activities	1000
Functions (green)	**Range**
	1
New variables, input, functions (pink)	**Range**
Impact community state on the workforce	From E.2
Effect of health on the workforce	From health

E.2   CAPACITY MODULE (NEW)

Impact community state on removing the veg cover	1.2–0.8
Impact community state on capacity education	−0.5 to 2
Impact community state on capacity	−2 to 2
Varies for different services (health, food, water, wastewater treatment, energy, agriculture, construction)	
Impact community state on birth	0.8–1.2
Impact community state on death	1.2–0.8
Impact community state on migration	0.5–1
Impact community state on the workforce	0.8–1.2
Impact community state on land productivity	0.8–1.2
Impact community state on adding LUs	0.8–1.4
Impact community state on losing land	1.2–1
Impact community state on forestry	1.2–0.2
Impact community state on veg growing cover	0.8–1.2
Effect of water on PSC	1–2
Effect of grain security ratio on PSC	1–2
Effect of LU security ratio on PSC	1–2
PSC weights	1/3,1/3,1/3
Impact of climate change on PSC	2 to −1

Influence-dependence capacity analysis: see Table 10.1. Same for all services.

E.2.1   VARIATION OF P, S, AND C SECTORS

The effect of each sector on the adjustment rates of the other two varies linearly: $y = 0.012x - 0.2$.

Sectors	Initial Values	Desirable Values	Basic Adjustment Rate /Year
Peace	20 pu	100 pu	0.02
Sustainability	30 su	100 su	0.01
Climate security	40 cu	100 cu	0.03

E.2.2   CAPACITY MODULE HEALTH

Capacity Type	Initial Value	Desired Value	Basic Adjustment Rate
Institutional	70	100	0.005
Human	70	100	0.005
Technical	70	100	0.005
Financial	70	100	0.005
Energy	70	100	0.005
Environmental	70	100	0.005
Sociocultural	70	100	0.005

E.2.3 CAPACITY MODULE EDUCATION

Capacity Type	Initial Value	Desired Value	Basic Adjustment Rate
Institutional	70	100	0.01
Human	70	100	0.01
Technical	70	100	0.01
Financial	70	100	0.01
Energy	70	100	0.01
Environmental	70	100	0.01
Sociocultural	70	100	0.01

E.2.4 CAPACITY MODULE PLANT-BASED FOOD

Capacity Type	Initial Value	Desired Value	Basic Adjustment Rate
Institutional	80	100	0.01
Human	80	100	0.01
Technical	80	100	0.01
Financial	80	100	0.01
Energy	80	100	0.01
Environmental	80	100	0.01
Sociocultural	80	100	0.01

E.2.5 CAPACITY MODULE MEAT-BASED FOOD

Capacity Type	Initial Value	Desired Value	Basic Adjustment Rate
Institutional	70	100	0.01
Human	70	100	0.01
Technical	70	100	0.01
Financial	70	100	0.01
Energy	70	100	0.01
Environmental	70	100	0.01
Sociocultural	70	100	0.01

E.2.6 CAPACITY MODULE CONSTRUCTION

Capacity Type	Initial Value	Desired Value	Basic Adjustment Rate
Institutional	80	100	0.01
Human	80	100	0.01
Technical	80	100	0.01
Financial	80	100	0.01
Energy	80	100	0.01
Environmental	80	100	0.01
Sociocultural	80	100	0.01

E.2.7   Capacity Module Water

Capacity Type	Initial Value	Desired Value	Basic Adjustment Rate
Institutional	70	100	0.005
Human	70	100	0.005
Technical	70	100	0.005
Financial	70	100	0.005
Energy	70	100	0.005
Environmental	70	100	0.005
Sociocultural	70	100	0.005

E.2.8   Capacity Module Wastewater

Capacity Type	Initial Value	Desired Value	Basic Adjustment Rate
Institutional	70	100	0.008
Human	70	100	0.008
Technical	70	100	0.008
Financial	70	100	0.008
Energy	70	100	0.008
Environmental	70	100	0.008
Sociocultural	70	100	0.008

E.2.9   Capacity Module Energy

Capacity Type	Initial Value	Desired Value	Basic Adjustment Rate
Institutional	70	100	0.01
Human	70	100	0.01
Technical	70	100	0.01
Financial	70	100	0.01
Energy	70	100	0.01
Environmental	70	100	0.01
Sociocultural	70	100	0.01

E.2.10   Capacity Module Agriculture

Capacity Type	Initial Value	Desired Value	Basic Adjustment Rate
Institutional	60	100	0.05
Human	60	100	0.05
Technical	60	100	0.05
Financial	60	100	0.05
Energy	60	100	0.05
Environmental	60	100	0.05
Sociocultural	60	100	0.05

E.3 FOOD RESOURCES MODULE

Variables	Initial Values
Crops (tons) (grains, vegetables, fruits)	$4\times10^4, 4\times10^4, 4\times10^4$
Livestock units LU (three types)	4000,4000,4000
Input Parameters (red)	**Values**
Diet fraction meat vs. plant-based	0.1,0.9
kJ food demand per person per day	10,000
Days per year	365
Basic kJ of animal-based food per LU	$4\times10^6, 4\times10^6, 4\times10^6$
Basic fraction LU lost (/year)	0.1,0.1,0.1
Basic rate adding LU (/year)	0.9,0.9,0.9
Basic pasture land yield (tons/ha/year)	40
Basic arable land yield (tons/ha/year)	10,10,10
Fraction crops used for biofuel (/year)	0,0,0
The average weight of LUs (tons)	0.5,0.1,0.1
Daily livestock utilization rate	0.02,0.01,0.01
Basic kJ of plant-based food per ton of crops	$4\times10^6, 3\times10^6, 3\times10^6$
Fraction crop wasted or lost (/year)	0.01,0.01,0.01
Fraction cash crops (/year)	0.01,0.01,0.01
Fraction cash cattle (/year)	0,0,0
Price value crops ($/ton)	150,150,150
Price value livestock ($/LU)	1000,1000,1000
Desired crops available for plant-based food (tons)	$2\times10^5, 2\times10^5, 2\times10^5$
Desired total LUs available for meat-based food	15000
Crop energy input-output ratio	0.025,0.04,0.04
LU energy input-output ratio	0.01,0.01,0.01
Forage energy input-output ratio	0.025
kJ per ton of forage	1000
Functions (green)	**Range**
Efficiency converting LU into meat-based food	1–20
Efficiency converting crops into plant-based food	1–10
New variables, input, functions (pink)	**Range**
Minimum capacity plant-based food	From E.2
Minimum capacity meat-based food	From E.2
Impact of climate change on land productivity	1–0.001
Impact of climate change on adding LUs	1–0.1
Impact of climate change on losing LUs	1–3
Service delivery factor plant-based food	0–1.2
Service delivery factor meat-based food	0–1.5

E.4   LAND RESOURCES MODULE

E.4.1   LAND DISTRIBUTION ZONING

Variables	Initial Values
Zoned land (km^2) (wild, arable, pasture, residential, industrial)	30,15,15,20,20
Input Parameters (red)	**Values**
Losing land (sq km per year)	0,0,0,0,0
Functions (green)	**Range**

E.4.2   SOIL/VEGETATION

Variables	Initial Values
Soil thickness (m) (wild, arable, pasture, residential, industrial)	5,5,5,5,5,5
Vegetation cover (km^2) (wild, arable, pasture, residential, industrial)	14,14,14,10,5
Input parameters (red)	**Values**
Soil porosity (wild, arable, pasture, residential, industrial)	0.5,0.5,0.5, 0.5,0.5
Basic soil erosion rate (per sector) ($\times 10^{-3}$)	1,1,1,1,1
Basic rate disappearing vegetation cover (per sector) ($\times 10^{-2}$)	1,1,1,1,1
Basic vegetation growing rate (per sector) ($\times 10^{-2}$)	2,2,2,2,2
Fraction soil clay content (per soil type)	0.5,0.5,0.5,0.5,0.5
Fraction of soil organic matter (per soil type)	0.5,0.5,0.5,0.5,0.5
Functions (green)	**Range**
Effect of soil erosion on removing vegetation cover	[0–2]
Effect of farming on removing vegetation cover	[0–2]
Effect of deforestation on removing vegetation cover	[0–2]
Effect of soil thickness on vegetation growth	[0–2]
Effect of clay content on vegetation growth	[0–2]
Effect of organic matter on vegetation growth	[0–2]
Effect of soil water content on vegetation growth	[1–1.2]
Effect of desertification on soil erosion rate	[1–2]
Effect of vegetation cover on soil erosion rate	[0–2]
Effect of non-natural processes on soil erosion rate	[0–2]
Effect of topography on soil erosion rate	[0–2]
Effect of rainfall and runoff on soil erosion rate	[0–2]
New variables, input, functions (pink)	**Range**
Impact of climate change on vegetation growth rate	1–0.5
Impact of climate change on desertification	1–2
Impact of community state on removing the veg cover	From E.2
Impact of community state on growing veg cover	From E.2
Impact of community state on losing soil	From E.2

E.4.3 RESIDENTIAL LAND

Variables	Initial Values
Homes under construction	100
Completed homes	0
Homes in disrepair	0
Repaired homes	0
Removed homes	0
Available home construction material (tons)	10^5
Land used for homes (ha)	10
Land used for infrastructure (ha)	100
Input Parameters (red)	**Values**
Material required per home (tons)	5
Home completion time (months)	6
Time homes degrading (years)	20
Time homes repaired (years)	2
Time homes removed (years)	2
Basic construction rate (homes/year)	20
Land area per home (ha)	1
Fraction of residential land zoned for homes	0.6
Fraction of residential land zoned for infrastructure	0.2
Fraction of residential land zoned for other uses	0.1
Basic infrastructure land claiming rate	0.01
Infrastructure land reclaiming rate	0.02
Energy required for each home lifecycle (kWh per home)	100,100,100
Energy required for infrastructure (kWh/year)	1000
Functions (green)	**Range**
Material supplying rate (/year)	0–0.1
New variables, input, functions (pink)	**Range**
Minimum capacity construction	From E.2
Service delivery factor construction	0.8–2

E.4.4 AGRICULTURAL LAND

Variables	Initial Values
Land for agriculture (ha) Grain, Veg, Fruit, Pasture	300,300,300,300
Farmland equipment units working	5,5,5,5
Farm livestock equipment units working	5,5,5
Input Parameters (red)	**Values**
Basic agricultural land adjustment rate	0.02,0.02,0.02,0.02
Fraction arable land for crops (grain, veg, fruit)	1/3,1/3,1/3
Desired agricultural land productivity (tons)	$10^4,10^4,10^4,10^4$
Basic rate losing ag land	0.01,0.01,0.01,0.01
Fraction pasture land occupied	1/3,1/3,1/3
Farmland equipment life span (years)	20,20,20
Livestock equipment life span (years)	20,20,20
Required farmland equipment	10,10,10,10
Required livestock equipment	10,10,10
LU max per hectare	5,20,20

Functions (green)	Value/Range
Effect farmland equipment multiplier	[0–2]
Effect livestock equipment multiplier	[0–2]
Effect land/veg on adding LU	1,1,1
Buying pattern for farmland equipment (units)	[50–10]
Buying pattern for livestock equipment (units)	[50–10]
Other effects on arable and pasture land productivity	1,1,1,1
Effect use of fertilizers	[0–2]
Other land effects of adding LU	[0–2]
Effect arable soil thickness	1,1,1,1
Effect pastureland thickness	1
Effect soil contamination	[0–2]
Effect of poor land practices	[0–2]
New variables, input, functions (pink)	**Range**
Minimum capacity agriculture	From E.2
Service delivery factor ag pasture	0.8–1.2
Service delivery factor LU	0.8–1.2
Ag land loss factor	1.2–1.0

E.4.5   INDUSTRIAL/COMMERCIAL LAND

Variables	Initial Values
Land for Ind/Com (ha)	300,300,300
Input Parameters (red)	**Values**
Desired Ind/com land productivity ($)	10000,10000
Basic Ind/com land adjustment rate	0.01,0.01
Productivity Ind/com land ($ per ha)	10,10
Fractions Ind/com types	1/3,1/3
Energy demand by industry/commerce (kWh/year)	10^5, 10^5
Functions (green)	**Range**
New variables, input, functions (pink)	**Range**
Impact community state on losing land	From E.2

E.4.6   WILDLAND

Variables	Initial Values
New trees (two tree types)	1000,1000
Mature trees (two tree types)	1.2×10^6, 1.2×10^6
Timber industry revenue ($)	10000,10000
Equipment units in the timber industry	1000
Input parameters (red)	**Values**
Desired forested land (ha)	2000,2000
Trees per hectare	2000,2000
Tree longevity (years)	20,20
Basic rate adding trees (/year)	0.1,0.1

Fraction new trees lost (/year)	0.05,0.05
Time for trees to mature	2,2
Basic industrial tree-harvesting rate	0.01,0.01
Domestic tree lumber cutting rate	0.01,0.01
Fuel wood required per household (tons/year)	5,5
Fuel wood (tons per tree)	1,1
Basic equipment deteriorating time (years)	20
Buying pattern for equipment units	[50–10]
Cost per equipment unit ($)	100000
O&M equipment cost per unit/year	1000
Labor cost ($/year)	100000
Spending tree-type fraction	0.5,0.5
Required timber industry equipment (units)	1500
Tree clearing rate (/year)	0.01,0.01
Revenue per ton of wood ($/ton)	200,200
Energy demand from the timber industry (kWh/year)	100
Energy demand to manage forested land (kWh/ha/year)	100,100
Functions (green)	**Range**
Effect soil thickness	1,1
Effect canopy	1,1
Effect leaf biomass	1,1
Effect of timber industry equipment multiplier	[0–2]
New variables, input, functions (pink)	**Range**
Impact community state on forestry	From E.2
Effect of climate change on tree dying	1–2

E.5   WATER RESOURCES MODULE

E.5.1   WATER BALANCE

Variables	Initial Values
Precipitation water (cu m)	0
Soil water (cu m)	Calculated
Groundwater GW (cu m)	1×10^{10}
Available SW for non-irrigation (cu m)	2×10^{6}
Available GW for non-irrigation (cu m)	2×10^{6}
Available SW for irrigation (cu m)	2×10^{6}
Available GW for irrigation (cu m)	4×10^{6}
Total stream runoff (cu m)	100
Input parameters (red)	**Values**
Initial soil saturation level	0.9,0.9,0.9,0.9,0.9
Average precipitation per year (mm)	800
Evaporation rate (/year)	0.2
Runoff rate (/year)	0.1998
Fraction allocated as SW for non-irrigation (/year)	0.002
Fraction allocated as SW for irrigation (/year)	0.1
Fraction allocated as GW for non-irrigation (/year)	0.0002
Fraction allocated as GW for irrigation (/year)	0.005

Percolating rate in soil (/year)   0.1,0.1,0.1,0.1,0.1
Percolating rate to GW (/year)   0.1,0.1,0.01,0.1,0.1
Energy required to supply non-irrigation water (kWh/m³)   0.2
Energy required to supply irrigation water (kWh/m³)   0.5
Energy required for water purification (kWh/m³)   0.2
Desired available non-irrigation water 5×10^9
Desired available irrigation water 7×10^8
Functions (green)   **Range**
Effect water available on adding LUs   0.5–1.5
Effect of water on birth   0.5–1.5
Effect of water on death   1.2–0.5
Effect of soil water on crops and pasture production   1–1.2
New variables, input, functions (pink)   **Range**
Effect of climate change on precipitation   1–0.25
Effect of climate change on evaporation   1–1.2
Service delivery factor water   0–10
Minimum capacity water   From E.2

E.5.2   WATER DEMAND

Variables	Initial Values
Input Parameters (red)	**Values**
DW demand (L/pp/day)	100
Fraction DW used (ND, D)	0.7,0.3
Fraction NDDW from non-irrigation SW, GW	0.5,0.5
Fraction DDW from non-irrigation SW, GW	0.1,0.9
AWL demand per LU (L/day)	50,10,5
Fraction AWL from non-irrigation SW, GW	0.5,0.5
Available arable land evapotranspiration (mm/year/m²)	365
Used arable land evapotranspiration (mm/year/m²)	365
Wildland forested evapotranspiration (mm/year/m²)	36.5
Wildland non-forested evapotranspiration (mm/year/m²)	36.5
Pasture land evapotranspiration (mm per year/m²)	73
Residential land evapotranspiration (mm per year/m²)	36.5
Industrial land evapotranspiration (mm per year/m²)	36.5
Minimum soil water (m³) 10⁷	5,5,5,5,5
Unit converter (m³/km²) 10⁵	0.51,3.04,0.25,0,0
Fraction irrigation from SW, GW	0.2,0.8
Water demand by industry/commerce (m³/year)	1000,500
Fraction IW from non-irrigation SW, GW	0.8,0.2
Functions (green)	**Range**
New variables, input, functions (pink)	**Range**
Impact of climate change on water demand	1–1.1

E.5.3 WASTEWATER

Variables	Initial Values
Raw blackwater	0
Raw graywater	0
Blackwater subject to primary treatment	0
Blackwater subject to secondary treatment	0
Untreated sewage released in the environment	0
Total sewage released in streams	0
Sewage infiltrating in soils	0
Sewage in groundwater	0
Treated graywater	0
Treated graywater reused in irrigation	0
Untreated graywater in the environment	0
Graywater infiltrating in soils	0
Graywater in groundwater	0
Total graywater released in streams	0
Input Parameters (red)	**Values**
Fraction of SW returned as wastewater	0.9,0.9,0.9,0.9
Fraction of GW returned as wastewater	0.9,0.9,0.9,0.9
Blackwater treatment rate per year	0.05
Days for secondary treatment	25
Fraction of sewage flowing in streams (/year)	0.1
Graywater treatment rate per year	0.05
Fraction of graywater released in streams (/year)	0.1
Fraction of treated graywater reusable in irrigation (/year)	0.8
Fraction of treated blackwater reusable in irrigation (/year)	0.8
Energy required to collect and treat sewage water (kWh/m^3)	1
Energy required to collect and treat graywater (kWh/m^3)	1
Functions (green)	**Range**
New variables, input, functions (pink)	**Range**
Minimum capacity WWT	From E.2
Service delivery factor WWT	0–1.2

E.6 ENERGY RESOURCES MODULE

E.6.1 ENERGY BALANCE

Variables	Initial Values
Energy resources (kWh)	5×10^7
Energy resources for water use (kWh)	
(non-irrigation, irrigation, wastewater treatment) 10^7	0.5,50,0.5
Energy resources for agricultural uses (kWh)	
(crops, pasture, LU) 10^4	3000,1,1
Energy resources for other uses (kWh)	
(household, residential land, ind/com, wildland) 10^6	1,1,1,1

Input Parameters (Red)	Values
Renewable energy supply (kWh/year)	20×10^6
Non-renewable energy supply (kWh/year)	10×10^6
Desired energy for water uses (kWh) 10^8	6,50,7
Desired energy for ag uses (kWh) 10^8	30,3,3
Desired energy for other uses (kWh) 10^8	5,5,5,5
Fraction energy for water uses	0.02,0.15,0.03
Fraction energy for ag uses	0.05,0.005,0.005
Fraction energy for other uses	0.01,0.01,0.01,0.01
Multipliers (green)	**Range**
Energy factor on wild land	[1–2]
Energy factor on residential land	[1–2]
Energy factor on industry/commerce land	[1–2]
Energy factor on household	[1–2]
Energy factor in supplying crops	[1–2]
Energy factor on pasture production	[1–2]
Energy factor on adding LU	[1–2]
Energy factor in supplying irrigation water	[1–2]
Energy factor in supplying non-irrigation water	[1–2]
Energy factor in providing wastewater treatment	[1–2]
New variables, input, functions (pink)	**Range**
Minimum capacity energy	From E.2
Service delivery factor energy	0–10
Impact of climate change on supplying energy	1–0

Appendix F
The Syrian Conflict—Model PSC6

A user-friendly interactive user interface can be found on the website: https://exchange.iseesystems.com/public/bernardamadei/psc6

Time frame: 20 years

F.1 RURAL COMPONENT

Variables	Initial Values
Rural population (people)	4×10^6
Inward migration (people)	0
Rural livelihood resources (units)	2×10^7
Input parameters (Red)	**Values**
Birth rate rural (/year)	0.03
Basic death rate rural (/year)	0.005
Normal migration rate (/year)	0.005
Basic consumption of rural resources (units/pp/year)	1
Normal resources supply rate (/year)	0.1
Functions (green)	**Range**
Impact of climate change rural	0–4
Effect of climate change on resources supply rural	1–0.1
Effect of resources on consumption pp rural	0–1
Effect of resources on death rate rural	10–1
Resources management factors rural	0–5
Other resources limiting factors rural	0–2

F.2   URBAN COMPONENT

Variables	Initial Values
Urban population (people)	1.5×10^6
External migration (people)	0
Urban livelihood resources (units)	2×10^7
Urban jobs	0.3×10^6

Input parameters (Red)	Values
Fraction of migrants going to urban areas	0.8
Birth rate urban (/year)	0.02
Basic death rate urban (/year)	0.005
Normal leaving rate (/year)	0.015
Basic consumption of urban resources (units/pp/year)	1.5
Basic rate supplying livelihood resources (/year)	0.1
Fraction of urban pop as adult labor	0.7
Normal rate of decreasing jobs (/year)	0.01
Basic unrest level	20

Functions (green)	Range
Impact of climate change urban	0–4
Effect of climate change on resources supply urban	1–0.1
Effect of resources on consumption pp urban	0–1
Effect of resources on death rate urban	10–1
Unrest multiplier due to poverty	0–2
Other resources limiting factors urban	0–2
Unrest multiplier due to unemployment	0–3
Unrest multiplier due to government repression	0–2
Effect of unrest on supplying livelihood resources	1–0
Effect of unrest on job creation	1–0
Human insecurity	0–100
Effect of insecurity on external migration	1–3
Resources management factors urban	1–5
Basic rate creating jobs (/year)	0.01–0.1

Index

Note: **Bold** page numbers refer to tables; *italic* page numbers refer to figures.

For Product Safety Concerns and Information please contact our
EU representative GPSR@taylorandfrancis.com Taylor & Francis
Verlag GmbH, Kaufingerstraße 24, 80331 München, Germany